Works of Swami Vivekananda Vol. I

by

Swami Vivekananda

Double 9 BOOKS

Works of Swami Vivekananda
Vol. I
by Swami Vivekananda

ISBN: 978-93-59393-78-0

Published by

DOUBLE 9 BOOKS
2/13-B, Ansari Road
Daryaganj, New Delhi – 110002
info@double9books.com
www.double9books.com
Tel. 011-40042856

ABOUT THE AUTHOR

Swami Vivekananda was born Narendranath Datta in India on January 12, 1863. He died on July 4, 1902, and was the most important student of the Indian saint Ramakrishna. He was an important part of bringing Vedanta and Yoga to the West. He is also charged with making people more aware of other religions and making Hinduism a major world religion. Vivekananda had a lot of success at the Parliament. In the years that followed, he gave hundreds of lectures across the United States, England, and Europe to spread the main ideas of Hinduism. He also started the Vedanta Society of New York and the Vedanta Society of San Francisco, which is now the Vedanta Society of Northern California. Both of these groups became the basis for Vedanta Societies in the West. Vivekananda was one of the most important philosophers and social reformers in India at the time. He was also one of the most successful and powerful Vedanta missionaries in the West.People now think of him as one of the most important people in modern India and Hinduism. Mahatma Gandhi said that after reading Vivekananda's works, he loved his country a thousand times more.

CONTENTS

Addresses at The Parliament of Religions 9

Response To Welcome 9

Why We Disagree 11

Paper On Hinduism 12

Religion Not The Crying Need Of India 22

Buddhism, The Fulfilment Of Hinduism 23

Address At The Final Session 25

Karma-Yoga 27

Chapter I.
Karma In Its Effect On Character 27

Chapter II.
Each Is Great In His Own Place 33

Chapter III.
The Secret Of Work 44

Chapter IV.
What Is Duty? 51

Chapter V.
We Help Ourselves, Not The World 57

Chapter VI.
Non-Attachment Is Complete Self-Abnegation 64

Chapter VII.
Freedom 73

Chapter VIII.
The Ideal Of Karma-Yoga 82

Raja-Yoga

Preface....89

Chapter I.
Introductory....91

Chapter II.
The First Steps....100

Chapter III.
Prana....107

Chapter IV.
The Psychic Prana....116

Chapter V.
The Control Of Psychic Prana....120

Chapter VI.
Pratyahara And Dharana....124

Chapter VII.
Dhyana And Samadhi....130

Chapter VIII.
Raja-Yoga In Brief....137

Patanjali's Yoga Aphorisms....142

Introduction....142

Chapter I.
Concentration: Its Spiritual Uses....146

Chapter II.
Concentration: Its Practice....170

Chapter III.
Powers....193

Chapter IV.
Independence....206

Appendix....218

Lectures and Discourses....226

Soul, God And Religion....226

The Hindu Religion....235

What Is Religion?....238

Vedic Religious Ideals 246
The Vedanta Philosophy 255
Reason And Religion 261
Vedanta As A Factor In Civilisation 273
The Spirit And Influence Of Vedanta 276
Steps Of Hindu Philosophic Thought 280
Steps To Realisation 289
Vedanta And Privilege 297
Privilege 306
Krishna 311
The Gita I 317
The Gita II 326
The Gita III 331
Mohammed 340
Vilvamangala 343
The Soul And God 345
Breathing 355
Practical Religion:
Breathing And Meditation 363

Addresses at The Parliament of Religions

Response To Welcome

At the World's Parliament of Religions, Chicago
11th September, 1893

Sisters and Brothers of America,

It fills my heart with joy unspeakable to rise in response to the warm and cordial welcome which you have given us. I thank you in the name of the most ancient order of monks in the world; I thank you in the name of the mother of religions; and I thank you in the name of millions and millions of Hindu people of all classes and sects.

My thanks, also, to some of the speakers on this platform who, referring to the delegates from the Orient, have told you that these men from far-off nations may well claim the honour of bearing to different lands the idea of toleration. I am proud to belong to a religion which has taught the world both tolerance and universal acceptance. We believe not only in universal toleration, but we accept all religions as true. I am proud to belong to a nation which has sheltered the persecuted and the refugees of all religions and all nations of the earth. I am proud to tell you that we have gathered in our bosom the purest remnant of the Israelites, who came to Southern India and took refuge with us in the very year in which their holy temple was shattered to pieces by Roman tyranny. I am proud to belong to the religion which has sheltered and is still fostering the remnant of the grand Zoroastrian nation. I will quote to you, brethren, a few lines from a hymn which I remember to have repeated from my earliest boyhood, which is every day repeated by millions of human beings: "*As the different streams having their sources in different places all mingle their water in the sea, so, O Lord, the different paths which men take through different tendencies, various though they appear, crooked or straight, all lead to Thee.*"

The present convention, which is one of the most august assemblies ever held, is in itself a vindication, a declaration to the world of the wonderful doctrine preached in the Gita: "*Whosoever comes to Me, through whatsoever form, I reach him; all men are struggling through paths which in the end lead to me.*" Sectarianism, bigotry, and its horrible descendant, fanaticism, have long possessed this beautiful earth. They have filled the earth with violence, drenched it often and often with human blood, destroyed civilisation and sent whole nations to despair. Had it not been for these horrible demons, human society would be far more advanced than it is now. But their time is come; and I fervently hope that the bell that tolled this morning in honour of this convention may be the death-knell of all fanaticism, of all persecutions with the sword or with the pen, and of all uncharitable feelings between persons wending their way to the same goal.

Why We Disagree

15th September, 1893

I will tell you a little story. You have heard the eloquent speaker who has just finished say, "Let us cease from abusing each other," and he was very sorry that there should be always so much variance.

But I think I should tell you a story which would illustrate the cause of this variance. A frog lived in a well. It had lived there for a long time. It was born there and brought up there, and yet was a little, small frog. Of course the evolutionists were not there then to tell us whether the frog lost its eyes or not, but, for our story's sake, we must take it for granted that it had its eyes, and that it every day cleansed the water of all the worms and bacilli that lived in it with an energy that would do credit to our modern bacteriologists. In this way it went on and became a little sleek and fat. Well, one day another frog that lived in the sea came and fell into the well.

"Where are you from?"

"I am from the sea."

"The sea! How big is that? Is it as big as my well?" and he took a leap from one side of the well to the other.

"My friend," said the frog of the sea, "how do you compare the sea with your little well?"

Then the frog took another leap and asked, "Is your sea so big?"

"What nonsense you speak, to compare the sea with your well!"

"Well, then," said the frog of the well, "nothing can be bigger than my well; there can be nothing bigger than this; this fellow is a liar, so turn him out."

That has been the difficulty all the while.

I am a Hindu. I am sitting in my own little well and thinking that the whole world is my little well. The Christian sits in his little well and thinks the whole world is his well. The Mohammedan sits in his little well and thinks that is the whole world. I have to thank you of America for the great attempt you are making to break down the barriers of this little world of ours, and hope that, in the future, the Lord will help you to accomplish your purpose.

Paper On Hinduism

Read at the Parliament on 19th September, 1893

Three religions now stand in the world which have come down to us from time prehistoric – Hinduism, Zoroastrianism and Judaism. They have all received tremendous shocks and all of them prove by their survival their internal strength. But while Judaism failed to absorb Christianity and was driven out of its place of birth by its all-conquering daughter, and a handful of Parsees is all that remains to tell the tale of their grand religion, sect after sect arose in India and seemed to shake the religion of the Vedas to its very foundations, but like the waters of the seashore in a tremendous earthquake it receded only for a while, only to return in an all-absorbing flood, a thousand times more vigorous, and when the tumult of the rush was over, these sects were all sucked in, absorbed, and assimilated into the immense body of the mother faith.

From the high spiritual flights of the Vedanta philosophy, of which the latest discoveries of science seem like echoes, to the low ideas of idolatry with its multifarious mythology, the agnosticism of the Buddhists, and the atheism of the Jains, each and all have a place in the Hindu's religion.

Where then, the question arises, where is the common centre to which all these widely diverging radii converge? Where is the common basis upon which all these seemingly hopeless contradictions rest? And this is the question I shall attempt to answer.

The Hindus have received their religion through revelation, the Vedas. They hold that the Vedas are without beginning and without end. It may sound ludicrous to this audience, how a book can be without beginning or end. But by the Vedas no books are meant. They mean the accumulated treasury of spiritual laws discovered by different persons in different times. Just as the law of gravitation existed before its discovery, and would exist if all humanity forgot it, so is it with the laws that govern the spiritual world. The moral, ethical, and spiritual relations between soul and soul and between individual spirits and the Father of all spirits, were there before their discovery, and would remain even if we forgot them.

The discoverers of these laws are called Rishis, and we honour them as perfected beings. I am glad to tell this audience that some of the very greatest of them were women. Here it may be said that these laws as laws may be without end, but they must have had a beginning. The Vedas teach us that creation is without beginning or end. Science is said to have proved that the sum total of cosmic energy is always the same. Then, if there was a time when nothing existed, where was all this manifested energy? Some say it was in a potential form in God. In that case God is sometimes potential and sometimes kinetic, which would make Him mutable. Everything mutable is a compound, and everything compound must undergo that change which is called destruction. So God would die, which is absurd. Therefore there never was a time when there was no creation.

If I may be allowed to use a simile, creation and creator are two lines, without beginning and without end, running parallel to each other. God is the ever active providence, by whose power systems after systems are being evolved out of chaos, made to run for a time and again destroyed. This is what the Brâhmin boy repeats every day: "*The sun and the moon, the Lord created like the suns and moons of previous cycles.*" And this agrees with modern science.

Here I stand and if I shut my eyes, and try to conceive my existence, "I", "I", "I", what is the idea before me? The idea of a body. Am I, then, nothing but a combination of material substances? The Vedas declare, "No". I am a spirit living in a body. I am not the body. The body will die, but I shall not die. Here am I in this body; it will fall, but I shall go on living. I had also a past. The soul was not created, for creation means a combination which means a certain future dissolution. If then the soul was created, it must die. Some are born happy, enjoy perfect health, with beautiful body, mental vigour and all wants supplied. Others are born miserable, some are without hands or feet, others again are idiots and only drag on a wretched existence. Why, if they are all created, why does a just and merciful God create one happy and another unhappy, why is He so partial? Nor would it mend matters in the least to hold that those who are miserable in this life will be happy in a future one. Why should a man be miserable even here in the reign of a just and merciful God?

In the second place, the idea of a creator God does not explain the anomaly, but simply expresses the cruel fiat of an all-powerful being. There must have been causes, then, before his birth, to make a man miserable or happy and those were his past actions.

Are not all the tendencies of the mind and the body accounted for by inherited aptitude? Here are two parallel lines of existence — one of the mind, the other of matter. If matter and its transformations answer for all that we have, there is no necessity for supposing the existence of a soul. But it cannot be proved that thought has been evolved out of matter, and if a philosophical monism is inevitable, spiritual monism is certainly logical and no less desirable than a materialistic monism; but neither of these is necessary here.

We cannot deny that bodies acquire certain tendencies from heredity, but those tendencies only mean the physical configuration, through which a peculiar mind alone can act in a peculiar way. There are other tendencies peculiar to a soul caused by its past actions. And a soul with a certain tendency would by the laws of affinity take birth in a body which is the fittest instrument for the display of that tendency. This is in accord with science, for science wants to explain everything by habit, and habit is got through repetitions. So repetitions are necessary to explain the natural habits of a new-born soul. And since they were not obtained in this present life, they must have come down from past lives.

There is another suggestion. Taking all these for granted, how is it that I do not remember anything of my past life ? This can be easily explained. I am now speaking English. It is not my mother tongue, in fact no words of my mother tongue are now present in my consciousness; but let me try to bring them up, and they rush in. That shows that consciousness is only the surface of the mental ocean, and within its depths are stored up all our experiences. Try and struggle, they would come up and you would be conscious even of your past life.

This is direct and demonstrative evidence. Verification is the perfect proof of a theory, and here is the challenge thrown to the world by the Rishis. We have discovered the secret by which the very depths of the ocean of memory can be stirred up — try it and you would get a complete reminiscence of your past life.

So then the Hindu believes that he is a spirit. Him the sword cannot pierce — him the fire cannot burn — him the water cannot melt — him the air cannot dry. The Hindu believes that every soul is a circle whose circumference is nowhere, but whose centre is located in the body, and that death means the change of this centre from body to body. Nor is the soul bound by the conditions of matter. In its very essence it is free, unbounded, holy, pure, and perfect. But somehow or other it finds itself tied down to matter, and thinks of itself as matter.

Why should the free, perfect, and pure being be thus under the thraldom of matter, is the next question. How can the perfect soul be deluded into the belief that it is imperfect? We have been told that the Hindus shirk the question and say that no such question can be there. Some thinkers want to answer it by positing one or more quasi-perfect beings, and use big scientific names to fill up the gap. But naming is not explaining. The question remains the same. How can the perfect become the quasi-perfect; how can the pure, the absolute, change even a microscopic particle of its nature? But the Hindu is sincere. He does not want to take shelter under sophistry. He is brave enough to face the question in a manly fashion; and his answer is: "I do not know. I do not know how the perfect being, the soul, came to think of itself as imperfect, as joined to and conditioned by matter." But the fact is a fact for all that. It is a fact in everybody's consciousness that one thinks of oneself as the body. The Hindu does not attempt to explain why one thinks one is the body. The answer that it is the will of God is no explanation. This is nothing more than what the Hindu says, "I do not know."

Well, then, the human soul is eternal and immortal, perfect and infinite, and death means only a change of centre from one body to another. The present is determined by our past actions, and the future by the present. The soul will go on evolving up or reverting back from birth to birth and death to death. But here is another question: Is man a tiny boat in a tempest, raised one moment on the foamy crest of a billow and dashed down into a yawning chasm the next, rolling to and fro at the mercy of good and bad actions — a powerless, helpless wreck in an ever-raging, ever-rushing, uncompromising current of cause and effect; a little moth placed under the wheel of causation which rolls on crushing everything in its way and waits not for the widow's tears or the orphan's cry? The heart sinks at the idea, yet this is the law of Nature. Is there no hope? Is there no escape? — was the cry that went up from the bottom of the heart of despair. It reached the throne of mercy, and words of hope and consolation came down and inspired a Vedic sage, and he stood up before the world and in trumpet voice proclaimed the glad tidings: "Hear, ye children of immortal bliss! even ye that reside in higher spheres! I have found the Ancient One who is beyond all darkness, all delusion: knowing Him alone you shall be saved from death over again." "Children of immortal bliss" — what a sweet, what a hopeful name! Allow me to call you, brethren, by that sweet name — heirs of immortal bliss — yea, the Hindu refuses to call you sinners. Ye are the Children of God, the sharers of immortal bliss, holy and perfect beings. Ye divinities on earth — sinners! It is a sin to call a man so; it is a standing libel on human nature. Come up, O lions, and shake off the delusion that you are sheep; you are souls immortal, spirits free, blest and eternal; ye are not matter, ye are not bodies; matter is your servant, not you the servant of matter.

Thus it is that the Vedas proclaim not a dreadful combination of unforgiving laws, not an endless prison of cause and effect, but that at the head of all these laws, in and through every particle of matter and force, stands One "by whose command the wind blows, the fire burns, the clouds rain, and death stalks upon the earth."

And what is His nature?

He is everywhere, the pure and formless One, the Almighty and the All-merciful. "Thou art our father, Thou art our mother, Thou art our beloved friend, Thou art the source of all strength; give us strength. Thou art He that beareth the burdens of the universe; help me bear the little burden of this life." Thus sang the Rishis of the Vedas. And how to worship Him? Through love. "He is to be worshipped as the one beloved, dearer than everything in this and the next life."

This is the doctrine of love declared in the Vedas, and let us see how it is fully developed and taught by Krishna, whom the Hindus believe to have been God incarnate on earth.

He taught that a man ought to live in this world like a lotus leaf, which grows in water but is never moistened by water; so a man ought to live in the world — his heart to God and his hands to work.

It is good to love God for hope of reward in this or the next world, but it is better to love God for love's sake, and the prayer goes: "Lord, I do not want wealth, nor children, nor learning. If it be Thy will, I shall go from birth to birth, but grant me this, that I may love Thee without the hope of reward — love unselfishly for love's sake." One of the disciples of Krishna, the then Emperor of India, was driven from his kingdom by his enemies and had to take shelter with his queen in a forest in the Himalayas, and there one day the queen asked him how it was that he, the most virtuous of men, should suffer so much misery. Yudhishthira answered, "Behold, my queen, the Himalayas, how grand and beautiful they are; I love them. They do not give me anything, but my nature is to love the grand, the beautiful, therefore I love them. Similarly, I love the Lord. He is the source of all beauty, of all sublimity. He is the only object to be loved; my nature is to love Him, and therefore I love. I do not pray for anything; I do not ask for anything. Let Him place me wherever He likes. I must love Him for love's sake. I cannot trade in love."

The Vedas teach that the soul is divine, only held in the bondage of matter; perfection will be reached when this bond will burst, and the word they use for it is therefore, Mukti — freedom, freedom from the bonds of imperfection, freedom from death and misery.

And this bondage can only fall off through the mercy of God, and this mercy comes on the pure. So purity is the condition of His mercy. How does that mercy act? He reveals Himself to the pure heart; the pure and the stainless see God, yea, even in this life; then and then only all the crookedness of the heart is made straight. Then all doubt ceases. He is no more the freak of a terrible law of causation. This is the very centre, the very vital conception of Hinduism. The Hindu does not want to live upon words and theories. If there are existences beyond the ordinary sensuous existence, he wants to come face to face with them. If there is a soul in him which is not matter, if there is an all-merciful universal Soul, he will go to Him direct. He must see Him, and that alone can destroy all doubts. So the best proof a Hindu sage gives about the soul, about God, is: "I have seen the soul; I have seen God." And that is the only condition of perfection. The Hindu religion does not consist in struggles and attempts to believe a certain doctrine or dogma, but in realising — not in believing, but in being and becoming.

Thus the whole object of their system is by constant struggle to become perfect, to become divine, to reach God and see God, and this reaching God, seeing God, becoming perfect even as the Father in Heaven is perfect, constitutes the religion of the Hindus.

And what becomes of a man when he attains perfection? He lives a life of bliss infinite. He enjoys infinite and perfect bliss, having obtained the only thing in which man ought to have pleasure, namely God, and enjoys the bliss with God.

So far all the Hindus are agreed. This is the common religion of all the sects of India; but, then, perfection is absolute, and the absolute cannot be two or three. It cannot have any qualities. It cannot be an individual. And so when a soul becomes perfect and absolute, it must become one with Brahman, and it would only realise the Lord as the perfection, the reality, of its own nature and existence, the existence absolute, knowledge absolute, and bliss absolute. We have often and often read this called the losing of individuality and becoming a stock or a stone.

"He jests at scars that never felt a wound."

I tell you it is nothing of the kind. If it is happiness to enjoy the consciousness of this small body, it must be greater happiness to enjoy the consciousness of two bodies, the measure of happiness increasing with the consciousness of an increasing number of bodies, the aim, the ultimate of happiness being reached when it would become a universal consciousness.

Therefore, to gain this infinite universal individuality, this miserable little prison-individuality must go. Then alone can death cease when I am alone with life, then alone can misery cease when I am one with happiness itself, then alone can all errors cease when I am one with knowledge itself; and this is the necessary scientific conclusion. Science has proved to me that physical individuality is a delusion, that really my body is one little continuously changing body in an unbroken ocean of matter; and Advaita (unity) is the necessary conclusion with my other counterpart, soul.

Science is nothing but the finding of unity. As soon as science would reach perfect unity, it would stop from further progress, because it would reach the goal. Thus Chemistry could not progress farther when it would discover one element out of which all other could be made. Physics would stop when it would be able to fulfill its services in discovering one energy of which all others are but manifestations, and the science of religion become perfect when it would discover Him who is the one life in a universe of death, Him who is the constant basis of an ever-changing world. One who is the only Soul of which all souls are but delusive manifestations. Thus is it, through multiplicity and duality, that the ultimate unity is reached. Religion can go no farther. This is the goal of all science.

All science is bound to come to this conclusion in the long run. Manifestation, and not creation, is the word of science today, and the Hindu is only glad that what he has been cherishing in his bosom for ages is going to be taught in more forcible language, and with further light from the latest conclusions of science.

Descend we now from the aspirations of philosophy to the religion of the ignorant. At the very outset, I may tell you that there is no *polytheism* in India. In every temple, if one stands by and listens, one will find the worshippers applying all the attributes of God, including omnipresence, to the images. It is not polytheism, nor would the name henotheism explain the situation. "The rose called by any other name would smell as sweet." Names are not explanations.

I remember, as a boy, hearing a Christian missionary preach to a crowd in India. Among other sweet things he was telling them was that if he gave a blow to their idol with his stick, what could it do? One of his hearers sharply answered, "If I abuse your God, what can He do?" "You would be punished," said the preacher, "when you die." "So my idol will punish you when you die," retorted the Hindu.

The tree is known by its fruits. When I have seen amongst them that are called idolaters, men, the like of whom in morality and spirituality and love I have never seen anywhere, I stop and ask myself, "Can sin beget holiness?"

Superstition is a great enemy of man, but bigotry is worse. Why does a Christian go to church? Why is the cross holy? Why is the face turned toward the sky in prayer? Why are there so many images in the Catholic Church? Why are there so many images in the minds of Protestants when they pray? My brethren, we can no more think about anything without a mental image than we can live without breathing. By the law of association, the material image calls up the mental idea and *vice versa*. This is why the Hindu uses an external symbol when he worships. He will tell you, it helps to keep his mind fixed on the Being to whom he prays. He knows as well as you do that the image is not God, is not omnipresent. After all, how much does omnipresence mean to almost the whole world? It stands merely as a word, a symbol. Has God superficial area? If not, when we repeat that word "omnipresent", we think of the extended sky or of space, that is all.

As we find that somehow or other, by the laws of our mental constitution, we have to associate our ideas of infinity with the image of the blue sky, or of the sea, so we naturally connect our idea of holiness with the image of a church, a mosque, or a cross. The Hindus have associated the idea of holiness, purity, truth, omnipresence, and such other ideas with different images and forms. But with this difference that while some people devote their whole lives to their idol of a church and never rise higher, because with them religion means an intellectual assent to certain doctrines and doing good to their fellows, the whole religion of the Hindu is centred in realisation. Man is to become divine by realising the divine. Idols or temples or churches or books are only the supports, the helps, of his spiritual childhood: but on and on he must progress.

He must not stop anywhere. "External worship, material worship," say the scriptures, "is the lowest stage; struggling to rise high, mental prayer is the next stage, but the highest stage is when the Lord has been realised." Mark, the same earnest man who is kneeling before the idol tells you, "Him the Sun cannot express, nor the moon, nor the stars, the lightning cannot express Him, nor what we speak of as fire; through Him they shine." But he does not abuse any one's idol or call its worship sin. He recognises in it a necessary stage of life. "The child is father of the man." Would it be right for an old man to say that childhood is a sin or youth a sin?

If a man can realise his divine nature with the help of an image, would it be right to call that a sin? Nor even when he has passed that stage, should he call it an error. To the Hindu, man is not travelling from error to truth, but from truth to truth, from lower to higher truth. To him all the religions, from the lowest fetishism to the highest absolutism, mean so many attempts of the human soul to grasp and realise the Infinite, each determined by the conditions of its birth and association, and each of these marks a stage of progress; and every soul is a young eagle soaring higher and higher, gathering more and more strength, till it reaches the Glorious Sun.

Unity in variety is the plan of nature, and the Hindu has recognised it. Every other religion lays down certain fixed dogmas, and tries to force society to adopt them. It places before society only one coat which must fit Jack and John and Henry, all alike. If it does not fit John or Henry, he must go without a coat to cover his body. The Hindus have discovered that the absolute can only be realised, or thought of, or stated, through the relative, and the images, crosses, and crescents are simply so many symbols — so many pegs to hang the spiritual ideas on. It is not that this help is necessary for every one, but those that do not need it have no right to say that it is wrong. Nor is it compulsory in Hinduism.

One thing I must tell you. Idolatry in India does not mean anything horrible. It is not the mother of harlots. On the other hand, it is the attempt of undeveloped minds to grasp high spiritual truths. The Hindus have their faults, they sometimes have their exceptions; but mark this, they are always for punishing their own bodies, and never for cutting the throats of their neighbours. If the Hindu fanatic burns himself on the pyre, he never lights the fire of Inquisition. And even this cannot be laid at the door of his religion any more than the burning of witches can be laid at the door of Christianity.

To the Hindu, then, the whole world of religions is only a travelling, a coming up, of different men and women, through various conditions and circumstances, to the same goal. Every religion is only evolving a God out of the material man, and the same God is the inspirer of all of them. Why, then, are there so many contradictions? They are only apparent, says the Hindu. The contradictions come from the same truth adapting itself to the varying circumstances of different natures.

It is the same light coming through glasses of different colours. And these little variations are necessary for purposes of adaptation. But in the heart of everything the same truth reigns. The Lord has declared to the Hindu in His incarnation as Krishna, *"I am in every religion as the thread through a string of pearls. Wherever thou seest extraordinary holiness and extraordinary power raising and purifying humanity, know thou that I am there."* And what has been the result? I challenge the world to find, throughout the whole system of Sanskrit philosophy, any such expression as that the Hindu alone will be saved and not others. Says Vyasa, *"We find perfect men even beyond the pale of our caste and creed."* One thing more. How, then, can the Hindu, whose whole fabric of thought centres in God, believe in Buddhism which is agnostic, or in Jainism which is atheistic?

The Buddhists or the Jains do not depend upon God; but the whole force of their religion is directed to the great central truth in every religion, to evolve a God out of man. They have not seen the Father, but they have seen the Son. And he that hath seen the Son hath seen the Father also.

This, brethren, is a short sketch of the religious ideas of the Hindus. The Hindu may have failed to carry out all his plans, but if there is ever to be a universal religion, it must be one which will have no location in place or time; which will be infinite like the God it will preach, and whose sun will shine upon the followers of Krishna and of Christ, on saints and sinners alike; which will not be Brahminic or Buddhistic, Christian or Mohammedan, but the sum total of all these, and still have infinite space for development; which in its catholicity will embrace in its infinite arms, and find a place for, every human being, from the lowest grovelling savage not far removed from the brute, to the highest man towering by the virtues of his head and heart almost above humanity, making society stand in awe of him and doubt his human nature. It will be a religion which will have no place for persecution or intolerance in its polity, which will recognise divinity in every man and woman, and whose whole scope, whose whole force, will be created in aiding humanity to realise its own true, divine nature.

Offer such a religion, and all the nations will follow you. Asoka's council was a council of the Buddhist faith. Akbar's, though more to the purpose, was only a parlour-meeting. It was reserved for America to proclaim to all quarters of the globe that the Lord is in every religion.

May He who is the Brahman of the Hindus, the Ahura-Mazda of the Zoroastrians, the Buddha of the Buddhists, the Jehovah of the Jews, the Father in Heaven of the Christians, give strength to you to carry out your noble idea! The star arose in the East; it travelled steadily towards the West, sometimes dimmed and sometimes effulgent, till it made a circuit of the world; and now it is again rising on the very horizon of the East, the borders of the Sanpo, a thousandfold more effulgent than it ever was before.

Hail, Columbia, motherland of liberty! It has been given to thee, who never dipped her hand in her neighbour's blood, who never found out that the shortest way of becoming rich was by robbing one's neighbours, it has been given to thee to march at the vanguard of civilisation with the flag of harmony.

Religion Not The Crying Need Of India

20th September, 1893

Christians must always be ready for good criticism, and I hardly think that you will mind if I make a little criticism. You Christians, who are so fond of sending out missionaries to save the soul of the heathen — why do you not try to save their bodies from starvation? In India, during the terrible famines, thousands died from hunger, yet you Christians did nothing. You erect churches all through India, but the crying evil in the East is not religion — they have religion enough — but it is bread that the suffering millions of burning India cry out for with parched throats. They ask us for bread, but we give them stones. It is an insult to a starving people to offer them religion; it is an insult to a starving man to teach him metaphysics. In India a priest that preached for money would lose caste and be spat upon by the people. I came here to seek aid for my impoverished people, and I fully realised how difficult it was to get help for heathens from Christians in a Christian land.

Buddhism, The Fulfilment Of Hinduism

26th September, 1893

I am not a Buddhist, as you have heard, and yet I am. If China, or Japan, or Ceylon follow the teachings of the Great Master, India worships him as God incarnate on earth. You have just now heard that I am going to criticise Buddhism, but by that I wish you to understand only this. Far be it from me to criticise him whom I worship as God incarnate on earth. But our views about Buddha are that he was not understood properly by his disciples. The relation between Hinduism (by Hinduism, I mean the religion of the Vedas) and what is called Buddhism at the present day is nearly the same as between Judaism and Christianity. Jesus Christ was a Jew, and Shâkya Muni was a Hindu. The Jews rejected Jesus Christ, nay, crucified him, and the Hindus have accepted Shâkya Muni as God and worship him. But the real difference that we Hindus want to show between modern Buddhism and what we should understand as the teachings of Lord Buddha lies principally in this: Shâkya Muni came to preach nothing new. He also, like Jesus, came to fulfil and not to destroy. Only, in the case of Jesus, it was the old people, the Jews, who did not understand him, while in the case of Buddha, it was his own followers who did not realise the import of his teachings. As the Jew did not understand the fulfilment of the Old Testament, so the Buddhist did not understand the fulfilment of the truths of the Hindu religion. Again, I repeat, Shâkya Muni came not to destroy, but he was the fulfilment, the logical conclusion, the logical development of the religion of the Hindus.

The religion of the Hindus is divided into two parts: the ceremonial and the spiritual. The spiritual portion is specially studied by the monks.

In that there is no caste. A man from the highest caste and a man from the lowest may become a monk in India, and the two castes become equal. In religion there is no caste; caste is simply a social institution. Shâkya Muni himself was a monk, and it was his glory that he had the large-heartedness to bring out the truths from the hidden Vedas and through them broadcast all over the world. He was the first being in the world who brought missionarising into practice — nay, he was the first to conceive the idea of proselytising.

The great glory of the Master lay in his wonderful sympathy for everybody, especially for the ignorant and the poor. Some of his disciples were Brahmins. When Buddha was teaching, Sanskrit was no more the spoken language in India. It was then only in the books of the learned. Some of Buddha's Brahmins disciples wanted to translate his teachings into Sanskrit, but he distinctly told them, "I am for the poor, for the people; let me speak in the tongue of the people." And so to this day the great bulk of his teachings are in the vernacular of that day in India.

Whatever may be the position of philosophy, whatever may be the position of metaphysics, so long as there is such a thing as death in the world, so long as there is such a thing as weakness in the human heart, so long as there is a cry going out of the heart of man in his very weakness, there shall be a faith in God.

On the philosophic side the disciples of the Great Master dashed themselves against the eternal rocks of the Vedas and could not crush them, and on the other side they took away from the nation that eternal God to which every one, man or woman, clings so fondly. And the result was that Buddhism had to die a natural death in India. At the present day there is not one who calls oneself a Buddhist in India, the land of its birth.

But at the same time, Brahminism lost something — that reforming zeal, that wonderful sympathy and charity for everybody, that wonderful heaven which Buddhism had brought to the masses and which had rendered Indian society so great that a Greek historian who wrote about India of that time was led to say that no Hindu was known to tell an untruth and no Hindu woman was known to be unchaste.

Hinduism cannot live without Buddhism, nor Buddhism without Hinduism. Then realise what the separation has shown to us, that the Buddhists cannot stand without the brain and philosophy of the Brahmins, nor the Brahmin without the heart of the Buddhist. This separation between the Buddhists and the Brahmins is the cause of the downfall of India. That is why India is populated by three hundred millions of beggars, and that is why India has been the slave of conquerors for the last thousand years. Let us then join the wonderful intellect of the Brahmins with the heart, the noble soul, the wonderful humanising power of the Great Master.

Address At The Final Session

27th September, 1893

The World's Parliament of Religions has become an accomplished fact, and the merciful Father has helped those who laboured to bring it into existence, and crowned with success their most unselfish labour.

My thanks to those noble souls whose large hearts and love of truth first dreamed this wonderful dream and then realised it. My thanks to the shower of liberal sentiments that has overflowed this platform. My thanks to his enlightened audience for their uniform kindness to me and for their appreciation of every thought that tends to smooth the friction of religions. A few jarring notes were heard from time to time in this harmony. My special thanks to them, for they have, by their striking contrast, made general harmony the sweeter

Much has been said of the common ground of religious unity. I am not going just now to venture my own theory. But if any one here hopes that this unity will come by the triumph of any one of the religions and the destruction of the others, to him I say, "Brother, yours is an impossible hope." Do I wish that the Christian would become Hindu? God forbid. Do I wish that the Hindu or Buddhist would become Christian? God forbid.

The seed is put in the ground, and earth and air and water are placed around it. Does the seed become the earth; or the air, or the water? No. It becomes a plant, it develops after the law of its own growth, assimilates the air, the earth, and the water, converts them into plant substance, and grows into a plant.

Similar is the case with religion. The Christian is not to become a Hindu or a Buddhist, nor a Hindu or a Buddhist to become a Christian. But each must assimilate the spirit of the others and yet preserve his individuality and grow according to his own law of growth.

If the Parliament of Religions has shown anything to the world it is this: It has proved to the world that holiness, purity and charity are not the exclusive possessions of any church in the world, and that every system has produced men and women of the most exalted character. In the face of this evidence, if anybody dreams of the exclusive survival of his own religion and the destruction of the others, I pity him from the bottom of my heart, and point out to him that upon the banner of every religion will soon be written, in spite of resistance: "Help and not Fight," "Assimilation and not Destruction," "Harmony and Peace and not Dissension."

Karma-Yoga

Chapter I.
Karma In Its Effect On Character

The word Karma is derived from the Sanskrit Kri, to do; all action is Karma. Technically, this word also means the effects of actions. In connection with metaphysics, it sometimes means the effects, of which our past actions were the causes. But in Karma-Yoga we have simply to do with the word Karma as meaning work. The goal of mankind is knowledge. That is the one ideal placed before us by Eastern philosophy. Pleasure is not the goal of man, but knowledge. Pleasure and happiness come to an end. It is a mistake to suppose that pleasure is the goal. The cause of all the miseries we have in the world is that men foolishly think pleasure to be the ideal to strive for. After a time man finds that it is not happiness, but knowledge, towards which he is going, and that both pleasure and pain are great teachers, and that he learns as much from evil as from good. As pleasure and pain pass before his soul they have upon it different pictures, and the result of these combined impressions is what is called man's "character". If you take the character of any man, it really is but the aggregate of tendencies, the sum total of the bent of his mind; you will find that misery and happiness are equal factors in the formation of that character. Good and evil have an equal share in moulding character, and in some instances misery is a greater teacher than happiness. In studying the great characters the world has produced, I dare say, in the vast majority of cases, it would be found that it was misery that taught more than happiness, it was poverty that taught more than wealth, it was blows that brought out their inner fire more than praise.

Now this knowledge, again, is inherent in man. No knowledge comes from outside; it is all inside. What we say a man "knows", should, in strict psychological language, be what he "discovers" or "unveils"; what a man "learns" is really what he "discovers", by taking the cover off his own soul, which is a mine of infinite knowledge.

We say Newton discovered gravitation. Was it sitting anywhere in a corner waiting for him? It was in his own mind; the time came and he found it out. All knowledge that the world has ever received comes from the mind; the infinite library of the universe is in your own mind. The external world is simply the suggestion, the occasion, which sets you to study your own mind, but the object of your study is always your own mind. The falling of an apple gave the suggestion to Newton, and he studied his own mind. He rearranged all the previous links of thought in his mind and discovered a new link among them, which we call the law of gravitation. It was not in the apple nor in anything in the centre of the earth.

All knowledge, therefore, secular or spiritual, is in the human mind. In many cases it is not discovered, but remains covered, and when the covering is being slowly taken off, we say, "We are learning," and the advance of knowledge is made by the advance of this process of uncovering. The man from whom this veil is being lifted is the more knowing man, the man upon whom it lies thick is ignorant, and the man from whom it has entirely gone is all-knowing, omniscient. There have been omniscient men, and, I believe, there will be yet; and that there will be myriads of them in the cycles to come. Like fire in a piece of flint, knowledge exists in the mind; suggestion is the friction which brings it out. So with all our feelings and action — our tears and our smiles, our joys and our griefs, our weeping and our laughter, our curses and our blessings, our praises and our blames — every one of these we may find, if we calmly study our own selves, to have been brought out from within ourselves by so many blows. The result is what we are. All these blows taken together are called Karma — work, action. Every mental and physical blow that is given to the soul, by which, as it were, fire is struck from it, and by which its own power and knowledge are discovered, is Karma, this word being used in its widest sense. Thus we are all doing Karma all the time. I am talking to you: that is Karma. You are listening: that is Karma. We breathe: that is Karma. We walk: Karma. Everything we do, physical or mental, is Karma, and it leaves its marks on us.

There are certain works which are, as it were, the aggregate, the sum total, of a large number of smaller works. If we stand near the seashore and hear the waves dashing against the shingle, we think it is such a great noise, and yet we know that one wave is really composed of millions and millions of minute waves. Each one of these is making a noise, and yet we do not catch it; it is only when they become the big aggregate that we hear. Similarly, every pulsation of the heart is work. Certain kinds of work we feel and they become tangible to us; they are, at the same time, the aggregate of a number of small works. If you really want to judge of the character of a man, look not at his great performances. Every fool may become a hero at one time or another. Watch a man do his most common actions; those are indeed the things which will tell you the real character of a great man. Great occasions rouse even the lowest of human beings to some kind of greatness, but he alone is the really great man whose character is great always, the same wherever he be.

Karma in its effect on character is the most tremendous power that man has to deal with. Man is, as it were, a centre, and is attracting all the powers of the universe towards himself, and in this centre is fusing them all and again sending them off in a big current. Such a centre is the *real* man — the almighty, the omniscient — and he draws the whole universe towards him. Good and bad, misery and happiness, all are running towards him and clinging round him; and out of them he fashions the mighty stream of tendency called character and throws it outwards. As he has the power of drawing in anything, so has he the power of throwing it out.

All the actions that we see in the world, all the movements in human society, all the works that we have around us, are simply the display of thought, the manifestation of the will of man. Machines or instruments, cities, ships, or men-of-war, all these are simply the manifestation of the will of man; and this will is caused by character, and character is manufactured by Karma. As is Karma, so is the manifestation of the will. The men of mighty will the world has produced have all been tremendous workers — gigantic souls, with wills powerful enough to overturn worlds, wills they got by persistent work, through ages, and ages. Such a gigantic will as that of a Buddha or a Jesus could not be obtained in one life, for we know who their fathers were. It is not known that their fathers ever spoke a word for the good of mankind. Millions and millions of carpenters like Joseph had gone; millions are still living. Millions and millions of petty kings like Buddha's father had been in the world. If it was only a case of hereditary transmission, how do you account for this petty prince, who was not, perhaps, obeyed by his own servants, producing this son, whom half a world worships? How do you explain the gulf between the carpenter and his son, whom millions of human beings worship as God? It cannot be solved by the theory of heredity. The gigantic will which Buddha and Jesus threw over the world, whence did it come? Whence came this accumulation of power? It must have been there through ages and ages, continually growing bigger and bigger, until it burst on society in a Buddha or a Jesus, even rolling down to the present day.

All this is determined by Karma, work. No one can get anything unless he earns it. This is an eternal law. We may sometimes think it is not so, but in the long run we become convinced of it. A man may struggle all his life for riches; he may cheat thousands, but he finds at last that he did not deserve to become rich, and his life becomes a trouble and a nuisance to him. We may go on accumulating things for our physical enjoyment, but only what we earn is really ours. A fool may buy all the books in the world, and they will be in his library; but he will be able to read only those that he deserves to; and this deserving is produced by Karma. Our Karma determines what we deserve and what we can assimilate. We are responsible for what we are; and whatever we wish ourselves to be, we have the power to make ourselves. If what we are now has been the result of our own past actions, it certainly follows that whatever we wish to be in future can be produced by our present actions; so we have to know how to act. You will say, "What is the use of learning how to work? Everyone works in some way or other in this world." But there is such a thing as frittering away our energies. With regard to Karma-Yoga, the Gita says that it is doing work with cleverness and as a science; by knowing how to work, one can obtain the greatest results. You must remember that all work is simply to bring out the power of the mind which is already there, to wake up the soul. The power is inside every man, so is knowing; the different works are like blows to bring them out, to cause these giants to wake up.

Man works with various motives. There cannot be work without motive. Some people want to get fame, and they work for fame. Others want money, and they work for money. Others want to have power, and they work for power. Others want to get to heaven, and they work for the same. Others want to leave a name when they die, as they do in China, where no man gets a title until he is dead; and that is a better way, after all, than with us. When a man does something very good there, they give a title of nobility to his father, who is dead, or to his grandfather. Some people work for that. Some of the followers of certain Mohammedan sects work all their lives to have a big tomb built for them when they die. I know sects among whom, as soon as a child is born, a tomb is prepared for it; that is among them the most important work a man has to do, and the bigger and the finer the tomb, the better off the man is supposed to be. Others work as a penance; do all sorts of wicked things, then erect a temple, or give something to the priests to buy them off and obtain from them a passport to heaven. They think that this kind of beneficence will clear them and they will go scot-free in spite of their sinfulness. Such are some of the various motives for work.

Work for work's sake. There are some who are really the salt of the earth in every country and who work for work's sake, who do not care for name, or fame, or even to go to heaven. They work just because good will come of it. There are others who do good to the poor and help mankind from still higher motives, because they believe in doing good and love good. The motive for name and fame seldom brings immediate results, as a rule;

they come to us when we are old and have almost done with life. If a man works without any selfish motive in view, does he not gain anything? Yes, he gains the highest. Unselfishness is more paying, only people have not the patience to practice it. It is more paying from the point of view of health also. Love, truth, and unselfishness are not merely moral figures of speech, but they form our highest ideal, because in them lies such a manifestation of power. In the first place, a man who can work for five days, or even for five minutes, without any selfish motive whatever, without thinking of future, of heaven, of punishment, or anything of the kind, has in him the capacity to become a powerful moral giant. It is hard to do it, but in the heart of our hearts we know its value, and the good it brings. It is the greatest manifestation of power — this tremendous restraint; self-restraint is a manifestation of greater power than all outgoing action. A carriage with four horses may rush down a hill unrestrained, or the coachman may curb the horses. Which is the greater manifestation of power, to let them go or to hold them? A cannonball flying through the air goes a long distance and falls. Another is cut short in its flight by striking against a wall, and the impact generates intense heat. All outgoing energy following a selfish motive is frittered away; it will not cause power to return to you; but if restrained, it will result in development of power. This self-control will tend to produce a mighty will, a character which makes a Christ or a Buddha. Foolish men do not know this secret; they nevertheless want to rule mankind. Even a fool may rule the whole world if he works and waits. Let him wait a few years, restrain that foolish idea of governing; and when that idea is wholly gone, he will be a power in the world. The majority of us cannot see beyond a few years, just as some animals cannot see beyond a few steps. Just a little narrow circle — that is our world. We have not the patience to look beyond, and thus become immoral and wicked. This is our weakness, our powerlessness.

Even the lowest forms of work are not to be despised. Let the man, who knows no better, work for selfish ends, for name and fame; but everyone should always try to get towards higher and higher motives and to understand them. "To work we have the right, but not to the fruits thereof:" Leave the fruits alone. Why care for results? If you wish to help a man, never think what that man's attitude should be towards you. If you want to do a great or a good work, do not trouble to think what the result will be.

There arises a difficult question in this ideal of work. Intense activity is necessary; we must always work. We cannot live a minute without work. What then becomes of rest? Here is one side of the life-struggle — work, in which we are whirled rapidly round. And here is the other — that of calm, retiring renunciation: everything is peaceful around, there is very little of noise and show, only nature with her animals and flowers and mountains. Neither of them is a perfect picture. A man used to solitude, if brought in contact with the surging whirlpool of the world, will be crushed by it; just as the fish that lives in the deep sea water, as soon as it is brought to the surface, breaks into pieces, deprived of the weight of water on it that had kept it together. Can a man who has been used to the turmoil and the rush of life live at ease if he comes to a quiet place? He suffers and perchance may lose his mind. The ideal man is he who, in the midst of the greatest silence and solitude, finds the intensest activity, and in the midst of the intensest activity finds the silence and solitude of the desert. He has learnt the secret of restraint, he has controlled himself. He goes through the streets of a big city with all its traffic, and his mind is as calm as if he were in a cave, where not a sound could reach him; and he is intensely working all the time. That is the ideal of Karma-Yoga, and if you have attained to that you have really learnt the secret of work.

But we have to begin from the beginning, to take up the works as they come to us and slowly make ourselves more unselfish every day. We must do the work and find out the motive power that prompts us; and, almost without exception, in the first years, we shall find that our motives are always selfish; but gradually this selfishness will melt by persistence, till at last will come the time when we shall be able to do really unselfish work. We may all hope that some day or other, as we struggle through the paths of life, there will come a time when we shall become perfectly unselfish; and the moment we attain to that, all our powers will be concentrated, and the knowledge which is ours will be manifest.

Chapter II.
Each Is Great In His Own Place

According to the Sânkhya philosophy, nature is composed of three forces called, in Sanskrit, Sattva, Rajas, and Tamas. These as manifested in the physical world are what we may call equilibrium, activity, and inertness. Tamas is typified as darkness or inactivity; Rajas is activity, expressed as attraction or repulsion; and Sattva is the equilibrium of the two.

In every man there are these three forces. Sometimes Tamas prevails. We become lazy, we cannot move, we are inactive, bound down by certain ideas or by mere dullness. At other times activity prevails, and at still other times that calm balancing of both. Again, in different men, one of these forces is generally predominant. The characteristic of one man is inactivity, dullness and laziness; that of another, activity, power, manifestation of energy; and in still another we find the sweetness, calmness, and gentleness, which are due to the balancing of both action and inaction. So in all creation — in animals, plants, and men — we find the more or less typical manifestation of all these different forces.

Karma-Yoga has specially to deal with these three factors. By teaching what they are and how to employ them, it helps us to do our work better. Human society is a graded organization. We all know about morality, and we all know about duty, but at the same time we find that in different countries the significance of morality varies greatly. What is regarded as moral in one country may in another be considered perfectly immoral. For instance, in one country cousins may marry; in another, it is thought to be very immoral; in one, men may marry their sisters-in-law; in another, it is regarded as immoral; in one country people may marry only once; in another, many times; and so forth. Similarly, in all other departments of morality, we find the standard varies greatly — yet we have the idea that there must be a universal standard of morality.

So it is with duty. The idea of duty varies much among different nations. In one country, if a man does not do certain things, people will say he has acted wrongly; while if he does those very things in another country, people will say that he did not act rightly — and yet we know that there must be some universal idea of duty. In the same way, one class of society thinks that certain things are among its duty, while another class thinks quite the opposite and would be horrified if it had to do those things. Two ways are left open to us — the way of the ignorant, who think that there is only one way to truth and that all the rest are wrong, and the way of the wise, who admit that, according to our mental constitution or the different planes of existence in which we are, duty and morality may vary. The important thing is to know that there are gradations of duty and of morality — that the duty of one state of life, in one set of circumstances, will not and cannot be that of another.

To illustrate: All great teachers have taught, "Resist not evil," that non-resistance is the highest moral ideal. We all know that, if a certain number of us attempted to put that maxim fully into practice, the whole social fabric would fall to pieces, the wicked would take possession of our properties and our lives, and would do whatever they liked with us. Even if only one day of such non-resistance were practiced, it would lead to disaster. Yet, intuitively, in our heart of hearts we feel the truth of the teaching "Resist not evil." This seems to us to be the highest ideal; yet to teach this doctrine only would be equivalent to condemning a vast portion of mankind. Not only so, it would be making men feel that they were always doing wrong, and cause in them scruples of conscience in all their actions; it would weaken them, and that constant self-disapproval would breed more vice than any other weakness would. To the man who has begun to hate himself the gate to degeneration has already opened; and the same is true of a nation.

Our first duty is not to hate ourselves, because to advance we must have faith in ourselves first and then in God. He who has no faith in himself can never have faith in God. Therefore, the only alternative remaining to us is to recognise that duty and morality vary under different circumstances; not that the man who resists evil is doing what is always and in itself wrong, but that in the different circumstances in which he is placed it may become even his duty to resist evil.

In reading the Bhagavad-Gita, many of you in Western countries may have felt astonished at the second chapter, wherein Shri Krishna calls Arjuna a hypocrite and a coward because of his refusal to fight, or offer resistance, on account of his adversaries being his friends and relatives, making the plea that non-resistance was the highest ideal of love. This is a great lesson for us all to learn, that in all matters the two extremes are alike. The extreme positive and the extreme negative are always similar. When the vibrations of light are too slow, we do not see them, nor do we see them when they are too rapid. So with sound; when very low in pitch, we do not hear it; when very high, we do not hear it either. Of like nature is the difference between resistance and non-resistance. One man does not resist because he is weak, lazy, and cannot, not because he will not; the other man knows that he can strike an irresistible blow if he likes; yet he not only does not strike, but blesses his enemies. The one who from weakness resists not commits a sin, and as such cannot receive any benefit from the non-resistance; while the other would commit a sin by offering resistance. Buddha gave up his throne and renounced his position, that was true renunciation; but there cannot be any question of renunciation in the case of a beggar who has nothing to renounce. So we must always be careful about what we really mean when we speak of this non-resistance and ideal love. We must first take care to understand whether we have the power of resistance or not. Then, having the power, if we renounce it and do not resist, we are doing a grand act of love; but if we cannot resist, and yet, at the same time, try to deceive ourselves into the belief that we are actuated by motives of the highest love, we are doing the exact opposite. Arjuna became a coward at the sight of the mighty array against him; his "love" made him forget his duty towards his country and king. That is why Shri Krishna told him that he was a hypocrite: Thou talkest like a wise man, but thy actions betray thee to be a coward; therefore stand up and fight!

Such is the central idea of Karma-Yoga. The Karma-Yogi is the man who understands that the highest ideal is non-resistance, and who also knows that this non-resistance is the highest manifestation of power in actual possession, and also what is called the resisting of evil is but a step on the way towards the manifestation of this highest power, namely, non-resistance. Before reaching this highest ideal, man's duty is to resist evil; let him work, let him fight, let him strike straight from the shoulder. Then only, when he has gained the power to resist, will non-resistance be a virtue.

I once met a man in my country whom I had known before as a very stupid, dull person, who knew nothing and had not the desire to know anything, and was living the life of a brute. He asked me what he should do to know God, how he was to get free. "Can you tell a lie?" I asked him. "No," he replied. "Then you must learn to do so. It is better to tell a lie than to be a brute, or a log of wood. You are inactive; you have not certainly reached the highest state, which is beyond all actions, calm and serene; you are too dull even to do something wicked." That was an extreme case, of course, and I was joking with him; but what I meant was that a man must be active in order to pass through activity to perfect calmness.

Inactivity should be avoided by all means. Activity always means resistance. Resist all evils, mental and physical; and when you have succeeded in resisting, then will calmness come. It is very easy to say, "Hate nobody, resist not evil," but we know what that kind of thing generally means in practice. When the eyes of society are turned towards us, we may make a show of non-resistance, but in our hearts it is canker all the time. We feel the utter want of the calm of non-resistance; we feel that it would be better for us to resist. If you desire wealth, and know at the same time that the whole world regards him who aims at wealth as a very wicked man, you, perhaps, will not dare to plunge into the struggle for wealth, yet your mind will be running day and night after money. This is hypocrisy and will serve no purpose. Plunge into the world, and then, after a time, when you have suffered and enjoyed all that is in it, will renunciation come; then will calmness come. So fulfil your desire for power and everything else, and after you have fulfilled the desire, will come the time when you will know that they are all very little things; but until you have fulfilled this desire, until you have passed through that activity, it is impossible for you to come to the state of calmness, serenity, and self-surrender. These ideas of serenity and renunciation have been preached for thousands of years; everybody has heard of them from childhood, and yet we see very few in the world who have really reached that stage. I do not know if I have seen twenty persons in my life who are really calm and non-resisting, and I have travelled over half the world.

Every man should take up his own ideal and endeavour to accomplish it. That is a surer way of progress than taking up other men's ideals, which he can never hope to accomplish. For instance, we take a child and at once give him the task of walking twenty miles. Either the little one dies, or one in a thousand crawls the twenty miles, to reach the end exhausted and half-dead. That is like what we generally try to do with the world. All the men and women, in any society, are not of the same mind, capacity, or of the same power to do things; they must have different ideals, and we have no right to sneer at any ideal. Let every one do the best he can for realising his own ideal. Nor is it right that I should be judged by your standard or you by mine. The apple tree should not be judged by the standard of the oak, nor the oak by that of the apple. To judge the apple tree you must take the apple standard, and for the oak, its own standard.

Unity in variety is the plan of creation. However men and women may vary individually, there is unity in the background. The different individual characters and classes of men and women are natural variations in creation. Hence, we ought not to judge them by the same standard or put the same ideal before them. Such a course creates only an unnatural struggle, and the result is that man begins to hate himself and is hindered from becoming religious and good. Our duty is to encourage every one in his struggle to live up to his own highest ideal, and strive at the same time to make the ideal as near as possible to the truth.

In the Hindu system of morality we find that this fact has been recognised from very ancient times; and in their scriptures and books on ethics different rules are laid down for the different classes of men — the householder, the Sannyâsin (the man who has renounced the world), and the student.

The life of every individual, according to the Hindu scriptures, has its peculiar duties apart from what belongs in common to universal humanity. The Hindu begins life as a student; then he marries and becomes a householder; in old age he retires; and lastly he gives up the world and becomes a Sannyasin. To each of these stages of life certain duties are attached. No one of these stages is intrinsically superior to another. The life of the married man is quite as great as that of the celibate who has devoted himself to religious work. The scavenger in the street is quite as great and glorious as the king on his throne. Take him off his throne, make him do the work of the scavenger, and see how he fares. Take up the scavenger and see how he will rule. It is useless to say that the man who lives out of the world is a greater man than he who lives in the world; it is much more difficult to live in the world and worship God than to give it up and live a free and easy life. The four stages of life in India have in later times been reduced to two — that of the householder and of the monk. The householder marries and carries on his duties as a citizen, and the duty of the other is to devote his energies wholly to religion, to preach and to worship God. I shall read to you a few passages from the Mahâ-Nirvâna-Tantra, which treats of this subject, and you will see that it is a very difficult task for a man to be a householder, and perform all his duties perfectly:

The householder should be devoted to God; the knowledge of God should be his goal of life. Yet he must work constantly, perform all his duties; he must give up the fruits of his actions to God.

It is the most difficult thing in this world to work and not care for the result, to help a man and never think that he ought to be grateful, to do some good work and at the same time never look to see whether it brings you name or fame, or nothing at all. Even the most arrant coward becomes brave when the world praises him. A fool can do heroic deeds when the approbation of society is upon him, but for a man to constantly do good without caring for the approbation of his fellow men is indeed the highest sacrifice man can perform. The great duty of the householder is to earn a living, but he must take care that he does not do it by telling lies, or by cheating, or by robbing others; and he must remember that his life is for the service of God, and the poor.

Knowing that mother and father are the visible representatives of God, the householder, always and by all means, must please them. If the mother is pleased, and the father, God is pleased with the man. That child is really a good child who never speaks harsh words to his parents.

Before parents one must not utter jokes, must not show restlessness, must not show anger or temper. Before mother or father, a child must bow down low, and stand up in their presence, and must not take a seat until they order him to sit.

If the householder has food and drink and clothes without first seeing that his mother and his father, his children, his wife, and the poor, are supplied, he is committing a sin. The mother and the father are the causes of this body; so a man must undergo a thousand troubles in order to do good to them.

Even so is his duty to his wife. No man should scold his wife, and he must always maintain her as if she were his own mother. And even when he is in the greatest difficulties and troubles, he must not show anger to his wife.

He who thinks of another woman besides his wife, if he touches her even with his mind — that man goes to dark hell.

Before women he must not talk improper language, and never brag of his powers. He must not say, "I have done this, and I have done that."

The householder must always please his wife with money, clothes, love, faith, and words like nectar, and never do anything to disturb her. That man who has succeeded in getting the love of a chaste wife has succeeded in his religion and has all the virtues.

The following are duties towards children:

A son should be lovingly reared up to his fourth year; he should be educated till he is sixteen. When he is twenty years of age he should be employed in some work; he should then be treated affectionately by his father as his equal. Exactly in the same manner the daughter should be brought up, and should be educated with the greatest care. And when she marries, the father ought to give her jewels and wealth.

Then the duty of the man is towards his brothers and sisters, and towards the children of his brothers and sisters, if they are poor, and towards his other relatives, his friends and his servants. Then his duties are towards the people of the same village, and the poor, and any one that comes to him for help. Having sufficient means, if the householder does not take care to give to his relatives and to the poor, know him to be only a brute; he is not a human being.

Excessive attachment to food, clothes, and the tending of the body, and dressing of the hair should be avoided. The householder must be pure in heart and clean in body, always active and always ready for work.

To his enemies the householder must be a hero. Them he must resist. That is the duty of the householder. He must not sit down in a corner and weep, and talk nonsense about non-resistance. If he does not show himself a hero to his enemies he has not done his duty. And to his friends and relatives he must be as gentle as a lamb.

It is the duty of the householder not to pay reverence to the wicked; because, if he reverences the wicked people of the world, he patronizes wickedness; and it will be a great mistake if he disregards those who are worthy of respect, the good people. He must not be gushing in his friendship; he must not go out of the way making friends everywhere; he must watch the actions of the men he wants to make friends with, and their dealings with other men, reason upon them, and then make friends.

These three things he must not talk of. He must not talk in public of his own fame; he must not preach his own name or his own powers; he must not talk of his wealth, or of anything that has been told to him privately.

A man must not say he is poor, or that he is wealthy — he must not brag of his wealth. Let him keep his own counsel; this is his religious duty. This is not mere worldly wisdom; if a man does not do so, he may be held to be immoral.

The householder is the basis, the prop, of the whole society. He is the principal earner. The poor, the weak, the children and the women who do not work — all live upon the householder; so there must be certain duties that he has to perform, and these duties must make him feel strong to perform them, and not make him think that he is doing things beneath his ideal. Therefore, if he has done something weak, or has made some mistake, he must not say so in public; and if he is engaged in some enterprise and knows he is sure to fail in it, he must not speak of it. Such self-exposure is not only uncalled for, but also unnerves the man and makes him unfit for the performance of his legitimate duties in life. At the same time, he must struggle hard to acquire these things — firstly, knowledge, and secondly, wealth. It is his duty, and if he does not do his duty, he is nobody. A householder who does not struggle to get wealth is immoral. If he is lazy and content to lead an idle life, he is immoral, because upon him depend hundreds. If he gets riches, hundreds of others will be thereby supported.

If there were not in this city hundreds who had striven to become rich, and who had acquired wealth, where would all this civilization, and these alms-houses and great houses be?

Going after wealth in such a case is not bad, because that wealth is for distribution. The householder is the centre of life and society. It is a worship for him to acquire and spend wealth nobly, for the householder who struggles to become rich by good means and for good purposes is doing practically the same thing for the attainment of salvation as the anchorite does in his cell when he is praying; for in them we see only the different aspects of the same virtue of self-surrender and self-sacrifice prompted by the feeling of devotion to God and to all that is His.

He must struggle to acquire a good name by all means. He must not gamble, he must not move in the company of the wicked, he must not tell lies, and must not be the cause of trouble to others.

Often people enter into things they have not the means to accomplish, with the result that they cheat others to attain their own ends. Then there is in all things the time factor to be taken into consideration; what at one time might be a failure, would perhaps at another time be a very great success.

The householder must speak the truth, and speak gently, using words which people like, which will do good to others; nor should he talk of the business of other men.

The householder by digging tanks, by planting trees on the roadsides, by establishing rest-houses for men and animals, by making roads and building bridges, goes towards the same goal as the greatest Yogi.

This is one part of the doctrine of Karma-Yoga — activity, the duty of the householder. There is a passage later on, where it says that "if the householder dies in battle, fighting for his country or his religion, he comes to the same goal as the Yogi by meditation," showing thereby that what is duty for one is not duty for another. At the same time, it does not say that this duty is lowering and the other elevating. Each duty has its own place, and according to the circumstances in which we are placed, we must perform our duties.

One idea comes out of all this — the condemnation of all weakness. This is a particular idea in all our teachings which I like, either in philosophy, or in religion, or in work. If you read the Vedas, you will find this word always repeated — fearlessness — fear nothing. Fear is a sign of weakness. A man must go about his duties without taking notice of the sneers and the ridicule of the world.

If a man retires from the world to worship God, he must not think that those who live in the world and work for the good of the world are not worshipping God: neither must those who live in the world, for wife and children, think that those who give up the world are low vagabonds. Each is great in his own place. This thought I will illustrate by a story.

A certain king used to inquire of all the Sannyasins that came to his country, "Which is the greater man — he who gives up the world and becomes a Sannyasin, or he who lives in the world and performs his duties as a house holder?" Many wise men sought to solve the problem. Some asserted that the Sannyasin was the greater, upon which the king demanded that they should prove their assertion. When they could not, he ordered them to marry and become householders. Then others came and said, "The householder who performs his duties is the greater man." Of them, too, the king demanded proofs. When they could not give them, he made them also settle down as householders.

At last there came a young Sannyasin, and the king similarly inquired of him also. He answered, "Each, O king, is equally great in his place." "Prove this to me," asked the king. "I will prove it to you," said the Sannyasin, "but you must first come and live as I do for a few days, that I may be able to prove to you what I say." The king consented and followed the Sannyasin out of his own territory and passed through many other countries until they came to a great kingdom. In the capital of that kingdom a great ceremony was going on. The king and the Sannyasin heard the noise of drums and music, and heard also the criers; the people were assembled in the streets in gala dress, and a great proclamation was being made. The king and the Sannyasin stood there to see what was going on. The crier was proclaiming loudly that the princess, daughter of the king of that country, was about to choose a husband from among those assembled before her.

It was an old custom in India for princesses to choose husbands in this way. Each princess had certain ideas of the sort of man she wanted for a husband. Some would have the handsomest man, others would have only the most learned, others again the richest, and so on. All the princes of the neighbourhood put on their bravest attire and presented themselves before her. Sometimes they too had their own criers to enumerate their advantages and the reasons why they hoped the princess would choose them. The princess was taken round on a throne, in the most splendid array, and looked at and heard about them. If she was not pleased with what she saw and heard, she said to her bearers, "Move on," and no more notice was taken of the rejected suitors. If, however, the princess was pleased with any one of them, she threw a garland of flowers over him and he became her husband.

The princess of the country to which our king and the Sannyasin had come was having one of these interesting ceremonies. She was the most beautiful princess in the world, and the husband of the princess would be ruler of the kingdom after her father's death. The idea of this princess was to marry the handsomest man, but she could not find the right one to please her. Several times these meetings had taken place, but the princess could not select a husband. This meeting was the most splendid of all; more people than ever had come to it. The princess came in on a throne, and the bearers carried her from place to place. She did not seem to care for any one, and every one became disappointed that this meeting also was going to be a failure. Just then came a young man, a Sannyasin, handsome as if the sun had come down to the earth, and stood in one corner of the assembly, watching what was going on. The throne with the princess came near him, and as soon as she saw the beautiful Sannyasin, she stopped and threw the garland over him. The young Sannyasin seized the garland and threw it off, exclaiming, "What nonsense is this? I am a Sannyasin. What is marriage to me?" The king of that country thought that perhaps this man was poor and so dared not marry the princess, and said to him, "With my daughter goes half my kingdom now, and the whole kingdom after my death!" and put the garland again on the Sannyasin. The young man threw it off once more, saying, "Nonsense! I do not want to marry," and walked quickly away from the assembly.

Now the princess had fallen so much in love with this young man that she said, "I must marry this man or I shall die"; and she went after him to bring him back. Then our other Sannyasin, who had brought the king there, said to him, "King, let us follow this pair"; so they walked after them, but at a good distance behind. The young Sannyasin who had refused to marry the princess walked out into the country for several miles. When he came to a forest and entered into it, the princess followed him, and the other two followed them. Now this young Sannyasin was well acquainted with that forest and knew all the intricate paths in it. He suddenly passed into one of these and disappeared, and the princess could not discover him. After trying for a long time to find him she sat down under a tree and began to weep, for she did not know the way out. Then our king and the other Sannyasin came up to her and said, "Do not weep; we will show you the way out of this forest, but it is too dark for us to find it now. Here is a big tree; let us rest under it, and in the morning we will go early and show you the road."

Now a little bird and his wife and their three little ones lived on that tree, in a nest. This little bird looked down and saw the three people under the tree and said to his wife, "My dear, what shall we do? Here are some guests in the house, and it is winter, and we have no fire." So he flew away and got a bit of burning firewood in his beak and dropped it before the guests, to which they added fuel and made a blazing fire. But the little bird was not satisfied. He said again to his wife, "My dear, what shall we do? There is nothing to give these people to eat, and they are hungry. We are householders; it is our duty to feed any one who comes to the house. I must do what I can, I will give them my body." So he plunged into the midst of the fire and perished. The guests saw him falling and tried to save him, but he was too quick for them.

The little bird's wife saw what her husband did, and she said, "Here are three persons and only one little bird for them to eat. It is not enough; it is my duty as a wife not to let my husband's effort go in vain; let them have my body also." Then she fell into the fire and was burned to death.

Then the three baby-birds, when they saw what was done and that there was still not enough food for the three guests, said, "Our parents have done what they could and still it is not enough. It is our duty to carry on the work of our parents; let our bodies go too." And they all dashed down into the fire also.

Amazed at what they saw, the three people could not of course eat these birds. They passed the night without food, and in the morning the king and the Sannyasin showed the princess the way, and she went back to her father.

Then the Sannyasin said to the king, "King, you have seen that each is great in his own place. If you want to live in the world, live like those birds, ready at any moment to sacrifice yourself for others. If you want to renounce the world, be like that young man to whom the most beautiful woman and a kingdom were as nothing. If you want to be a householder, hold your life a sacrifice for the welfare of others; and if you choose the life of renunciation, do not even look at beauty and money and power. Each is great in his own place, but the duty of the one is not the duty of the other.

Chapter III.
The Secret Of Work

Helping others physically, by removing their physical needs, is indeed great, but the help is great according as the need is greater and according as the help is far reaching. If a man's wants can be removed for an hour, it is helping him indeed; if his wants can be removed for a year, it will be more help to him; but if his wants can be removed for ever, it is surely the greatest help that can be given him. Spiritual knowledge is the only thing that can destroy our miseries for ever; any other knowledge satisfies wants only for a time. It is only with the knowledge of the spirit that the faculty of want is annihilated for ever; so helping man spiritually is the highest help that can be given to him. He who gives man spiritual knowledge is the greatest benefactor of mankind and as such we always find that those were the most powerful of men who helped man in his spiritual needs, because spirituality is the true basis of all our activities in life. A spiritually strong and sound man will be strong in every other respect, if he so wishes. Until there is spiritual strength in man even physical needs cannot be well satisfied. Next to spiritual comes intellectual help. The gift of knowledge is a far higher gift than that of food and clothes; it is even higher than giving life to a man, because the real life of man consists of knowledge. Ignorance is death, knowledge is life. Life is of very little value, if it is a life in the dark, groping through ignorance and misery. Next in order comes, of course, helping a man physically. Therefore, in considering the question of helping others, we must always strive not to commit the mistake of thinking that physical help is the only help that can be given. It is not only the last but the least, because it cannot bring about permanent satisfaction. The misery that I feel when I am hungry is satisfied by eating, but hunger returns; my misery can cease only when I am satisfied beyond all want. Then hunger will not make me miserable; no distress, no sorrow will be able to move me. So, that help which tends to make us strong spiritually is the highest, next to it comes intellectual help, and after that physical help.

The miseries of the world cannot be cured by physical help only. Until man's nature changes, these physical needs will always arise, and miseries will always be felt, and no amount of physical help will cure them completely. The only solution of this problem is to make mankind pure. Ignorance is the mother of all the evil and all the misery we see. Let men have light, let them be pure and spiritually strong and educated, then alone will misery cease in the world, not before. We may convert every house in the country into a charity asylum, we may fill the land with hospitals, but the misery of man will still continue to exist until man's character changes.

We read in the Bhagavad-Gita again and again that we must all work incessantly. All work is by nature composed of good and evil. We cannot do any work which will not do some good somewhere; there cannot be any work which will not cause some harm somewhere. Every work must necessarily be a mixture of good and evil; yet we are commanded to work incessantly. Good and evil will both have their results, will produce their Karma. Good action will entail upon us good effect; bad action, bad. But good and bad are both bondages of the soul. The solution reached in the Gita in regard to this bondage-producing nature of work is that, if we do not attach ourselves to the work we do, it will not have any binding effect on our soul. We shall try to understand what is meant by this "non-attachment to" to work.

This is the one central idea in the Gita: work incessantly, but be not attached to it. Samskâra can be translated very nearly by "inherent tendency". Using the simile of a lake for the mind, every ripple, every wave that rises in the mind, when it subsides, does not die out entirely, but leaves a mark and a future possibility of that wave coming out again. This mark, with the possibility of the wave reappearing, is what is called Samskâra. Every work that we do, every movement of the body, every thought that we think, leaves such an impression on the mind-stuff, and even when such impressions are not obvious on the surface, they are sufficiently strong to work beneath the surface, subconsciously. What we are every moment is determined by the sum total of these impressions on the mind. What I am just at this moment is the effect of the sum total of all the impressions of my past life. This is really what is meant by character; each man's character is determined by the sum total of these impressions. If good impressions prevail, the character becomes good; if bad, it becomes bad. If a man continuously hears bad words, thinks bad thoughts, does bad actions, his mind will be full of bad impressions; and they will influence his thought and work without his being conscious of the fact. In fact, these bad impressions are always working, and their resultant must be evil, and that man will be a bad man; he cannot help it. The sum total of these impressions in him will create the strong motive power for doing bad actions. He will be like a machine in the hands of his impressions, and they will force him to do evil. Similarly, if a man thinks good thoughts and does good works, the sum total of these impressions will be good; and they, in a similar manner, will force him to do good even in spite of himself. When a man has done so much good work and thought so many good thoughts that there is an irresistible tendency in him to do good in spite of himself and even if he wishes to do evil, his mind, as the sum total of his tendencies, will not allow him to do so; the tendencies will turn him back; he is completely under the influence of the good tendencies. When such is the case, a man's good character is said to be established.

As the tortoise tucks its feet and head inside the shell, and you may kill it and break it in pieces, and yet it will not come out, even so the character of that man who has control over his motives and organs is unchangeably established. He controls his own inner forces, and nothing can draw them out against his will. By this continuous reflex of good thoughts, good impressions moving over the surface of the mind, the tendency for doing good becomes strong, and as the result we feel able to control the Indriyas (the sense-organs, the nerve-centres). Thus alone will character be established, then alone a man gets to truth. Such a man is safe for ever; he cannot do any evil. You may place him in any company, there will be no danger for him. There is a still higher state than having this good tendency, and that is the desire for liberation. You must remember that freedom of the soul is the goal of all Yogas, and each one equally leads to the same result. By work alone men may get to where Buddha got largely by meditation or Christ by prayer. Buddha was a working Jnâni, Christ was a Bhakta, but the same goal was reached by both of them. The difficulty is here. Liberation means entire freedom — freedom from the bondage of good, as well as from the bondage of evil. A golden chain is as much a chain as an iron one. There is a thorn in my finger, and I use another to take the first one out; and when I have taken it out, I throw both of them aside; I have no necessity for keeping the second thorn, because both are thorns after all. So the bad tendencies are to be counteracted by the good ones, and the bad impressions on the mind should be removed by the fresh waves of good ones, until all that is evil almost disappears, or is subdued and held in control in a corner of the mind; but after that, the good tendencies have also to be conquered. Thus the "attached" becomes the "unattached". Work, but let not the action or the thought produce a deep impression on the mind. Let the ripples come and go, let huge actions proceed from the muscles and the brain, but let them not make any deep impression on the soul.

How can this be done? We see that the impression of any action, to which we attach ourselves, remains. I may meet hundreds of persons during the day, and among them meet also one whom I love; and when I retire at night, I may try to think of all the faces I saw, but only that face comes before the mind — the face which I met perhaps only for one minute, and which I loved; all the others have vanished. My attachment to this particular person caused a deeper impression on my mind than all the other faces. Physiologically the impressions have all been the same; every one of the faces that I saw pictured itself on the retina, and the brain took the pictures in, and yet there was no similarity of effect upon the mind. Most of the faces, perhaps, were entirely new faces, about which I had never thought before, but that one face of which I got only a glimpse found associations inside. Perhaps I had pictured him in my mind for years, knew hundreds of things about him, and this one new vision of him awakened hundreds of sleeping memories in my mind; and this one impression having been repeated perhaps a hundred times more than those of the different faces together, will produce a great effect on the mind.

Therefore, be "unattached"; let things work; let brain centres work; work incessantly, but let not a ripple conquer the mind. Work as if you were a stranger in this land, a sojourner; work incessantly, but do not bind yourselves; bondage is terrible. This world is not our habitation, it is only one of the many stages through which we are passing. Remember that great saying of the Sânkhya, "The whole of nature is for the soul, not the soul for nature." The very reason of nature's existence is for the education of the soul; it has no other meaning; it is there because the soul must have knowledge, and through knowledge free itself. If we remember this always, we shall never be attached to nature; we shall know that nature is a book in which we are to read, and that when we have gained the required knowledge, the book is of no more value to us. Instead of that, however, we are identifying ourselves with nature; we are thinking that the soul is for nature, that the spirit is for the flesh, and, as the common saying has it, we think that man "lives to eat" and not "eats to live". We are continually making this mistake; we are regarding nature as ourselves and are becoming attached to it; and as soon as this attachment comes, there is the deep impression on the soul, which binds us down and makes us work not from freedom but like slaves.

The whole gist of this teaching is that you should work like a *master* and not as a *slave*; work incessantly, but do not do slave's work. Do you not see how everybody works? Nobody can be altogether at rest; ninety-nine per cent of mankind work like slaves, and the result is misery; it is all selfish work. Work through freedom! Work through love! The word "love" is very difficult to understand; love never comes until there is freedom. There is no true love possible in the slave. If you buy a slave and tie him down in chains and make him work for you, he will work like a drudge, but there will be no love in him. So when we ourselves work for the things of the world as slaves, there can be no love in us, and our work is not true work. This is true of work done for relatives and friends, and is true of work done for our own selves. Selfish work is slave's work; and here is a test. Every act of love brings happiness; there is no act of love which does not bring peace and blessedness as its reaction. Real existence, real knowledge, and real love are eternally connected with one another, the three in one: where one of them is, the others also must be; they are the three aspects of the One without a second — the Existence - Knowledge - Bliss. When that existence becomes relative, we see it as the world; that knowledge becomes in its turn modified into the knowledge of the things of the world; and that bliss forms the foundation of all true love known to the heart of man. Therefore true love can never react so as to cause pain either to the lover or to the beloved. Suppose a man loves a woman; he wishes to have her all to himself and feels extremely jealous about her every movement; he wants her to sit near him, to stand near him, and to eat and move at his bidding. He is a slave to her and wishes to have her as his slave. That is not love; it is a kind of morbid affection of the slave, insinuating itself as love. It cannot be love, because it is painful; if she does not do what he wants, it brings him pain. With love there is no painful reaction; love only brings a reaction of bliss; if it does not, it is not love; it is mistaking something else for love. When you have succeeded in loving your husband, your wife, your children, the whole world, the universe, in such a manner that there is no reaction of pain or jealousy, no selfish feeling, then you are in a fit state to be unattached.

Krishna says, "Look at Me, Arjuna! If I stop from work for one moment, the whole universe will die. I have nothing to gain from work; I am the one Lord, but why do I work? Because I love the world." God is unattached because He loves; that real love makes us unattached. Wherever there is attachment, the clinging to the things of the world, you must know that it is all physical attraction between sets of particles of matter — something that attracts two bodies nearer and nearer all the time and, if they cannot get near enough, produces pain; but where there is *real* love, it does not rest on physical attachment at all. Such lovers may be a thousand miles away from one another, but their love will be all the same; it does not die, and will never produce any painful reaction.

To attain this unattachment is almost a life-work, but as soon as we have reached this point, we have attained the goal of love and become free; the bondage of nature falls from us, and we see nature as she is; she forges no more chains for us; we stand entirely free and take not the results of work into consideration; who then cares for what the results may be?

Do you ask anything from your children in return for what you have given them? It is your duty to work for them, and there the matter ends. In whatever you do for a particular person, a city, or a state, assume the same attitude towards it as you have towards your children — expect nothing in return. If you can invariably take the position of a giver, in which everything given by you is a free offering to the world, without any thought of return, then will your work bring you no attachment. Attachment comes only where we expect a return.

If working like slaves results in selfishness and attachment, working as master of our own mind gives rise to the bliss of non-attachment. We often talk of right and justice, but we find that in the world right and justice are mere baby's talk. There are two things which guide the conduct of men: might and mercy. The exercise of might is invariably the exercise of selfishness. All men and women try to make the most of whatever power or advantage they have. Mercy is heaven itself; to be good, we have all to be merciful. Even justice and right should stand on mercy. All thought of obtaining return for the work we do hinders our spiritual progress; nay, in the end it brings misery. There is another way in which this idea of mercy and selfless charity can be put into practice; that is, by looking upon work as "worship" in case we believe in a Personal God. Here we give up all the fruits our work unto the Lord, and worshipping Him thus, we have no right to expect anything from man kind for the work we do. The Lord Himself works incessantly and is ever without attachment. Just as water cannot wet the lotus leaf, so work cannot bind the unselfish man by giving rise to attachment to results. The selfless and unattached man may live in the very heart of a crowded and sinful city; he will not be touched by sin.

This idea of complete self-sacrifice is illustrated in the following story: After the battle of Kurukshetra the five Pândava brothers performed a great sacrifice and made very large gifts to the poor. All people expressed amazement at the greatness and richness of the sacrifice, and said that such a sacrifice the world had never seen before. But, after the ceremony, there came a little mongoose, half of whose body was golden, and the other half brown; and he began to roll on the floor of the sacrificial hall. He said to those around, "You are all liars; this is no sacrifice." "What!" they exclaimed, "you say this is no sacrifice; do you not know how money and jewels were poured out to the poor and every one became rich and happy? This was the most wonderful sacrifice any man ever performed." But the mongoose said, "There was once a little village, and in it there dwelt a poor Brahmin with his wife, his son, and his son's wife. They were very poor and lived on small gifts made to them for preaching and teaching. There came in that land a three years' famine, and the poor Brahmin suffered more than ever. At last when the family had starved for days, the father brought home one morning a little barley flour, which he had been fortunate enough to obtain, and he divided it into four parts, one for each member of the family. They prepared it for their meal, and just as they were about to eat, there was a knock at the door. The father opened it, and there stood a guest. Now in India a guest is a sacred person; he is as a god for the time being, and must be treated as such. So the poor Brahmin said, 'Come in, sir; you are welcome,' He set before the guest his own portion of the food, which the guest quickly ate and said, 'Oh, sir, you have killed me; I have been starving for ten days, and this little bit has but increased my hunger.' Then the wife said to her husband, 'Give him my share,' but the husband said, 'Not so.' The wife however insisted, saying, 'Here is a poor man, and it is our duty as householders to see that he is fed, and it is my duty as a wife to give him my portion, seeing that you have no more to offer him.' Then she gave her share to the guest, which he ate, and said he was still burning with hunger. So the son said, 'Take my portion also; it is the duty of a son to help his father to fulfil his obligations.' The guest ate that, but remained still unsatisfied; so the son's wife gave him her portion also. That was sufficient, and the guest departed, blessing them. That night those four people died of starvation. A few granules of that flour had fallen on the floor; and when I rolled my body on them, half of it became golden, as you see. Since then I have been travelling all over the world, hoping to find another sacrifice like that, but nowhere have I found one; nowhere else has the other half of my body been turned into gold. That is why I say this is no sacrifice."

This idea of charity is going out of India; great men are becoming fewer and fewer. When I was first learning English, I read an English story book in which there was a story about a dutiful boy who had gone out to work and had given some of his money to his old mother, and this was praised in three or four pages. What was that? No Hindu boy can ever understand the moral of that story. Now I understand it when I hear the Western idea — every man for himself. And some men take everything for themselves, and fathers and mothers and wives and children go to the wall. That should never and nowhere be the ideal of the householder.

Now you see what Karma-Yoga means; even at the point of death to help any one, without asking questions. Be cheated millions of times and never ask a question, and never think of what you are doing. Never vaunt of your gifts to the poor or expect their gratitude, but rather be grateful to them for giving you the occasion of practicing charity to them. Thus it is plain that to be an ideal householder is a much more difficult task than to be an ideal Sannyasin; the true life of work is indeed as hard as, if not harder than, the equally true life of renunciation.

Chapter IV.
What Is Duty?

It is necessary in the study of Karma-Yoga to know what duty is. If I have to do something I must first know that it is my duty, and then I can do it. The idea of duty again is different in different nations. The Mohammedan says what is written in his book, the Koran, is his duty; the Hindu says what is in the Vedas is his duty; and the Christian says what is in the Bible is his duty. We find that there are varied ideas of duty, differing according to different states in life, different historical periods and different nations. The term "duty", like every other universal abstract term, is impossible clearly to define; we can only get an idea of it by knowing its practical operations and results. When certain things occur before us, we have all a natural or trained impulse to act in a certain manner towards them; when this impulse comes, the mind begins to think about the situation. Sometimes it thinks that it is good to act in a particular manner under the given conditions; at other times it thinks that it is wrong to act in the same manner even in the very same circumstances. The ordinary idea of duty everywhere is that every good man follows the dictates of his conscience. But what is it that makes an act a duty? If a Christian finds a piece of beef before him and does not eat it to save his own life, or will not give it to save the life of another man, he is sure to feel that he has not done his duty. But if a Hindu dares to eat that piece of beef or to give it to another Hindu, he is equally sure to feel that he too has not done his duty; the Hindu's training and education make him feel that way. In the last century there were notorious bands of robbers in India called thugs; they thought it their duty to kill any man they could and take away his money; the larger the number of men they killed, the better they thought they were. Ordinarily if a man goes out into the street and shoots down another man, he is apt to feel sorry for it, thinking that he has done wrong. But if the very same man, as a soldier in his regiment, kills not one but twenty, he is certain to feel glad and think that he has done his duty remarkably well. Therefore we see that it is not the thing done that defines a duty. To give an objective definition of duty is thus entirely impossible. Yet there is duty from the subjective side. Any action that makes us go Godward is a good action, and is our duty; any action that makes us go downward is evil, and is not our duty. From the subjective standpoint we may see that certain acts have a tendency to exalt and ennoble us, while certain other acts have a tendency to degrade and to brutalise us. But it is not possible to make out with certainty which acts have which kind of tendency in relation to all persons, of all sorts and conditions. There is, however, only one idea of duty which has been universally accepted by all mankind, of all ages and sects and countries, and that has been summed up in a Sanskrit aphorism thus: "Do not injure any being; not injuring any being is virtue, injuring any being is sin."

The Bhagavad-Gita frequently alludes to duties dependent upon birth and position in life. Birth and position in life and in society largely determine the mental and moral attitude of individuals towards the various activities of life. It is therefore our duty to do that work which will exalt and ennoble us in accordance with the ideals and activities of the society in which we are born. But it must be particularly remembered that the same ideals and activities do not prevail in all societies and countries; our ignorance of this is the main cause of much of the hatred of one nation towards another. An American thinks that whatever an American does in accordance with the custom of his country is the best thing to do, and that whoever does not follow his custom must be a very wicked man. A Hindu thinks that his customs are the only right ones and are the best in the world, and that whosoever does not obey them must be the most wicked man living. This is quite a natural mistake which all of us are apt to make. But it is very harmful; it is the cause of half the uncharitableness found in the world. When I came to this country and was going through the Chicago Fair, a man from behind pulled at my turban. I looked back and saw that he was a very gentlemanly-looking man, neatly dressed. I spoke to him; and when he found that I knew English, he became very much abashed. On another occasion in the same Fair another man gave me a push. When I asked him the reason, he also was ashamed and stammered out an apology saying, "Why do you dress that way?" The sympathies of these men were limited within the range of their own language and their own fashion of dress. Much of the oppression of powerful nations on weaker ones is caused by this prejudice. It dries up their fellow feeling for fellow men. That very man who asked me why I did not dress as he did and wanted to ill-treat me because of my dress may have been a very good man, a good father, and a good citizen; but the kindliness of his nature died out as soon as he saw a man in a different dress. Strangers are exploited in all countries, because they do not know how to defend themselves; thus they carry home false impressions of the peoples they have seen. Sailors, soldiers, and traders behave in foreign lands in very queer ways, although they would not dream of doing so in their own country;

perhaps this is why the Chinese call Europeans and Americans "foreign devils". They could not have done this if they had met the good, the kindly sides of Western life.

Therefore the one point we ought to remember is that we should always try to see the duty of others through their own eyes, and never judge the customs of other peoples by our own standard. I am not the standard of the universe. I have to accommodate myself to the world, and not the world to me. So we see that environments change the nature of our duties, and doing the duty which is ours at any particular time is the best thing we can do in this world. Let us do that duty which is ours by birth; and when we have done that, let us do the duty which is ours by our position in life and in society. There is, however, one great danger in human nature, viz that man never examines himself. He thinks he is quite as fit to be on the throne as the king. Even if he is, he must first show that he has done the duty of his own position; and then higher duties will come to him. When we begin to work earnestly in the world, nature gives us blows right and left and soon enables us to find out our position. No man can long occupy satisfactorily a position for which he is not fit. There is no use in grumbling against nature's adjustment. He who does the lower work is not therefore a lower man. No man is to be judged by the mere nature of his duties, but all should be judged by the manner and the spirit in which they perform them.

Later on we shall find that even this idea of duty undergoes change, and that the greatest work is done only when there is no selfish motive to prompt it. Yet it is work through the sense of duty that leads us to work without any idea of duty; when work will become worship — nay, something higher — then will work be done for its own sake. We shall find that the philosophy of duty, whether it be in the form of ethics or of love, is the same as in every other Yoga — the object being the attenuating of the lower self, so that the real higher Self may shine forth — the lessening of the frittering away of energies on the lower plane of existence, so that the soul may manifest itself on the higher ones. This is accomplished by the continuous denial of low desires, which duty rigorously requires. The whole organisation of society has thus been developed, consciously or unconsciously, in the realms of action and experience, where, by limiting selfishness, we open the way to an unlimited expansion of the real nature of man.

Duty is seldom sweet. It is only when love greases its wheels that it runs smoothly; it is a continuous friction otherwise. How else could parents do their duties to their children, husbands to their wives, and vice versa? Do we not meet with cases of friction every day in our lives? Duty is sweet only through love, and love shines in freedom alone. Yet is it freedom to be a slave to the senses, to anger, to jealousies and a hundred other petty things that must occur every day in human life? In all these little roughnesses that we meet with in life, the highest expression of freedom is to forbear. Women, slaves to their own irritable, jealous tempers, are apt to blame their husbands, and assert their own "freedom", as they think, not knowing that thereby they only prove that they are slaves. So it is with husbands who eternally find fault with their wives.

Chastity is the first virtue in man or woman, and the man who, however he may have strayed away, cannot be brought to the right path by a gentle and loving and chaste wife is indeed very rare. The world is not yet as bad as that. We hear much about brutal husbands all over the world and about the impurity of men, but is it not true that there are quite as many brutal and impure women as men? If all women were as good and pure as their own constant assertions would lead one to believe, I am perfectly satisfied that there would not be one impure man in the world. What brutality is there which purity and chastity cannot conquer? A good, chaste wife, who thinks of every other man except her own husband as her child and has the attitude of a mother towards all men, will grow so great in the power of her purity that there cannot be a single man, however brutal, who will not breathe an atmosphere of holiness in her presence. Similarly, every husband must look upon all women, except his own wife, in the light of his own mother or daughter or sister. That man, again, who wants to be a teacher of religion must look upon every woman as his mother, and always behave towards her as such.

The position of the mother is the highest in the world, as it is the one place in which to learn and exercise the greatest unselfishness. The love of God is the only love that is higher than a mother's love; all others are lower. It is the duty of the mother to think of her children first and then of herself. But, instead of that, if the parents are always thinking of themselves first, the result is that the relation between parents and children becomes the same as that between birds and their offspring which, as soon as they are fledged, do not recognise any parents. Blessed, indeed, is the man who is able to look upon woman as the representative of the motherhood of God. Blessed, indeed, is the woman to whom man represents the fatherhood of God. Blessed are the children who look upon their parents as Divinity manifested on earth.

The only way to rise is by doing the duty next to us, and thus gathering strength go on until we reach the highest state. A young Sannyâsin went to a forest; there he meditated, worshipped, and practiced Yoga for a long time. After years of hard work and practice, he was one day sitting under a tree, when some dry leaves fell upon his head. He looked up and saw a crow and a crane fighting on the top of the tree, which made him very angry. He said, "What! Dare you throw these dry leaves upon my head!" As with these words he angrily glanced at them, a flash of fire went out of his head — such was the Yogi's power — and burnt the birds to ashes. He was very glad, almost overjoyed at this development of power — he could burn the crow and the crane by a look. After a time he had to go to the town to beg his bread. He went, stood at a door, and said, "Mother, give me food." A voice came from inside the house, "Wait a little, my son." The young man thought, "You wretched woman, how dare you make me wait! You do not know my power yet." While he was thinking thus the voice came again: "Boy, don't be thinking too much of yourself. Here is neither crow nor crane." He was astonished; still he had to wait. At last the woman came, and he fell at her feet and said, "Mother, how did you know that?" She said, "My boy, I do not know your Yoga or your practices. I am a common everyday woman. I made you wait because my husband is ill, and I was nursing him. All my life I have struggled to do my duty. When I was unmarried, I did my duty to my parents; now that I am married, I do my duty to my husband; that is all the Yoga I practice. But by doing my duty I have become illumined; thus I could read your thoughts and know what you had done in the forest. If you want to know something higher than this, go to the market of such and such a town where you will find a Vyâdha (The lowest class of people in India who used to live as hunters and butchers.) who will tell you something that you will be very glad to learn." The Sannyasin thought, "Why should I go to that town and to a Vyadha?" But after what he had seen, his mind opened a little, so he went. When he came near the town, he found the market and there saw, at a distance, a big fat Vyadha cutting meat with big knives, talking and bargaining with different people. The young man said, "Lord help me! Is this the man from whom I am going to learn? He is the incarnation of a demon, if he is anything." In the meantime this man looked up and said, "O Swami, did that lady send you here? Take a seat until I have done my business." The Sannyasin thought, "What comes to me here?" He took his seat; the man went on with his work, and after he had finished he took his money and said to the Sannyasin, "Come sir, come to my home." On reaching home the Vyadha gave him a seat, saying, "Wait here," and went into the house. He then washed his old father and mother, fed them, and did all he could to please them, after which he came to the Sannyasin and said, "Now, sir, you have come here to see me; what can I do for you?" The Sannyasin asked him a few questions about soul and about God, and the Vyadha gave him a lecture which forms a part of the Mahâbhârata, called the *Vyâdha-Gitâ*. It contains one of the highest flights of the Vedanta. When the Vyadha finished his teaching, the Sannyasin felt astonished. He said, "Why are you in that body? With such knowledge as yours why are you in a Vyadha's body, and doing such filthy, ugly work?"

"My son," replied the Vyadha, "no duty is ugly, no duty is impure. My birth placed me in these circumstances and environments. In my boyhood I learnt the trade; I am unattached, and I try to do my duty well. I try to do my duty as a householder, and I try to do all I can to make my father and mother happy. I neither know your Yoga, nor have I become a Sannyasin, nor did I go out of the world into a forest; nevertheless, all that you have heard and seen has come to me through the unattached doing of the duty which belongs to my position."

There is a sage in India, a great Yogi, one of the most wonderful men I have ever seen in my life. He is a peculiar man, he will not teach any one; if you ask him a question he will not answer. It is too much for him to take up the position of a teacher, he will not do it. If you ask a question, and wait for some days, in the course of conversation he will bring up the subject, and wonderful light will he throw on it. He told me once the secret of work, "Let the end and the means be joined into one." When you are doing any work, do not think of anything beyond. Do it as worship, as the highest worship, and devote your whole life to it for the time being. Thus, in the story, the Vyadha and the woman did their duty with cheerfulness and whole-heartedness; and the result was that they became illuminated, clearly showing that the right performance of the duties of any station in life, without attachment to results, leads us to the highest realisation of the perfection of the soul.

It is the worker who is attached to results that grumbles about the nature of the duty which has fallen to his lot; to the unattached worker all duties are equally good, and form efficient instruments with which selfishness and sensuality may be killed, and the freedom of the soul secured. We are all apt to think too highly of ourselves. Our duties are determined by our desires to a much larger extent than we are willing to grant. Competition rouses envy, and it kills the kindliness of the heart. To the grumbler all duties are distasteful; nothing will ever satisfy him, and his whole life is doomed to prove a failure. Let us work on, doing as we go whatever happens to be our duty, and being ever ready to put our shoulders to the wheel. Then surely shall we see the Light!

Chapter V.
We Help Ourselves, Not The World

Before considering further how devotion to duty helps us in our spiritual progress, let me place before you in a brief compass another aspect of what we in India mean by Karma. In every religion there are three parts: philosophy, mythology, and ritual. Philosophy of course is the essence of every religion; mythology explains and illustrates it by means of the more or less legendary lives of great men, stories and fables of wonderful things, and so on; ritual gives to that philosophy a still more concrete form, so that every one may grasp it — ritual is in fact concretised philosophy. This ritual is Karma; it is necessary in every religion, because most of us cannot understand abstract spiritual things until we grow much spiritually. It is easy for men to think that they can understand anything; but when it comes to practical experience, they find that abstract ideas are often very hard to comprehend. Therefore symbols are of great help, and we cannot dispense with the symbolical method of putting things before us. From time immemorial symbols have been used by all kinds of religions. In one sense we cannot think but in symbols; words themselves are symbols of thought. In another sense everything in the universe may be looked upon as a symbol. The whole universe is a symbol, and God is the essence behind. This kind of symbology is not simply the creation of man; it is not that certain people belonging to a religion sit down together and think out certain symbols, and bring them into existence out of their own minds. The symbols of religion have a natural growth. Otherwise, why is it that certain symbols are associated with certain ideas in the mind of almost every one? Certain symbols are universally prevalent. Many of you may think that the cross first came into existence as a symbol in connection with the Christian religion, but as a matter of fact it existed before Christianity was, before Moses was born, before the Vedas were given out, before there was any human record of human things. The cross may be found to have been in existence among the Aztecs and the Phoenicians; every race seems to have had the cross. Again, the symbol of the crucified Saviour, of a man crucified upon a cross, appears to have been known to almost every nation. The circle has been a great symbol throughout the world. Then there is the most universal of all symbols, the Swastika. At one time it was thought that the Buddhists carried it all over the world with them, but it has been found out that ages before Buddhism it was used among nations. In Old Babylon and in Egypt it was to be found. What does this show? All these symbols could not have been purely conventional. There must be some reason for them; some natural association between them and the human mind. Language is not the result of convention; it is not that people ever agreed to represent certain ideas by certain words; there never was an idea without a corresponding word or a word without a corresponding idea; ideas and words are in their nature inseparable. The symbols to represent ideas may be sound symbols or colour symbols. Deaf and dumb people have to think with other than sound symbols. Every thought in the mind has a form as its counterpart. This is called in Sanskrit philosophy Nâma-Rupa — name and form. It is as impossible to create by convention a system of symbols as it is to create a language. In the world's ritualistic symbols we have an expression of the religious thought of humanity. It is easy to say that there is no use of rituals and temples and all such paraphernalia; every baby says that in modern times. But it must be easy for all to see that those who worship inside a temple are in many respects different from those who will not worship there. Therefore the association of particular temples, rituals, and other concrete forms with particular religions has a tendency to bring into the minds of the followers of those religions the thoughts for which those concrete things stand as symbols; and it is not wise to ignore rituals and symbology altogether. The study and practice of these things form naturally a part of Karma-Yoga.

There are many other aspects of this science of work. One among them is to know the relation between thought and word and what can be achieved by the power of the word. In every religion the power of the word is recognised, so much so that in some of them creation itself is said to have come out of the word. The external aspect of the thought of God is the Word, and as God thought and willed before He created, creation came out of the Word. In this stress and hurry of our materialistic life, our nerves lose sensibility and become hardened. The older we grow, the longer we are knocked about in the world, the more callous we become; and we are apt to neglect things that even happen persistently and prominently around us. Human nature, however, asserts itself sometimes, and we are led to inquire into and wonder at some of these common occurrences; wondering thus is the first step in the acquisition of light. Apart from the higher philosophic and religious value of the Word, we may see that sound symbols play a prominent part in the drama of human life. I am talking to you. I am not touching you; the pulsations of the air caused by my speaking go into your ear, they touch your nerves and produce effects in your minds. You cannot resist this. What can be more wonderful than this? One man calls another a fool, and at this the other stands up and clenches his fist and lands a blow on his nose. Look at the power of the word! There is a woman weeping and miserable; another woman comes along and speaks to her a few gentle words, the doubled up frame of the weeping woman becomes straightened at once, her sorrow is gone and she already begins to smile. Think of the power of words! They are a great force in higher philosophy as well as in common life. Day and night we manipulate this force without thought and without inquiry. To know the nature of this force and to use it well is also a part of Karma-Yoga.

Our duty to others means helping others; doing good to the world. Why should we do good to the world? Apparently to help the world, but really to help ourselves. We should always try to help the world, that should be the highest motive in us; but if we consider well, we find that the world does not require our help at all. This world was not made that you or I should come and help it. I once read a sermon in which it was said, "All this beautiful world is very good, because it gives us time and opportunity to help others." Apparently, this is a very beautiful sentiment, but is it not a blasphemy to say that the world needs our help? We cannot deny that there is much misery in it; to go out and help others is, therefore, the best thing we can do, although in the long run, we shall find that helping others is only helping ourselves. As a boy I had some white mice. They were kept in a little box in which there were little wheels, and when the mice tried to cross the wheels, the wheels turned and turned, and the mice never got anywhere. So it is with the world and our helping it. The only help is that we get moral exercise. This world is neither good nor evil; each man manufactures a world for himself. If a blind man begins to think of the world, it is either as soft or hard, or as cold or hot. We are a mass of happiness or misery; we have seen that hundreds of times in our lives. As a rule, the young are optimistic and the old pessimistic. The young have life before them; the old complain their day is gone; hundreds of desires, which they cannot fulfil struggle in their hearts. Both are foolish nevertheless. Life is good or evil according to the state of mind in which we look at it, it is neither by itself. Fire, by itself, is neither good nor evil. When it keeps us warm we say, "How beautiful is fire!" When it burns our fingers, we blame it. Still, in itself it is neither good nor bad. According as we use it, it produces in us the feeling of good or bad; so also is this world. It is perfect. By perfection is meant that it is perfectly fitted to meet its ends. We may all be perfectly sure that it will go on beautifully well without us, and we need not bother our heads wishing to help it.

Yet we must do good; the desire to do good is the highest motive power we have, if we know all the time that it is a privilege to help others. Do not stand on a high pedestal and take five cents in your hand and say, "Here, my poor man," but be grateful that the poor man is there, so that by making a gift to him you are able to help yourself. It is not the receiver that is blessed, but it is the giver. Be thankful that you are allowed to exercise your power of benevolence and mercy in the world, and thus become pure and perfect. All good acts tend to make us pure and perfect. What can we do at best? Build a hospital, make roads, or erect charity asylums. We may organise a charity and collect two or three millions of dollars, build a hospital with one million, with the second give balls and drink champagne, and of the third let the officers steal half, and leave the rest finally to reach the poor; but what are all these? One mighty wind in five minutes can break all your buildings up. What shall we do then? One volcanic eruption may sweep away all our roads and hospitals and cities and buildings. Let us give up all this foolish talk of doing good to the world. It is not waiting for your or my help; yet we must work and constantly do good, because it is a blessing to ourselves. That is the only way we can become perfect. No beggar whom we have helped has ever owed a single cent to us; we owe everything to him, because he has allowed us to exercise our charity on him. It is entirely wrong to think that we have done, or can do, good to the world, or to think that we have helped such and such people. It is a foolish thought, and all foolish thoughts bring misery. We think that we have helped some man and expect him to thank us, and because he does not, unhappiness comes to us. Why should we expect anything in return for what we do? Be grateful to the man you help, think of him as God. Is it not a great privilege to be allowed to worship God by helping our fellow men? If we were really unattached, we should escape all this pain of vain expectation, and could cheerfully do good work in the world. Never will unhappiness or misery come through work done without attachment. The world will go on with its happiness and misery through eternity.

There was a poor man who wanted some money; and somehow he had heard that if he could get hold of a ghost, he might command him to bring money or anything else he liked; so he was very anxious to get hold of a ghost. He went about searching for a man who would give him a ghost, and at last he found a sage with great powers, and besought his help. The sage asked him what he would do with a ghost. I want a ghost to work for me; teach me how to get hold of one, sir; I desire it very much," replied the man. But the sage said, "Don't disturb yourself, go home." The next day the man went again to the sage and began to weep and pray, "Give me a ghost; I must have a ghost, sir, to help me." At last the sage was disgusted, and said, "Take this charm, repeat this magic word, and a ghost will come, and whatever you say to him he will do. But beware; they are terrible beings, and must be kept continually busy. If you fail to give him work, he will take your life." The man replied, "That is easy; I can give him work for all his life." Then he went to a forest, and after long repetition of the magic word, a huge ghost appeared before him, and said, "I am a ghost. I have been conquered by your magic; but you must keep me constantly employed. The moment you fail to give me work I will kill you." The man said, "Build me a palace," and the ghost said, "It is done; the palace is built." "Bring me money," said the man. "Here is your money," said the ghost. "Cut this forest down, and build a city in its place." "That is done," said the ghost, "anything more?" Now the man began to be frightened and thought he could give him nothing more to do; he did everything in a trice. The ghost said, "Give me something to do or I will eat you up." The poor man could find no further occupation for him, and was frightened. So he ran and ran and at last reached the sage, and said, "Oh, sir, protect my life!" The sage asked him what the matter was, and the man replied, "I have nothing to give the ghost to do. Everything I tell him to do he does in a moment, and he threatens to eat me up if I do not give him work." Just then the ghost arrived, saying, "I'll eat you up," and he would have swallowed the man. The man began to shake, and begged the sage to save his life. The sage said, "I will find you a way out. Look at that dog with a curly tail. Draw your sword quickly and cut the tail off and give it to the ghost to straighten out." The man cut off the dog's tail and gave it to the ghost, saying, "Straighten that out for me." The ghost took it and slowly and carefully straightened it out, but as soon as he let it go, it instantly curled up again. Once more he laboriously straightened it out, only to find it again curled up as soon as he attempted to let go of it. Again he patiently straightened it out, but as soon as he let it go, it curled up again. So he went on for days and days, until he was exhausted and said, "I was never in such trouble before in my life. I am an old veteran ghost, but never before was I in such trouble." "I will make a compromise with you ;" he said to the man, "you let me off and I will let you keep all I have given you and will promise not to harm you." The man was much pleased, and accepted the offer gladly.

This world is like a dog's curly tail, and people have been striving to straighten it out for hundreds of years; but when they let it go, it has curled up again. How could it be otherwise? One must first know how to work without attachment, then one will not be a fanatic. When we know that this world is like a dog's curly tail and will never get straightened, we shall not become fanatics. If there were no fanaticism in the world, it would make much more progress than it does now. It is a mistake to think that fanaticism can make for the progress of mankind. On the contrary, it is a retarding element creating hatred and anger, and causing people to fight each other, and making them unsympathetic. We think that whatever we do or possess is the best in the world, and what we do not do or possess is of no value. So, always remember the instance of the curly tail of the dog whenever you have a tendency to become a fanatic. You need not worry or make yourself sleepless about the world; it will go on without you. When you have avoided fanaticism, then alone will you work well. It is the level-headed man, the calm man, of good judgment and cool nerves, of great sympathy and love, who does good work and so does good to himself. The fanatic is foolish and has no sympathy; he can never straighten the world, nor himself become pure and perfect.

To recapitulate the chief points in today's lecture: First, we have to bear in mind that we are all debtors to the world and the world does not owe us anything. It is a great privilege for all of us to be allowed to do anything for the world. In helping the world we really help ourselves. The second point is that there is a God in this universe. It is not true that this universe is drifting and stands in need of help from you and me. God is ever present therein, He is undying and eternally active and infinitely watchful. When the whole universe sleeps, He sleeps not; He is working incessantly; all the changes and manifestations of the world are His. Thirdly, we ought not to hate anyone. This world will always continue to be a mixture of good and evil. Our duty is to sympathise with the weak and to love even the wrongdoer. The world is a grand moral gymnasium wherein we have all to take exercise so as to become stronger and stronger spiritually. Fourthly, we ought not to be fanatics of any kind, because fanaticism is opposed to love. You hear fanatics glibly saying, "I do not hate the sinner. I hate the sin," but I am prepared to go any distance to see the face of that man who can really make a distinction between the sin and the sinner. It is easy to say so. If we can distinguish well between quality and substance, we may become perfect men. It is not easy to do this. And further, the calmer we are and the less disturbed our nerves, the more shall we love and the better will our work be.

Chapter VI.
Non-Attachment Is Complete Self-Abnegation

Just as every action that emanates from us comes back to us as reaction, even so our actions may act on other people and theirs on us. Perhaps all of you have observed it as a fact that when persons do evil actions, they become more and more evil, and when they begin to do good, they become stronger and stronger and learn to do good at all times. This intensification of the influence of action cannot be explained on any other ground than that we can act and react upon each other. To take an illustration from physical science, when I am doing a certain action, my mind may be said to be in a certain state of vibration; all minds which are in similar circumstances will have the tendency to be affected by my mind. If there are different musical instruments tuned alike in one room, all of you may have noticed that when one is struck, the others have the tendency to vibrate so as to give the same note. So all minds that have the same tension, so to say, will be equally affected by the same thought. Of course, this influence of thought on mind will vary according to distance and other causes, but the mind is always open to affection. Suppose I am doing an evil act, my mind is in a certain state of vibration, and all minds in the universe, which are in a similar state, have the possibility of being affected by the vibration of my mind. So, when I am doing a good action, my mind is in another state of vibration; and all minds similarly strung have the possibility of being affected by my mind; and this power of mind upon mind is more or less according as the force of the tension is greater or less.

Following this simile further, it is quite possible that, just as light waves may travel for millions of years before they reach any object, so thought waves may also travel hundreds of years before they meet an object with which they vibrate in unison. It is quite possible, therefore, that this atmosphere of ours is full of such thought pulsations, both good and evil. Every thought projected from every brain goes on pulsating, as it were, until it meets a fit object that will receive it. Any mind which is open to receive some of these impulses will take them immediately. So, when a man is doing evil actions, he has brought his mind to a certain state of tension and all the waves which correspond to that state of tension, and which may be said to be already in the atmosphere, will struggle to enter into his mind. That is why an evil-doer generally goes on doing more and more evil. His actions become intensified. Such, also will be the case with the doer of good; he will open himself to all the good waves that are in the atmosphere, and his good actions also will become intensified. We run, therefore, a twofold danger in doing evil: first, we open ourselves to all the evil influences surrounding us; secondly, we create evil which affects others, may be hundreds of years hence. In doing evil we injure ourselves and others also. In doing good we do good to ourselves and to others as well; and, like all other forces in man, these forces of good and evil also gather strength from outside.

According to Karma-Yoga, the action one has done cannot be destroyed until it has borne its fruit; no power in nature can stop it from yielding its results. If I do an evil action, I must suffer for it; there is no power in this universe to stop or stay it. Similarly, if I do a good action, there is no power in the universe which can stop its bearing good results. The cause must have its effect; nothing can prevent or restrain this. Now comes a very fine and serious question about Karma-Yoga — namely, that these actions of ours, both good and evil, are intimately connected with each other. We cannot put a line of demarcation and say, this action is entirely good and this entirely evil. There is no action which does not bear good and evil fruits at the same time. To take the nearest example: I am talking to you, and some of you, perhaps, think I am doing good; and at the same time I am, perhaps, killing thousands of microbes in the atmosphere; I am thus doing evil to something else. When it is very near to us and affects those we know, we say that it is very good action if it affects them in a good manner. For instance, you may call my speaking to you very good, but the microbes will not; the microbes you do not see, but yourselves you do see. The way in which my talk affects you is obvious to you, but how it affects the microbes is not so obvious. And so, if we analyse our evil actions also, we may find that some good possibly results from them somewhere. He who in good action sees that there is something evil in it, and in the midst of evil sees that there is something good in it somewhere, has known the secret of work.

But what follows from it? That, howsoever we may try, there cannot be any action which is perfectly pure, or any which is perfectly impure, taking purity and impurity in the sense of injury and non-injury. We cannot breathe or live without injuring others, and every bit of the food we eat is taken away from another's mouth. Our very lives are crowding out other lives. It may be men, or animals, or small microbes, but some one or other of these we have to crowd out. That being the case, it naturally follows that perfection can never be attained by work. We may work through all eternity, but there will be no way out of this intricate maze. You may work on, and on, and on; there will be no end to this inevitable association of good and evil in the results of work.

The second point to consider is, what is the end of work? We find the vast majority of people in every country believing that there will be a time when this world will become perfect, when there will be no disease, nor death, nor unhappiness, nor wickedness. That is a very good idea, a very good motive power to inspire and uplift the ignorant; but if we think for a moment, we shall find on the very face of it that it cannot be so. How can it be, seeing that good and evil are the obverse and reverse of the same coin? How can you have good without evil at the same time? What is meant by perfection? A perfect life is a contradiction in terms. Life itself is a state of continuous struggle between ourselves and everything outside. Every moment we are fighting actually with external nature, and if we are defeated, our life has to go. It is, for instance, a continuous struggle for food and air. If food or air fails, we die. Life is not a simple and smoothly flowing thing, but it is a compound effect. This complex struggle between something inside and the external world is what we call life. So it is clear that when this struggle ceases, there will be an end of life.

What is meant by ideal happiness is the cessation of this struggle. But then life will cease, for the struggle can only cease when life itself has ceased. We have seen already that in helping the world we help ourselves. The main effect of work done for others is to purify ourselves. By means of the constant effort to do good to others we are trying to forget ourselves; this forgetfulness of self is the one great lesson we have to learn in life. Man thinks foolishly that he can make himself happy, and after years of struggle finds out at last that true happiness consists in killing selfishness and that no one can make him happy except himself. Every act of charity, every thought of sympathy, every action of help, every good deed, is taking so much of self-importance away from our little selves and making us think of ourselves as the lowest and the least, and, therefore, it is all good. Here we find that Jnâna, Bhakti, and Karma — all come to one point. The highest ideal is eternal and entire self-abnegation, where there is no "I," but all is "Thou"; and whether he is conscious or unconscious of it, Karma-Yoga leads man to that end. A religious preacher may become horrified at the idea of an Impersonal God; he may insist on a Personal God and wish to keep up his own identity and individuality, whatever he may mean by that. But his ideas of ethics, if they are really good, cannot but be based on the highest self-abnegation. It is the basis of all morality; you may extend it to men, or animals, or angels, it is the one basic idea, the one fundamental principle running through all ethical systems.

You will find various classes of men in this world. First, there are the God-men, whose self-abnegation is complete, and who do only good to others even at the sacrifice of their own lives. These are the highest of men. If there are a hundred of such in any country, that country need never despair. But they are unfortunately too few. Then there are the good men who do good to others so long as it does not injure themselves. And there is a third class who, to do good to themselves, injure others. It is said by a Sanskrit poet that there is a fourth unnamable class of people who injure others merely for injury's sake. Just as there are at one pole of existence the highest good men, who do good for the sake of doing good, so, at the other pole, there are others who injure others just for the sake of the injury. They do not gain anything thereby, but it is their nature to do evil.

Here are two Sanskrit words. The one is Pravritti, which means revolving towards, and the other is Nivritti, which means revolving away. The "revolving towards" is what we call the world, the "I and mine"; it includes all those things which are always enriching that "me" by wealth and money and power, and name and fame, and which are of a grasping nature, always tending to accumulate everything in one centre, that centre being "myself". That is the Pravritti, the natural tendency of every human being; taking everything from everywhere and heaping it around one centre, that centre being man's own sweet self. When this tendency begins to break, when it is Nivritti or "going away from," then begin morality and religion. Both Pravritti and Nivritti are of the nature of work: the former is evil work, and the latter is good work. This Nivritti is the fundamental basis of all morality and all religion, and the very perfection of it is entire self-abnegation, readiness to sacrifice mind and body and everything for another being. When a man has reached that state, he has attained to the perfection of Karma-Yoga. This is the highest result of good works. Although a man has not studied a single system of philosophy, although he does not believe in any God, and never has believed, although he has not prayed even once in his whole life, if the simple power of good actions has brought him to that state where he is ready to give up his life and all else for others, he has arrived at the same point to which the religious man will come through his prayers and the philosopher through his knowledge; and so you may find that the philosopher, the worker, and the devotee, all meet at one point, that one point being self-abnegation. However much their systems of philosophy and religion may differ, all mankind stand in reverence and awe before the man who is ready to sacrifice himself for others. Here, it is not at all any question of creed, or doctrine — even men who are very much opposed to all religious ideas, when they see one of these acts of complete self-sacrifice, feel that they must revere it. Have you not seen even a most bigoted

Christian, when he reads Edwin Arnold's *Light of Asia*, stand in reverence of Buddha, who Preached no God, preached nothing but self-sacrifice? The only thing is that the bigot does not know that his own end and aim in life is exactly the same as that of those from whom he differs. The worshipper, by keeping constantly before him the idea of God and a surrounding of good, comes to the same point at last and says, "Thy will be done," and keeps nothing to himself. That is self-abnegation. The philosopher, with his knowledge, sees that the seeming self is a delusion and easily gives it up. It is self-abnegation. So Karma, Bhakti, and Jnana all meet here; and this is what was meant by all the great preachers of ancient times, when they taught that God is not the world. There is one thing which is the world and another which is God; and this distinction is very true. What they mean by world is selfishness. Unselfishness is God. One may live on a throne, in a golden palace, and be perfectly unselfish; and then he is in God. Another may live in a hut and wear rags, and have nothing in the world; yet, if he is selfish, he is intensely merged in the world.

To come back to one of our main points, we say that we cannot do good without at the same time doing some evil, or do evil without doing some good. Knowing this, how can we work? There have, therefore, been sects in this world who have in an astoundingly preposterous way preached slow suicide as the only means to get out of the world, because if a man lives, he has to kill poor little animals and plants or do injury to something or some one. So according to them the only way out of the world is to die. The Jains have preached this doctrine as their highest ideal. This teaching seems to be very logical. But the true solution is found in the Gita. It is the theory of non-attachment, to be attached to nothing while doing our work of life. Know that you are separated entirely from the world, though you are in the world, and that whatever you may be doing in it, you are not doing that for your own sake. Any action that you do for yourself will bring its effect to bear upon you. If it is a good action, you will have to take the good effect, and if bad, you will have to take the bad effect; but any action that is not done for your own sake, whatever it be, will have no effect on you. There is to be found a very expressive sentence in our scriptures embodying this idea: "Even if he kill the whole universe (or be himself killed), he is neither the killer nor the killed, when he knows that he is not acting for himself at all." Therefore Karma-Yoga teaches, "Do not give up the world; live in the world, imbibe its influences as much as you can; but if it be for your own enjoyment's sake, work not at all." Enjoyment should not be the goal. First kill your self and then take the whole world as yourself; as the old Christians used to say, "The old man must die." This old man is the selfish idea that the whole world is made for our enjoyment. Foolish parents teach their children to pray, "O Lord, Thou hast created this sun for me and this moon for me," as if the Lord has had nothing else to do than to create everything for these babies. Do not teach your children such nonsense. Then again, there are people who are foolish in another way: they teach us that all these animals were created for us to kill and eat, and that this universe is for the enjoyment of men. That is all foolishness. A tiger may say, "Man was created for me" and pray, "O Lord, how wicked are these men who do not come and place themselves before me to be eaten; they are breaking Your law." If the world is created for us, we are also created for the world. That this world is created for our enjoyment is the most wicked idea that holds us down. This world is not for our sake. Millions pass out of it every year; the world does not feel it; millions of others are supplied in their place. Just as much as the world is for us, so we also are for the world.

To work properly, therefore, you have first to give up the idea of attachment. Secondly, do not mix in the fray, hold yourself as a witness and go on working. My master used to say, "Look upon your children as a nurse does." The nurse will take your baby and fondle it and play with it and behave towards it as gently as if it were her own child; but as soon as you give her notice to quit, she is ready to start off bag and baggage from the house. Everything in the shape of attachment is forgotten; it will not give the ordinary nurse the least pang to leave your children and take up other children. Even so are you to be with all that you consider your own. You are the nurse, and if you believe in God, believe that all these things which you consider yours are really His. The greatest weakness often insinuates itself as the greatest good and strength. It is a weakness to think that any one is dependent on me, and that I can do good to another. This belief is the mother of all our attachment, and through this attachment comes all our pain. We must inform our minds that no one in this universe depends upon us; not one beggar depends on our charity; not one soul on our kindness; not one living thing on our help. All are helped on by nature, and will be so helped even though millions of us were not here. The course of nature will not stop for such as you and me; it is, as already pointed out, only a blessed privilege to you and to me that we are allowed, in the way of helping others, to educate ourselves. This is a great lesson to learn in life, and when we have learned it fully, we shall never be unhappy; we can go and mix without harm in society anywhere and everywhere. You may have wives and husbands, and regiments of servants, and kingdoms to govern; if only you act on the principle that the world is not for you and does not inevitably need you, they can do you no harm. This very year some of your friends may have died. Is the world waiting without going on, for them to come again? Is its current stopped? No, it goes on. So drive out of your mind the idea that you have to do something for the world; the world does not require any help from you. It is sheer nonsense on the part of any man to think that he is born to help the world; it is simply pride, it is selfishness insinuating itself in the form of virtue. When you have trained your mind and your nerves to realise this idea of the world's non-dependence on you or on anybody, there will then be no reaction in the form of pain resulting from work. When you give something to a man and expect nothing — do not even expect the man to be grateful — his ingratitude will not tell upon you, because you never expected anything, never thought you had any right to anything in the way of a return. You gave him what he deserved; his own Karma got it for him; your Karma made you the carrier thereof. Why should you be proud of having given away something? You are the porter that carried the money or other kind of gift, and the world deserved it by its own Karma. Where is then the reason for pride in you? There is nothing very great in what you give to the world. When you have acquired the feeling of non-attachment, there will then be neither good nor evil for you. It is only selfishness that causes the difference between good and evil. It is a very hard thing to understand, but you will come to learn in time that nothing in the universe has power over you until you allow it to exercise such a power. Nothing has power over the Self of man, until the Self becomes a fool and loses independence. So, by non-attachment, you overcome and deny the power of anything to act upon you. It is very easy to say that nothing has the right to act upon you until you allow it to do so; but what is the true sign of the man who really does not allow anything to work upon him, who is neither happy nor unhappy when acted upon by the external world? The sign is that good or ill fortune causes no change in his mind: in all conditions he continues to remain the same.

There was a great sage in India called Vyâsa. This Vyâsa is known as the author of the Vedanta aphorisms, and was a holy man. His father had tried to become a very perfect man and had failed. His grandfather had also tried and failed. His great-grandfather had similarly tried and failed. He himself did not succeed perfectly, but his son, Shuka, was born perfect. Vyasa taught his son wisdom; and after teaching him the knowledge of truth himself, he sent him to the court of King Janaka. He was a great king and was called Janaka Videha. Videha means "without a body". Although a king, he had entirely forgotten that he was a body; he felt that he was a spirit all the time. This boy Shuka was sent to be taught by him. The king knew that Vyasa's son was coming to him to learn wisdom: so he made certain arrangements beforehand. And when the boy presented himself at the gates of the palace, the guards took no notice of him whatsoever. They only gave him a seat, and he sat there for three days and nights, nobody speaking to him, nobody asking him who he was or whence he was. He was the son of a very great sage, his father was honoured by the whole country, and he himself was a most respectable person; yet the low, vulgar guards of the palace would take no notice of him. After that, suddenly, the ministers of the king and all the big officials came there and received him with the greatest honours. They conducted him in and showed him into splendid rooms, gave him the most fragrant baths and wonderful dresses, and for eight days they kept him there in all kinds of luxury. That solemnly serene face of Shuka did not change even to the smallest extent by the change in the treatment accorded to him; he was the same in the midst of this luxury as when waiting at the door. Then he was brought before the king. The king was on his throne, music was playing, and dancing and other amusements were going on. The king then gave him a cup of milk, full to the brim, and asked him to go seven times round the hall without spilling even a drop. The boy took the cup and proceeded in the midst of the music and the attraction of the beautiful faces. As desired by the king, seven times did he go round, and not a drop of the milk was spilt. The boy's mind could not be attracted by anything in the world, unless he allowed it to affect him. And when he brought the cup to the king, the king said to him, "What your father has taught you, and what you have learned yourself, I can only repeat. You have known the Truth; go home."

Thus the man that has practiced control over himself cannot be acted upon by anything outside; there is no more slavery for him. His mind has become free. Such a man alone is fit to live well in the world. We generally find men holding two opinions regarding the world. Some are pessimists and say, "How horrible this world is, how wicked!" Some others are optimists and say, "How beautiful this world is, how wonderful!" To those who have not controlled their own minds, the world is either full of evil or at best a mixture of good and evil. This very world will become to us an optimistic world when we become masters of our own minds. Nothing will then work upon us as good or evil; we shall find everything to be in its proper place, to be harmonious. Some men, who begin by saying that the world is a hell, often end by saying that it is a heaven when they succeed in the practice of self-control. If we are genuine Karma-Yogis and wish to train ourselves to that attainment of this state, wherever we may begin we are sure to end in perfect self-abnegation; and as soon as this seeming self has gone, the whole world, which at first appears to us to be filled with evil, will appear to be heaven itself and full of blessedness. Its very atmosphere will be blessed; every human face there will be god. Such is the end and aim of Karma-Yoga, and such is its perfection in practical life.

Our various Yogas do not conflict with each other; each of them leads us to the same goal and makes us perfect. Only each has to be strenuously practiced. The whole secret is in practicing. First you have to hear, then think, and then practice. This is true of every Yoga. You have first to hear about it and understand what it is; and many things which you do not understand will be made clear to you by constant hearing and thinking. It is hard to understand everything at once. The explanation of everything is after all in yourself. No one was ever really taught by another; each of us has to teach himself. The external teacher offers only the suggestion which rouses the internal teacher to work to understand things. Then things will be made clearer to us by our own power of perception and thought, and we shall realise them in our own souls; and that realisation will grow into the intense power of will. First it is feeling, then it becomes willing, and out of that willing comes the tremendous force for work that will go through every vein and nerve and muscle, until the whole mass of your body is changed into an instrument of the unselfish Yoga of work, and the desired result of perfect self-abnegation and utter unselfishness is duly attained. This attainment does not depend on any dogma, or doctrine, or belief. Whether one is Christian, or Jew, or Gentile, it does not matter. Are you unselfish? That is the question. If you are, you will be perfect without reading a single religious book, without going into a single church or temple. Each one of our Yogas is fitted to make man perfect even without the help of the others, because they have all the same goal in view. The Yogas of work, of wisdom, and of devotion are all capable of serving as direct and independent means for the attainment of Moksha. "Fools alone say that work and philosophy are different, not the learned." The learned know that, though apparently different from each other, they at last lead to the same goal of human perfection.

Chapter VII.
Freedom

In addition to meaning work, we have stated that psychologically the word Karma also implies causation. Any work, any action, any thought that produces an effect is called a Karma. Thus the law of Karma means the law of causation, of inevitable cause and sequence. Wheresoever there is a cause, there an effect must be produced; this necessity cannot be resisted, and this law of Karma, according to our philosophy, is true throughout the whole universe. Whatever we see, or feel, or do, whatever action there is anywhere in the universe, while being the effect of past work on the one hand, becomes, on the other, a cause in its turn, and produces its own effect. It is necessary, together with this, to consider what is meant by the word "law". By law is meant the tendency of a series to repeat itself. When we see one event followed by another, or sometimes happening simultaneously with another, we expect this sequence or co-existence to recur. Our old logicians and philosophers of the Nyâyâ school call this law by the name of Vyâpti. According to them, all our ideas of law are due to association. A series of phenomena becomes associated with things in our mind in a sort of invariable order, so that whatever we perceive at any time is immediately referred to other facts in the mind. Any one idea or, according to our psychology, any one wave that is produced in the mind-stuff, Chitta, must always give rise to many similar waves. This is the psychological idea of association, and causation is only an aspect of this grand pervasive principle of association. This pervasiveness of association is what is, in Sanskrit, called Vyâpti. In the external world the idea of law is the same as in the internal — the expectation that a particular phenomenon will be followed by another, and that the series will repeat itself. Really speaking, therefore, law does not exist in nature. Practically it is an error to say that gravitation exists in the earth, or that there is any law existing objectively anywhere in nature. Law is the method, the manner in which our mind grasps a series of phenomena; it is all in the mind. Certain phenomena, happening one after another or together, and followed by the conviction of the regularity of their recurrence — thus enabling our minds to grasp the method of the whole series — constitute what we call law.

The next question for consideration is what we mean by law being universal. Our universe is that portion of existence which is characterized by what the Sanskrit psychologists call Desha-kâla-nimitta, or what is known to European psychology as space, time, and causation. This universe is only a part of infinite existence, thrown into a peculiar mould, composed of space, time, and causation. It necessarily follows that law is possible only within this conditioned universe; beyond it there cannot be any law. When we speak of the universe, we only mean that portion of existence which is limited by our mind — the universe of the senses, which we can see, feel, touch, hear, think of, imagine. This alone is under law; but beyond it existence cannot be subject to law, because causation does not extend beyond the world of our minds. Anything beyond the range of our mind and our senses is not bound by the law of causation, as there is no mental association of things in the region beyond the senses, and no causation without association of ideas. It is only when "being" or existence gets moulded into name and form that it obeys the law of causation, and is said to be under law; because all law has its essence in causation. Therefore we see at once that there cannot be any such thing as free will; the very words are a contradiction, because will is what we know, and everything that we know is within our universe, and everything within our universe is moulded by the conditions of space, time, and causation. Everything that we know, or can possibly know, must be subject to causation, and that which obeys the law of causation cannot be free. It is acted upon by other agents, and becomes a cause in its turn. But that which has become converted into the will, which was not the will before, but which, when it fell into this mould of space, time, and causation, became converted into the human will, is free; and when this will gets out of this mould of space, time, and causation, it will be free again. From freedom it comes, and becomes moulded into this bondage, and it gets out and goes back to freedom again.

The question has been raised as to from whom this universe comes, in whom it rests, and to whom it goes; and the answer has been given that from freedom it comes, in bondage it rests, and goes back into that freedom again. So, when we speak of man as no other than that infinite being which is manifesting itself, we mean that only one very small part thereof is man; this body and this mind which we see are only one part of the whole, only one spot of the infinite being. This whole universe is only one speck of the infinite being; and all our laws, our bondages, our joys and our sorrows, our happinesses and our expectations, are only within this small universe; all our progression and digression are within its small compass. So you see how childish it is to expect a continuation of this universe — the creation of our minds — and to expect to go to heaven, which after all must mean only a repetition of this world that we know. You see at once that it is an impossible and childish desire to make the whole of infinite existence conform to the limited and conditioned existence which we know. When a man says that he will have again and again this same thing which he is hating now, or, as I sometimes put it, when he asks for a *comfortable* religion, you may know that he has become so degenerate that he cannot think of anything higher than what he is now; he is just his little present surroundings and nothing more. He has forgotten his infinite nature, and his whole idea is confined to these little joys, and sorrows, and heart-jealousies of the moment. He thinks that this finite thing is the infinite; and not only so, he will not let this foolishness go. He clings on desperately unto Trishnâ, and the thirst after life, what the Buddhists call Tanhâ and Tissâ. There may be millions of kinds of happiness, and beings, and laws, and progress, and causation, all acting outside the little universe that we know; and, after all, the whole of this comprises but one section of our infinite nature.

To acquire freedom we have to get beyond the limitations of this universe; it cannot be found here. Perfect equilibrium, or what the Christians call the peace that passeth all understanding, cannot be had in this universe, nor in heaven, nor in any place where our mind and thoughts can go, where the senses can feel, or which the imagination can conceive. No such place can give us that freedom, because all such places would be within our universe, and it is limited by space, time, and causation. There may be places that are more ethereal than this earth of ours, where enjoyments may be keener, but even those places must be in the universe and, therefore, in bondage to law; so we have to go beyond, and real religion begins where this little universe ends. These little joys, and sorrows, and knowledge of things end there, and the reality begins. Until we give up the thirst after life, the strong attachment to this our transient conditioned existence we have no hope of catching even a glimpse of that infinite freedom beyond. It stands to reason then that there is only one way to attain to that freedom which is the goal of all the noblest aspirations of mankind, and that is by giving up this little life, giving up this little universe, giving up this earth, giving up heaven, giving up the body, giving up the mind, giving up everything that is limited and conditioned. If we give up our attachment to this little universe of the senses or of the mind, we shall be free immediately. The only way to come out of bondage is to go beyond the limitations of law, to go beyond causation.

But it is a most difficult thing to give up the clinging to this universe; few ever attain to that. There are two ways to do that mentioned in our books. One is called the "Neti, Neti" (not this, not this), the other is called "Iti" (this); the former is the negative, and the latter is the positive way. The negative way is the most difficult. It is only possible to the men of the very highest, exceptional minds and gigantic wills who simply stand up and say, "No, I will not have this," and the mind and body obey their will, and they come out successful. But such people are very rare. The vast majority of mankind choose the positive way, the way through the world, making use of all the bondages themselves to break those very bondages. This is also a kind of giving up; only it is done slowly and gradually, by knowing things, enjoying things and thus obtaining experience, and knowing the nature of things until the mind lets them all go at last and becomes unattached. The former way of obtaining non-attachment is by reasoning, and the latter way is through work and experience. The first is the path of Jnâna-Yoga, and is characterized by the refusal to do any work; the second is that of Karma-Yoga, in which there is no cessation from work. Every one must work in the universe. Only those who are perfectly satisfied with the Self, whose desires do not go beyond the Self, whose mind never strays out of the Self, to whom the Self is all in all, only those do not work. The rest must work. A current rushing down of its own nature falls into a hollow and makes a whirlpool, and, after running a little in that whirlpool, it emerges again in the form of the free current to go on unchecked. Each human life is like that current. It gets into the whirl, gets involved in this world of space, time, and causation, whirls round a little, crying out, "my father, my brother, my name, my fame", and so on, and at last emerges out of it and regains its original freedom. The whole universe is doing that. Whether we know it or not, whether we are conscious or unconscious of it, we are all working to get out of the dream of the world. Man's experience in the world is to enable him to get out of its whirlpool.

What is Karma-Yoga? The knowledge of the secret of work. We see that the whole universe is working. For what? For salvation, for liberty; from the atom to the highest being, working for the one end, liberty for the mind, for the body, for the spirit. All things are always trying to get freedom, flying away from bondage. The sun, the moon, the earth, the planets, all are trying to fly away from bondage. The centrifugal and the centripetal forces of nature are indeed typical of our universe. Instead of being knocked about in this universe, and after long delay and thrashing, getting to know things as they are, we learn from Karma-Yoga the secret of work, the method of work, the organising power of work. A vast mass of energy may be spent in vain if we do not know how to utilise it. Karma-Yoga makes a science of work; you learn by it how best to utilise all the workings of this world. Work is inevitable, it must be so; but we should work to the highest purpose. Karma-Yoga makes us admit that this world is a world of five minutes, that it is a something we have to pass through; and that freedom is not here, but is only to be found beyond. To find the way out of the bondages of the world we have to go through it slowly and surely. There may be those exceptional persons about whom I just spoke, those who can stand aside and give up the world, as a snake casts off its skin and stands aside and looks at it. There are no doubt these exceptional beings; but the rest of mankind have to go slowly through the world of work. Karma-Yoga shows the process, the secret, and the method of doing it to the best advantage.

What does it say? "Work incessantly, but give up all attachment to work." Do not identify yourself with anything. Hold your mind free. All this that you see, the pains and the miseries, are but the necessary conditions of this world; poverty and wealth and happiness are but momentary; they do not belong to our real nature at all. Our nature is far beyond misery and happiness, beyond every object of the senses, beyond the imagination; and yet we must go on working all the time. "Misery comes through attachment, not through work." As soon as we identify ourselves with the work we do, we feel miserable; but if we do not identify ourselves with it, we do not feel that misery. If a beautiful picture belonging to another is burnt, a man does not generally become miserable; but when his own picture is burnt, how miserable he feels! Why? Both were beautiful pictures, perhaps copies of the same original; but in one case very much more misery is felt than in the other. It is because in one case he identifies himself with the picture, and not in the other. This "I and mine" causes the whole misery. With the sense of possession comes selfishness, and selfishness brings on misery. Every act of selfishness or thought of selfishness makes us attached to something, and immediately we are made slaves. Each wave in the Chitta that says "I and mine" immediately puts a chain round us and makes us slaves; and the more we say "I and mine", the more slavery grows, the more misery increases. Therefore Karma-Yoga tells us to enjoy the beauty of all the pictures in the world, but not to identify ourselves with any of them. Never say "mine". Whenever we say a thing is "mine", misery will immediately come. Do not even say "my child" in your mind. Possess the child, but do not say "mine". If you do, then will come the misery. Do not say "my house," do not say "my body". The whole difficulty is there. The body is neither yours, nor mine, nor anybody's. These bodies are coming and going by the laws of nature, but we are free, standing as witness. This body is no more free than a picture or a wall. Why should we be attached so much to a body? If somebody paints a picture, he does it and passes on. Do not project that tentacle of selfishness, "I must possess it". As soon as that is projected, misery will begin.

So Karma-Yoga says, first destroy the tendency to project this tentacle of selfishness, and when you have the power of checking it, hold it in and do not allow the mind to get into the ways of selfishness. Then you may go out into the world and work as much as you can. Mix everywhere, go where you please; you will never be contaminated with evil. There is the lotus leaf in the water; the water cannot touch and adhere to it; so will you be in the world. This is called "Vairâgya", dispassion or non-attachment. I believe I have told you that without non-attachment there cannot be any kind of Yoga. Non-attachment is the basis of all the Yogas. The man who gives up living in houses, wearing fine clothes, and eating good food, and goes into the desert, may be a most attached person. His only possession, his own body, may become everything to him; and as he lives he will be simply struggling for the sake of his body. Non-attachment does not mean anything that we may do in relation to our external body, it is all in the mind. The binding link of "I and mine" is in the mind. If we have not this link with the body and with the things of the senses, we are non-attached, wherever and whatever we may be. A man may be on a throne and perfectly non-attached; another man may be in rags and still very much attached. First, we have to attain this state of non-attachment and then to work incessantly. Karma-Yoga gives us the method that will help us in giving up all attachment, though it is indeed very hard.

Here are the two ways of giving up all attachment. The one is for those who do not believe in God, or in any outside help. They are left to their own devices; they have simply to work with their own will, with the powers of their mind and discrimination, saying, "I must be non-attached". For those who believe in God there is another way, which is much less difficult. They give up the fruits of work unto the Lord; they work and are never attached to the results. Whatever they see, feel, hear, or do, is for Him. For whatever good work we may do, let us not claim any praise or benefit. It is the Lord's; give up the fruits unto Him. Let us stand aside and think that we are only servants obeying the Lord, our Master, and that every impulse for action comes from Him every moment. Whatever thou worshippest, whatever thou perceivest, whatever thou doest, give up all unto Him and be at rest. Let us be at peace, perfect peace, with ourselves, and give up our whole body and mind and everything as an eternal sacrifice unto the Lord. Instead of the sacrifice of pouring oblations into the fire, perform this one great sacrifice day and night — the sacrifice of your little self. "In search of wealth in this world, Thou art the only wealth I have found; I sacrifice myself unto Thee. In search of some one to be loved, Thou art the only one beloved I have found; I sacrifice myself unto Thee." Let us repeat this day and night, and say, "Nothing for me; no matter whether the thing is good, bad, or indifferent; I do not care for it; I sacrifice all unto Thee." Day and night let us renounce our seeming self until it becomes a habit with us to do so, until it gets into the blood, the nerves, and the brain, and the whole body is every moment obedient to this idea of self-renunciation. Go then into the midst of the battlefield, with the roaring cannon and the din of war, and you will find yourself to be free and at peace.

Karma-Yoga teaches us that the ordinary idea of duty is on the lower plane; nevertheless, all of us have to do our duty. Yet we may see that this peculiar sense of duty is very often a great cause of misery. Duty becomes a disease with us; it drags us ever forward. It catches hold of us and makes our whole life miserable. It is the bane of human life. This duty, this idea of duty is the midday summer sun which scorches the innermost soul of mankind. Look at those poor slaves to duty! Duty leaves them no time to say prayers, no time to bathe. Duty is ever on them. They go out and work. Duty is on them! They come home and think of the work for the next day. Duty is on them! It is living a slave's life, at last dropping down in the street and dying in harness, like a horse. This is duty as it is understood. The only true duty is to be unattached and to work as free beings, to give up all work unto God. All our duties are His. Blessed are we that we are ordered out here. We serve our time; whether we do it ill or well, who knows? If we do it well, we do not get the fruits. If we do it ill, neither do we get the care. Be at rest, be free, and work. This kind of freedom is a very hard thing to attain. How easy it is to interpret slavery as duty — the morbid attachment of flesh for flesh as duty! Men go out into the world and struggle and fight for money or for any other thing to which they get attached. Ask them why they do it. They say, "It is a duty". It is the absurd greed for gold and gain, and they try to cover it with a few flowers.

What is duty after all? It is really the impulsion of the flesh, of our attachment; and when an attachment has become established, we call it duty. For instance, in countries where there is no marriage, there is no duty between husband and wife; when marriage comes, husband and wife live together on account of attachment; and that kind of living together becomes settled after generations; and when it becomes so settled, it becomes a duty. It is, so to say, a sort of chronic disease. When it is acute, we call it disease; when it is chronic, we call it nature. It is a disease. So when attachment becomes chronic, we baptise it with the high sounding name of duty. We strew flowers upon it, trumpets sound for it, sacred texts are said over it, and then the whole world fights, and men earnestly rob each other for this duty's sake. Duty is good to the extent that it checks brutality. To the lowest kinds of men, who cannot have any other ideal, it is of some good; but those who want to be Karma-Yogis must throw this idea of duty overboard. There is no duty for you and me. Whatever you have to give to the world, do give by all means, but not as a duty. Do not take any thought of that. Be not compelled. Why should you be compelled? *Everything that you do under compulsion goes to build up attachment.* Why should you have any duty? Resign everything unto God. In this tremendous fiery furnace where the fire of duty scorches everybody, drink this cup of nectar and be happy. We are all simply working out His will, and have nothing to do with rewards and punishments. If you want the reward, you must also have the punishment; the only way to get out of the punishment is to give up the reward. The only way of getting out of misery is by giving up the idea of happiness, because these two are linked to each other. On one side there is happiness, on the other there is misery. On one side there is life, on the other there is death. The only way to get beyond death is to give up the love of life. Life and death are the same thing, looked at from different points. So the idea of happiness without misery, or of life without death, is very good for school-boys and children; but the thinker sees that it is all a contradiction in terms and gives up both. Seek no praise, no reward, for anything you do. No sooner do we perform a good action than we begin to desire credit for it. No sooner do we give money to some charity than we want to see our names blazoned in the papers. Misery must come as the result of such desires. The greatest men in the world have passed away unknown. The Buddhas and the Christs that we know are but second-rate heroes in comparison with the greatest men of whom the world knows nothing. Hundreds of these unknown heroes have lived in every country working silently. Silently they live and silently they pass away; and in time their thoughts find expression in Buddhas or Christs, and it is these latter that become known to us. The highest men do not seek to get any name or fame from their knowledge. They leave their ideas to the world; they put forth no claims for themselves and establish no schools or systems in their name. Their whole nature shrinks from such a thing. They are the pure Sâttvikas, who can never make any stir, but only melt down in love. I have seen one such Yogi who lives in a cave in India. He is one of the most wonderful men I have ever seen. He has so completely lost the sense of his own individuality that we may say that the man in him is completely gone, leaving behind only the all comprehending sense of the divine. If an animal bites one of his arms, he is ready to give it his other arm also, and say that it is the Lord's will. Everything that comes to him is from the Lord. He does not show himself to men, and yet he is a magazine of love and of true and sweet ideas.

Next in order come the men with more Rajas, or activity, combative natures, who take up the ideas of the perfect ones and preach them to the world. The highest kind of men silently collect true and noble ideas, and others — the Buddhas and Christs — go from place to place preaching them and working for them. In the life of Gautama Buddha we notice him constantly saying that he is the twenty-fifth Buddha. The twenty-four before him are unknown to history, although the Buddha known to history must have built upon foundations laid by them. The highest men are calm, silent, and unknown. They are the men who really know the power of thought; they are sure that, even if they go into a cave and close the door and simply think five true thoughts and then pass away, these five thoughts of theirs will live through eternity. Indeed such thoughts will penetrate through the mountains, cross the oceans, and travel through the world. They will enter deep into human hearts and brains and raise up men and women who will give them practical expression in the workings of human life. These Sattvika men are too near the Lord to be active and to fight, to be working, struggling, preaching and doing good, as they say, here on earth to humanity. The active workers, however good, have still a little remnant of ignorance left in them. When our nature has yet some impurities left in it, then alone can we work. It is in the nature of work to be impelled ordinarily by motive and by attachment. In the presence of an ever active Providence who notes even the sparrow's fall, how can man attach any importance to his own work? Will it not be a blasphemy to do so when we know that He is taking care of the minutest things in the world? We have only to stand in awe and reverence before Him saying, "Thy will be done". The highest men cannot work, for in them there is no attachment. Those whose whole soul is gone into the Self, those whose desires are confined in the Self, who have become ever associated with the Self, for them there is no work. Such are indeed the highest of mankind; but apart from them every one else has to work. In so working we should never think that we can help on even the least thing in this universe. We cannot. We only help ourselves in this gymnasium of the world. This is the proper attitude of work. If we work in this way, if we always remember that our present opportunity to work thus is a privilege which has been given to us, we shall never be attached to anything. Millions like you and me think that we are great people in the world; but we all die, and in five minutes the world forgets us. But the life of God is infinite. "Who can live a moment, breathe a moment, if this all-powerful One does not will it?" He is the ever active Providence. All power is His and within His command. Through His command the winds blow, the sun shines, the earth lives, and death stalks upon the earth. He is the all in all; He is all and in all. We can only worship Him. Give up all fruits of work; do good for its own sake; then alone will come perfect non-attachment. The bonds of the heart will thus break, and we shall reap perfect freedom. This freedom is indeed the goal of Karma-Yoga.

Chapter VIII. The Ideal Of Karma-Yoga

The grandest idea in the religion of the Vedanta is that we may reach the same goal by different paths; and these paths I have generalised into four, viz those of work, love, psychology, and knowledge. But you must, at the same time, remember that these divisions are not very marked and quite exclusive of each other. Each blends into the other. But according to the type which prevails, we name the divisions. It is not that you can find men who have no other faculty than that of work, nor that you can find men who are no more than devoted worshippers only, nor that there are men who have no more than mere knowledge. These divisions are made in accordance with the type or the tendency that may be seen to prevail in a man. We have found that, in the end, all these four paths converge and become one. All religions and all methods of work and worship lead us to one and the same goal.

I have already tried to point out that goal. It is freedom as I understand it. Everything that we perceive around us is struggling towards freedom, from the atom to the man, from the insentient, lifeless particle of matter to the highest existence on earth, the human soul. The whole universe is in fact the result of this struggle for freedom. In all combinations every particle is trying to go on its own way, to fly from the other particles; but the others are holding it in check. Our earth is trying to fly away from the sun, and the moon from the earth. Everything has a tendency to infinite dispersion. All that we see in the universe has for its basis this one struggle towards freedom; it is under the impulse of this tendency that the saint prays and the robber robs. When the line of action taken is not a proper one, we call it evil; and when the manifestation of it is proper and high, we call it good. But the impulse is the same, the struggle towards freedom. The saint is oppressed with the knowledge of his condition of bondage, and he wants to get rid of it; so he worships God. The thief is oppressed with the idea that he does not possess certain things, and he tries to get rid of that want, to obtain freedom from it; so he steals. Freedom is the one goal of all nature, sentient or insentient; and consciously or unconsciously, everything is struggling towards that goal. The freedom which the saint seeks is very different from that which the robber seeks; the freedom loved by the saint leads him to the enjoyment of infinite, unspeakable bliss, while that on which the robber has set his heart only forges other bonds for his soul.

There is to be found in every religion the manifestation of this struggle towards freedom. It is the groundwork of all morality, of unselfishness, which means getting rid of the idea that men are the same as their little body. When we see a man doing good work, helping others, it means that he cannot be confined within the limited circle of "me and mine". There is no limit to this getting out of selfishness. All the great systems of ethics preach absolute unselfishness as the goal. Supposing this absolute unselfishness can be reached by a man, what becomes of him? He is no more the little Mr. So-and-so; he has acquired infinite expansion. The little personality which he had before is now lost to him for ever; he has become infinite, and the attainment of this infinite expansion is indeed the goal of all religions and of all moral and philosophical teachings. The personalist, when he hears this idea philosophically put, gets frightened. At the same time, if he preaches morality, he after all teaches the very same idea himself. He puts no limit to the unselfishness of man. Suppose a man becomes perfectly unselfish under the personalistic system, how are we to distinguish him from the perfected ones in other system? He has become one with the universe and to become that is the goal of all; only the poor personalist has not the courage to follow out his own reasoning to its right conclusion. Karma-Yoga is the attaining through unselfish work of that freedom which is the goal of all human nature. Every selfish action, therefore, retards our reaching the goal, and every unselfish action takes us towards the goal; that is why the only definition that can be given of morality is this: *That which is selfish is immoral, and that which is unselfish is moral.*

But, if you come to details, the matter will not be seen to be quite so simple. For instance, environment often makes the details different as I have already mentioned. The same action under one set of circumstances may be unselfish, and under another set quite selfish. So we can give only a general definition, and leave the details to be worked out by taking into consideration the differences in time, place, and circumstances. In one country one kind of conduct is considered moral, and in another the very same is immoral, because the circumstances differ. The goal of all nature is freedom, and freedom is to be attained only by perfect unselfishness; every thought, word, or deed that is unselfish takes us towards the goal, and, as such, is called moral. That definition, you will find, holds good in every religion and every system of ethics. In some systems of thought morality is derived from a Superior Being — God. If you ask why a man ought to do this and not that, their answer is: "Because such is the command of God."

But whatever be the source from which it is derived, their code of ethics also has the same central idea — not to think of self but to give up self. And yet some persons, in spite of this high ethical idea, are frightened at the thought of having to give up their little personalities. We may ask the man who clings to the idea of little personalities to consider the case of a person who has become perfectly unselfish, who has no thought for himself, who does no deed for himself, who speaks no word for himself, and then say where his "himself" is. That "himself" is known to him only so long as he thinks, acts, or speaks for himself. If he is only conscious of others, of the universe, and of the all, where is his "himself"? It is gone for ever.

Karma-Yoga, therefore, is a system of ethics and religion intended to attain freedom through unselfishness, and by good works. The Karma-Yogi need not believe in any doctrine whatever. He may not believe even in God, may not ask what his soul is, nor think of any metaphysical speculation. He has got his own special aim of realising selflessness; and he has to work it out himself. Every moment of his life must be realisation, because he has to solve by mere work, without the help of doctrine or theory, the very same problem to which the Jnâni applies his reason and inspiration and the Bhakta his love.

Now comes the next question: What is this work? What is this doing good to the world? Can we do good to the world? In an absolute sense, no; in a relative sense, yes. No permanent or everlasting good can be done to the world; if it could be done, the world would not be this world. We may satisfy the hunger of a man for five minutes, but he will be hungry again. Every pleasure with which we supply a man may be seen to be momentary. No one can permanently cure this ever-recurring fever of pleasure and pain. Can any permanent happiness be given to the world? In the ocean we cannot raise a wave without causing a hollow somewhere else. The sum total of the good things in the world has been the same throughout in its relation to man's need and greed. It cannot be increased or decreased. Take the history of the human race as we know it today. Do we not find the same miseries and the same happiness, the same pleasures and pains, the same differences in position? Are not some rich, some poor, some high, some low, some healthy, some unhealthy? All this was just the same with the Egyptians, the Greeks, and the Romans in ancient times as it is with the Americans today. So far as history is known, it has always been the same; yet at the same time we find that, running along with all these incurable differences of pleasure and pain, there has ever been the struggle to alleviate them. Every period of history has given birth to thousands of men and women who have worked hard to smooth the passage of life for others. And how far have they succeeded? We can only play at driving the ball from one place to another. We take away pain from the physical plane, and it goes to the mental one. It is like that picture in Dante's hell where the misers were given a mass of gold to roll up a hill. Every time they rolled it up a little, it again rolled down. All our talks about the millennium are very nice as school-boys' stories, but they are no better than that. All nations that dream of the millennium also think that, of all peoples in the world, they will have the best of it then for themselves. This is the wonderfully unselfish idea of the millennium!

We cannot add happiness to this world; similarly, we cannot add pain to it either. The sum total of the energies of pleasure and pain displayed here on earth will be the same throughout. We just push it from this side to the other side, and from that side to this, but it will remain the same, because to remain so is its very nature. This ebb and flow, this rising and falling, is in the world's very nature; it would be as logical to hold otherwise as to say that we may have life without death. This is complete nonsense, because the very idea of life implies death and the very idea of pleasure implies pain. The lamp is constantly burning out, and that is its life. If you want to have life, you have to die every moment for it. Life and death are only different expressions of the same thing looked at from different standpoints; they are the falling and the rising of the same wave, and the two form one whole. One looks at the "fall" side and becomes a pessimist another looks at the "rise" side and becomes an optimist. When a boy is going to school and his father and mother are taking care of him, everything seems blessed to him; his wants are simple, he is a great optimist. But the old man, with his varied experience, becomes calmer and is sure to have his warmth considerably cooled down. So, old nations, with signs of decay all around them, are apt to be less hopeful than new nations. There is a proverb in India: "A thousand years a city, and a thousand years a forest." This change of city into forest and vice versa is going on everywhere, and it makes people optimists or pessimists according to the side they see of it.

The next idea we take up is the idea of equality. These millennium ideas have been great motive powers to work. Many religions preach this as an element in them — that God is coming to rule the universe, and that then there will be no difference at all in conditions. The people who preach this doctrine are mere fanatics, and fanatics are indeed the sincerest of mankind. Christianity was preached just on the basis of the fascination of this fanaticism, and that is what made it so attractive to the Greek and the Roman slaves. They believed that under the millennial religion there would be no more slavery, that there would be plenty to eat and drink; and, therefore, they flocked round the Christian standard. Those who preached the idea first were of course ignorant fanatics, but very sincere. In modern times this millennial aspiration takes the form of equality — of liberty, equality, and fraternity. This is also fanaticism. True equality has never been and never can be on earth. How can we all be equal here? This impossible kind of equality implies total death. What makes this world what it is? Lost balance. In the primal state, which is called chaos, there is perfect balance. How do all the formative forces of the universe come then? By struggling, competition, conflict. Suppose that all the particles of matter were held in equilibrium, would there be then any process of creation? We know from science that it is impossible. Disturb a sheet of water, and there you find every particle of the water trying to become calm again, one rushing against the other; and in the same way all the phenomena which we call the universe — all things therein — are struggling to get back to the state of perfect balance. Again a disturbance comes, and again we have combination and creation. Inequality is the very basis of creation. At the same time the forces struggling to obtain equality are as much a necessity of creation as those which destroy it.

Absolute equality, that which means a perfect balance of all the struggling forces in all the planes, can never be in this world. Before you attain that state, the world will have become quite unfit for any kind of life, and no one will be there. We find, therefore, that all these ideas of the millennium and of absolute equality are not only impossible but also that, if we try to carry them out, they will lead us surely enough to the day of destruction. What makes the difference between man and man? It is largely the difference in the brain. Nowadays no one but a lunatic will say that we are all born with the same brain power. We come into the world with unequal endowments; we come as greater men or as lesser men, and there is no getting away from that pre-natally determined condition. The American Indians were in this country for thousands of years, and a few handfuls of your ancestors came to their land. What difference they have caused in the appearance of the country! Why did not the Indians make improvements and build cities, if all were equal? With your ancestors a different sort of brain power came into the land, different bundles of past impressions came, and they worked out and manifested themselves. Absolute non-differentiation is death. So long as this world lasts, differentiation there will and must be, and the millennium of perfect equality will come only when a cycle of creation comes to its end. Before that, equality cannot be. Yet this idea of realising the millennium is a great motive power. Just as inequality is necessary for creation itself, so the struggle to limit it is also necessary. If there were no struggle to become free and get back to God, there would be no creation either. It is the difference between these two forces that determines the nature of the motives of men. There will always be these motives to work, some tending towards bondage and others towards freedom.

This world's wheel within wheel is a terrible mechanism; if we put our hands in it, as soon as we are caught we are gone. We all think that when we have done a certain duty, we shall be at rest; but before we have done a part of that duty, another is already in waiting. We are all being dragged along by this mighty, complex world-machine. There are only two ways out of it; one is to give up all concerns with the machine, to let it go and stand aside, to give up our desires. That is very easy to say, but is almost impossible to do. I do not know whether in twenty millions of men one can do that. The other way is to plunge into the world and learn the secret of work, and that is the way of Karma-Yoga. Do not fly away from the wheels of the world-machine, but stand inside it and learn the secret of work. Through proper work done inside, it is also possible to come out. Through this machinery itself is the way out.

We have now seen what work is. It is a part of natures foundation, and goes on always. Those that believe in God understand this better, because they know that God is not such an incapable being as will need our help. Although this universe will go on always, our goal is freedom, our goal is unselfishness; and according to Karma-Yoga, that goal is to be reached through work. All ideas of making the world perfectly happy may be good as motive powers for fanatics; but we must know that fanaticism brings forth as much evil as good. The Karma-Yogi asks why you require any motive to work other than the inborn love of freedom. Be beyond the common worldly motives. "To work you have the right, but not to the fruits thereof." Man can train himself to know and to practice that, says the Karma-Yogi. When the idea of doing good becomes a part of his very being, then he will not seek for any motive outside. Let us do good because it is good to do good; he who does good work even in order to get to heaven binds himself down, says the Karma-Yogi. Any work that is done with any the least selfish motive, instead of making us free, forges one more chain for our feet.

So the only way is to give up all the fruits of work, to be unattached to them. Know that this world is not we, nor are we this world; that we are really not the body; that we really do not work. We are the Self, eternally at rest and at peace. Why should we be bound by anything? It is very good to say that we should be perfectly non-attached, but what is the way to do it? Every good work we do without any ulterior motive, instead of forging a new chain, will break one of the links in the existing chains. Every good thought that we send to the world without thinking of any return, will be stored up there and break one link in the chain, and make us purer and purer, until we become the purest of mortals. Yet all this may seem to be rather quixotic and too philosophical, more theoretical than practical. I have read many arguments against the Bhagavad-Gita, and many have said that without motives you cannot work. They have never seen unselfish work except under the influence of fanaticism, and, therefore, they speak in that way.

Let me tell you in conclusion a few words about one man who actually carried this teaching of Karma-Yoga into practice. That man is Buddha. He is the one man who ever carried this into perfect practice. All the prophets of the world, except Buddha, had external motives to move them to unselfish action. The prophets of the world, with this single exception, may be divided into two sets, one set holding that they are incarnations of God come down on earth, and the other holding that they are only messengers from God; and both draw their impetus for work from outside, expect reward from outside, however highly spiritual may be the language they use. But Buddha is the only prophet who said, "I do not care to know your various theories about God. What is the use of discussing all the subtle doctrines about the soul? Do good and be good. And this will take you to freedom and to whatever truth there is." He was, in the conduct of his life, absolutely without personal motives; and what man worked more than he? Show me in history one character who has soared so high above all. The whole human race has produced but one such character, such high philosophy, such wide sympathy. This great philosopher, preaching the highest philosophy, yet had the deepest sympathy for the lowest of animals, and never put forth any claims for himself. He is the ideal Karma-Yogi, acting entirely without motive, and the history of humanity shows him to have been the greatest man ever born; beyond compare the greatest combination of heart and brain that ever existed, the greatest soul-power that has even been manifested. He is the first great reformer the world has seen. He was the first who dared to say, "Believe not because some old manuscripts are produced, believe not because it is your national belief, because you have been made to believe it from your childhood; but reason it all out, and after you have analysed it, then, if you find that it will do good to one and all, believe it, live up to it, and help others to live up to it." He works best who works without any motive, neither for money, nor for fame, nor for anything else; and when a man can do that, he will be a Buddha, and out of him will come the power to work in such a manner as will transform the world. This man represents the very highest ideal of Karma-Yoga.

Raja-Yoga

Preface

Since the dawn of history, various extraordinary phenomena have been recorded as happening amongst human beings. Witnesses are not wanting in modern times to attest to the fact of such events, even in societies living under the full blaze of modern science. The vast mass of such evidence is unreliable, as coming from ignorant, superstitious, or fraudulent persons. In many instances the so-called miracles are imitations. But what do they imitate? It is not the sign of a candid and scientific mind to throw overboard anything without proper investigation. Surface scientists, unable to explain the various extraordinary mental phenomena, strive to ignore their very existence. They are, therefore, more culpable than those who think that their prayers are answered by a being, or beings, above the clouds, or than those who believe that their petitions will make such beings change the course of the universe. The latter have the excuse of ignorance, or at least of a defective system of education, which has taught them dependence upon such beings, a dependence which has become a part of their degenerate nature. The former have no such excuse.

For thousands of years such phenomena have been studied, investigated, and generalised, the whole ground of the religious faculties of man has been analysed, and the practical result is the science of Râja-Yoga. Raja-Yoga does not, after the unpardonable manner of some modern scientists, deny the existence of facts which are difficult to explain; on the other hand, it gently yet in no uncertain terms tells the superstitious that miracles, and answers to prayers, and powers of faith, though true as facts, are not rendered comprehensible through the superstitious explanation of attributing them to the agency of a being, or beings, above the clouds. It declares that each man is only a conduit for the infinite ocean of knowledge and power that lies behind mankind. It teaches that desires and wants are in man, that the power of supply is also in man; and that wherever and whenever a desire, a want, a prayer has been fulfilled, it was out of this infinite magazine that the supply came, and not from any supernatural being. The idea of supernatural beings may rouse to a certain extent the power of action in man, but it also brings spiritual decay. It brings dependence; it brings fear; it brings superstition. It degenerates into a horrible belief in the natural weakness of man. There is no supernatural, says the Yogi, but there are in nature gross manifestations and subtle manifestations. The subtle are the causes, the gross the effects. The gross can be easily perceived by the senses; not so the subtle. The practice of Raja-Yoga will lead to the acquisition of the more subtle perceptions.

All the orthodox systems of Indian philosophy have one goal in view, the liberation of the soul through perfection. The method is by Yoga. The word Yoga covers an immense ground, but both the Sânkhya and the Vedanta Schools point to Yoga in some form or other.

The subject of the present book is that form of Yoga known as Raja-Yoga. The aphorisms of Patanjali are the highest authority on Raja-Yoga, and form its textbook. The other philosophers, though occasionally differing from Patanjali in some philosophical points, have, as a rule, acceded to his method of practice a decided consent. The first part of this book comprises several lectures to classes delivered by the present writer in New York. The second part is a rather free translation of the aphorisms (Sutras) of Patanjali, with a running commentary. Effort has been made to avoid technicalities as far as possible, and to keep to the free and easy style of conversation. In the first part some simple and specific directions are given for the student who wants to practice, *but all such are especially and earnestly reminded that, with few exceptions, Yoga can only be safely learnt by direct contact with a teacher*. If these conversations succeed in awakening a desire for further information on the subject, the teacher will not be wanting.

The system of Patanjali is based upon the system of the Sankhyas, the points of difference being very few. The two most important differences are, first, that Patanjali admits a Personal God in the form of a first teacher, while the only God the Sankhyas admit is a nearly perfected being, temporarily in charge of a cycle of creation. Second, the Yogis hold the mind to be equally all-pervading with the soul, or Purusha, and the Sankhyas do not.

THE AUTHOR

Each soul is potentially divine.

The goal is to manifest this Divinity within by controlling nature, external and internal.

Do this either by work, or worship, or psychic control, or philosophy — by one, or more, or all of these — and be free.

This is the whole of religion. Doctrines, or dogmas, or rituals, or books, or temples, or forms, are but secondary details.

Chapter I.
Introductory

All our knowledge is based upon experience. What we call inferential knowledge, in which we go from the less to the more general, or from the general to the particular, has experience as its basis. In what are called the exact sciences, people easily find the truth, because it appeals to the particular experiences of every human being. The scientist does not tell you to believe in anything, but he has certain results which come from his own experiences, and reasoning on them when he asks us to believe in his conclusions, he appeals to some universal experience of humanity. In every exact science there is a basis which is common to all humanity, so that we can at once see the truth or the fallacy of the conclusions drawn therefrom. Now, the question is: Has religion any such basis or not? I shall have to answer the question both in the affirmative and in the negative.

Religion, as it is generally taught all over the world, is said to be based upon faith and belief, and, in most cases, consists only of different sets of theories, and that is the reason why we find all religions quarrelling with one another. These theories, again, are based upon belief. One man says there is a great Being sitting above the clouds and governing the whole universe, and he asks me to believe that solely on the authority of his assertion. In the same way, I may have my own ideas, which I am asking others to believe, and if they ask a reason, I cannot give them any. This is why religion and metaphysical philosophy have a bad name nowadays. Every educated man seems to say, "Oh, these religions are only bundles of theories without any standard to judge them by, each man preaching his own pet ideas." Nevertheless, there is a basis of universal belief in religion, governing all the different theories and all the varying ideas of different sects in different countries. Going to their basis we find that they also are based upon universal experiences.

In the first place, if you analyse all the various religions of the world, you will find that these are divided into two classes, those with a book and those without a book. Those with a book are the strongest, and have the largest number of followers. Those without books have mostly died out, and the few new ones have very small following. Yet, in all of them we find one consensus of opinion, that the truths they teach are the results of the experiences of particular persons. The Christian asks you to believe in his religion, to believe in Christ and to believe in him as the incarnation of God, to believe in a God, in a soul, and in a better state of that soul. If I ask him for reason, he says he believes in them. But if you go to the fountain-head of Christianity, you will find that it is based upon experience. Christ said he saw God; the disciples said they felt God; and so forth. Similarly, in Buddhism, it is Buddha's experience. He experienced certain truths, saw them, came in contact with them, and preached them to the world. So with the Hindus. In their books the writers, who are called Rishis, or sages, declare they experienced certain truths, and these they preach. Thus it is clear that all the religions of the world have been built upon that one universal and adamantine foundation of all our knowledge — direct experience. The teachers all saw God; they all saw their own souls, they saw their future, they saw their eternity, and what they saw they preached. Only there is this difference that by most of these religions especially in modern times, a peculiar claim is made, namely, that these experiences are impossible at the present day; they were only possible with a few men, who were the first founders of the religions that subsequently bore their names. At the present time these experiences have become obsolete, and, therefore, we have now to take religion on belief. This I entirely deny. If there has been one experience in this world in any particular branch of knowledge, it absolutely follows that that experience has been possible millions of times before, and will be repeated eternally. Uniformity is the rigorous law of nature; what once happened can happen always.

The teachers of the science of Yoga, therefore, declare that religion is not only based upon the experience of ancient times, but that no man can be religious until he has the same perceptions himself. Yoga is the science which teaches us how to get these perceptions. It is not much use to talk about religion until one has felt it. Why is there so much disturbance, so much fighting and quarrelling in the name of God? There has been more bloodshed in the name of God than for any other cause, because people never went to the fountain-head; they were content only to give a mental assent to the customs of their forefathers, and wanted others to do the same. What right has a man to say he has a soul if he does not feel it, or that there is a God if he does not see Him? If there is a God we must see Him, if there is a soul we must perceive it; otherwise it is better not to believe. It is better to be an outspoken atheist than a hypocrite. The modern idea, on the one hand, with the "learned" is that religion and metaphysics and all search after a Supreme Being are futile; on the other hand, with the semi-educated, the idea seems to be that these things really have no basis; their only value consists in the fact that they furnish strong motive powers for doing good to the world. If men believe in a God, they may become good, and moral, and so make good citizens. We cannot blame them for holding such ideas, seeing that all the teaching these men get is simply to believe in an eternal rigmarole of words, without any substance behind them. They are asked to live upon words; can they do it? If they could, I should not have the least regard for human nature. Man wants truth, wants to experience truth for himself; when he has grasped it, realised it, felt it within his heart of hearts, then alone, declare the Vedas, would all doubts vanish, all darkness be scattered, and all crookedness be made straight. "Ye children of immortality, even those who live in the highest sphere, the way is found; there is a way out of all this darkness, and that is by perceiving Him who is beyond all darkness; there is no other way."

The science of Râja-Yoga proposes to put before humanity a practical and scientifically worked out method of reaching this truth. In the first place, every science must have its own method of investigation. If you want to become an astronomer and sit down and cry "Astronomy! Astronomy!" it will never come to you. The same with chemistry. A certain method must be followed. You must go to a laboratory, take different substances, mix them up, compound them, experiment with them, and out of that will come a knowledge of chemistry. If you want to be an astronomer, you must go to an observatory, take a telescope, study the stars and planets, and then you will become an astronomer. Each science must have its own methods. I could preach you thousands of sermons, but they would not make you religious, until you practiced the method. These are the truths of the sages of all countries, of all ages, of men pure and unselfish, who had no motive but to do good to the world. They all declare that they have found some truth higher than what the senses can bring to us, and they invite verification. They ask us to take up the method and practice honestly, and then, if we do not find this higher truth, we will have the right to say there is no truth in the claim, but before we have done that, we are not rational in denying the truth of their assertions. So we must work faithfully using the prescribed methods, and light will come.

In acquiring knowledge we make use of generalisations, and generalisation is based upon observation. We first observe facts, then generalise, and then draw conclusions or principles. The knowledge of the mind, of the internal nature of man, of thought, can never be had until we have first the power of observing the facts that are going on within. It is comparatively easy to observe facts in the external world, for many instruments have been invented for the purpose, but in the internal world we have no instrument to help us. Yet we know we must observe in order to have a real science. Without a proper analysis, any science will be hopeless — mere theorising. And that is why all the psychologists have been quarrelling among themselves since the beginning of time, except those few who found out the means of observation.

The science of Raja-Yoga, in the first place, proposes to give us such a means of observing the internal states. The instrument is the mind itself. The power of attention, when properly guided, and directed towards the internal world, will analyse the mind, and illumine facts for us. The powers of the mind are like rays of light dissipated; when they are concentrated, they illumine. This is our only means of knowledge. Everyone is using it, both in the external and the internal world; but, for the psychologist, the same minute observation has to be directed to the internal world, which the scientific man directs to the external; and this requires a great deal of practice. From our childhood upwards we have been taught only to pay attention to things external, but never to things internal; hence most of us have nearly lost the faculty of observing the internal mechanism. To turn the mind as it were, inside, stop it from going outside, and then to concentrate all its powers, and throw them upon the mind itself, in order that it may know its own nature, analyse itself, is very hard work. Yet that is the only way to anything which will be a scientific approach to the subject.

What is the use of such knowledge? In the first place, knowledge itself is the highest reward of knowledge, and secondly, there is also utility in it. It will take away all our misery. When by analysing his own mind, man comes face to face, as it were, with something which is never destroyed, something which is, by its own nature, eternally pure and perfect, he will no more be miserable, no more unhappy. All misery comes from fear, from unsatisfied desire. Man will find that he never dies, and then he will have no more fear of death. When he knows that he is perfect, he will have no more vain desires, and both these causes being absent, there will be no more misery — there will be perfect bliss, even while in this body.

There is only one method by which to attain this knowledge, that which is called concentration. The chemist in his laboratory concentrates all the energies of his mind into one focus, and throws them upon the materials he is analysing, and so finds out their secrets. The astronomer concentrates all the energies of his mind and projects them through his telescope upon the skies; and the stars, the sun, and the moon, give up their secrets to him. The more I can concentrate my thoughts on the matter on which I am talking to you, the more light I can throw upon you. You are listening to me, and the more you concentrate your thoughts, the more clearly you will grasp what I have to say.

How has all the knowledge in the world been gained but by the concentration of the powers of the mind? The world is ready to give up its secrets if we only know how to knock, how to give it the necessary blow. The strength and force of the blow come through concentration. There is no limit to the power of the human mind. The more concentrated it is, the more power is brought to bear on one point; that is the secret.

It is easy to concentrate the mind on external things, the mind naturally goes outwards; but not so in the case of religion, or psychology, or metaphysics, where the subject and the object, are one. The object is internal, the mind itself is the object, and it is necessary to study the mind itself — mind studying mind. We know that there is the power of the mind called reflection. I am talking to you. At the same time I am standing aside, as it were, a second person, and knowing and hearing what I am talking. You work and think at the same time, while a portion of your mind stands by and sees what you are thinking. The powers of the mind should be concentrated and turned back upon itself, and as the darkest places reveal their secrets before the penetrating rays of the sun, so will this concentrated mind penetrate its own innermost secrets. Thus will we come to the basis of belief, the real genuine religion. We will perceive for ourselves whether we have souls, whether life is of five minutes or of eternity, whether there is a God in the universe or more. It will all be revealed to us. This is what Raja-Yoga proposes to teach. The goal of all its teaching is how to concentrate the minds, then, how to discover the innermost recesses of our own minds, then, how to generalise their contents and form our own conclusions from them. It, therefore, never asks the question what our religion is, whether we are Deists or Atheists, whether Christians, Jews, or Buddhists. We are human beings; that is sufficient. Every human being has the right and the power to seek for religion. Every human being has the right to ask the reason, why, and to have his question answered by himself, if he only takes the trouble.

So far, then, we see that in the study of this Raja-Yoga no faith or belief is necessary. Believe nothing until you find it out for yourself; that is what it teaches us. Truth requires no prop to make it stand. Do you mean to say that the facts of our awakened state require any dreams or imaginings to prove them? Certainly not. This study of Raja-Yoga takes a long time and constant practice. A part of this practice is physical, but in the main it is mental. As we proceed we shall find how intimately the mind is connected with the body. If we believe that the mind is simply a finer part of the body, and that mind acts upon the body, then it stands to reason that the body must react upon the mind. If the body is sick, the mind becomes sick also. If the body is healthy, the mind remains healthy and strong. When one is angry, the mind becomes disturbed. Similarly when the mind is disturbed, the body also becomes disturbed. With the majority of mankind the mind is greatly under the control of the body, their mind being very little developed. The vast mass of humanity is very little removed from the animals. Not only so, but in many instances, the power of control in them is little higher than that of the lower animals. We have very little command of our minds. Therefore to bring that command about, to get that control over body and mind, we must take certain physical helps. When the body is sufficiently controlled, we can attempt the manipulation of the mind. By manipulating the mind, we shall be able to bring it under our control, make it work as we like, and compel it to concentrate its powers as we desire.

According to the Raja-Yogi, the external world is but the gross form of the internal, or subtle. The finer is always the cause, the grosser the effect. So the external world is the effect, the internal the cause. In the same way external forces are simply the grosser parts, of which the internal forces are the finer. The man who has discovered and learned how to manipulate the internal forces will get the whole of nature under his control. The Yogi proposes to himself no less a task than to master the whole universe, to control the whole of nature. He wants to arrive at the point where what we call "nature's laws" will have no influence over him, where he will be able to get beyond them all. He will be master of the whole of nature, internal and external. The progress and civilisation of the human race simply mean controlling this nature.

Different races take to different processes of controlling nature. Just as in the same society some individuals want to control the external nature, and others the internal, so, among races, some want to control the external nature, and others the internal. Some say that by controlling internal nature we control everything. Others that by controlling external nature we control everything. Carried to the extreme both are right, because in nature there is no such division as internal or external. These are fictitious limitations that never existed. The externalists and the internalists are destined to meet at the same point, when both reach the extreme of their knowledge. Just as a physicist, when he pushes his knowledge to its limits, finds it melting away into metaphysics, so a metaphysician will find that what he calls mind and matter are but apparent distinctions, the reality being One.

The end and aim of all science is to find the unity, the One out of which the manifold is being manufactured, that One existing as many. Raja-Yoga proposes to start from the internal world, to study internal nature, and through that, control the whole — both internal and external. It is a very old attempt. India has been its special stronghold, but it was also attempted by other nations. In Western countries it was regarded as mysticism and people who wanted to practice it were either burned or killed as witches and sorcerers. In India, for various reasons, it fell into the hands of persons who destroyed ninety per cent of the knowledge, and tried to make a great secret of the remainder. In modern times many so-called teachers have arisen in the West worse than those of India, because the latter knew something, while these modern exponents know nothing.

Anything that is secret and mysterious in these systems of Yoga should be at once rejected. The best guide in life is strength. In religion, as in all other matters, discard everything that weakens you, have nothing to do with it. Mystery-mongering weakens the human brain. It has well-nigh destroyed Yoga — one of the grandest of sciences. From the time it was discovered, more than four thousand years ago, Yoga was perfectly delineated, formulated, and preached in India. It is a striking fact that the more modern the commentator the greater the mistakes he makes, while the more ancient the writer the more rational he is. Most of the modern writers talk of all sorts of mystery. Thus Yoga fell into the hands of a few persons who made it a secret, instead of letting the full blaze of daylight and reason fall upon it. They did so that they might have the powers to themselves.

In the first place, there is no mystery in what I teach. What little I know I will tell you. So far as I can reason it out I will do so, but as to what I do not know I will simply tell you what the books say. It is wrong to believe blindly. You must exercise your own reason and judgment; you must practice, and see whether these things happen or not. Just as you would take up any other science, exactly in the same manner you should take up this science for study. There is neither mystery nor danger in it. So far as it is true, it ought to be preached in the public streets, in broad daylight. Any attempt to mystify these things is productive of great danger.

Before proceeding further, I will tell you a little of the Sânkhya philosophy, upon which the whole of Raja-Yoga is based. According to the Sankhya philosophy, the genesis of perception is as follows: the affections of external objects are carried by the outer instruments to their respective brain centres or organs, the organs carry the affections to the mind, the mind to the determinative faculty, from this the Purusha (the soul) receives them, when perception results. Next he gives the order back, as it were, to the motor centres to do the needful. With the exception of the Purusha all of these are material, but the mind is much finer matter than the external instruments. That material of which the mind is composed goes also to form the subtle matter called the Tanmâtras. These become gross and make the external matter. That is the psychology of the Sankhya. So that between the intellect and the grosser matter outside there is only a difference in degree. The Purusha is the only thing which is immaterial. The mind is an instrument, as it were, in the hands of the soul, through which the soul catches external objects. The mind is constantly changing and vacillating, and can, when perfected, either attach itself to several organs, to one, or to none. For instance, if I hear the clock with great attention, I will not, perhaps, see anything although my eyes may be open, showing that the mind was not attached to the seeing organ, while it was to the hearing organ. But the perfected mind can be attached to all the organs simultaneously. It has the reflexive power of looking back into its own depths. This reflexive power is what the Yogi wants to attain; by concentrating the powers of the mind, and turning them inward, he seeks to know what is happening inside. There is in this no question of mere belief; it is the analysis arrived at by certain philosophers. Modern physiologists tell us that the eyes are not the organ of vision, but that the organ is in one of the nerve centres of the brain, and so with all the senses; they also tell us that these centres are formed of the same material as the brain itself. The Sankhyas also tell us the same thing The former is a statement on the physical side, and the latter on the psychological side; yet both are the same. Our field of research lies beyond this.

The Yogi proposes to attain that fine state of perception in which he can perceive all the different mental states. There must be mental perception of all of them. One can perceive how the sensation is travelling, how the mind is receiving it, how it is going to the determinative faculty, and how this gives it to the Purusha. As each science requires certain preparations and has its own method, which must be followed before it could be understood, even so in Raja-Yoga.

Certain regulations as to food are necessary; we must use that food which brings us the purest mind. If you go into a menagerie, you will find this demonstrated at once. You see the elephants, huge animals, but calm and gentle; and if you go towards the cages of the lions and tigers, you find them restless, showing how much difference has been made by food. All the forces that are working in this body have been produced out of food; we see that every day. If you begin to fast, first your body will get weak, the physical forces will suffer; then after a few days, the mental forces will suffer also. First, memory will fail. Then comes a point, when you are not able to think, much less to pursue any course of reasoning. We have, therefore, to take care what sort of food we eat at the beginning, and when we have got strength enough, when our practice is well advanced, we need not be so careful in this respect. While the plant is growing it must be hedged round, lest it be injured; but when it becomes a tree, the hedges are taken away. It is strong enough to withstand all assaults.

A Yogi must avoid the two extremes of luxury and austerity. He must not fast, nor torture his flesh. He who does so, says the Gita, cannot be a Yogi: He who fasts, he who keeps awake, he who sleeps much, he who works too much, he who does no work, none of these can be a Yogi (Gita, VI, 16).

Chapter II.
The First Steps

Râja-Yoga is divided into eight steps. The first is Yama — non-killing, truthfulness, non-stealing, continence, and non-receiving of any gifts. Next is Niyama — cleanliness, contentment, austerity, study, and self-surrender to God. Then comes Âsana, or posture; Prânâyâma, or control of Prâna; Pratyâhâra, or restraint of the senses from their objects; Dhâranâ, or fixing the mind on a spot; Dhyâna, or meditation; and Samâdhi, or superconsciousness. The Yama and Niyama, as we see, are moral trainings; without these as the basis no practice of Yoga will succeed. As these two become established, the Yogi will begin to realise the fruits of his practice; without these it will never bear fruit. A Yogi must not think of injuring anyone, by thought, word, or deed. Mercy shall not be for men alone, but shall go beyond, and embrace the whole world.

The next step is Asana, posture. A series of exercises, physical and mental, is to be gone through every day, until certain higher states are reached. Therefore it is quite necessary that we should find a posture in which we can remain long. That posture which is the easiest for one should be the one chosen. For thinking, a certain posture may be very easy for one man, while to another it may be very difficult. We will find later on that during the study of these psychological matters a good deal of activity goes on in the body. Nerve currents will have to be displaced and given a new channel. New sorts of vibrations will begin, the whole constitution will be remodelled as it were. But the main part of the activity will lie along the spinal column, so that the one thing necessary for the posture is to hold the spinal column free, sitting erect, holding the three parts — the chest, neck, and head — in a straight line. Let the whole weight of the body be supported by the ribs, and then you have an easy natural postures with the spine straight. You will easily see that you cannot think very high thoughts with the chest in. This portion of the Yoga is a little similar to the Hatha-Yoga which deals entirely with the physical body, its aim being to make the physical body very strong. We have nothing to do with it here, because its practices are very difficult, and cannot be learned in a day, and, after all, do not lead to much spiritual growth. Many of these practices you will find in

Delsarte and other teachers, such as placing the body in different postures, but the object in these is physical, not psychological. There is not one muscle in the body over which a man cannot establish a perfect control. The heart can be made to stop or go on at his bidding, and each part of the organism can be similarly controlled.

The result of this branch of Yoga is to make men live long; health is the chief idea, the one goal of the Hatha-Yogi. He is determined not to fall sick, and he never does. He lives long; a hundred years is nothing to him; he is quite young and fresh when he is 150, without one hair turned grey. But that is all. A banyan tree lives sometimes 5000 years, but it is a banyan tree and nothing more. So, if a man lives long, he is only a healthy animal. One or two ordinary lessons of the Hatha-Yogis are very useful. For instance, some of you will find it a good thing for headaches to drink cold water through the nose as soon as you get up in the morning; the whole day your brain will be nice and cool, and you will never catch cold. It is very easy to do; put your nose into the water, draw it up through the nostrils and make a pump action in the throat.

After one has learned to have a firm erect seat, one has to perform, according to certain schools, a practice called the purifying of the nerves. This part has been rejected by some as not belonging to Raja-Yoga, but as so great an authority as the commentator Shankarâchârya advises it, I think fit that it should be mentioned, and I will quote his own directions from his commentary on the Shvetâshvatara Upanishad: "The mind whose dross has been cleared away by Pranayama, becomes fixed in Brahman; therefore Pranayama is declared. First the nerves are to be purified, then comes the power to practice Pranayama. Stopping the right nostril with the thumb, through the left nostril fill in air, according to capacity; then, without any interval, throw the air out through the right nostril, closing the left one. Again inhaling through the right nostril eject through the left, according to capacity; practicing this three or five times at four hours of the day, before dawn, during midday, in the evening, and at midnight, in fifteen days or a month purity of the nerves is attained; then begins Pranayama."

Practice is absolutely necessary. You may sit down and listen to me by the hour every day, but if you do not practice, you will not get one step further. It all depends on practice. We never understand these things until we experience them. We will have to see and feel them for ourselves. Simply listening to explanations and theories will not do. There are several obstructions to practice. The first obstruction is an unhealthy body: if the body is not in a fit state, the practice will be obstructed. Therefore we have to keep the body in good health; we have to take care of what we eat and drink, and what we do. Always use a mental effort, what is usually called

"Christian Science," to keep the body strong. That is all — nothing further of the body. We must not forget that health is only a means to an end. If health were the end, we would be like animals; animals rarely become unhealthy.

The second obstruction is doubt; we always feel doubtful about things we do not see. Man cannot live upon words, however he may try. So, doubt comes to us as to whether there is any truth in these things or not; even the best of us will doubt sometimes: With practice, within a few days, a little glimpse will come, enough to give one encouragement and hope. As a certain commentator on Yoga philosophy says, "When one proof is obtained, however little that may be, it will give us faith in the whole teaching of Yoga." For instance, after the first few months of practice, you will begin to find you can read another's thoughts; they will come to you in picture form. Perhaps you will hear something happening at a long distance, when you concentrate your mind with a wish to hear. These glimpses will come, by little bits at first, but enough to give you faith, and strength, and hope. For instance, if you concentrate your thoughts on the tip of your nose, in a few days you will begin to smell most beautiful fragrance, which will be enough to show you that there are certain mental perceptions that can be made obvious without the contact of physical objects. But we must always remember that these are only the means; the aim, the end, the goal, of all this training is liberation of the soul. Absolute control of nature, and nothing short of it, must be the goal. We must be the masters, and not the slaves of nature; neither body nor mind must be our master, nor must we forget that the body is mine, and not I the body's.

A god and a demon went to learn about the Self from a great sage. They studied with him for a long time. At last the sage told them, "You yourselves are the Being you are seeking." Both of them thought that their bodies were the Self. They went back to their people quite satisfied and said, "We have learned everything that was to be learned; eat, drink, and be merry; we are the Self; there is nothing beyond us." The nature of the demon was ignorant, clouded; so he never inquired any further, but was perfectly contented with the idea that he was God, that by the Self was meant the body. The god had a purer nature. He at first committed the mistake of thinking: I, this body, am Brahman: so keep it strong and in health, and well dressed, and give it all sorts of enjoyments. But, in a few days, he found out that that could not be the meaning of the sage, their master; there must be something higher. So he came back and said, "Sir, did you teach me that this body was the Self? If so, I see all bodies die; the Self cannot die." The sage said, "Find it out; thou art That." Then the god thought that the vital forces which work the body were what the sage meant. But. after a time, he found that if he ate, these vital forces remained strong, but, if he starved, they became weak. The god then went back to the sage and said, "Sir, do you mean that the vital forces are the Self ?" The sage said, "Find out for yourself; thou art That." The god returned home once more, thinking that it was the mind, perhaps, that was the Self. But in a short while he saw that thoughts were so various, now good, again bad; the mind was too changeable to be the Self. He went back to the sage and said, "Sir, I do not think that the mind is the Self; did you mean that?" "No," replied the sage, "thou art That; find out for yourself." The god went home, and at last found that he was the Self, beyond all thought, one without birth or death, whom the sword cannot pierce or the fire burn, whom the air cannot dry or the water melt, the beginningless and endless, the immovable, the intangible, the omniscient, the omnipotent Being; that It was neither the body nor the mind, but beyond them all. So he was satisfied; but the poor demon did not get the truth, owing to his fondness for the body.

This world has a good many of these demoniac natures, but there are some gods too. If one proposes to teach any science to increase the power of sense-enjoyment, one finds multitudes ready for it. If one undertakes to show the supreme goal, one finds few to listen to him. Very few have the power to grasp the higher, fewer still the patience to attain to it. But there are a few also who know that even if the body can be made to live for a thousand years, the result in the end will be the same. When the forces that hold it together go away, the body must fall. No man was ever born who could stop his body one moment from changing. Body is the name of a series of changes. "As in a river the masses of water are changing before you every moment, and new masses are coming, yet taking similar form, so is it with this body." Yet the body must be kept strong and healthy. It is the best instrument we have.

This human body is the greatest body in the universe, and a human being the greatest being. Man is higher than all animals, than all angels; none is greater than man. Even the Devas (gods) will have to come down again and attain to salvation through a human body. Man alone attains to perfection, not even the Devas. According to the Jews and Mohammedans, God created man after creating the angels and everything else, and after creating man He asked the angels to come and salute him, and all did so except Iblis; so God cursed him and he became Satan. Behind this allegory is the great truth that this human birth is the greatest birth we can have. The lower creation, the animal, is dull, and manufactured mostly out of Tamas. Animals cannot have any high thoughts; nor can the angels, or Devas, attain to direct freedom without human birth. In human society, in the same way, too much wealth or too much poverty is a great impediment to the higher development of the soul. It is from the middle classes that the great ones of the world come. Here the forces are very equally adjusted and balanced.

Returning to our subject, we come next to Pranayarna, controlling the breathing. What has that to do with concentrating the powers of the mind? Breath is like the fly-wheel of this machine, the body. In a big engine you find the fly-wheel first moving, and that motion is conveyed to finer and finer machinery until the most delicate and finest mechanism in the machine is in motion. The breath is that fly-wheel, supplying and regulating the motive power to everything in this body.

There was once a minister to a great king. He fell into disgrace. The king, as a punishment, ordered him to be shut up in the top of a very high tower. This was done, and the minister was left there to perish. He had a faithful wife, however, who came to the tower at night and called to her husband at the top to know what she could do to help him. He told her to return to the tower the following night and bring with her a long rope, some stout twine, pack thread, silken thread, a beetle, and a little honey. Wondering much, the good wife obeyed her husband, and brought him the desired articles. The husband directed her to attach the silken thread firmly to the beetle, then to smear its horns with a drop of honey, and to set it free on the wall of the tower, with its head pointing upwards. She obeyed all these instructions, and the beetle started on its long journey. Smelling the honey ahead it slowly crept onwards, in the hope of reaching the honey, until at last it reached the top of the tower, when the minister grasped the beetle, and got possession of the silken thread. He told his wife to tie the other end to the pack thread, and after he had drawn up the pack thread, he repeated the process with the stout twine, and lastly with the rope. Then the rest was easy. The minister descended from the tower by means of the rope, and made his escape. In this body of ours the breath motion is the "silken thread"; by laying hold of and learning to control it we grasp the pack thread of the nerve currents, and from these the stout twine of our thoughts, and lastly the rope of Prana, controlling which we reach freedom.

We do not know anything about our own bodies; we cannot know. At best we can take a dead body, and cut it in pieces, and there are some who can take a live animal and cut it in pieces in order to see what is inside the body. Still, that has nothing to do with our own bodies. We know very little about them. Why do we not? Because our attention is not discriminating enough to catch the very fine movements that are going on within. We can know of them only when the mind becomes more subtle and enters, as it were, deeper into the body. To get the subtle perception we have to begin with the grosser perceptions. We have to get hold of that which is setting the whole engine in motion. That is the Prana, the most obvious manifestation of which is the breath. Then, along with the breath, we shall slowly enter the body, which will enable us to find out about the subtle forces, the nerve currents that are moving all over the body. As soon as we perceive and learn to feel them, we shall begin to get control over them, and over the body. The mind is also set in motion: by these different nerve currents, so at last we shall reach the state of perfect control over the body and the mind, making both our servants. Knowledge is power. We have to get this power. So we must begin at the beginning, with Pranayama, restraining the Prana. This Pranayama is a long subject, and will take several lessons to illustrate it thoroughly. We shall take it part by part.

We shall gradually see the reasons for each exercise and what forces in the body are set in motion. All these things will come to us, but it requires constant practice, and the proof will come by practice. No amount of reasoning which I can give you will be proof to you, until you have demonstrated it for yourselves. As soon as you begin to feel these currents in motion all over you, doubts will vanish, but it requires hard practice every day. You must practice at least twice every day, and the best times are towards the morning and the evening. When night passes into day, and day into night, a state of relative calmness ensues. The early morning and the early evening are the two periods of calmness. Your body will have a like tendency to become calm at those times. We should take advantage of that natural condition and begin then to practice. Make it a rule not to eat until you have practiced; if you do this, the sheer force of hunger will break your laziness. In India they teach children never to eat until they have practiced or worshipped, and it becomes natural to them after a time; a boy will not feel hungry until he has bathed and practiced.

Those of you who can afford it will do better to have a room for this practice alone. Do not sleep in that room, it must be kept holy. You must not enter the room until you have bathed, and are perfectly clean in body and mind. Place flowers in that room always; they are the best surroundings for a Yogi; also pictures that are pleasing. Burn incense morning and evening. Have no quarrelling, nor anger, nor unholy thought in that room. Only allow those persons to enter it who are of the same thought as you. Then gradually there will be an atmosphere of holiness in the room, so that when you are miserable, sorrowful, doubtful, or your mind is disturbed, the very fact of entering that room will make you calm. This was the idea of the temple and the church, and in some temples and churches you will find it even now, but in the majority of them the very idea has been lost. The idea is that by keeping holy vibrations there the place becomes and remains illumined. Those who cannot afford to have a room set apart can practice anywhere they like. Sit in a straight posture, and the first thing to do is to send a current of holy thought to all creation. Mentally repeat, "Let all beings be happy; let all beings be peaceful; let all beings be blissful." So do to the east, south, north and west. The more you do that the better you will feel yourself. You will find at last that the easiest way to make ourselves healthy is to see that others are healthy, and the easiest way to make ourselves happy is to see that others are happy. After doing that, those who believe in God should pray — not for money, not for health, nor for heaven; pray for knowledge and light; every other prayer is selfish. Then the next thing to do is to think of your own body, and see that it is strong and healthy; it is the best instrument you have. Think of it as being as strong as adamant, and that with the help of this body you will cross the ocean of life. Freedom is never to be reached by the weak. Throw away all weakness. Tell your body that it is strong, tell your mind that it is strong, and have unbounded faith and hope in yourself.

Chapter III.
Prana

Prânâyâma is not, as many think, something about breath; breath indeed has very little to do with it, if anything. Breathing is only one of the many exercises through which we get to the real Pranayama. Pranayama means the control of Prâna. According to the philosophers of India, the whole universe is composed of two materials, one of which they call Âkâsha. It is the omnipresent, all-penetrating existence. Everything that has form, everything that is the result of combination, is evolved out of this Akasha. It is the Akasha that becomes the air, that becomes the liquids, that becomes the solids; it is the Akasha that becomes the sun, the earth, the moon, the stars, the comets; it is the Akasha that becomes the human body, the animal body, the plants, every form that we see, everything that can be sensed, everything that exists. It cannot be perceived; it is so subtle that it is beyond all ordinary perception; it can only be seen when it has become gross, has taken form. At the beginning of creation there is only this Akasha. At the end of the cycle the solids, the liquids, and the gases all melt into the Akasha again, and the next creation similarly proceeds out of this Akasha.

By what power is this Akasha manufactured into this universe? By the power of Prana. Just as Akasha is the infinite, omnipresent material of this universe, so is this Prana the infinite, omnipresent manifesting power of this universe. At the beginning and at the end of a cycle everything becomes Akasha, and all the forces that are in the universe resolve back into the Prana; in the next cycle, out of this Prana is evolved everything that we call energy, everything that we call force. It is the Prana that is manifesting as motion; it is the Prana that is manifesting as gravitation, as magnetism. It is the Prana that is manifesting as the actions of the body, as the nerve currents, as thought force. From thought down to the lowest force, everything is but the manifestation of Prana. The sum total of all forces in the universe, mental or physical, when resolved back to their original state, is called Prana. "When there was neither aught nor naught, when darkness was covering darkness, what existed then? That Akasha existed without motion." The physical motion of the Prana was stopped, but it existed all the same.

At the end of a cycle the energies now displayed in the universe quiet down and become potential. At the beginning of the next cycle they start up, strike upon the Akasha, and out of the Akasha evolve these various forms, and as the Akasha changes, this Prana changes also into all these manifestations of energy. The knowledge and control of this Prana is really what is meant by Pranayama.

This opens to us the door to almost unlimited power. Suppose, for instance, a man understood the Prana perfectly, and could control it, what power on earth would not be his? He would be able to move the sun and stars out of their places, to control everything in the universe, from the atoms to the biggest suns, because he would control the Prana. This is the end and aim of Pranayama. When the Yogi becomes perfect, there will be nothing in nature not under his control. If he orders the gods or the souls of the departed to come, they will come at his bidding. All the forces of nature will obey him as slaves. When the ignorant see these powers of the Yogi, they call them the miracles. One peculiarity of the Hindu mind is that it always inquires for the last possible generalisation, leaving the details to be worked out afterwards. The question is raised in the Vedas, "What is that, knowing which, we shall know everything?" Thus, all books, and all philosophies that have been written, have been only to prove that by knowing which everything is known. If a man wants to know this universe bit by bit he must know every individual grain of sand, which means infinite time; he cannot know all of them. Then how can knowledge be? How is it possible for a man to be all-knowing through particulars? The Yogis say that behind this particular manifestation there is a generalisation. Behind all particular ideas stands a generalised, an abstract principle; grasp it, and you have grasped everything. Just as this whole universe has been generalised in the Vedas into that One Absolute Existence, and he who has grasped that Existence has grasped the whole universe, so all forces have been generalised into this Prana, and he who has grasped the Prana has grasped all the forces of the universe, mental or physical. He who has controlled the Prana has controlled his own mind, and all the minds that exist. He who has controlled the Prana has controlled his body, and all the bodies that exist, because the Prana is the generalised manifestation of force.

How to control the Prana is the one idea of Pranayama. All the trainings and exercises in this regard are for that one end. Each man must begin where he stands, must learn how to control the things that are nearest to him. This body is very near to us, nearer than anything in the external universe, and this mind is the nearest of all. The Prana which is working this mind and body is the nearest to us of all the Prana in this universe. This little wave of the Prana which represents our own energies, mental and physical, is the nearest to us of all the waves of the infinite ocean of Prana. If we can succeed in controlling that little wave, then alone we can hope to control the whole of Prana. The Yogi who has done this gains perfection; no longer is he under any power. He becomes almost almighty, almost all-knowing. We see sects in every country who have attempted this control of Prana. In this country there are Mind-healers, Faith-healers, Spiritualists, Christian Scientists, Hypnotists, etc., and if we examine these different bodies, we shall find at the back of each this control of the Prana, whether they know it or not. If you boil all their theories down, the residuum will be that. It is the one and the same force they are manipulating, only unknowingly. They have stumbled on the discovery of a force and are using it unconsciously without knowing its nature, but it is the same as the Yogi uses, and which comes from Prana.

The Prana is the vital force in every being. Thought is the finest and highest action of Prana. Thought, again, as we see, is not all. There is also what we call instinct or unconscious thought, the lowest plane of action. If a mosquito stings us, our hand will strike it automatically, instinctively. This is one expression of thought. All reflex actions of the body belong to this plane of thought. There is again the other plane of thought, the conscious. I reason, I judge, I think, I see the pros and cons of certain things, yet that is not all. We know that reason is limited. Reason can go only to a certain extent, beyond that it cannot reach. The circle within which it runs is very very limited indeed. Yet at the same time, we find facts rush into this circle. Like the coming of comets certain things come into this circle; it is certain they come from outside the limit, although our reason cannot go beyond. The causes of the phenomena intruding themselves in this small limit are outside of this limit. The mind can exist on a still higher plane, the superconscious. When the mind has attained to that state, which is called Samâdhi — perfect concentration, superconsciousness — it goes beyond the limits of reason, and comes face to face with facts which no instinct or reason can ever know. All manipulations of the subtle forces of the body, the different manifestations of Prana, if trained, give a push to the mind, help it to go up higher, and become superconscious, from where it acts.

In this universe there is one continuous substance on every plane of existence. Physically this universe is one: there is no difference between the sun and you. The scientist will tell you it is only a fiction to say the contrary. There is no real difference between the table and me; the table is one point in the mass of matter, and I another point. Each form represents, as it were, one whirlpool in the infinite ocean of matter, of which not one is constant. Just as in a rushing stream there may be millions of whirlpools, the water in each of which is different every moment, turning round and round for a few seconds, and then passing out, replaced by a fresh quantity, so the whole universe is one constantly changing mass of matter, in which all forms of existence are so many whirlpools. A mass of matter enters into one whirlpool, say a human body, stays there for a period, becomes changed, and goes out into another, say an animal body this time, from which again after a few years, it enters into another whirlpool, called a lump of mineral. It is a constant change. Not one body is constant. There is no such thing as my body, or your body, except in words. Of the one huge mass of matter, one point is called a moon, another a sun, another a man, another the earth, another a plant, another a mineral. Not one is constant, but everything is changing, matter eternally concreting and disintegrating. So it is with the mind. Matter is represented by the ether; when the action of Prana is most subtle, this very ether, in the finer state of vibration, will represent the mind and there it will be still one unbroken mass. If you can simply get to that subtle vibration, you will see and feel that the whole universe is composed of subtle vibrations. Sometimes certain drugs have the power to take us, while as yet in the senses, to that condition. Many of you may remember the celebrated experiment of Sir Humphrey Davy, when the laughing gas overpowered him — how, during the lecture, he remained motionless, stupefied and after that, he said that the whole universe was made up of ideas. For, the time being, as it were, the gross vibrations had ceased, and only the subtle vibrations which he called ideas, were present to him. He could only see the subtle vibrations round him; everything had become thought; the whole universe was an ocean of thought, he and everyone else had become little thought whirlpools.

Thus, even in the universe of thought we find unity, and at last, when we get to the Self, we know that that Self can only be One. Beyond the vibrations of matter in its gross and subtle aspects, beyond motion there is but One. Even in manifested motion there is only unity. These facts can no more be denied. Modern physics also has demonstrated that the sum total of the energies in the universe is the same throughout. It has also been proved that this sum total of energy exists in two forms. It becomes potential, toned down, and calmed, and next it comes out manifested as all these various forces; again it goes back to the quiet state, and again it manifests. Thus it goes on evolving and involving through eternity. The control of this Prana, as before stated, is what is called Pranayama.

The most obvious manifestation of this Prana in the human body is the motion of the lungs. If that stops, as a rule all the other manifestations of force in the body will immediately stop. But there are persons who can train themselves in such a manner that the body will live on, even when this motion has stopped. There are some persons who can bury themselves for days, and yet live without breathing. To reach the subtle we must take the help of the grosser, and so, slowly travel towards the most subtle until we gain our point. Pranayama really means controlling this motion of the lungs and this motion is associated with the breath. Not that breath is producing it; on the contrary it is producing breath. This motion draws in the air by pump action. The Prana is moving the lungs, the movement of the lungs draws in the air. So Pranayama is not breathing, but controlling that muscular power which moves the lungs. That muscular power which goes out through the nerves to the muscles and from them to the lungs, making them move in a certain manner, is the Prana, which we have to control in the practice of Pranayama. When the Prana has become controlled, then we shall immediately find that all the other actions of the Prana in the body will slowly come under control. I myself have seen men who have controlled almost every muscle of the body; and why not? If I have control over certain muscles, why not over every muscle and nerve of the body? What impossibility is there? At present the control is lost, and the motion has become automatic. We cannot move our ears at will, but we know that animals can. We have not that power because we do not exercise it. This is what is called atavism.

Again, we know that motion which has become latent can be brought back to manifestation. By hard work and practice certain motions of the body which are most dormant can be brought back under perfect control. Reasoning thus we find there is no impossibility, but, on the other hand. every probability that each part of the body can be brought under perfect control. This the Yogi does through Pranayama. Perhaps some of you have read that in Pranayama, when drawing in the breath, you must fill your whole body with Prana. In the English translations Prana is given as breath, and you are inclined to ask how that is to be done. The fault is with the translator. Every part of the body can be filled with Prana, this vital force, and when you are able to do that, you can control the whole body. All the sickness and misery felt in the body will be perfectly controlled; not only so, you will be able to control another's body. Everything is infectious in this world, good or bad. If your body be in a certain state of tension, it will have a tendency to produce the same tension in others. If you are strong and healthy, those that live near you will also have the tendency to become strong and healthy, but if you are sick and weak, those around you will have the tendency to become the same. In the case of one man trying to heal another, the first idea is simply transferring his own health to the other. This is the primitive sort of healing. Consciously or unconsciously, health can be transmitted. A very strong man, living with a weak man, will make him a little stronger, whether he knows it or not. When consciously done, it becomes quicker and better in its action. Next come those cases in which a man may not be very healthy himself, yet we know that he can bring health to another. The first man, in such a case, has a little more control over the Prana, and can rouse, for the time being, his Prana, as it were, to a certain state of vibration, and transmit it to another person.

There have been cases where this process has been carried on at a distance, but in reality there is no distance in the sense of a break. Where is the distance that has a break? Is there any break between you and the sun? It is a continuous mass of matter, the sun being one part, and you another. Is there a break between one part of a river and another? Then why cannot any force travel? There is no reason against it. Cases of healing from a distance are perfectly true. The Prana can be transmitted to a very great distance; but to one genuine case, there are hundreds of frauds. This process of healing is not so easy as it is thought to be. In the most ordinary cases of such healing you will find that the healers simply take advantage of the naturally healthy state of the human body. An allopath comes and treats cholera patients, and gives them his medicines. The homoeopath comes and gives his medicines, and cures perhaps more than the allopath does, because the homoeopath does not disturb his patients, but allows nature to deal with them. The Faith-healer cures more still, because he brings the strength of his mind to bear, and rouses, through faith, the dormant Prana of the patient.

There is a mistake constantly made by Faith-healers: they think that faith directly heals a man. But faith alone does not cover all the ground. There are diseases where the worst symptoms are that the patient never thinks that he has that disease. That tremendous faith of the patient is itself one symptom of the disease, and usually indicates that he will die quickly. In such cases the principle that faith cures does not apply. If it were faith alone that cured, these patients also would be cured. It is by the Prana that real curing comes. The pure man, who has controlled the Prana, has the power of bringing it into a certain state of vibration, which can be conveyed to others, arousing in them a similar vibration. You see that in everyday actions. I am talking to you. What am I trying to do? I am, so to say, bringing my mind to a certain state of vibration, and the more I succeed in bringing it to that state, the more you will be affected by what I say. All of you know that the day I am more enthusiastic, the more you enjoy the lecture; and when I am less enthusiastic, you feel lack of interest.

The gigantic will-powers of the world, the world-movers, can bring their Prana into a high state of vibration, and it is so great and powerful that it catches others in a moment, and thousands are drawn towards them, and half the world think as they do. Great prophets of the world had the most wonderful control of the Prana, which gave them tremendous will-power; they had brought their Prana to the highest state of motion, and this is what gave them power to sway the world. All manifestations of power arise from this control. Men may not know the secret, but this is the one explanation. Sometimes in your own body the supply of Prana gravitates more or less to one part; the balance is disturbed, and when the balance of Prana is disturbed, what we call disease is produced. To take away the superfluous Prana, or to supply the Prana that is wanting, will be curing the disease. That again is Pranayama — to learn when there is more or less Prana in one part of the body than there should be. The feelings will become so subtle that the mind will feel that there is less Prana in the toe or the finger than there should be, and will possess the power to supply it. These are among the various functions of Pranayama. They have to be learned slowly and gradually, and as you see, the whole scope of Raja-Yoga is really to teach the control and direction in different planes of the Prana. When a man has concentrated his energies, he masters the Prana that is in his body. When a man is meditating, he is also concentrating the Prana.

In an ocean there are huge waves, like mountains, then smaller waves, and still smaller, down to little bubbles, but back of all these is the infinite ocean. The bubble is connected with the infinite ocean at one end, and the huge wave at the other end. So, one may be a gigantic man, and another a little bubble, but each is connected with that infinite ocean of energy, which is the common birthright of every animal that exists. Wherever there is life, the storehouse of infinite energy is behind it. Starting as some fungus, some very minute, microscopic bubble, and all the time drawing from that infinite store-house of energy, a form is changed slowly and steadily until in course of time it becomes a plant, then an animal, then man, ultimately God. This is attained through millions of aeons, but what is time? An increase of speed, an increase of struggle, is able to bridge the gulf of time. That which naturally takes a long time to accomplish can be shortened by the intensity of the action, says the Yogi. A man may go on slowly drawing in this energy from the infinite mass that exists in the universe, and, perhaps, he will require a hundred thousand years to become a Deva, and then, perhaps, five hundred thousand years to become still higher, and, perhaps, five millions of years to become perfect. Given rapid growth, the time will be lessened. Why is it not possible, with sufficient effort, to reach this very perfection in six months or six years? There is no limit. Reason shows that. If an engine, with a certain amount of coal, runs two miles an hour, it will run the distance in less time with a greater supply of coal. Similarly, why shall not the soul, by intensifying its action, attain perfection in this very life? All beings will at last attain to that goal, we know. But who cares to wait all these millions of aeons? Why not reach it immediately, in this body even, in this human form? Why shall I not get that infinite knowledge, infinite power, now?

The ideal of the Yogi, the whole science of Yoga, is directed to the end of teaching men how, by intensifying the power of assimilation, to shorten the time for reaching perfection, instead of slowly advancing from point to point and waiting until the whole human race has become perfect. All the great prophets, saints, and seers of the world — what did they do? In one span of life they lived the whole life of humanity, traversed the whole length of time that it takes ordinary humanity to come to perfection. In one life they perfect themselves; they have no thought for anything else, never live a moment for any other idea, and thus the way is shortened for them. This is what is meant by concentration, intensifying the power of assimilation, thus shortening the time. Raja-Yoga is the science which teaches us how to gain the power of concentration.

What has Pranayama to do with spiritualism? Spiritualism is also a manifestation of Pranayama. If it be true that the departed spirits exist, only we cannot see them, it is quite probable that there may be hundreds and millions of them about us we can neither see, feel, nor touch. We may be continually passing and repassing through their bodies, and they do not see or feel us. It is a circle within a circle, universe within universe. We have five senses, and we represent Prana in a certain state of vibration. All beings in the same state of vibration will see one another, but if there are beings who represent Prana in a higher state of vibration, they will not be seen. We may increase the intensity of a light until we cannot see it at all, but there may be beings with eyes so powerful that they can see such light. Again, if its vibrations are very low, we do not see a light, but there are animals that may see it, as cats and owls. Our range of vision is only one plane of the vibrations of this Prana. Take this atmosphere, for instance; it is piled up layer on layer, but the layers nearer to the earth are denser than those above, and as you go higher the atmosphere becomes finer and finer. Or take the case of the ocean; as you go deeper and deeper the pressure of the water increases, and animals which live at the bottom of the sea can never come up, or they will be broken into pieces.

Think of the universe as an ocean of ether, consisting of layer after layer of varying degrees of vibration under the action of Prana; away from the centre the vibrations are less, nearer to it they become quicker and quicker; one order of vibration makes one plane. Then suppose these ranges of vibrations are cut into planes, so many millions of miles one set of vibration, and then so many millions of miles another still higher set of vibration, and so on. It is, therefore, probable, that those who live on the plane of a certain state of vibration will have the power of recognising one another, but will not recognise those above them. Yet, just as by the telescope and the microscope we can increase the scope of our vision, similarly we can by Yoga bring ourselves to the state of vibration of another plane, and thus enable ourselves to see what is going on there. Suppose this room is full of beings whom we do not see. They represent Prana in a certain state of vibration while we represent another. Suppose they represent a quick one, and we the opposite. Prana is the material of which the: are composed, as well as we. All are parts of the same ocean of Prana, they differ only in their rate of vibration. If I can bring myself to the quick vibration, this plane will immediately change for me: I shall not see you any more; you vanish and they appear. Some of you, perhaps, know this to be true. All this bringing of the mind into a higher state of vibration is included in one word in Yoga — Samadhi. All these states of higher vibration, superconscious vibrations of the mind, are grouped in that one word, Samadhi, and the lower states of Samadhi give us visions of these beings. The highest grade of Samadhi is when we see the real thing, when we see the material out of which the whole of these grades of beings are composed, and that one lump of clay being known, we know all the clay in the universe.

Thus we see that Pranayama includes all that is true of spiritualism even. Similarly, you will find that wherever any sect or body of people is trying to search out anything occult and mystical, or hidden, what they are doing is really this Yoga, this attempt to control the Prana. You will find that wherever there is any extraordinary display of power, it is the manifestation of this Prana. Even the physical sciences can be included in Pranayama. What moves the steam engine? Prana, acting through the steam. What are all these phenomena of electricity and so forth but Prana? What is physical science? The science of Pranayama, by external means. Prana, manifesting itself as mental power, can only be controlled by mental means. That part of Pranayama which attempts to control the physical manifestations of the Prana by physical means is called physical science, and that part which tries to control the manifestations of the Prana as mental force by mental means is called Raja-Yoga.

Chapter IV.
The Psychic Prana

According to the Yogis, there are two nerve currents in the spinal column, called Pingalâ and Idâ, and a hollow canal called Sushumnâ running through the spinal cord. At the lower end of the hollow canal is what the Yogis call the "Lotus of the Kundalini". They describe it as triangular in form in which, in the symbolical language of the Yogis, there is a power called the Kundalini, coiled up. When that Kundalini awakes, it tries to force a passage through this hollow canal, and as it rises step by step, as it were, layer after layer of the mind becomes open and all the different visions and wonderful powers come to the Yogi. When it reaches the brain, the Yogi is perfectly detached from the body and mind; the soul finds itself free. We know that the spinal cord is composed in a peculiar manner. If we take the figure eight horizontally (∞) there are two parts which are connected in the middle. Suppose you add eight after eight, piled one on top of the other, that will represent the spinal cord. The left is the Ida, the right Pingala, and that hollow canal which runs through the centre of the spinal cord is the Sushumna. Where the spinal cord ends in some of the lumbar vertebrae, a fine fibre issues downwards, and the canal runs up even within that fibre, only much finer. The canal is closed at the lower end, which is situated near what is called the sacral plexus, which, according to modern physiology, is triangular in form. The different plexuses that have their centres in the spinal canal can very well stand for the different "lotuses" of the Yogi.

The Yogi conceives of several centres, beginning with the Mulâdhâra, the basic, and ending with the Sahasrâra, the thousand-petalled Lotus in the brain. So, if we take these different plexuses as representing these lotuses, the idea of the Yogi can be understood very easily in the language of modern physiology. We know there are two sorts of actions in these nerve currents, one afferent, the other efferent; one sensory and the other motor; one centripetal, and the other centrifugal. One carries the sensations to the brain, and the other from the brain to the outer body. These vibrations are all connected with the brain in the long run. Several other facts we have to remember, in order to clear the way for the explanation which is to come. This spinal cord, at the brain, ends in a sort of bulb, in the medulla, which is not attached to the brain, but floats in a fluid in the brain, so that if there be a blow on the head the force of that blow will be dissipated in the fluid, and will not hurt the bulb. This is an important fact to remember. Secondly, we have also to know that, of all the centres, we have particularly to remember three, the Muladhara (the basic), the Sahasrara (the thousand-petalled lotus of the brain) and the Manipura (the lotus of the navel).

Next we shall take one fact from physics. We all hear of electricity and various other forces connected with it. What electricity is no one knows, but so far as it is known, it is a sort of motion. There are various other motions in the universe; what is the difference between them and electricity? Suppose this table moves — that the molecules which compose this table are moving in different directions; if they are all made to move in the same direction, it will be through electricity. Electric motion makes the molecules of a body move in the same direction. If all the air molecules in a room are made to move in the same direction, it will make a gigantic battery of electricity of the room. Another point from physiology we must remember, that the centre which regulates the respiratory system, the breathing system, has a sort of controlling action over the system of nerve currents.

Now we shall see why breathing is practised. In the first place, from rhythmical breathing comes a tendency of all the molecules in the body to move in the same direction. When mind changes into will, the nerve currents change into a motion similar to electricity, because the nerves have been proved to show polarity under the action of electric currents. This shows that when the will is transformed into the nerve currents, it is changed into something like electricity. When all the motions of the body have become perfectly rhythmical, the body has, as it were, become a gigantic battery of will. This tremendous will is exactly what the Yogi wants. This is, therefore, a physiological explanation of the breathing exercise. It tends to bring a rhythmic action in the body, and helps us, through the respiratory centre, to control the other centres. The aim of Prânâyâma here is to rouse the coiled-up power in the Muladhara, called the Kundalini.

Everything that we see, or imagine, or dream, we have to perceive in space. This is the ordinary space, called the Mahâkâsha, or elemental space. When a Yogi reads the thoughts of other men, or perceives supersensuous objects he sees them in another sort of space called the Chittâkâsha, the mental space. When perception has become objectless, and the soul shines in its own nature, it is called the Chidâkâsha, or knowledge space. When the Kundalini is aroused, and enters the canal of the Sushumna, all the perceptions are in the mental space. When it has reached that end of the canal which opens out into the brain, the objectless perception is in the knowledge space. Taking the analogy of electricity, we find that man can send a current only along a wire, (The reader should remember that this was spoken before the discovery of wireless telegraphy. — Ed.) but nature requires no wires to send her tremendous currents. This proves that the wire is not really necessary, but that only our inability to dispense with it compels us to use it.

Similarly, all the sensations and motions of the body are being sent into the brain, and sent out of it, through these wires of nerve fibres. The columns of sensory and motor fibres in the spinal cord are the Ida and Pingala of the Yogis. They are the main channels through which the afferent and efferent currents travel. But why should not the mind send news without any wire, or react without any wire? We see this is done in nature. The Yogi says, if you can do that, you have got rid of the bondage of matter. How to do it? If you can make the current pass through the Sushumna, the canal in the middle of the spinal column, you have solved the problem. The mind has made this network of the nervous system, and has to break it, so that no wires will be required to work through. Then alone will all knowledge come to us — no more bondage of body; that is why it is so important that we should get control of that Sushumna. If we can send the mental current through the hollow canal without any nerve fibres to act as wires, the Yogi says, the problem is solved, and he also says it can be done.

This Sushumna is in ordinary persons closed up at the lower extremity; no action comes through it. The Yogi proposes a practice by which it can be opened, and the nerve currents made to travel through. When a sensation is carried to a centre, the centre reacts. This reaction, in the case of automatic centres, is followed by motion; in the case of conscious centres it is followed first by perception, and secondly by motion. All perception is the reaction to action from outside. How, then, do perceptions in dreams arise? There is then no action from outside. The sensory motions, therefore, are coiled up somewhere. For instance, I see a city; the perception of that city is from the reaction to the sensations brought from outside objects comprising that city. That is to say, a certain motion in the brain molecules has been set up by the motion in the incarrying nerves, which again are set in motion by external objects in the city. Now, even after a long time I can remember the city. This memory is exactly the same phenomenon, only it is in a milder form. But whence is the action that sets up even the milder form of similar vibrations in the brain? Not certainly from the primary sensations. Therefore it must be that the sensations are coiled up somewhere, and they, by their acting, bring out the mild reaction which we call dream perception.

Now the centre where all these residual sensations are, as it were, stored up, is called the Muladhara, the root receptacle, and the coiled-up energy of action is Kundalini, "the coiled up". It is very probable that the residual motor energy is also stored up in the same centre, as, after deep study or meditation on external objects, the part of the body where the Muladhara centre is situated (probably the sacral plexus) gets heated. Now, if this coiled-up energy be roused and made active, and then consciously made to travel up the Sushumna canal, as it acts upon centre after centre, a tremendous reaction will set in. When a minute portion of energy travels along a nerve fibre and causes reaction from centres, the perception is either dream or imagination. But when by the power of long internal meditation the vast mass of energy stored up travels along the Sushumna, and strikes the centres, the reaction is tremendous, immensely superior to the reaction of dream or imagination, immensely more intense than the reaction of sense-perception. It is super-sensuous perception. And when it reaches the metropolis of all sensations, the brain, the whole brain, as it were, reacts, and the result is the full blaze of illumination, the perception of the Self. As this Kundalini force travels from centre to centre, layer after layer of the mind, as it were, opens up, and this universe is perceived by the Yogi in its fine, or causal form. Then alone the causes of this universe, both as sensation and reaction, are known as they are, and hence comes all knowledge. The causes being known, the knowledge of the effects is sure to follow.

Thus the rousing of the Kundalini is the one and only way to attaining Divine Wisdom, superconscious perception, realisation of the spirit. The rousing may come in various ways, through love for God, through the mercy of perfected sages, or through the power of the analytic will of the philosopher. Wherever there was any manifestation of what is ordinarily called supernatural power or wisdom, there a little current of Kundalini must have found its way into the Sushumna. Only, in the vast majority of such cases, people had ignorantly stumbled on some practice which set free a minute portion of the coiled-up Kundalini. All worship, consciously or unconsciously, leads to this end. The man who thinks that he is receiving response to his prayers does not know that the fulfilment comes from his own nature, that he has succeeded by the mental attitude of prayer in waking up a bit of this infinite power which is coiled up within himself. What, thus, men ignorantly worship under various names, through fear and tribulation, the Yogi declares to the world to be the real power coiled up in every being, the mother of eternal happiness, if we but know how to approach her. And Râja-Yoga is the science of religion, the rationale of all worship, all prayers, forms, ceremonies, and miracles.

Chapter V.
The Control Of Psychic Prana

We have now to deal with the exercises in Prânâyâma. We have seen that the first step, according to the Yogis, is to control the motion of the lungs. What we want to do is to feel the finer motions that are going on in the body. Our minds have become externalised, and have lost sight of the fine motions inside. If we can begin to feel them, we can begin to control them. These nerve currents go on all over the body, bringing life and vitality to every muscle, but we do not feel them. The Yogi says we can learn to do so. How? By taking up and controlling the motion of the lungs; when we have done that for a sufficient length of time, we shall be able to control the finer motions.

We now come to the exercises in Pranayama. Sit upright; the body must be kept straight. The spinal cord, although not attached to the vertebral column, is yet inside of it. If you sit crookedly you disturb this spinal cord, so let it be free. Any time that you sit crookedly and try to meditate you do yourself an injury. The three parts of the body, the chest, the neck, and the head, must be always held straight in one line. You will find that by a little practice this will come to you as easy as breathing. The second thing is to get control of the nerves. We have said that the nerve centre that controls the respiratory organs has a sort of controlling effect on the other nerves, and rhythmical breathing is, therefore, necessary. The breathing that we generally use should not be called breathing at all. It is very irregular. Then there are some natural differences of breathing between men and women.

The first lesson is just to breathe in a measured way, in and out. That will harmonise the system. When you have practiced this for some time, you will do well to join to it the repetition of some word as "Om," or any other sacred word. In India we use certain symbolical words instead of counting one, two, three, four. That is why I advise you to join the mental repetition of the "Om," or some other sacred word to the Pranayama. Let the word flow in and out with the breath, rhythmically, harmoniously, and you will find the whole body is becoming rhythmical. Then you will learn what rest is. Compared with it, sleep is not rest. Once this rest comes the most tired nerves will be calmed down, and you will find that you have never before really rested.

The first effect of this practice is perceived in the change of expression of one's face; harsh lines disappear; with calm thought calmness comes over the face. Next comes beautiful voice. I never saw a Yogi with a croaking voice. These signs come after a few months' practice. After practicing the above mentioned breathing for a few days, you should take up a higher one. Slowly fill the lungs with breath through the Idâ, the left nostril, and at the same time concentrate the mind on the nerve current. You are, as it were, sending the nerve current down the spinal column, and striking violently on the last plexus, the basic lotus which is triangular in form, the seat of the Kundalini. Then hold the current there for some time. Imagine that you are slowly drawing that nerve current with the breath through the other side, the Pingalâ, then slowly throw it out through the right nostril. This you will find a little difficult to practice. The easiest way is to stop the right nostril with the thumb, and then slowly draw in the breath through the left; then close both nostrils with thumb and forefinger, and imagine that you are sending that current down, and striking the base of the Sushumnâ; then take the thumb off, and let the breath out through the right nostril. Next inhale slowly through that nostril, keeping the other closed by the forefinger, then close both, as before. The way the Hindus practice this would be very difficult for this country, because they do it from their childhood, and their lungs are prepared for it. Here it is well to begin with four seconds, and slowly increase. Draw in four seconds, hold in sixteen seconds, then throw out in eight seconds. This makes one Pranayama. At the same time think of the basic lotus, triangular in form; concentrate the mind on that centre. The imagination can help you a great deal. The next breathing is slowly drawing the breath in, and then immediately throwing it out slowly, and then stopping the breath out, using the same numbers. The only difference is that in the first case the breath was held in, and in the second, held out. This last is the easier one. The breathing in which you hold the breath in the lungs must not be practiced too much. Do it only four times in the morning, and four times in the evening. Then you can slowly increase the time and number. You will find that you have the power to do so, and that you take pleasure in it. So very carefully and cautiously increase as you feel that you have the power, to six instead of four. It may injure you if you practice it irregularly.

Of the three processes for the purification of the nerves, described above, the first and the last are neither difficult nor dangerous. The more you practice the first one the calmer you will be. Just think of "Om," and you can practice even while you are sitting at your work. You will be all the better for it. Some day, if you practice hard, the Kundalini will be aroused. For those who practice once or twice a day, just a little calmness of the body and mind will come, and beautiful voice; only for those who can go on further with it will Kundalini be aroused, and the whole of nature will begin to change, and the book of knowledge will open. No more will you need to go to books for knowledge; your own mind will have become your book, containing infinite knowledge. I have already spoken of the Ida and Pingala currents, flowing through either side of the spinal column, and also of the Sushumna, the passage through the centre of the spinal cord. These three are present in every animal; whatever being has a spinal column has these three lines of action. But the Yogis claim that in an ordinary man the Sushumna is closed; its action is not evident while that of the other two is carrying power to different parts of the body.

The Yogi alone has the Sushumna open. When this Sushumna current opens, and begins to rise, we get beyond the sense, our minds become supersensuous, superconscious — we get beyond even the intellect, where reasoning cannot reach. To open that Sushumna is the prime object of the Yogi. According to him, along this Sushumna are ranged these centres, or, in more figurative language, these lotuses, as they are called. The lowest one is at the lower end of the spinal cord, and is called Mulâdhâra, the next higher is called Svâdhishthâna, the third Manipura, the fourth Anâhata, the fifth Vishuddha, the sixth Âjnâ and the last, which is in the brain, is the Sahasrâra, or "the thousand-petalled". Of these we have to take cognition just now of two centres only, the lowest, the Muladhara, and the highest, the Sahasrara. All energy has to be taken up from its seat in the Muladhara and brought to the Sahasrara. The Yogis claim that of all the energies that are in the human body the highest is what they call "Ojas". Now this Ojas is stored up in the brain, and the more Ojas is in a man's head, the more powerful he is, the more intellectual, the more spiritually strong. One man may speak beautiful language and beautiful thoughts, but they, do not impress people; another man speaks neither beautiful language nor beautiful thoughts, yet his words charm. Every movement of his is powerful. That is the power of Ojas.

Now in every man there is more or less of this Ojas stored up. All the forces that are working in the body in their highest become Ojas. You must remember that it is only a question of transformation. The same force which is working outside as electricity or magnetism will become changed into inner force; the same forces that are working as muscular energy will be changed into Ojas. The Yogis say that that part of the human energy which is expressed as sex energy, in sexual thought, when checked and controlled, easily becomes changed into Ojas, and as the Muladhara guides these, the

Yogi pays particular attention to that centre. He tries to take up all his sexual energy and convert it into Ojas. It is only the chaste man or woman who can make the Ojas rise and store it in the brain; that is why chastity has always been considered the highest virtue. A man feels that if he is unchaste, spirituality goes away, he loses mental vigour and moral stamina. That is why in all the religious orders in the world which have produced spiritual giants you will always find absolute chastity insisted upon. That is why the monks came into existence, giving up marriage. There must be perfect chastity in thought, word, and deed; without it the practice of Raja-Yoga is dangerous, and may lead to insanity. If people practice Raja-Yoga and at the same time lead an impure life, how can they expect to become Yogis?

Chapter VI.
Pratyahara And Dharana

The next step is called Pratyâhâra. What is this? You know how perceptions come. First of all there are the external instruments, then the internal organs acting in the body through the brain centres, and there is the mind. When these come together and attach themselves to some external object, then we perceive it. At the same time it is a very difficult thing to concentrate the mind and attach it to one organ only; the mind is a slave.

We hear "Be good," and "Be good," and "Be good," taught all over the world. There is hardly a child, born in any country in the world, who has not been told, "Do not steal," "Do not tell a lie," but nobody tells the child how he can help doing them. Talking will not help him. Why should he not become a thief? We do not teach him how not to steal; we simply tell him, "Do not steal." Only when we teach him to control his mind do we really help him. All actions, internal and external, occur when the mind joins itself to certain centres, called the organs. Willingly or unwillingly it is drawn to join itself to the centres, and that is why people do foolish deeds and feel miserable, which, if the mind were under control, they would not do. What would be the result of controlling the mind? It then would not join itself to the centres of perception, and, naturally, feeling and willing would be under control. It is clear so far. Is it possible? It is perfectly possible. You see it in modern times; the faith-healers teach people to deny misery and pain and evil. Their philosophy is rather roundabout, but it is a part of Yoga upon which they have somehow stumbled. Where they succeed in making a person throw off suffering by denying it, they really use a part of Pratyahara, as they make the mind of the person strong enough to ignore the senses. The hypnotists in a similar manner, by their suggestion, excite in the patient a sort of morbid Pratyahara for the time being. The so-called hypnotic suggestion can only act upon a weak mind. And until the operator, by means of fixed gaze or otherwise, has succeeded in putting the mind of the subject in a sort of passive, morbid condition, his suggestions never work.

Now the control of the centres which is established in a hypnotic patient or the patient of faith-healing, by the operator, for a time, is reprehensible, because it leads to ultimate ruin. It is not really controlling the brain centres by the power of one's own will, but is, as it were, stunning the patient's mind for a time by sudden blows which another's will delivers to it. It is not checking by means of reins and muscular strength the mad career of a fiery team, but rather by asking another to deliver heavy blows on the heads of the horses, to stun them for a time into gentleness. At each one of these processes the man operated upon loses a part of his mental energies, till at last, the mind, instead of gaining the power of perfect control, becomes a shapeless, powerless mass, and the only goal of the patient is the lunatic asylum.

Every attempt at control which is not voluntary, not with the controller's own mind, is not only disastrous, but it defeats the end. The goal of each soul is freedom, mastery — freedom from the slavery of matter and thought, mastery of external and internal nature. Instead of leading towards that, every will-current from another, in whatever form it comes, either as direct control of organs, or as forcing to control them while under a morbid condition, only rivets one link more to the already existing heavy chain of bondage of past thoughts, past superstitions. Therefore, beware how you allow yourselves to be acted upon by others. Beware how you unknowingly bring another to ruin. True, some succeed in doing good to many for a time, by giving a new trend to their propensities, but at the same time, they bring ruin to millions by the unconscious suggestions they throw around, rousing in men and women that morbid, passive, hypnotic condition which makes them almost soulless at last. Whosoever, therefore, asks any one to believe blindly, or drags people behind him by the controlling power of his superior will, does an injury to humanity, though he may not intend it.

Therefore use your own minds, control body and mind yourselves, remember that until you are a diseased person, no extraneous will can work upon you; avoid everyone, however great and good he may be, who asks you to believe blindly. All over the world there have been dancing and jumping and howling sects, who spread like infection when they begin to sing and dance and preach; they also are a sort of hypnotists. They exercise a singular control for the time being over sensitive persons, alas! often, in the long run, to degenerate whole races. Ay, it is healthier for the individual or the race to remain wicked than be made apparently good by such morbid extraneous control. One's heart sinks to think of the amount of injury done to humanity by such irresponsible yet well-meaning religious fanatics. They little know that the minds which attain to sudden spiritual upheaval under their suggestions, with music and prayers, are simply making themselves passive, morbid, and powerless, and opening themselves to any other suggestion, be it ever so evil. Little do these ignorant, deluded persons dream that whilst they are congratulating themselves upon their miraculous power to transform human hearts, which power they think was poured upon them by some Being above the clouds, they are sowing the seeds of future decay, of crime, of lunacy, and of death. Therefore, beware of everything that takes away your freedom. Know that it is dangerous, and avoid it by all the means in your power.

He who has succeeded in attaching or detaching his mind to or from the centres at will has succeeded in Pratyahara, which means, "gathering towards," checking the outgoing powers of the mind, freeing it from the thraldom of the senses. When we can do this, we shall really possess character; then alone we shall have taken a long step towards freedom; before that we are mere machines.

How hard it is to control the mind! Well has it been compared to the maddened monkey. There was a monkey, restless by his own nature, as all monkeys are. As if that were not enough some one made him drink freely of wine, so that he became still more restless. Then a scorpion stung him. When a man is stung by a scorpion, he jumps about for a whole day; so the poor monkey found his condition worse than ever. To complete his misery a demon entered into him. What language can describe the uncontrollable restlessness of that monkey? The human mind is like that monkey, incessantly active by its own nature; then it becomes drunk with the wine of desire, thus increasing its turbulence. After desire takes possession comes the sting of the scorpion of jealousy at the success of others, and last of all the demon of pride enters the mind, making it think itself of all importance. How hard to control such a mind!

The first lesson, then, is to sit for some time and let the mind run on. The mind is bubbling up all the time. It is like that monkey jumping about. Let the monkey jump as much as he can; you simply wait and watch. Knowledge is power, says the proverb, and that is true. Until you know what the mind is doing you cannot control it. Give it the rein; many hideous thoughts may come into it; you will be astonished that it was possible for you to think such thoughts. But you will find that each day the mind's vagaries are becoming less and less violent, that each day it is becoming calmer. In the first few months you will find that the mind will have a great many thoughts, later you will find that they have somewhat decreased, and in a few more months they will be fewer and fewer, until at last the mind will be under perfect control; but we must patiently practice every day. As soon as the steam is turned on, the engine must run; as soon as things are before us we must perceive; so a man, to prove that he is not a machine, must demonstrate that he is under the control of nothing. This controlling of the mind, and not allowing it to join itself to the centres, is Pratyahara. How is this practised? It is a tremendous work, not to be done in a day. Only after a patient, continuous struggle for years can we succeed.

After you have practised Pratyahara for a time, take the next step, the Dhâranâ, holding the mind to certain points. What is meant by holding the mind to certain points? Forcing the mind to feel certain parts of the body to the exclusion of others. For instance, try to feel only the hand, to the exclusion of other parts of the body. When the Chitta, or mind-stuff, is confined and limited to a certain place it is Dharana. This Dharana is of various sorts, and along with it, it is better to have a little play of the imagination. For instance, the mind should be made to think of one point in the heart. That is very difficult; an easier way is to imagine a lotus there. That lotus is full of light, effulgent light. Put the mind there. Or think of the lotus in the brain as full of light, or of the different centres in the Sushumna mentioned before.

The Yogi must always practice. He should try to live alone; the companionship of different sorts of people distracts the mind; he should not speak much, because to speak distracts the mind; not work much, because too much work distracts the mind; the mind cannot be controlled after a whole day's hard work. One observing the above rules becomes a Yogi. Such is the power of Yoga that even the least of it will bring a great amount of benefit. It will not hurt anyone, but will benefit everyone. First of all, it will tone down nervous excitement, bring calmness, enable us to see things more clearly. The temperament will be better, and the health will be better. Sound health will be one of the first signs, and a beautiful voice. Defects in the voice will be changed. This will be among the first of the many effects that will come. Those who practise hard will get many other signs. Sometimes there will be sounds, as a peal of bells heard at a distance, commingling, and falling on the ear as one continuous sound. Sometimes things will be seen, little specks of light floating and becoming bigger and bigger; and when these things come, know that you are progressing fast.

Those who want to be Yogis, and practice hard, must take care of their diet at first. But for those who want only a little practice for everyday business sort of life, let them not eat too much; otherwise they may eat whatever they please. For those who want to make rapid progress, and to practice hard, a strict diet is absolutely necessary. They will find it advantageous to live only on milk and cereals for some months. As the organisation becomes finer and finer, it will be found in the beginning that the least irregularity throws one out of balance. One bit of food more or less will disturb the whole system, until one gets perfect control, and then one will be able to eat whatever one likes.

When one begins to concentrate, the dropping of a pin will seem like a thunderbolt going through the brain. As the organs get finer, the perceptions get finer. These are the stages through which we have to pass, and all those who persevere will succeed. Give up all argumentation and other distractions. Is there anything in dry intellectual jargon? It only throws the mind off its balance and disturbs it. Things of subtler planes have to be realised. Will talking do that? So give up all vain talk. Read only those books which have been written by persons who have had realisation.

Be like the pearl oyster. There is a pretty Indian fable to the effect that if it rains when the star Svâti is in the ascendant, and a drop of rain falls into an oyster, that drop becomes a pearl. The oysters know this, so they come to the surface when that star shines, and wait to catch the precious raindrop. When a drop falls into them, quickly the oysters close their shells and dive down to the bottom of the sea, there to patiently develop the drop into the pearl. We should be like that. First hear, then understand, and then, leaving all distractions, shut your minds to outside influences, and devote yourselves to developing the truth within you. There is the danger of frittering away your energies by taking up an idea only for its novelty, and then giving it up for another that is newer. Take one thing up and do it, and see the end of it, and before you have seen the end, do not give it up. He who can become mad with an idea, he alone sees light. Those that only take a nibble here and a nibble there will never attain anything. They may titillate their nerves for a moment, but there it will end. They will be slaves in the hands of nature, and will never get beyond the senses.

Those who really want to be Yogis must give up, once for all, this nibbling at things. Take up one idea. Make that one idea your life — think of it, dream of it, live on that idea. Let the brain, muscles, nerves, every part of your body, be full of that idea, and just leave every other idea alone. This is the way to success, and this is the way great spiritual giants are produced. Others are mere talking machines. If we really want to be blessed, and make others blessed, we must go deeper. The first step is not to disturb the mind, not to associate with persons whose ideas are disturbing. All of you know that certain persons, certain places, certain foods, repel you. Avoid them; and those who want to go to the highest, must avoid all company, good or bad. Practise hard; whether you live or die does not matter. You have to plunge in and work, without thinking of the result. If you are brave enough, in six months you will be a perfect Yogi. But those who take up just a bit of it and a little of everything else make no progress. It is of no use simply to take a course of lessons. To those who are full of Tamas, ignorant and dull — those whose minds never get fixed on any idea, who only crave for something to amuse them — religion and philosophy are simply objects of entertainment. These are the unpersevering. They hear a talk, think it very nice, and then go home and forget all about it. To succeed, you must have tremendous perseverance, tremendous will. "I will drink the ocean," says the persevering soul, "at my will mountains will crumble up." Have that sort of energy, that sort of will, work hard, and you will reach the goal.

Chapter VII.
Dhyana And Samadhi

We have taken a cursory view of the different steps in Râja-Yoga, except the finer ones, the training in concentration, which is the goal to which Raja-Yoga will lead us. We see, as human beings, that all our knowledge which is called rational is referred to consciousness. My consciousness of this table, and of your presence, makes me know that the table and you are here. At the same time, there is a very great part of my existence of which I am not conscious. All the different organs inside the body, the different parts of the brain — nobody is conscious of these.

When I eat food, I do it consciously; when I assimilate it, I do it unconsciously. When the food is manufactured into blood, it is done unconsciously. When out of the blood all the different parts of my body are strengthened, it is done unconsciously. And yet it is I who am doing all this; there cannot be twenty people in this one body. How do I know that I do it, and nobody else? It may be urged that my business is only in eating and assimilating the food, and that strengthening the body by the food is done for me by somebody else. That cannot be, because it can be demonstrated that almost every action of which we are now unconscious can be brought up to the plane of consciousness. The heart is beating apparently without our control. None of us here can control the heart; it goes on its own way. But by practice men can bring even the heart under control, until it will just beat at will, slowly, or quickly, or almost stop. Nearly every part of the body can be brought under control. What does this show? That the functions which are beneath consciousness are also performed by us, only we are doing it unconsciously. We have, then, two planes in which the human mind works. First is the conscious plane, in which all work is always accompanied with the feeling of egoism. Next comes the unconscious plane, where all work is unaccompanied by the feeling of egoism. That part of mind-work which is unaccompanied with the feeling of egoism is unconscious work, and that part which is accompanied with the feeling of egoism is conscious work. In the lower animals this unconscious work is called instinct. In higher animals, and in the highest of all animals, man, what is called conscious work prevails.

But it does not end here. There is a still higher plane upon which the mind can work. It can go beyond consciousness. Just as unconscious work is beneath consciousness, so there is another work which is above consciousness, and which also is not accompanied with the feeling of egoism. The feeling of egoism is only on the middle plane. When the mind is above or below that line, there is no feeling of "I", and yet the mind works. When the mind goes beyond this line of self-consciousness, it is called Samâdhi or superconsciousness. How, for instance, do we know that a man in Samadhi has not gone below consciousness, has not degenerated instead of going higher? In both cases the works are unaccompanied with egoism. The answer is, by the effects, by the results of the work, we know that which is below, and that which is above. When a man goes into deep sleep, he enters a plane beneath consciousness. He works the body all the time, he breathes, he moves the body, perhaps, in his sleep, without any accompanying feeling of ego; he is unconscious, and when he returns from his sleep, he is the same man who went into it. The sum total of the knowledge which he had before he went into the sleep remains the same; it does not increase at all. No enlightenment comes. But when a man goes into Samadhi, if he goes into it a fool, he comes out a sage.

What makes the difference? From one state a man comes out the very same man that he went in, and from another state the man comes out enlightened, a sage, a prophet, a saint, his whole character changed, his life changed, illumined. These are the two effects. Now the effects being different, the causes must be different. As this illumination with which a man comes back from Samadhi is much higher than can be got from unconsciousness, or much higher than can be got by reasoning in a conscious state, it must, therefore, be superconsciousness, and Samadhi is called the superconscious state.

This, in short, is the idea of Samadhi. What is its application? The application is here. The field of reason, or of the conscious workings of the mind, is narrow and limited. There is a little circle within which human reason must move. It cannot go beyond. Every attempt to go beyond is impossible, yet it is beyond this circle of reason that there lies all that humanity holds most dear. All these questions, whether there is an immortal soul, whether there is a God, whether there is any supreme intelligence guiding this universe or not, are beyond the field of reason. Reason can never answer these questions. What does reason say? It says, "I am agnostic; I do not know either yea or nay." Yet these questions are so important to us. Without a proper answer to them, human life will be purposeless. All our ethical theories, all our moral attitudes, all that is good and great in human nature, have been moulded upon answers that have come from beyond the circle. It is very important, therefore, that we should have answers to these questions. If life is only a short play, if the universe is only a "fortuitous combination of atoms," then why should I do good to another? Why should there be mercy, justice, or fellow-feeling? The best thing for this world would be to make hay while the sun shines, each man for himself. If there is no hope, why should I love my brother, and not cut his throat? If there is nothing beyond, if there is no freedom, but only rigorous dead laws, I should only try to make myself happy here. You will find people saying nowadays that they have utilitarian grounds as the basis of morality. What is this basis? Procuring the greatest amount of happiness to the greatest number. Why should I do this? Why should I not produce the greatest unhappiness to the greatest number, if that serves my purpose? How will utilitarians answer this question? How do you know what is right, or what is wrong? I am impelled by my desire for happiness, and I fulfil it, and it is in my nature; I know nothing beyond. I have these desires, and must fulfil them; why should you complain? Whence come all these truths about human life, about morality, about the immortal soul, about God, about love and sympathy, about being good, and, above all, about being unselfish?

All ethics, all human action and all human thought, hang upon this one idea of unselfishness. The whole idea of human life can be put into that one word, unselfishness. Why should we be unselfish? Where is the necessity, the force, the power, of my being unselfish? You call yourself a rational man, a utilitarian; but if you do not show me a reason for utility, I say you are irrational. Show me the reason why I should not be selfish. To ask one to be unselfish may be good as poetry, but poetry is not reason. Show me a reason. Why shall I be unselfish, and why be good? Because Mr. and Mrs. So-and-so say so does not weigh with me. Where is the utility of my being unselfish? My utility is to be selfish if utility means the greatest amount of happiness. What is the answer? The utilitarian can never give it. The answer is that this world is only one drop in an infinite ocean, one link in an infinite chain. Where did those that preached unselfishness, and taught it to the human race, get this idea? We know it is not instinctive; the animals, which have instinct, do not know it. Neither is it reason; reason does not know anything about these ideas. Whence then did they come?

We find, in studying history, one fact held in common by all the great teachers of religion the world ever had. They all claim to have got their truths from beyond, only many of them did not know where they got them from. For instance, one would say that an angel came down in the form of a human being, with wings, and said to him, "Hear, O man, this is the message." Another says that a Deva, a bright being, appeared to him. A third says he dreamed that his ancestor came and told him certain things. He did not know anything beyond that. But this is common that all claim that this knowledge has come to them from beyond, not through their reasoning power. What does the science of Yoga teach? It teaches that they were right in claiming that all this knowledge came to them from beyond reasoning, but that it came from within themselves.

The Yogi teaches that the mind itself has a higher state of existence, beyond reason, a superconscious state, and when the mind gets to that higher state, then this knowledge, beyond reasoning, comes to man. Metaphysical and transcendental knowledge comes to that man. This state of going beyond reason, transcending ordinary human nature, may sometimes come by chance to a man who does not understand its science; he, as it were, stumbles upon it. When he stumbles upon it, he generally interprets it as coming from outside. So this explains why an inspiration, or transcendental knowledge, may be the same in different countries, but in one country it will seem to come through an angel, and in another through a Deva, and in a third through God. What does it mean? It means that the mind brought the knowledge by its own nature, and that the finding of the knowledge was interpreted according to the belief and education of the person through whom it came. The real fact is that these various men, as it were, stumbled upon this superconscious state.

The Yogi says there is a great danger in stumbling upon this state. In a good many cases there is the danger of the brain being deranged, and, as a rule, you will find that all those men, however great they were, who had stumbled upon this superconscious state without understanding it, groped in the dark, and generally had, along with their knowledge, some quaint superstition. They opened themselves to hallucinations. Mohammed claimed that the Angel Gabriel came to him in a cave one day and took him on the heavenly horse, Harak, and he visited the heavens. But with all that, Mohammed spoke some wonderful truths. If you read the Koran, you find the most wonderful truths mixed with superstitions. How will you explain it? That man was inspired, no doubt, but that inspiration was, as it were, stumbled upon. He was not a trained Yogi, and did not know the reason of what he was doing. Think of the good Mohammed did to the world, and think of the great evil that has been done through his fanaticism! Think of the millions massacred through his teachings, mothers bereft of their children, children made orphans, whole countries destroyed, millions upon millions of people killed!

So we see this danger by studying the lives of great teachers like Mohammed and others. Yet we find, at the same time, that they were all inspired. Whenever a prophet got into the superconscious state by heightening his emotional nature, he brought away from it not only some truths, but some fanaticism also, some superstition which injured the world as much as the greatness of the teaching helped. To get any reason out of the mass of incongruity we call human life, we have to transcend our reason, but we must do it scientifically, slowly, by regular practice, and we must cast off all superstition. We must take up the study of the superconscious state just as any other science. On reason we must have to lay our foundation, we must follow reason as far as it leads, and when reason fails, reason itself will show us the way to the highest plane. When you hear a man say, "I am inspired," and then talk irrationally, reject it. Why? Because these three states — instinct, reason, and superconsciousness, or the unconscious, conscious, and superconscious states — belong to one and the same mind. There are not three minds in one man, but one state of it develops into the others. Instinct develops into reason, and reason into the transcendental consciousness; therefore, not one of the states contradicts the others. Real inspiration never contradicts reason, but fulfils it. Just as you find the great prophets saying, "I come not to destroy but to fulfil," so inspiration always comes to fulfil reason, and is in harmony with it.

All the different steps in Yoga are intended to bring us scientifically to the superconscious state, or Samadhi. Furthermore, this is a most vital point to understand, that inspiration is as much in every man's nature as it was in that of the ancient prophets. These prophets were not unique; they were men as you or I. They were great Yogis. They had gained this superconsciousness, and you and I can get the same. They were not peculiar people. The very fact that one man ever reached that state, proves that it is possible for every man to do so. Not only is it possible, but every man must, eventually, get to that state, and that is religion. Experience is the only teacher we have. We may talk and reason all our lives, but we shall not understand a word of truth, until we experience it ourselves. You cannot hope to make a man a surgeon by simply giving him a few books. You cannot satisfy my curiosity to see a country by showing me a map; I must have actual experience. Maps can only create curiosity in us to get more perfect knowledge. Beyond that, they have no value whatever. Clinging to books only degenerates the human mind. Was there ever a more horrible blasphemy than the statement that all the knowledge of God is confined to this or that book? How dare men call God infinite, and yet try to compress Him within the covers of a little book! Millions of people have been killed because they did not believe what the books said, because they would not see all the knowledge of God within the covers of a book. Of course this killing and murdering has gone by, but the world is still tremendously bound up in a belief in books.

In order to reach the superconscious state in a scientific manner it is necessary to pass through the various steps of Raja-Yoga I have been teaching. After Pratyâhâra and Dhâranâ, we come to Dhyâna, meditation. When the mind has been trained to remain fixed on a certain internal or external location, there comes to it the power of flowing in an unbroken current, as it were, towards that point. This state is called Dhyana. When one has so intensified the power of Dhyana as to be able to reject the external part of perception and remain meditating only on the internal part, the meaning, that state is called Samadhi. The three — Dharana, Dhyana, and Samadhi — together, are called Samyama. That is, if the mind can first concentrate upon an object, and then is able to continue in that concentration for a length of time, and then, by continued concentration, to dwell only on the internal part of the perception of which the object was the effect, everything comes under the control of such a mind.

This meditative state is the highest state of existence. So long as there is desire, no real happiness can come. It is only the contemplative, witness-like study of objects that brings to us real enjoyment and happiness. The animal has its happiness in the senses, the man in his intellect, and the god in spiritual contemplation. It is only to the soul that has attained to this contemplative state that the world really becomes beautiful. To him who desires nothing, and does not mix himself up with them, the manifold changes of nature are one panorama of beauty and sublimity.

These ideas have to be understood in Dhyana, or meditation. We hear a sound. First, there is the external vibration; second, the nerve motion that carries it to the mind; third, the reaction from the mind, along with which flashes the knowledge of the object which was the external cause of these different changes from the ethereal vibrations to the mental reactions. These three are called in Yoga, Shabda (sound), Artha (meaning), and Jnâna (knowledge). In the language of physics and physiology they are called the ethereal vibration, the motion in the nerve and brain, and the mental reaction. Now these, though distinct processes, have become mixed up in such a fashion as to become quite indistinct. In fact, we cannot now perceive any of these, we only perceive their combined effect, what we call the external object. Every act of perception includes these three, and there is no reason why we should not be able to distinguish them.

When, by the previous preparations, it becomes strong and controlled, and has the power of finer perception, the mind should be employed in meditation. This meditation must begin with gross objects and slowly rise to finer and finer, until it becomes objectless. The mind should first be employed in perceiving the external causes of sensations, then the internal motions, and then its own reaction. When it has succeeded in perceiving the external causes of sensations by themselves, the mind will acquire the power of perceiving all fine material existences, all fine bodies and forms.

When it can succeed in perceiving the motions inside by themselves, it will gain the control of all mental waves, in itself or in others, even before they have translated themselves into physical energy; and when he will be able to perceive the mental reaction by itself, the Yogi will acquire the knowledge of everything, as every sensible object, and every thought is the result of this reaction. Then will he have seen the very foundations of his mind, and it will be under his perfect control. Different powers will come to the Yogi, and if he yields to the temptations of any one of these, the road to his further progress will be barred. Such is the evil of running after enjoyments. But if he is strong enough to reject even these miraculous powers, he will attain to the goal of Yoga, the complete suppression of the waves in the ocean of the mind. Then the glory of the soul, undisturbed by the distractions of the mind, or motions of the body, will shine in its full effulgence; and the Yogi will find himself as he is and as he always was, the essence of knowledge, the immortal, the all-pervading.

Samadhi is the property of every human being — nay, every animal. From the lowest animal to the highest angel, some time or other, each one will have to come to that state, and then, and then alone, will real religion begin for him. Until then we only struggle towards that stage. There is no difference now between us and those who have no religion, because we have no experience. What is concentration good for, save to bring us to this experience? Each one of the steps to attain Samadhi has been reasoned out, properly adjusted, scientifically organised, and, when faithfully practiced, will surely lead us to the desired end. Then will all sorrows cease, all miseries vanish; the seeds for actions will be burnt, and the soul will be free for ever.

Chapter VIII.
Raja-Yoga In Brief

The following is a summary of Râja-Yoga freely translated from the Kurma-Purâna.

The fire of Yoga burns the cage of sin that is around a man. Knowledge becomes purified and Nirvâna is directly obtained. From Yoga comes knowledge; knowledge again helps the Yogi. He who combines in himself both Yoga and knowledge, with him the Lord is pleased. Those that practice Mahâyoga, either once a day, or twice a day, or thrice, or always, know them to be gods. Yoga is divided into two parts. One is called Abhâva, and the other, Mahayoga. Where one's self is meditated upon as zero, and bereft of quality, that is called Abhava. That in which one sees the self as full of bliss and bereft of all impurities, and one with God, is called Mahayoga. The Yogi, by each one, realises his Self. The other Yogas that we read and hear of, do not deserve to be ranked with the excellent Mahayoga in which the Yogi finds himself and the whole universe as God. This is the highest of all Yogas.

Yama, Niyama, Âsana, Prânâyâma, Pratyâhâra, Dhârâna, Dhyâna, and Samâdhi are the steps in Raja-Yoga, of which non-injury, truthfulness, non-covetousness, chastity, not receiving anything from another are called Yama. This purifies the mind, the Chitta. Never producing pain by thought, word, and deed, in any living being, is what is called Ahimsâ, non-injury. There is no virtue higher than non-injury. There is no happiness higher than what a man obtains by this attitude of non-offensiveness, to all creation. By truth we attain fruits of work. Through truth everything is attained. In truth everything is established. Relating facts as they are — this is truth. Not taking others' goods by stealth or by force, is called Asteya, non-covetousness. Chastity in thought, word, and deed, always, and in all conditions, is what is called Brahmacharya. Not receiving any present from anybody, even when one is suffering terribly, is what is called Aparigraha. The idea is, when a man receives a gift from another, his heart becomes impure, he becomes low, he loses his independence, he becomes bound and attached.

The following are helps to success in Yoga and are called Niyama or regular habits and observances; Tapas, austerity; Svâdhyâya, study; Santosha, contentment; Shaucha, purity; Ishvara-pranidhâna, worshipping God. Fasting, or in other ways controlling the body, is called physical Tapas. Repeating the Vedas and other Mantras, by which the Sattva material in the body is purified, is called study, Svadhyaya. There are three sorts of repetitions of these Mantras. One is called the verbal, another semi-verbal, and the third mental. The verbal or audible is the lowest, and the inaudible is the highest of all. The repetition which is loud is the verbal; the next one is where only the lips move, but no sound is heard. The inaudible repetition of the Mantra, accompanied with the thinking of its meaning, is called the "mental repetition," and is the highest. The sages have said that there are two sorts of purification, external and internal. The purification of the body by water, earth, or other materials is the external purification, as bathing etc. Purification of the mind by truth, and by all the other virtues, is what is called internal purification. Both are necessary. It is not sufficient that a man should be internally pure and externally dirty. When both are not attainable the internal purity is the better, but no one will be a Yogi until he has both. Worship of God is by praise, by thought, by devotion.

We have spoken about Yama and Niyama. The next is Asana (posture). The only thing to understand about it is leaving the body free, holding the chest, shoulders, and head straight. Then comes Pranayama. Prana means the vital forces in one's own body, Âyâma means controlling them. There are three sorts of Pranayama, the very simple, the middle, and the very high. Pranayama is divided into three parts: filling, restraining, and emptying. When you begin with twelve seconds it is the lowest Pranayama; when you begin with twenty-four seconds it is the middle Pranayama; that Pranayama is the best which begins with thirty-six seconds. In the lowest kind of Pranayama there is perspiration, in the medium kind, quivering of the body, and in the highest Pranayama levitation of the body and influx of great bliss. There is a Mantra called the Gâyatri. It is a very holy verse of the Vedas. "We meditate on the glory of that Being who has produced this universe; may He enlighten our minds." Om is joined to it at the beginning and the end. In one Pranayama repeat three Gayatris. In all books they speak of Pranayama being divided into Rechaka (rejecting or exhaling), Puraka (inhaling), and Kurnbhaka (restraining, stationary). The Indriyas, the organs of the senses, are acting outwards and coming in contact with external objects. Bringing them under the control of the will is what is called Pratyahara or gathering towards oneself. Fixing the mind on the lotus of the heart, or on the centre of the head, is what is called Dharana. Limited to one spot, making that spot the base, a particular kind of mental waves rises; these are not swallowed up by other kinds of waves, but by degrees become prominent, while all the others recede and finally disappear. Next the multiplicity of these waves gives place to unity and one wave only is left in the mind. This is Dhyana, meditation. When no basis is necessary, when the whole of the mind has become one wave, one-formedness, it is called Samadhi. Bereft of all help from places and centres, only the meaning of the thought is present. If the mind can be fixed on the centre for twelve seconds it will be a Dharana, twelve such Dharanas will be a Dhyana, and twelve such Dhyanas will be a Samadhi.

Where there is fire, or in water or on ground which is strewn with dry leaves, where there are many ant-hills, where there are wild animals, or danger, where four streets meet, where there is too much noise, where there are many wicked persons, Yoga must not be practiced. This applies more particularly to India. Do not practice when the body feels very lazy or ill, or when the mind is very miserable and sorrowful. Go to a place which is well hidden, and where people do not come to disturb you. Do not choose dirty places. Rather choose beautiful scenery, or a room in your own house which is beautiful. When you practice, first salute all the ancient Yogis, and your own Guru, and God, and then begin.

Dhyana is spoken of, and a few examples are given of what to meditate upon. Sit straight, and look at the tip of your nose. Later on we shall come to know how that concentrates the mind, how by controlling the two optic nerves one advances a long way towards the control of the arc of reaction, and so to the control of the will. Here are a few specimens of meditation. Imagine a lotus upon the top of the head, several inches up, with virtue as its centre, and knowledge as its stalk. The eight petals of the lotus are the eight powers of the Yogi. Inside, the stamens and pistils are renunciation. If the Yogi refuses the external powers he will come to salvation. So the eight petals of the lotus are the eight powers, but the internal stamens and pistils are extreme renunciation, the renunciation of all these powers. Inside of that lotus think of the Golden One, the Almighty, the Intangible, He whose name is Om, the Inexpressible, surrounded with effulgent light. Meditate on that. Another meditation is given. Think of a space in your heart, and in the midst of that space think that a flame is burning. Think of that flame as your own soul and inside the flame is another effulgent light, and that is the Soul of your soul, God. Meditate upon that in the heart. Chastity, non-injury, forgiving even the greatest enemy, truth, faith in the Lord, these are all different Vrittis. Be not afraid if you are not perfect in all of these; work, they will come. He who has given up all attachment, all fear, and all anger, he whose whole soul has gone unto the Lord, he who has taken refuge in the Lord, whose heart has become purified, with whatsoever desire he comes to the Lord, He will grant that to him. Therefore worship Him through knowledge, love, or renunciation.

"He who hates none, who is the friend of all, who is merciful to all, who has nothing of his own, who is free from egoism, who is even-minded in pain and pleasure, who is forbearing, who is always satisfied, who works always in Yoga, whose self has become controlled, whose will is firm, whose mind and intellect are given up unto Me, such a one is My beloved Bhakta. From whom comes no disturbance, who cannot be disturbed by others, who is free from joy, anger, fear, and anxiety, such a one is My beloved. He who does not depend on anything, who is pure and active, who does not care whether good comes or evil, and never becomes miserable, who has given up all efforts for himself; who is the same in praise or in blame, with a silent, thoughtful mind, blessed with what little comes in his way, homeless, for the whole world is his home, and who is steady in his ideas, such a one is My beloved Bhakta." Such alone become Yogis.

* * * *

There was a great god-sage called Nârada. Just as there are sages among mankind, great Yogis, so there are great Yogis among the gods. Narada was a good Yogi, and very great. He travelled everywhere. One day he was passing through a forest, and saw a man who had been meditating until the white ants had built a huge mound round his body — so long had he been sitting in that position. He said to Narada, "Where are you going?" Narada replied, "I am going to heaven." "Then ask God when He will be merciful to me; when I shall attain freedom." Further on Narada saw another man. He was jumping about, singing, dancing, and said, "Oh, Narada, where are you going?" His voice and his gestures were wild. Narada said, "I am going to heaven." "Then, ask when I shall be free." Narada went on. In the course of time he came again by the same road, and there was the man who had been meditating with the ant-hill round him. He said, "Oh, Narada, did you ask the Lord about me?" "Oh, yes." "What did He say?" "The Lord told me that you would attain freedom in four more births." Then the man began to weep and wail, and said, "I have meditated until an ant-hill has grown around me, and I have four more births yet!" Narada went to the other man. "Did you ask my question?" "Oh, yes. Do you see this tamarind tree? I have to tell you that as many leaves as there are on that tree, so many times, you shall be born, and then you shall attain freedom." The man began to dance for joy, and said, "I shall have freedom after such a short time!" A voice came, "My child, you will have freedom this minute." That was the reward for his perseverance. He was ready to work through all those births, nothing discouraged him. But the first man felt that even four more births were too long. Only perseverance, like that of the man who was willing to wait aeons brings about the highest result.

Patanjali's Yoga Aphorisms

Introduction

Before going into the Yoga aphorisms I shall try to discuss one great question, upon which rests the whole theory of religion for the Yogis. It seems the consensus of opinion of the great minds of the world, and it has been nearly demonstrated by researches into physical nature, that we are the outcome and manifestation of an absolute condition, back of our present relative condition, and are going forward, to return to that absolute. This being granted, the question is: Which is better, the absolute or this state? There are not wanting people who think that this manifested state is the highest state of man. Thinkers of great calibre are of the opinion that we are manifestations of undifferentiated being and the differentiated state is higher than the absolute. They imagine that in the absolute there cannot be any quality; that it must be insensate, dull, and lifeless; that only this life can be enjoyed, and, therefore, we must cling to it. First of all we want to inquire into other solutions of life. There was an old solution that man after death remained the same; that all his good sides, minus his evil sides, remained for ever. Logically stated, this means that man's goal is the world; this world carried a stage higher, and eliminated of its evils, is the state they call heaven. This theory, on the face of it, is absurd and puerile, because it cannot be. There cannot be good without evil, nor evil without good. To live in a world where it is all good and no evil is what Sanskrit logicians call a "dream in the air". Another theory in modern times has been presented by several schools, that man's destiny is to go on always improving, always struggling towards, but never reaching the goal. This statement, though apparently very nice, is also absurd, because there is no such thing as motion in a straight line. Every motion is in a circle. If you can take up a stone, and project it into space, and then live long enough, that stone, if it meets with no obstruction, will come back exactly to your hand. A straight line, infinitely projected must end in a circle. Therefore, this idea that the destiny of man is progressing ever forward and forward, and never stopping, is absurd. Although extraneous to the subject, I may remark that this idea explains the ethical theory that you must not hate, and must love. Because, just as in the case of electricity the modern theory is that the power leaves the dynamo and completes the circle back to the dynamo, so with hate and love; they must come back to the source. Therefore do not hate anybody, because that hatred which comes out from you, must, in the long run, come back to you. If you love, that love will come back to you, completing the circle. It is as certain as can be, that every bit of hatred that goes out of the heart of a man comes back to him in full force, nothing can stop it; similarly every impulse of love comes back to him.

On other and practical grounds we see that the theory of eternal progression is untenable, for destruction is the goal of everything earthly. All our struggles and hopes and fears and joys, what will they lead to? We shall all end in death. Nothing is so certain as this. Where, then, is this motion in a straight line — this infinite progression? It is only going out to a distance, and coming back to the centre from which it started. See how, from nebulae, the sun, moon, and stars are produced; then they dissolve and go back to nebulae. The same is being done everywhere. The plant takes material from the earth, dissolves, and gives it back. Every form in this world is taken out of surrounding atoms and goes back to these atoms. It cannot be that the same law acts differently in different places. Law is uniform. Nothing is more certain than that. If this is the law of nature, it also applies to thought. Thought will dissolve and go back to its origin. Whether we will it or not, we shall have to return to our origin which is called God or Absolute. We all came from God, and we are all bound to go back to God. Call that by any name you like, God, Absolute, or Nature, the fact remains the same. "From whom all this universe comes out, in whom all that is born lives, and to whom all returns." This is one fact that is certain. Nature works on the same plan; what is being worked out in one sphere is repeated in millions of spheres. What you see with the planets, the same will it be with this earth, with men, and with all. The huge wave is a mighty compound of small waves, it may be of millions; the life of the whole world is a compound of millions of little lives, and the death of the whole world is the compound of the deaths of these millions of little beings.

Now the question arises: Is going back to God the higher state, or not? The philosophers of the Yoga school emphatically answer that it is. They say that man's present state is a degeneration. There is not one religion on the face of the earth which says that man is an improvement. The idea is that his beginning is perfect and pure, that he degenerates until he cannot degenerate further, and that there must come a time when he shoots upward again to complete the circle. The circle must be described. However low he may go, he must ultimately take the upward bend and go back to the original source, which is God. Man comes from God in the beginning, in the middle he becomes man, and in the end he goes back to God. This is the method of putting it in the dualistic form. The monistic form is that man is God, and goes back to Him again. If our present state is the higher one, then why is there so much horror and misery, and why is there an end to it? If this is the higher state, why does it end? That which corrupts and degenerates cannot be the highest state. Why should it be so diabolical, so unsatisfying? It is only excusable, inasmuch as through it we are taking a higher groove; we have to pass through it in order to become regenerate again. Put a seed into the ground and it disintegrates, dissolves after a time, and out of that dissolution comes the splendid tree. Every soul must disintegrate to become God. So it follows that the sooner we get out of this state we call "man" the better for us Is it by committing suicide that we get out of this state? Not at all. That will be making it worse. Torturing our. selves, or condemning the world, is not the way to get out. We have to pass through the Slough of Despond, and the sooner we are through, the better. It must always be remembered that man-state is not the highest state.

The really difficult part to understand is that this state, the Absolute, which has been called the highest, is not, as some fear, that of the zoophyte or of the stone. According to them, there are only two states of existence, one of the stone, and the other of thought. What right have they to limit existence to these two? Is there not something infinitely superior to thought? The vibrations of light, when they are very low, we do not see; when they become a little more intense, they become light to us; when they become still more intense, we do not see them — it is dark to us. Is the darkness in the end the same darkness as in the beginning? Certainly not; they are different as the two poles. Is the thoughtlessness of the stone the same as the thoughtlessness of God? Certainly not. God does not think; He does not reason. Why should He? Is anything unknown to Him, that He should reason? The stone cannot reason; God does not. Such is the difference. These philosophers think it is awful if we go beyond thought; they find nothing beyond thought.

There are much higher states of existence beyond reasoning. It is really beyond the intellect that the first state of religious life is to be found. When you step beyond thought and intellect and all reasoning, then you have made the first step towards God; and that is the beginning of life. What is commonly called life is but an embryo state.

The next question will be: What proof is there that the state beyond thought and reasoning is the highest state? In the first place, all the great men of the world, much greater than those that only talk, men who moved the world, men who never thought of any selfish ends whatever, have declared that this life is but a little stage on the way towards Infinity which is beyond. In the second place, they not only say so, but show the way to every one, explain their methods, that all can follow in their steps. In the third place, there is no other way left. There is no other explanation. Taking for granted that there is no higher state, why are we going through this circle all the time; what reason can explain the world? The sensible world will be the limit to our knowledge if we cannot go farther, if we must not ask for anything more. This is what is called agnosticism. But what reason is there to believe in the testimony of the senses? I would call that man a true agnostic who would stand still in the street and die. If reason is all in all, it leaves us no place to stand on this side of nihilism. If a man is agnostic of everything but money, fame, and name, he is only a fraud. Kant has proved beyond all doubt that we cannot penetrate beyond the tremendous dead wall called reason. But that is the very first idea upon which all Indian thought takes its stand, and dares to seek, and succeeds in finding something higher than reason, where alone the explanation of the present state is to be found. This is the value of the study of something that will take us beyond the world. "Thou art our father, and wilt take us to the other shore of this ocean of ignorance." That is the science of religion, nothing else.

Chapter I.
Concentration: Its Spiritual Uses

अथ योगानुशासनम् ॥१॥

1. Now concentration is explained.

योगश्चित्तवृत्तिनिरोधः ॥२॥

2. Yoga is restraining the mind-stuff (Chitta) from taking various forms (Vrittis).

A good deal of explanation is necessary here. We have to understand what Chitta is, and what the Vrittis are. I have eyes. Eyes do not see. Take away the brain centre which is in the head, the eyes will still be there, the retinae complete, as also the pictures of objects on them, and yet the eyes will not see. So the eyes are only a secondary instrument, not the organ of vision. The organ of vision is in a nerve centre of the brain. The two eyes will not be sufficient. Sometimes a man is asleep with his eyes open. The light is there and the picture is there, but a third thing is necessary — the mind must be joined to the organ. The eye is the external instrument; we need also the brain centre and the agency of the mind. Carriages roll down a street, and you do not hear them. Why? Because your mind has not attached itself to the organ of hearing. First, there is the instrument, then there is the organ, and third, the mind attached to these two. The mind takes the impression farther in, and presents it to the determinative faculty — Buddhi — which reacts. Along with this reaction flashes the idea of egoism. Then this mixture of action and reaction is presented to the Purusha, the real Soul, who perceives an object in this mixture. The organs (Indriyas), together with the mind (Manas), the determinative faculty (Buddhi), and egoism (Ahamkâra), form the group called the Antahkarana (the internal instrument). They are but various processes in the mind-stuff, called Chitta. The waves of thought in the Chitta are called Vrittis (literally "whirlpool") . What is thought? Thought is a force, as is gravitation or repulsion. From the infinite storehouse of force in nature, the instrument called Chitta takes hold of some, absorbs it and sends it out as thought. Force is supplied to us through food, and out of that food the body obtains the power of motion etc. Others, the finer forces, it throws out in what we call thought. So we see that the mind is not intelligent; yet it appears to be intelligent. Why? Because the intelligent soul is behind it. You are the only sentient being; mind is only the instrument through which you catch the external world. Take this book; as a book it does not exist outside, what exists outside is unknown and unknowable. The unknowable furnishes the suggestion that gives a blow to the mind, and the mind gives out the reaction in the form of a book, in the same manner as when a stone is thrown into the water, the water is thrown against it in the form of waves. The real universe is the occasion of the reaction of the mind. A book form, or an elephant form, or a man form, is not outside; all that we know is our mental reaction from the outer suggestion. "Matter is the permanent possibility of sensations," said John Stuart Mill. It is only the suggestion that is outside. Take an oyster for example. You know how pearls are made. A parasite gets inside the shell and causes irritation, and the oyster throws a sort of enamelling round it, and this makes the pearl. The universe of experience is our own enamel, so to say, and the real universe is the parasite serving as nucleus. The ordinary man will never understand it, because when he tries to do so, he throws out an enamel, and sees only his own enamel. Now we understand what is meant by these Vrittis. The real man is behind the mind; the mind is the instrument his hands; it is his intelligence that is percolating through the mind. It is only when you stand behind the mind that it becomes intelligent. When man gives it up, it falls to pieces and is nothing. Thus you understand what is meant by Chitta. It is the mind-stuff, and Vrittis are the waves and ripples rising in it when external causes impinge on it. These Vrittis are our universe.

The bottom of a lake we cannot see, because its surface is covered with ripples. It is only possible for us to catch a glimpse of the bottom, when the ripples have subsided, and the water is calm. If the water is muddy or is agitated all the time, the bottom will not be seen. If it is clear, and there are no waves, we shall see the bottom. The bottom of the lake is our own true Self; the lake is the Chitta and the waves the Vrittis. Again, the mind is in three states, one of which is darkness, called Tamas, found in brutes and idiots; it only acts to injure. No other idea comes into that state of mind. Then there is the active state of mind, Rajas, whose chief motives are power and enjoyment. "I will be powerful and rule others." Then there is the state called Sattva, serenity, calmness, in which the waves cease, and the water of the mind-lake becomes clear. It is not inactive, but rather intensely active. It is the greatest manifestation of power to be calm. It is easy to be active. Let the reins go, and the horses will run away with you. Anyone can do that, but he who can stop the plunging horses is the strong man. Which requires the greater strength, letting go or restraining? The calm man is not the man who is dull. You must not mistake Sattva for dullness or laziness. The calm man is the one who has control over the mind waves. Activity is the manifestation of inferior strength, calmness, of the superior.

The Chitta is always trying to get back to its natural pure state, but the organs draw it out. To restrain it, to check this outward tendency, and to start it on the return journey to the essence of intelligence is the first step in Yoga, because only in this way can the Chitta get into its proper course.

Although the Chitta is in every animal, from the lowest to the highest, it is only in the human form that we find it as the intellect. Until the mind-stuff can take the form of intellect it is not possible for it to return through all these steps, and liberate the soul. Immediate salvation is impossible for the cow or the dog, although they have mind, because their Chitta cannot as yet take that form which we call intellect.

The Chitta manifests itself in the following forms — scattering, darkening, gathering, one-pointed, and concentrated. The scattering form is activity. Its tendency is to manifest in the form of pleasure or of pain. The darkening form is dullness which tends to injury. The commentator says, the third form is natural to the Devas, the angels, and the first and second to the demons. The gathering form is when it struggles to centre itself. The one-pointed form is when it tries to concentrate, and the concentrated form is what brings us to Samâdhi.

तदा द्रष्टुः स्वरूपेऽवस्थानम् ॥३॥

3. At that time (the time of concentration) the seer (Purusha) rests in his own (unmodified) state.

As soon as the waves have stopped, and the lake has become quiet, we see its bottom. So with the mind; when it is calm, we see what our own nature is; we do not mix ourselves but remain our own selves.

वृत्तिसारूप्यमितरत्र ॥४॥

4. At other times (other than that of concentration) the seer is identified with the modifications.

For instance, someone blames me; this produces a modification, Vritti, in my mind, and I identify myself with it and the result is misery.

वृत्तयः पंचतय्यः क्लिष्टा अक्लिष्टाः ॥५॥

5. There are five classes of modifications, (some) painful and (others) not painful.

प्रमाण – विपर्यय – विकल्प – निद्रा – स्मृतयः ॥६॥

6. (These are) right knowledge, indiscrimination, verbal delusion, sleep, and memory.

प्रत्यक्षानुमानागमाः प्रमाणानि ॥७॥

7. Direct perception, inference, and competent evidence are proofs.

When two of our perceptions do not contradict each other, we call it proof. I hear something, and if it contradicts something already perceived, I begin to fight it out, and do not believe it. There are also three kinds of proof. Pratyaksha, direct perception; whatever we see and feel, is proof, if there has been nothing to delude the senses. I see the world; that is sufficient proof that it exists. Secondly, Anumâna, inference; you see a sign, and from the sign you come to the thing signified. Thirdly, Âptavâkya, the direct evidence of the Yogis, of those who have seen the truth. We are all of us struggling towards knowledge. But you and I have to struggle hard, and come to knowledge through a long tedious process of reasoning, but the Yogi, the pure one, has gone beyond all this. Before his mind, the past, the present, and the future are alike, one book for him to read; he does not require to go through the tedious processes for knowledge we have to; his words are proof, because he sees knowledge in himself. These, for instance, are the authors of the sacred scriptures; therefore the scriptures are proof. If any such persons are living now their words will be proof. Other philosophers go into long discussions about Aptavakya and they say, "What is the proof of their words?" The proof is their direct perception. Because whatever I see is proof, and whatever you see is proof, if it does not contradict any past knowledge. There is knowledge beyond the senses, and whenever it does not contradict reason and past human experience, that knowledge is proof. Any madman may come into this room and say he sees angels around him; that would not be proof. In the first place, it must be true knowledge, and secondly, it must not contradict past knowledge, and thirdly, it must depend upon the character of the man who gives it out. I hear it said that the character of the man is not of so much importance as what he may say; we must first hear what he says. This may be true in other things. A man may be wicked, and yet make an astronomical discovery, but in religion it is different, because no impure man will ever have the power to reach the truths of religion. Therefore we have first of all to see that the man who declares himself to be an Âpta is a perfectly unselfish and holy person; secondly, that he has reached beyond the senses; and thirdly, that what he says does not contradict the past knowledge of humanity. Any new discovery of truth does not contradict the past truth, but fits into it. And fourthly, that truth must have a possibility of verification. If a man says, "I have seen a vision," and tells me that I have no right to see it, I believe him not. Everyone must have the power to see it for himself. No one who sells his knowledge is an Apta. All these conditions must be fulfilled; you must first see that the man is pure, and that he has no selfish motive; that he has no thirst for gain or fame. Secondly, he must show that he is superconscious. He must give us something that we cannot get from our senses, and which is for the benefit of the world. Thirdly, we must see that it does not contradict other truths; if it contradicts other scientific truths reject it at once. Fourthly, the man should never be singular; he should only represent what all men can attain. The three sorts of proof are, then, direct sense-perception, inference, and the words of an Apta. I cannot translate this word into English. It is not the word "inspired", because inspiration is believed to come from outside, while this knowledge comes from the man himself. The literal meaning is "attained".

विपर्ययो मिथ्याज्ञानमतद्रूपप्रतिष्ठम् ॥८॥

8. Indiscrimination is false knowledge not established in real nature.

The next class of Vrittis that arises is mistaking one thing for another, as a piece of mother-of-pearl is taken for a piece of silver.

शब्दज्ञानानुपाती वस्तुशून्यो विकल्पः ॥९॥

9. Verbal delusion follows from words having no (corresponding) reality.

There is another class of Vrittis called Vikalpa. A word is uttered, and we do not wait to consider its meaning; we jump to a conclusion immediately. It is the sign of weakness of the Chitta. Now you can understand the theory of restraint. The weaker the man, the less he has of restraint. Examine yourselves always by that test. When you are going to be angry or miserable, reason it out how it is that some news that has come to you is throwing your mind into Vrittis.

अभाव - प्रत्ययालम्बना - वृत्तिर्निद्रा ॥१०॥

10. Sleep is a Vritti which embraces the feeling of voidness.

The next class of Vrittis is called sleep and dream. When we awake, we know that we have been sleeping; we can only have memory of perception. That which we do not perceive we never can have any memory of. Every reaction is a wave in the lake. Now, if, during sleep, the mind had no waves, it would have no perceptions, positive or negative, and, therefore, we would not remember them. The very reason of our remembering sleep is that during sleep there was a certain class of waves in the mind. Memory is another class of Vrittis which is called Smriti.

अनुभूतविषयासम्प्रमोषः स्मृतिः ॥११॥

11. Memory is when the (Vrittis of) perceived subjects do not slip away (and through impressions come back to consciousness).

Memory can come from direct perception, false knowledge, verbal delusion, and sleep. For instance, you hear a word. That word is like a stone thrown into the lake of the Chitta; it causes a ripple, and that ripple rouses a series of ripples; this is memory. So in sleep. When the peculiar kind of ripple called sleep throws the Chitta into a ripple of memory, it is called a dream. Dream is another form of the ripple which in the waking state is called memory.

अभ्यासवैराग्याभ्यां तन्निरोधः ॥१२॥

12. Their control is by practice and nonattachment.

The mind, to have non-attachment, must be clear, good, and rational. Why should we practice? Because each action is like the pulsations quivering over the surface of the lake. The vibration dies out, and what is left? The Samskâras, the impressions. When a large number of these impressions are left on the mind, they coalesce and become a habit. It is said, "Habit is second nature", it is first nature also, and the whole nature of man; everything that we are is the result of habit. That gives us consolation, because, if it is only habit, we can make and unmake it at any time. The Samskaras are left by these vibrations passing out of our mind, each one of them leaving its result. Our character is the sum-total of these marks, and according as some particular wave prevails one takes that tone. If good prevails, one becomes good; if wickedness, one becomes wicked; if joyfulness, one becomes happy. The only remedy for bad habits is counter habits; all the bad habits that have left their impressions are to be controlled by good habits. Go on doing good, thinking holy thoughts continuously; that is the only way to suppress base impressions. Never say any man is hopeless, because he only represents a character, a bundle of habits, which can be checked by new and better ones. Character is repeated habits, and repeated habits alone can reform character.

तत्र स्थितौ यत्नोऽभ्यासः ॥१३॥

13. Continuous struggle to keep them (the Vrittis) perfectly restrained is practice.

What is practice? The attempt to restrain the mind in Chitta form, to prevent its going out into waves.

स तु दीर्घकालनैरन्तर्यसत्कारासेवितो दृढभूमिः ॥१४॥

14. It becomes firmly grounded by long constant efforts with great love (for the end to be attained).

Restraint does not come in one day, but by long continued practice.

दृष्टानुश्रविकविषयवितृष्णस्य वशीकारसंज्ञा वैराग्यम् ॥१५॥

15. That effect which comes to these who have given up their thirst after objects, either seen or heard, and which wills to control the objects, is non-attachment.

The two motive powers of our actions are (1) what we see ourselves, (2) the experience of others. These two forces throw the mind, the lake, into various waves. Renunciation is the power of battling against these forces and holding the mind in check. Their renunciation is what see want. I am passing through a street, and a man comes and takes away my watch. That is my own experience. I see it myself, and it immediately throws my Chitta into a wave, taking the form of anger. Allow not that to come. If you cannot prevent that, you are nothing; if you can, you have Vairâgya. Again, the experience of the worldly-minded teaches us that sense-enjoyments are the highest ideal. These are tremendous temptations. To deny them, and not allow the mind to come to a wave form with regard to them, is renunciation; to control the twofold motive powers arising from my own experience and from the experience of others, and thus prevent the Chitta from being governed by them, is Vairagya. These should be controlled by me, and not I by them. This sort of mental strength is called renunciation. Vairagya is the only way to freedom.

तत्परं पुरुषख्यातेर्गुणवैतृष्ण्यम् ॥१६॥

16. That is extreme non-attachment which gives up even the qualities, and comes from the knowledge of (the real nature of) the Purusha.

It is the highest manifestation of the power of Vairagya when it takes away even our attraction towards the qualities. We have first to understand what the Purusha, the Self, is and what the qualities are. According to Yoga philosophy, the whole of nature consists of three qualities or forces; one is called Tamas, another Rajas, and the third Sattva. These three qualities manifest themselves in the physical world as darkness or inactivity, attraction or repulsion, and equilibrium of the two. Everything that is in nature, all manifestations, are combinations and recombinations of these three forces. Nature has been divided into various categories by the Sânkhyas; the Self of man is beyond all these, beyond nature. It is effulgent, pure, and perfect. Whatever of intelligence we see in nature is but the reflection of this Self upon nature. Nature itself is insentient. You must remember that the word nature also includes the mind; mind is in nature; thought is in nature; from thought, down to the grossest form of matter, everything is in nature, the manifestation of nature. This nature has covered the Self of man, and when nature takes away the covering, the self appears in Its own glory. The non-attachment, as described in aphorism 15 (as being control of objects or nature) is the greatest help towards manifesting the Self. The next aphorism defines Samadhi, perfect concentration which is the goal of the Yogi.

वितर्कविचारानन्दास्मितानुगमात् सम्प्रज्ञातः ॥१७॥

17. The concentration called right knowledge is that which is followed by reasoning, discrimination bliss, unqualified egoism.

Samadhi is divided into two varieties. One is called the Samprajnâta, and the other the Asamprajnâta. In the Samprajnata Samadhi come all the powers of controlling nature. It is of four varieties. The first variety is called the Savitarka, when the mind meditates upon an object again and again, by isolating it from other objects. There are two sorts of objects for meditation in the twenty-five categories of the Sankhyas, (1) the twenty-four insentient categories of Nature, and (2) the one sentient Purusha. This part of Yoga is based entirely on Sankhya philosophy, about which I have already told you. As you will remember, egoism and will and mind have a common basis, the Chitta or the mind-stuff, out of which they are all manufactured. The mind-stuff takes in the forces of nature, and projects them as thought. There must be something, again, where both force and matter are one. This is called Avyakta, the unmanifested state of nature before creation, and to which, after the end of a cycle, the whole of nature returns, to come out again after another period. Beyond that is the Purusha, the essence of intelligence. Knowledge is power, and as soon as we begin to know a thing, we get power over it; so also when the mind begins to meditate on the different elements, it gains power over them. That sort of meditation where the external gross elements are the objects is called Savitarka. Vitarka means question; Savitarka, with question, questioning the elements, as it were, that they may give their truths and their powers to the man who meditates upon them. There is no liberation in getting powers. It is a worldly search after enjoyments, and there is no enjoyment in this life; all search for enjoyment is vain; this is the old, old lesson which man finds so hard to learn. When he does learn it, he gets out of the universe and becomes free. The possession of what are called occult powers is only intensifying the world, and in the end, intensifying suffering. Though as a scientist Patanjali is bound to point out the possibilities of this science, he never misses an opportunity to warn us against these powers.

Again, in the very same meditation, when one struggles to take the elements out of time and space, and think of them as they are, it is called Nirvitarka, without question. When the meditation goes a step higher, and takes the Tanmatras as its object, and thinks of them as in time and space, it is called Savichâra, with discrimination; and when in the same meditation one eliminates time and space, and thinks of the fine elements as they are, it is called Nirvichâra, without discrimination. The next step is when the elements are given up, both gross and fine, and the object of meditation is the interior organ, the thinking organ. When the thinking organ is thought of as bereft of the qualities of activity and dullness, it is then called Sânanda, the blissful Samadhi. When the mind itself is the object of meditation, when meditation becomes very ripe and concentrated, when all ideas of the gross and fine materials are given up, when the Sattva state only of the Ego remains, but differentiated from all other objects, it is called Sâsmita Samadhi. The man who has attained to this has attained to what is called in the Vedas "bereft of body". He can think of himself as without his gross body; but he will have to think of himself as with a fine body. Those that in this state get merged in nature without attaining the goal are called Prakritilayas, but those who do not stop even there reach the goal, which is freedom.

विरामप्रत्ययाभ्यासपूर्वः संस्कारशेषोऽन्यः ॥१८॥

18. There is another Samadhi which is attained by the constant practice of cessation of all mental activity, in which the Chitta retains only the unmanifested impressions.

This is the perfect superconscious Asamprajnata Samadhi, the state which gives us freedom. The first state does not give us freedom, does not liberate the soul. A man may attain to all powers, and yet fall again. There is no safeguard until the soul goes beyond nature. It is very difficult to do so, although the method seems easy. The method is to meditate on the mind itself, and whenever thought comes, to strike it down, allowing no thought to come into the mind, thus making it an entire vacuum. When we can really do this, that very moment we shall attain liberation. When persons without training and preparation try to make their minds vacant, they are likely to succeed only in covering themselves with Tamas, the material of ignorance, which makes the mind dull and stupid, and leads them to think that they are making a vacuum of the mind. To be able to really do that is to manifest the greatest strength, the highest control. When this state, Asamprajnata, superconsciousness, is reached, the Samadhi becomes seedless. What is meant by that? In a concentration where there is consciousness, where the mind succeeds only in quelling the waves in the Chitta and holding them down, the waves remain in the form of tendencies. These tendencies (or seeds) become waves again, when the time comes. But when you have destroyed all these tendencies, almost destroyed the mind, then the Samadhi becomes seedless; there are no more seeds in the mind out of which to manufacture again and again this plant of life, this ceaseless round of birth and death.

You may ask, what state would that be in which there is no mind, there is no knowledge? What we call knowledge is a lower state than the one beyond knowledge. You must always bear in mind that the extremes look very much alike. If a very low vibration of ether is taken as darkness, an intermediate state as light, very high vibration will be darkness again. Similarly, ignorance is the lowest state, knowledge is the middle state, and beyond knowledge is the highest state, the two extremes of which seem the same. Knowledge itself is a manufactured something, a combination; it is not reality.

What is the result of constant practice of this higher concentration? All old tendencies of restlessness and dullness will be destroyed, as well as the tendencies of goodness too. The case is similar to that of the chemicals used to take the dirt and alloy off gold. When the ore is smelted down, the dross is burnt along with the chemicals. So this constant controlling power will stop the previous bad tendencies, and eventually, the good ones also. Those good and evil tendencies will suppress each other, leaving alone the Soul, in its own splendour untrammelled by either good or bad, the omnipresent, omnipotent, and omniscient. Then the man will know that he had neither birth nor death, nor need for heaven or earth. He will know that he neither came nor went, it was nature which was moving, and that movement was reflected upon the soul. The form of the light reflected by the glass upon the wall moves, and the wall foolishly thinks it is moving. So with all of us; it is the Chitta constantly moving making itself into various forms, and we think that we are these various forms. All these delusions will vanish. When that free Soul will command — not pray or beg, but command — then whatever It desires will be immediately fulfilled; whatever It wants It will be able to do. According to the Sankhya philosophy, there is no God. It says that there can be no God of this universe, because if there were one, He must be a soul, and a soul must be either bound or free. How can the soul that is bound by nature, or controlled by nature, create? It is itself a slave. On the other hand, why should the Soul that is free create and manipulate all these things? It has no desires, so it cannot have any need to create. Secondly, it says the theory of God is an unnecessary one; nature explains all. What is the use of any God? But Kapila teaches that there are many souls, who, though nearly attaining perfection, fall short because they cannot perfectly renounce all powers. Their minds for a time merge in nature, to re-emerge as its masters. Such gods there are. We shall all become such gods, and, according to the Sankhyas, the God spoken of in the Vedas really means one of these free souls. Beyond them there is not an eternally free and blessed Creator of the universe. On the other hand, the Yogis say, "Not so, there is a God; there is one Soul separate from all other souls, and He is the eternal Master of all creation, the ever free, the Teacher of all teachers." The Yogis admit that those whom the Sankhyas call "the merged in nature" also exist. They are Yogis who have fallen short of perfection, and though, for a time, debarred from attaining the goal, remain as rulers of parts of the universe.

भव-प्रत्ययो विदेह-प्रकृतिलयानाम् ॥१९॥

19. (This Samadhi when not followed by extreme non-attachment) becomes the cause of the re-manifestation of the gods and of those that become merged in nature.

The gods in the Indian systems of philosophy represent certain high offices which are filled successively by various souls. But none of them is perfect.

श्रद्धा-वीर्य-स्मृति-समाधि-प्रज्ञा-पूर्वक-इतरेषाम् ॥२०॥

20. To others (this Samadhi) comes through faith, energy, memory, concentration, and discrimination of the real.

These are they who do not want the position of gods or even that of rulers of cycles. They attain to liberation.

तीव्रसंवेगानामासन्नः ॥२१॥

21. Success is speedy for the extremely energetic.

मृदुमध्याधिमात्रत्वात्ततोऽपि विशेषः ॥२२॥

22. The success of Yogis differs according as the means they adopt are mild, medium, or intense.

ईश्वरप्रणिधानाद्वा ॥२३॥

23. Or by devotion to Ishvara.

क्लेशकर्मविपाकाशयैरपरामृष्टः पुरुषविशेष ईश्वरः ॥२४॥

24. Ishvara (the Supreme Ruler) is a special Purusha, untouched by misery, actions, their results, and desires.

We must again remember that the Pâtanjala Yoga philosophy is based upon the Sankhya philosophy; only in the latter there is no place for God, while with the Yogis God has a place. The Yogis, however, do not mention many ideas about God, such as creating. God as the Creator of the universe is not meant by the Ishvara of the Yogis. According to the Vedas, Ishvara is the Creator of the universe; because it is harmonious, it must be the manifestation of one will. The Yogis want to establish a God, but they arrive at Him in a peculiar fashion of their own. They say:

तत्र निरतिशयं सर्वज्ञत्वबीजम् ॥२५॥

25. In Him becomes infinite that all-knowingness which in others is (only) a germ.

The mind must always travel between two extremes. You can think of limited space, but that very idea gives you also unlimited space. Close your eyes and think of a little space; at the same time that you perceive the little circle, you have a circle round it of unlimited dimensions. It is the same with time. Try to think of a second; you will have, with the same act of perception, to think of time which is unlimited. So with knowledge. Knowledge is only a germ in man, but you will have to think of infinite knowledge around it, so that the very constitution of our mind shows us that there is unlimited knowledge, and the Yogis call that unlimited knowledge God.

स पूर्वेषामपि गुरुः कालेनानवच्छेदात् ॥२६॥

26. He is the Teacher of even the ancient teachers, being not limited by time.

It is true that all knowledge is within ourselves, but this has to be called forth by another knowledge. Although the capacity to know is inside us, it must be called out, and that calling out of knowledge can only be done, a Yogi maintains, through another knowledge. Dead, insentient matter never calls out knowledge, it is the action of knowledge that brings out knowledge. Knowing beings must be with us to call forth what is in us, so these teachers were always necessary. The world was never without them, and no knowledge can come without them. God is the Teacher of all teachers, because these teachers, however great they may have been — gods or angels — were all bound and limited by time, while God is not. There are two peculiar deductions of the Yogis. The first is that in thinking of the limited, the mind must think of the unlimited; and that if one part of that perception is true, so also must the other be, for the reason that their value as perceptions of the mind is equal. The very fact that man has a little knowledge shows that God has unlimited knowledge. If I am to take one, why not the other? Reason forces me to take both or reject both. If I believe that there is a man with a little knowledge, I must also admit that there is someone behind him with unlimited knowledge. The second deduction is that no knowledge can come without a teacher. It is true, as the modern philosophers say, that there is something in man which evolves out of him; all knowledge is in man, but certain environments are necessary to call it out. We cannot find any knowledge without teachers. If there are men teachers, god teachers, or angel teachers, they are all limited; who was the teacher before them? We are forced to admit, as a last conclusion, one teacher who is not limited by time; and that One Teacher of infinite knowledge, without beginning or end, is called God.

तस्य वाचकः प्रणवः ॥२७॥

27. His manifesting word is Om.

Every idea that you have in the mind has a counterpart in a word; the word and the thought are inseparable. The external part of one and the same thing is what we call word, and the internal part is what we call thought. No man can, by analysis, separate thought from word. The idea that language was created by men — certain men sitting together and deciding upon words, has been proved to be wrong. So long as man has existed there have been words and language. What is the connection between an idea and a word? Although we see that there must always be a word with a thought, it is not necessary that the same thought requires the same word. The thought may be the same in twenty different countries, yet the language is different. We must have a word to express each thought, but these words need not necessarily have the same sound Sounds will vary in different nations. Our commentator says, "Although the relation between thought and word is perfectly natural, yet it does not mean a rigid connection between one sound and one idea." These sounds vary, yet the relation between the sounds and the thoughts is a natural one. The connection between thoughts and sounds is good only if there be a real connection between the thing signified and the symbol; until then that symbol will never come into general use. A symbol is the manifester of the thing signified, and if the thing signified has already an existence, and if, by experience, we know that the symbol has expressed that thing many times, then we are sure that there is a real relation between them. Even if the things are not present, there will be thousands who will know them by their symbols. There must be a natural connection between the symbol and the thing signified; then, when that symbol is pronounced, it recalls the thing signified. The commentator says the manifesting word of God is Om. Why does he emphasise this word? There are hundreds of words for God. One thought is connected with a thousand words; the idea "God" is connected with hundreds of words, and each one stands as a symbol for God. Very good. But there must be a generalization among all time words, some substratum, some common ground of all these symbols, and that which is the common symbol will be the best, and will really represent them all. In making a sound we use the larynx and the palate as a sounding board. Is there any material sound of which all other sounds must be manifestations, one which is the most natural sound? Om (Aum) is such a sound, the basis of all sounds. The first letter, *A*, is the root sound, the key, pronounced without touching any part of the tongue or palate; *M* represents the last sound in the series, being produced by the closed lips, and the *U* rolls from the very root to the end of the sounding board of the mouth. Thus, Om represents the whole phenomena of sound-producing. As such, it must be the natural symbol, the matrix of all the various sounds. It denotes the whole range and possibility of all the words that can be made. Apart from these speculations, we see that around this word Om are centred all the different religious ideas in India; all the various religious ideas of the Vedas have gathered themselves round this word Om. What has that to do with America and England, or any other country? Simply this, that the word has been retained at every stage of religious growth in India, and it has been manipulated to mean all the various ideas about God. Monists, dualists, mono-dualists, separatists, and even atheists took up this Om. Om has become the one symbol for the religious aspiration of the vast majority of human beings. Take, for instance, the English word God. It covers only a limited function, and if you go beyond it, you have to add adjectives, to make it Personal, or Impersonal, or Absolute God. So with the words for God in every other language; their signification is very small. This word Om, however, has around it all the various significances. As such it should be accepted by everyone.

तज्जपस्तदर्थभावनम् ॥२८॥

28. The repetition of this (Om) and meditating on its meaning (is the way).

Why should there be repetition? We have not forgotten the theory of Samskaras, that the sum-total of impressions lives in the mind. They become more and more latent but remain there, and as soon as they get the right stimulus, they come out. Molecular vibration never ceases. When this universe is destroyed, all the massive vibrations disappear; the sun, moon, stars, and earth, melt down; but the vibrations remain in the atoms. Each atom performs the same function as the big worlds do. So even when the vibrations of the Chitta subside, its molecular vibrations go on, and when they get the impulse, come out again. We can now understand what is meant by repetition. It is the greatest stimulus that can be given to the spiritual Samskaras. "One moment of company with the holy makes a ship to cross this ocean of life." Such is the power of association. So this repetition of Om, and thinking of its meaning, is keeping good company in your own mind. Study, and then meditate on what you have studied. Thus light will come to you, the Self will become manifest.

But one must think of Om, and of its meaning too. Avoid evil company, because the scars of old wounds are in you, and evil company is just the thing that is necessary to call them out. In the same way we are told that good company will call out the good impressions that are in us, but which have become latent. There is nothing holier in the world than to keep good company, because the good impressions will then tend to come to the surface.

ततः प्रत्यक्चेतनाधिगमोऽप्यन्तरायाभावश्च ॥२९॥

29. From that is gained (the knowledge of) introspection, and the destruction of obstacles.

The first manifestation of the repetition and thinking of Om is that the introspective power will manifest more and more, all the mental and physical obstacles will begin to vanish. What are the obstacles to the Yogi?

व्याधि - स्त्यान - संशय - प्रमादालस्याविरति - भ्रान्तिदर्शनालब्धभूमिकत्वान
- वस्थितत्वानि चित्तविक्षेपास्तेऽन्तरायाः ॥३०॥

30. Disease, mental laziness, doubt, lack of enthusiasm, lethargy, clinging to sense-enjoyments, false perception, non-attaining concentration, and falling away from the state when obtained, are the obstructing distractions.

Disease. This body is the boat which will carry us to the other shore of the ocean of life. It must be taken care of. Unhealthy persons cannot be Yogis. *Mental laziness* makes us lose all lively interest in the subject, without which there will neither be the will nor the energy to practise. *Doubts* will arise in the mind about the truth of the science, however strong one's intellectual conviction may be, until certain peculiar psychic experiences come, as hearing or seeing at a distance, etc. These glimpses strengthen the mind and make the student persevere. *Falling away ... when obtained*. Some days or weeks when you are practicing, the mind will be calm and easily concentrated, and you will find yourself progressing fast. All of a sudden the progress will stop one day, and you will find yourself, as it were, stranded. Persevere. All progress proceeds by such rise and fall.

दुःख - दौर्मनस्याङ्गमेजयत्व - श्वासप्रश्वासा विक्षेपसहभुवः ॥३१॥

31. Grief, mental distress, tremor of the body, irregular breathing, accompany non-retention of concentration.

Concentration will bring perfect repose to mind and body every time it is practised. When the practice has been misdirected, or not enough controlled, these disturbances come. Repetition of Om and self-surrender to the Lord will strengthen the mind, and bring fresh energy. The nervous shakings will come to almost everyone. Do not mind them at all, but keep on practising. Practice will cure them and make the seat firm.

तत्प्रतिषेधार्थमेकतत्त्वाभ्यासः ॥३२॥

32. To remedy this, the practice of one subject (should be made).

Making the mind take the form of one object for some time will destroy these obstacles. This is general advice. In the following aphorisms it will be expanded and particularized. As one practice cannot suit everyone, various methods will be advanced, and everyone by actual experience will find out that which helps him most.

मैत्री – करुणा मुदितोपेक्षाणां सुख – दुःखपुण्यापुण्य –
विषयाणां भावनातश्चित्तप्रसादनम् ॥३३॥

33. Friendship, mercy, gladness, and indifference, being thought of in regard to subjects, happy, unhappy, good, and evil respectively, pacify the Chitta.

We must have these four sorts of ideas. We must have friendship for all; we must be merciful towards those that are in misery; when people are happy, we ought to be happy; and to the wicked we must be indifferent. So with all subjects that come before us. If the subject is a good one, we shall feel friendly towards it; if the subject of thought is one that is miserable, we must be merciful towards it. If it is good, we must be glad; if it is evil, we must be indifferent. These attitudes of the mind towards the different subjects that come before it will make the mind peaceful. Most of our difficulties in our daily lives come from being unable to hold our minds in this way. For instance, if a man does evil to us, instantly we want to react evil, and every reaction of evil shows that we are not able to hold the Chitta down; it comes out in waves towards the object, and we lose our power. Every reaction in the form of hatred or evil is so much loss to the mind; and every evil thought or deed of hatred, or any thought of reaction, if it is controlled, will be laid in our favour. It is not that we lose by thus restraining ourselves; we are gaining infinitely more than we suspect. Each time we suppress hatred, or a feeling of anger, it is so much good energy stored up in our favour; that piece of energy will be converted into the higher powers.

प्रच्छर्दन – विधारणाभ्यां वा प्राणस्य ॥३४॥

34. By throwing out and restraining the Breath.

The word used is Prâna. Prana is not exactly breath. It is the name for the energy that is in the universe. Whatever you see in the universe, whatever moves or works, or has life, is a manifestation of this Prana. The sum-total of the energy displayed in the universe is called Prana. This Prana, before a cycle begins, remains in an almost motionless state; and when the cycle begins, this Prana begins to manifest itself. It is this Prana that is manifested as motion — as the nervous motion in human beings or animals; and the same Prana is manifesting as thought, and so on. The whole universe is a combination of Prana and Âkâsha; so is the human body. Out of Akasha you get the different materials that you feel and see, and out of Prana all the various forces. Now this throwing out and restraining the Prana is what is called Pranayama. Patanjali, the father of the Yoga philosophy, does not give very many particular directions about Pranayama, but later on other Yogis found out various things about this Pranayama, and made of it a great science. With Patanjali it is one of the many ways, but he does not lay much stress on it. He means that you simply throw the air out, and draw it in, and hold it for some time, that is all, and by that, the mind will become a little calmer. But, later on, you will find that out of this is evolved a particular science called Pranayama. We shall hear a little of what these later Yogis have to say.

Some of this I have told you before, but a little repetition will serve to fix it in your minds. First, you must remember that this Prana is not the breath; but that which causes the motion of the breath, that which is the vitality of the breath, is the Prana. Again, the word Prana is used for all the senses; they are all called Pranas, the mind is called Prana; and so we see that Prana is force. And yet we cannot call it force, because force is only the manifestation of it. It is that which manifests itself as force and everything else in the way of motion. The Chitta, the mind-stuff, is the engine which draws in the Prana from the surroundings, and manufactures out of Prana the various vital forces — those that keep the body in preservation — and thought, will, and all other powers. By the abovementioned process of breathing we can control all the various motions in the body, and the various nerve currents that are running through the body. First we begin to recognise them, and then we slowly get control over them.

Now, these later Yogis consider that there are three main currents of this Prana in the human body. One they call Idâ, another Pingalâ, and the third Sushumnâ. Pingala, according to them, is on the right side of the spinal column, and the Ida on the left, and in the middle of the spinal column is the Sushumna, an empty channel. Ida and Pingala, according to them, are the currents working in every man, and through these currents, we are performing all the functions of life. Sushumna is present in all, as a possibility; but it works only in the Yogi. You must remember that Yoga changes the body. As you go on practising, your body changes; it is not the same body that you had before the practice. That is very rational, and can be explained, because every new thought that we have must make, as it were, a new channel through the brain, and that explains the tremendous conservatism of human nature. Human nature likes to run through the ruts that are already there, because it is easy. If we think, just for example's sake, that the mind is like a needle, and the brain substance a soft lump before it, then each thought that we have makes a street, as it were, in the brain, and this street would close up, but for the grey matter which comes and makes a lining to keep it separate. If there were no grey matter, there would be no memory, because memory means going over these old streets, retracing a thought as it were. Now perhaps you have marked that when one talks on subjects in which one takes a few ideas that are familiar to everyone, and combines and recombines them, it is easy to follow because these channels are present in everyone's brain, and it is only necessary to recur to them. But whenever a new subject comes, new channels have to be made, so it is not understood readily. And that is why the brain (it is the brain, and not the people themselves) refuses unconsciously to be acted upon by new ideas. It resists. The Prana is trying to make new channels, and the brain will not allow it. This is the secret of conservatism. The fewer channels there have been in the brain, and the less the needle of the Prana has made these passages, the more conservative will be the brain, the more it will struggle against new thoughts. The more thoughtful the man, the more complicated will be the streets in his brain, and the more easily he will take to new ideas, and understand them. So with every fresh idea, we make a new impression in the brain, cut new channels through the brain-stuff, and that is why we find that in the practice of Yoga (it being an entirely new set of thoughts and motives) there is so much physical resistance at first. That is why we find that the part of religion which deals with the world-side of nature is so widely accepted, while the other part, the philosophy, or the psychology, which clears with the inner nature of man, is so frequently neglected.

We must remember the definition of this world of ours; it is only the Infinite Existence projected into the plane of consciousness. A little of the Infinite is projected into consciousness, and that we call our world. So there is an Infinite beyond; and religion has to deal with both — with the little lump we call our world, and with the Infinite beyond. Any religion which deals with one only of these two will be defective. It must deal with both. The part of religion which deals with the part of the Infinite which has come into the plane of consciousness, got itself caught, as it were, in the plane of consciousness, in the cage of time, space, and causation, is quite familiar to us, because we are in that already, and ideas about this world have been with us almost from time immemorial. The part of religion which deals with the Infinite beyond comes entirely new to us, and getting ideas about it produces new channels in the brain, disturbing the whole system, and that is why you find in the practice of Yoga ordinary people are at first turned out of their grooves. In order to lessen these disturbances as much as possible, all these methods are devised by Patanjali, that we may practice any one of them best suited to us.

विषयवती वा प्रवृत्तिरुत्पन्ना मनसः स्थितिनिबन्धिनी ॥३५॥

35. Those forms of concentration that bring extraordinary sense-perceptions cause perseverance of the mind.

This naturally comes with Dhâranâ, concentration; the Yogis say, if the mind becomes concentrated on the tip of the nose, one begins to smell, after a few days, wonderful perfumes. If it becomes concentrated at the root of the tongue, one begins to hear sounds; if on the tip of the tongue, one begins to taste wonderful flavours; if on the middle of the tongue, one feels as if one were coming in contact with something. If one concentrates one's mind on the palate, one begins to see peculiar things. If a man whose mind is disturbed wants to take up some of these practices of Yoga, yet doubts the truth of them, he will have his doubts set at rest when, after a little practice, these things come to him, and he will persevere.

विशोका वा ज्योतिष्मती ॥३६॥

36. Or (by the meditation on) the Effulgent Light, which is beyond all sorrow.

This is another sort of concentration. Think of the lotus of the heart, with petals downwards, and running through it, the Sushumna; take in the breath, and while throwing the breath out imagine that the lotus is turned with the petals upwards, and inside that lotus is an effulgent light. Meditate on that.

वीतरागविषयं वा चित्तम् ॥३७॥

37. Or (by meditation on) the heart that has given up all attachment to sense-objects.

Take some holy person, some great person whom you revere, some saint whom you know to be perfectly nonattached, and think of his heart. That heart has become non-attached, and meditate on that heart; it will calm the mind. If you cannot do that, there is the next way:

स्वप्ननिद्राज्ञानालम्बनं वा ॥३८॥

38. Or by meditating on the knowledge that comes in sleep.

Sometimes a man dreams that he has seen angels coming to him and talking to him, that he is in an ecstatic condition, that he has heard music floating through the air. He is in a blissful condition in that dream, and when he wakes, it makes a deep impression on him. Think of that dream as real, and meditate upon it. If you cannot do that, meditate on any holy thing that pleases you.

यथाभिमतध्यानाद्वा ॥३९॥

39. Or by the meditation on anything that appeals to one as good.

This does not mean any wicked subject, but anything good that you like, any place that you like best, any scenery that you like best, any idea that you like best, anything that will concentrate the mind.

परमाणु परममहत्त्वान्तोऽस्य वशीकारः ॥४०॥

40. The Yogi's mind thus meditating, becomes unobstructed from the atomic to the infinite.

The mind, by this practice, easily contemplates the most minute, as well as the biggest thing. Thus the mindwaves become fainter.

क्षीणवृत्तेरभिजातस्येव मणेर्ग्रहीतृ ग्रहण - ग्राह्येषु तत्स्थ -
तदञ्जनता समापत्तिः ॥४१॥

41. The Yogi whose Vrittis have thus become powerless (controlled) obtains in the receiver, (the instrument of) receiving, and the received (the Self, the mind, and external objects), concentratedness arid sameness like the crystal (before different coloured objects).

What results from this constant meditation? We must remember how in a previous aphorism Patanjali went into the various states of meditation, how the first would be the gross, the second the fine, and from them the advance was to still finer objects. The result of these meditations is that we can meditate as easily on the fine as on the gross objects. Here the Yogi sees the three things, the receiver, the received, and the receiving instrument, corresponding to the Soul, external objects, and the mind. There are three objects of meditation given us. First, the gross things, as bodies, or material objects; second, fine things, as the mind, the Chitta; and third, the Purusha qualified, not the Purusha itself, but the Egoism. By practice, the Yogi gets established in all these meditations. Whenever he meditates he can keep out all other thoughts; he becomes identified with that on which he meditates. When he meditates, he is like a piece of crystal. Before flowers the crystal becomes almost identified with the flowers. If the flower is red, the crystal looks red, or if the flower is blue, the crystal looks blue.

तत्र शब्दार्थज्ञानविकल्पैः सङ्कीर्णा सवितर्का समापत्तिः ॥४२॥

42. Sound, meaning, and resulting knowledge, being mixed up, is (called) Samadhi with question.

Sound here means vibration, meaning the nerve currents which conduct it; and knowledge, reaction. All the various meditations we have had so far, Patanjali calls Savitarka (meditation with question). Later on he gives us higher and higher Dhyânas. In these that are called "with question," we keep the duality of subject and object, which results from the mixture of word, meaning, and knowledge. There is first the external vibration, the word. This, carried inward by the sense currents, is the meaning. After that there comes a reactionary wave in the Chitta, which is knowledge, but the mixture of these three makes up what we call knowledge. In all the meditations up to this we get this mixture as objects of meditation. The next Samadhi is higher.

स्मृतिपरिशुद्धौ स्वरूपशून्येवार्थमात्रनिर्भासा निर्वितर्का ॥४३॥

43. The Samadhi called "without question" (comes) when the memory is purified, or devoid of qualities, expressing only the meaning (of the meditated object).

It is by the practice of meditation of these three that we come to the state where these three do not mix. We can get rid of them. We will first try to understand what these three are. Here is the Chitta; you will always remember the simile of the mind-stuff to a lake, and the vibration, the word, the sound, like a pulsation coming over it. You have that calm lake in you, and I pronounce a word, "Cow". As soon as it enters through your ears there is a wave produced in your Chitta along with it. So that wave represents the idea of the cow, the form or the meaning as we call it. The apparent cow that you know is really the wave in the mind-stuff that comes as a reaction to the internal and external sound vibrations. With the sound, the wave dies away; it can never exist without a word. You may ask how it is, when we only think of the cow, and do not hear a sound. You make that sound yourself. You are saying "cow" faintly in your mind, and with that comes a wave. There cannot be any wave without this impulse of sound; and when it is not from outside, it is from inside, and when the sound dies, the wave dies. What remains? The result of the reaction, and that is knowledge. These three are so closely combined in our mind that we cannot separate them. When the sound comes, the senses vibrate, and the wave rises in reaction; they follow so closely upon one another that there is no discerning one from the other. When this meditation has been practiced for a long time, memory, the receptacle of all impressions, becomes purified, and we are able clearly to distinguish them from one another. This is called Nirvitarka, concentration without question.

एतयैव सविचारा निर्विचारा च सूक्ष्मविषया व्याख्यता ॥४४॥

44. By this process (the concentrations) with discrimination and without discrimination, whose objects are finer, are (also) explained.

A process similar to the preceding is applied again; only, the objects to be taken up in the former meditations are gross; in this they are fine.

सूक्ष्मविषयत्वश्चालिङ्ग पर्यवसानम् ॥४५॥

45. The finer objects end with the Pradhâna.

The gross objects are only the elements and everything manufactured out of them. The fine objects begin with the Tanmatras or fine particles. The organs, the mind, (The mind, or common sensorium, the aggregate of all the senses), egoism, the mind-stuff (the cause of all manifestation), the equilibrium state of Sattva, Rajas, and Tamas materials — called Pradhâna (chief), Prakriti (nature), or Avyakta (unmanifest) — are all included within the category of fine objects, the Purusha (the Soul) alone being excepted.

ता एव सबीजः समाधिः ॥४६॥

46. These concentrations are with seed.

These do not destroy the seeds of past actions, and thus cannot give liberation, but what they bring to the Yogi is stated in the following aphorism.

निर्विचार - वैशारद्येऽध्यात्मप्रसादः ॥४७॥

47. The concentration "without discrimination" being purified, the Chitta becomes firmly fixed.

ऋतम्भरा तत्र प्रज्ञा ॥४८॥

48. The knowledge in that is called "filled with Truth".

The next aphorism will explain this.

श्रुतानुमानप्रज्ञाभ्यामन्यविषया विशेषार्थत्वात् ॥४९॥

49. The knowledge that is gained from testimony and inference is about common objects. That from the Samadhi just mentioned is of a much higher order, being able to penetrate where inference and testimony cannot go.

The idea is that we have to get our knowledge of ordinary objects by direct perception, and by inference therefrom, and from testimony of people who are competent. By "people who are competent," the Yogis always mean the Rishis, or the Seers of the thoughts recorded in the scriptures — the Vedas. According to them, the only proof of the scriptures is that they were the testimony of competent persons, yet they say the scriptures cannot take us to realisation. We can read all the Vedas, and yet will not realise anything, but when we practise their teachings, then we attain to that state which realises what the scriptures say, which penetrates where neither reason nor perception nor inference can go, and where the testimony of others cannot avail. This is what is meant by the aphorism.

Realisation is real religion, all the rest is only preparation — hearing lectures, or reading books, or reasoning is merely preparing the ground; it is not religion. Intellectual assent and intellectual dissent are not religion. The central idea of the Yogis is that just as we come in direct contact with objects of the senses, so religion even can be directly perceived in a far more intense sense. The truths of religion, as God and Soul, cannot be perceived by the external senses. I cannot see God with my eyes, nor can I touch Him with my hands, and we also know that neither can we reason beyond the senses. Reason leaves us at a point quite indecisive; we may reason all our lives, as the world has been doing for thousands of years, and the result is that we find we are incompetent to prove or disprove the facts of religion. What we perceive directly we take as the basis, and upon that basis we reason. So it is obvious that reasoning has to run within these bounds of perception. It can never go beyond. The whole scope of realisation, therefore, is beyond sense-perception. The Yogis say that man can go beyond his direct sense-perception, and beyond his reason also. Man has in him the faculty, the power, of transcending his intellect even, a power which is in every being, every creature. By the practice of Yoga that power is aroused, and then man transcends the ordinary limits of reason, and directly perceives things which are beyond all reason.

तज्जः संस्कारोऽन्यसंस्कारप्रतिबन्धी ॥५०॥

50. The resulting impression from this Samadhi obstructs all other impressions.

We have seen in the foregoing aphorism that the only way of attaining to that superconsciousness is by concentration, and we have also seen that what hinder the mind from concentration are the past Samskaras, impressions. All of you have observed that, when you are trying to concentrate your mind, your thoughts wander. When you are trying to think of God, that is the very time these Samskaras appear. At other times they are not so active; but when you want them not, they are sure to be there, trying their best to crowd in your mind. Why should that be so? Why should they be much more potent at the time of concentration? It is because you are repressing them, and they react with all their force. At other times they do not react. How countless these old past impressions must be, all lodged somewhere in the Chitta, ready, waiting like tigers, to jump up! These have to be suppressed that the one idea which we want may arise, to the exclusion of the others. Instead they are all struggling to come up at the same time. These are the various powers of the Samskaras in hindering concentration of the mind. So this Samadhi which has just been given is the best to be practised, on account of its power of suppressing the Samskaras. The Samskara which will be raised by this sort of concentration will be so powerful that it will hinder the action of the others, and hold them in check.

तस्यापि निरोधे सर्वनिरोधान्निर्बीजः समाधिः ॥५१॥

51. By the restraint of even this (impression, which obstructs all other impressions), all being restrained, comes the "seedless" Samadhi.

You remember that our goal is to perceive the Soul itself. We cannot perceive the Soul, because it has got mingled up with nature, with the mind, with the body. The ignorant man thinks his body is the Soul. The learned man thinks his mind is the Soul. But both of them are mistaken. What makes the Soul get mingled up with all this? Different waves in the Chitta rise and cover the Soul; we only see a little reflection of the Soul through these waves; so, if the wave is one of anger, we see the Soul as angry; "I am angry," one says. If it is one of love, we see ourselves reflected in that wave, and say we are loving. If that wave is one of weakness, and the Soul is reflected in it, we think we are weak. These various ideas come from these impressions, these Samskaras covering the Soul. The real nature of the Soul is not perceived as long as there is one single wave in the lake of the Chitta; this real nature will never be perceived until all the waves have subsided. So, first, Patanjali teaches us the meaning of these waves; secondly, the best way to repress them; and thirdly, how to make one wave so strong as to suppress all other waves, fire eating fire as it were. When only one remains, it will be easy to suppress that also, and when that is gone, this Samadhi or concentration is called seedless. It leaves nothing, and the Soul is manifested just as It is, in Its own glory. Then alone we know that the Soul is not a compound; It is the only eternal simple in the universe, and as such, It cannot be born, It cannot die; It is immortal, indestructible, the ever-living essence of intelligence.

Chapter II.
Concentration: Its Practice

तपः- स्वाध्यायेश्वरप्रणिधानानि क्रियायोगः ॥१॥

1. Mortification, study, and surrendering fruits of work to God are called Kriyâ-yoga.

Those Samâdhis with which we ended our last chapter are very difficult to attain; so we must take them up slowly. The first step, the preliminary step, is called Kriya-yoga. Literally this means work, working towards Yoga. The organs are the horses, the mind is the rein, the intellect is the charioteer, the soul is the rider, and the body is the chariot. The master of the household, the King, the Self of man, is sitting in this chariot. If the horses are very strong and do not obey the rein, if the charioteer, the intellect, does not know how to control the horses, then the chariot will come to grief. But if the organs, the horses, are well controlled, and if the rein, the mind, is well held in the hands of the charioteer, the intellect, the chariot reaches the goal. What is meant, therefore, by this mortification? Holding the rein firmly while guiding the body and the organs; not letting them do anything they like, but keeping them both under proper control. *Study*. What is meant by study in this case? No study of novels or story books, but study of those works which teach the liberation of the Soul. Then again this study does not mean controversial studies at all. The Yogi is supposed to have finished his period of controversy. He has had enough of that, and has become satisfied. He only studies to intensify his convictions. Vâda and Siddhânta — these are the two sorts of scriptural knowledge — Vada (the argumentative) and Siddhanta (the decisive). When a man is entirely ignorant he takes up the first of these, the argumentative fighting, and reasoning pro and con; and when he has finished that he takes up the Siddhanta, the decisive, arriving at a conclusion. Simply arriving at this conclusion will not do. It must be intensified. Books are infinite in number, and time is short; therefore the secret of knowledge is to take what is essential. Take that and try to live up to it. There is an old Indian legend that if you place a cup of milk and water before a Râja-Hamsa (swan), he will take all the milk and leave the water. In that way we should take what is of value in knowledge, and leave the dross. Intellectual gymnastics are necessary at first. We must not go blindly into anything. The Yogi has passed the argumentative state, and has come to a conclusion, which is, like the rocks, immovable. The only thing he now seeks to do is to intensify that conclusion. Do not argue, he says; if one forces arguments upon you, be silent. Do not answer any argument, but go away calmly, because arguments only disturb the mind. The only thing necessary is to train the intellect, what is the use of disturbing it for nothing? The intellect is but a weak instrument, and can give us only knowledge limited by the senses. The Yogi wants to go beyond the senses, therefore intellect is of no use to him. He is certain of this and, therefore, is silent, and does not argue. Every argument throws his mind out of balance, creates a disturbance in the Chitta, and a disturbance is a drawback. Argumentations and searchings of the reason are only by the way. There are much higher things beyond them. The whole of life is not for schoolboy fights and debating societies. "Surrendering the fruits of work to God" is to take to ourselves neither credit nor blame, but to give up both to the Lord and be at peace.

समाधि-भावनार्थः क्लेश-तनूकरणार्थश्च ॥२॥

2. (It is for) the practice of Samadhi and minimising the pain-bearing obstructions.

Most of us make our minds like spoilt children, allowing them to do whatever they want. Therefore it is necessary that Kriya-yoga should be constantly practised, in order to gain control of the mind, and bring it into subjection. The obstructions to Yoga arise from lack of control, and cause us pain. They can only be removed by denying the mind, and holding it in check, through the means of Kriya-yoga.

अविद्यास्मिता-राग-द्वेषाभिनिवेशाः क्लेशाः ॥३॥

3. The pain-bearing obstructions are — ignorance, egoism, attachment, aversion and clinging to life.

These are the five pains, the fivefold tie that binds us down, of which ignorance is the cause and the other four its effects. It is the only cause of all our misery. What else can make us miserable? The nature of the Soul is eternal bliss. What can make it sorrowful except ignorance, hallucination, delusion? All pain of the Soul is simply delusion.

अविद्या क्षेत्रमुत्तरेषां प्रसुप्त-तनु-विच्छिन्नोदाराणाम् ॥४॥

4. Ignorance is the productive field of all these that follow, whether they are dormant, attenuated, overpowered, or expanded.

Ignorance is the cause of egoism, attachment, aversion, and clinging to life. These impressions exist in different states. They are sometimes dormant. You often hear the expression "innocent as a baby," yet in the baby may be the state of a demon or of a god, which will come out by degrees. In the Yogi, these impressions, the Samskâras left by past actions, are attenuated, that is, exist in a very fine state, and he can control them, and not allow them to become manifest. "Overpowered" means that sometimes one set of impressions is held down for a while by those that are stronger, but they come out when that repressing cause is removed. The last state is the "expanded," when the Samskaras, having helpful surroundings, attain to a great activity, either as good or evil.

अनित्याशुचि – दुःखानात्मसु नित्य – शुचि – सुखात्मख्यातिरविद्या ॥५॥

5. Ignorance is taking the non-eternal, the impure, the painful, and the non-Self for the eternal, the pure, the happy, and the Âtman or Self (respectively).

All the different sorts of impressions have one source, ignorance. We have first to learn what ignorance is. All of us think, "I am the body, and not the Self, the pure, the effulgent, the ever blissful," and that is ignorance. We think of man, and see man as body. This is the great delusion.

दृग्दर्शनशक्त्योरेकात्मतेवास्मिता ॥६॥

6. Egoism is the identification of the seer with the instrument of seeing.

The seer is really the Self, the pure one, the ever holy, the infinite, the immortal. This is the Self of man. And what are the instruments? The Chitta or mind-stuff, the Buddhi or determinative faculty, the Manas or mind, and the Indriyas or sense-organs. These are the instruments for him to see the external world, and the identification of the Self with the instruments is what is called the ignorance of egoism. We say, "I am the mind," "I am thought," "I am angry," or "I am happy". How can we be angry and how can we hate? We should identify ourselves with the Self that cannot change. If It is unchangeable, how can It be one moment happy, and one moment unhappy? It is formless, infinite, omnipresent. What can change It ? It is beyond all law. What can affect it? Nothing in the universe can produce an effect on It. Yet through ignorance, we identify ourselves with the mind-stuff, and think we feel pleasure or pain.

सुखानुशयी रागः ॥७॥

7. Attachment is that which dwells on pleasure.

We find pleasure in certain things, and the mind like a current flows towards them; and this following the pleasure centre, as it were, is what is called attachment. We are never attached where we do not find pleasure. We find pleasure in very queer things sometimes, but the principle remains: wherever we find pleasure, there we are attached.

दुःखानुशयी द्वेषः ॥८॥

8. Aversion is that which dwells on pain.

That which gives us pain we immediately seek to get away from.

स्वरसवाही विदुषोऽपि तथारूढोऽभिनिवेशः ॥९॥

9. Flowing through its own nature, and established even in the learned, is the clinging to life.

This clinging to life you see manifested in every animal. Upon it many attempts have been made to build the theory of a future life, because men are so fond of life that they desire a future life also. Of course it goes without saying that this argument is without much value, but the most curious part of it is, that, in Western countries, the idea that this clinging to life indicates a possibility of future life applies only to men, but does not include animals. In India this clinging to life has been one of the arguments to prove past experience and existence. For instance, if it be true that all our knowledge has come from experience, then it is sure that that which we never experienced we cannot imagine or understand. As soon as chickens are hatched they begin to pick up food. Many times it has been seen, where ducks have been hatched by hens, that, as soon as they came out of the eggs they flew to water, and the mother thought they would be drowned. If experience be the only source of knowledge, where did these chickens learn to pick up food, or the ducklings that the water was their natural element? If you say it is instinct, it means nothing — it is simply giving a word, but is no explanation. What is this instinct? We have many instincts in ourselves. For instance, most of you ladies play the piano, and remember, when you first learned, how carefully you had to put your fingers on the black and the white keys, one after the other, but now, after long years of practice, you can talk with your friends while your fingers play mechanically. It has become instinct. So with every work we do; by practice it becomes instinct, it becomes automatic; but so far as we know, all the cases which we now regard as automatic are degenerated reason. In the language of the Yogi, instinct is involved reason. Discrimination becomes involved, and gets to be automatic Samskaras. Therefore it is perfectly logical to think that all we call instinct in this world is simply involved reason. As reason cannot come without experience, all instinct is, therefore, the result of past experience. Chickens fear the hawk, and ducklings love the water; these are both the results of past experience. Then the question is whether that experience belongs to a particular soul, or to the body simply, whether this experience which comes to the duck is the duck's forefathers' experience, or the duck's own experience. Modern scientific men hold that it belongs to the body, but the Yogis hold that it is the experience of the mind, transmitted through the body. This is called the theory of reincarnation.

We have seen that all our knowledge, whether we call it perception, or reason, or instinct, must come through that one channel called experience, and all that we now call instinct is the result of past experience, degenerated into instinct and that instinct regenerates into reason again. So on throughout the universe, and upon this has been built one of the chief arguments for reincarnation in India. The recurring experiences of various fears, in course of time, produce this clinging to life. That is why the child is instinctively afraid, because the past experience of pain is there in it. Even in the most learned men, who know that this body will go, and who say "never mind, we have had hundreds of bodies, the soul cannot die" — even in them, with all their intellectual convictions, we still find this clinging on to life. Why is this clinging to life? We have seen that it has become instinctive. In the psychological language of the Yogis it has become a Samskara. The Samskaras, fine and hidden, are sleeping in the Chitta. All this past experience of death, all that which we call instinct, is experience become subconscious. It lives in the Chitta, and is not inactive, but is working underneath.

The Chitta-Vrittis, the mind-waves, which are gross, we can appreciate and feel; they can be more easily controlled, but what about the finer instincts? How can they be controlled? When I am angry, my whole mind becomes a huge wave of anger. I feel it, see it, handle it, can easily manipulate it, can fight with it; but I shall not succeed perfectly in the fight until I can get down below to its causes. A man says something very harsh to me, and I begin to feel that I am getting heated, and he goes on till I am perfectly angry and forget myself, identify myself with anger. When he first began to abuse me, I thought, "I am going to be angry". Anger was one thing, and I was another; but when I became angry, I was anger. These feelings have to be controlled in the germ, the root, in their fine forms, before even we have become conscious that they are acting on us. With the vast majority of mankind the fine states of these passions are not even known — the states in which they emerge from subconsciousness. When a bubble is rising from the bottom of the lake, we do not see it, nor even when it is nearly come to the surface; it is only when it bursts and makes a ripple that we know it is there. We shall only be successful in grappling with the waves when we can get hold of them in their fine causes, and until you can get hold of them, and subdue them before they become gross, there is no hope of conquering any passion perfectly. To control our passions we have to control them at their very roots; then alone shall we be able to burn out their very seeds. As fried seeds thrown into the ground will never come up, so these passions will never arise.

ते प्रतिप्रसवहेयाः सूक्ष्माः ॥१०॥

10. The fine Samskaras are to be conquered by resolving them into their causal state.

Samskaras are the subtle impressions that manifest themselves into gross forms later on. How are these fine Samskaras to be controlled? By resolving the effect into its cause. When the Chitta, which is an effect, is resolved into its cause, Asmitâ or Egoism, then only, the fine impressions die along with it. Meditation cannot destroy these.

ध्यानहेयास्तद्वृत्तयः ॥११॥

11. By meditation, their (gross) modifications are to be rejected.

Meditation is one of the great means of controlling the rising of these waves. By meditation you can make the mind subdue these waves, and if you go on practicing meditation for days, and months, and years, until it has become a habit, until it will come in spite of yourself, anger and hatred will be controlled and checked.

क्लेशमूलः कर्माशयो दृष्टादृजन्मवेदनीयः ॥१२॥

12. The "receptacle of works" has its root in these pain-bearing obstructions, and their experience is in this visible life, or in the unseen life.

By the "receptacle of works" is meant the sum-total of Samskaras. Whatever work we do, the mind is thrown into a wave, and after the work is finished, we think the wave is gone. No. It has only become fine, but it is still there. When we try to remember the work, it comes up again and becomes a wave. So it was there; if not, there would not have been memory. Thus every action, every thought, good or bad, just goes down and becomes fine, and is there stored up. Both happy and unhappy thoughts are called pain-bearing obstructions, because according to the Yogis, they, in the long run, bring pain. All happiness which comes from the senses will, eventually, bring pain. All enjoyment will make us thirst for more, and that brings pain as its result. There is no limit to man's desires; he goes on desiring, and when he comes to a point where desire cannot be fulfilled, the result is pain. Therefore the Yogis regard the sum-total of the impressions, good or evil, as pain-bearing obstructions; they obstruct the way to freedom of the Soul.

It is the same with the Samskaras, the fine roots of all our works; they are the causes which will again bring effects, either in this life, or in the lives to come. In exceptional cases when these Samskaras are very strong, they bear fruit quickly; exceptional acts of wickedness, or of goodness, bring their fruits even in this life. The Yogis hold that men who are able to acquire a tremendous power of good Samskaras do not have to die, but, even in this life, can change their bodies into god-bodies. There are several such cases mentioned by the Yogis in their books. These men change the very material of their bodies; they re-arrange the molecules in such fashion that they have no more sickness, and what we call death does not come to them. Why should not this be? The physiological meaning of food is assimilation of energy from the sun. The energy has reached the plant, the plant is eaten by an animal, and the animal by man. The science of it is that we take so much energy from the sun, and make it part of ourselves. That being the case, why should there be only one way of assimilating energy? The plant's way is not the same as ours; the earth's process of assimilating energy differs from our own. But all assimilate energy in some form or other. The Yogis say that they are able to assimilate energy by the power of the mind alone, that they can draw in as much of it as they desire without recourse to the ordinary methods. As a spider makes its web out of its own substance, and becomes bound in it, and cannot go anywhere except along the lines of that web, so we have projected out of our own substance this network called the nerves, and we cannot work except through the channels of those nerves. The Yogi says we need not be bound by that.

Similarly, we can send electricity to any part of the world, but we have to send it by means of wires. Nature can send a vast mass of electricity without any wires at all. Why cannot we do the same? We can send mental electricity. What we call mind is very much the same as electricity. It is clear that this nerve fluid has some amount of electricity, because it is polarised, and it answers all electrical directions. We can only send our electricity through these nerve channels. Why not send the mental electricity without this aid? The Yogis say it is perfectly possible and practicable, and that when you can do that, you will work all over the universe. You will be able to work with any body anywhere, without the help of the nervous system. When the soul is acting through these channels, we say a man is living, and when these cease to work, a man is said to be dead. But when a man is able to act either with or without these channels, birth and death will have no meaning for him. All the bodies in the universe are made up of Tanmâtras, their difference lies in the arrangement of the latter. If you are the arranger, you can arrange a body in one way or another. Who makes up this body but you? Who eats the food? If another ate the food for you, you would not live long. Who makes the blood out of food? You, certainly. Who purifies the blood, and sends it through the veins? You. We are the masters of the body, and we live in it. Only we have lost the knowledge of how to rejuvenate it. We have become automatic, degenerate. We have forgotten the process of arranging its molecules. So, what we do automatically has to be done knowingly. We are the masters and we have to regulate that arrangement; and as soon as we can do that, we shall be able to rejuvenate just as we like, and then we shall have neither birth nor disease nor death.

सति मूलेतद्विपाको जात्यायुर्भोगाः ॥१३॥

13. The root being there, the fruition comes (in the form of) species, life, and experience of pleasure and pain.

The roots, the causes, the Samskaras being there, they manifest and form the effects. The cause dying down becomes the effect; the effect getting subtler becomes the cause of the next effect. A tree bears a seed, which becomes the cause of another tree, and so on. All our works now are the effects of past Samskaras; again, these works becoming Samskaras will be the causes of future actions, and thus we go on. So this aphorism says that the cause being there, the fruit must come, in the form of species of beings: one will be a man, another an angel, another an animal, another a demon. Then there are different effects of Karma in life. One man lives fifty years, another a hundred, another dies in two years, and never attains maturity; all these differences in life are regulated by past Karma. One man is born, as it were, for pleasure; if he buries himself in a forest, pleasure will follow him there. Another man, wherever he goes, is followed by pain; everything becomes painful for him. It is the result of their own past. According to the philosophy of the Yogis, all virtuous actions bring pleasure, and all vicious actions bring pain. Any man who does wicked deeds is sure to reap their fruit in the form of pain.

ते ह्लादपरितापफलाः पुण्यापुण्यहेतुत्वात् ॥१४॥

14. They bear fruit as pleasure or pain, caused by virtue or vice.

15. To the discriminating, all is, as it were, painful on account of everything bringing pain either as consequence, or as anticipation of loss of happiness, or as fresh craving arising from impressions of happiness, and also as counteraction of qualities.

The Yogis say that the man who has discriminating powers, the man of good sense, sees through all that are called pleasure and pain, and knows that they come to all, and that one follows and melts into the other; he sees that men follow an *ignis fatuus* all their lives, and never succeed in fulfilling their desires. The great king Yudhishthira once said that the most wonderful thing in life is that every moment we see people dying around us, and yet we think we shall never die. Surrounded by fools on every side, we think we are the only exceptions, the only learned men. Surrounded by all sorts of experiences of fickleness, we think our love is the only lasting love. How can that be? Even love is selfish, and the Yogi says that in the end we shall find that even the love of husbands and wives, and children and friends, slowly decays. Decadence seizes everything in this life. It is only when everything, even love, fails, that, with a flash, man finds out how vain, how dream-like is this world. Then he catches a glimpse of Vairâgya (renunciation), catches a glimpse of the Beyond. It is only by giving up this world that the other comes; never through holding on to this one. Never yet was there a great soul who had not to reject sense-pleasures and enjoyments to acquire his greatness. The cause of misery is the clash between the different forces of nature, one dragging one way, and another dragging another, rendering permanent happiness impossible.

हेयं दुःखमनागतम् ॥१६॥

16. The misery which is not yet come is to be avoided.

Some Karma we have worked out already, some we are working out now in the present, and some are waiting to bear fruit in the future. The first kind is past and gone. The second we will have to work out, and it is only that which is waiting to bear fruit in the future that we can conquer and control, towards which end all our forces should be directed. This is what Patanjali means when he says that Samskaras are to be controlled by resolving them into their causal state (II. 10).

द्रष्टृदृश्ययोः संयोगो हेयहेतुः ॥१७॥

17. The cause of that which is to be avoided is the junction of the seer and the seen.

Who is the seer? The Self of man, the Purusha. What is the seen? The whole of nature beginning with the mind, down to gross matter. All pleasure and pain arise from the junction between this Purusha and the mind. The Purusha, you must remember, according to this philosophy, is pure; when joined to nature, it appears to feel pleasure or pain by reflection.

प्रकाश – क्रिया – स्थितिशीलं भूतेन्द्रियात्मकं भोगापवर्गार्थं दृश्यम् ॥१८॥

18. The experienced is composed of elements and organs, is of the nature of illumination, action, and inertia, and is for the purpose of experience and release (of the experiencer).

The experienced, that is nature, is composed of elements and organs — the elements, gross and fine, which compose the whole of nature, and the organs of the senses, mind, etc. — and is of the nature of illumination (Sattva), action (Rajas), and inertia (Tamas). What is the purpose of the whole of nature? That the Purusha may gain experience. The Purusha has, as it were, forgotten its mighty, godly nature. There is a story that the king of the gods, Indra, once became a pig, wallowing in mire; he had a she-pig and a lot of baby pigs, and was very happy. Then some gods saw his plight, and came to him, and told him, "You are the king of the gods, you have all the gods under your command. Why are you here?" But Indra said, "Never mind; I am all right here; I do not care for heaven, while I have this sow and these little pigs." The poor gods were at their wits' end. After a time they decided to slay all the pigs one after another. When all were dead, Indra began to weep and mourn. Then the gods ripped his pig-body open and he came out of it, and began to laugh, when he realised what a hideous dream he had had — he, the king of the gods, to have become a pig, and to think that that pig-life was the only life! Not only so, but to have wanted the whole universe to come into the pig-life! The Purusha, when it identifies itself with nature, forgets that it is pure and infinite. The Purusha does not love, it is love itself. It does not exist, it is existence itself. The Soul does not know, It is knowledge itself. It is a mistake to say the Soul loves, exists, or knows. Love, existence, and knowledge are not the qualities of the Purusha, but its essence. When they get reflected upon something, you may call them the qualities of that something. They are not the qualities but the essence of the Purusha, the great Atman, the Infinite Being, without birth or death, established in its own glory. It appears to have become so degenerate that if you approach to tell it, "You are not a pig," it begins to squeal and bite.

Thus is it with us all in this Mâyâ, this dream world, where it is all misery, weeping and crying, where a few golden balls are rolled, and the world scrambles after them. You were never bound by laws, nature never had a bond for you. That is what the Yogi tells you. Have patience to learn it. And the Yogi shows how, by junction with nature, and identifying itself with the mind and the world, the Purusha thinks itself miserable. Then the Yogi goes on to show you that the way out is through experience. You have to get all this experience, but finish it quickly. We have placed ourselves in this net, and will have to get out. We have got ourselves caught in the trap, and we will have to work out our freedom. So get this experience of husbands, and wives, and friends, and little loves; you will get through them safely if you never forget what you really are. Never forget this is only a momentary state, and that w e have to pass through it. Experience is the one great teacher — experience of pleasure and pain — but know it is only experience. It leads, step by step, to that state where all things become small, and the Purusha so great that the whole universe seems as a drop in the ocean and falls off by its own nothingness. We have to go through different experiences, but let us never forget the ideal.

विशेषाविशेष लिङ्गमात्रालिङ्गानि गुणपर्वाणि ॥१९॥

19. The states of the qualities are the defined, the undefined, the indicated only, and the signless.

The system of Yoga is built entirely on the philosophy of the Sânkhyas, as I told you before, and here again I shall remind you of the cosmology of the Sankhya philosophy. According to the Sankhyas, nature is both the material and the efficient cause of the universe. In nature there are three sorts of materials, the Sattva, the Rajas, and the Tamas. The Tamas material is all that is dark, all that is ignorant and heavy. The Rajas is activity. The Sattva is calmness, light. Nature, before creation, is called by them Avyakta, undefined, or indiscrete; that is, in which there is no distinction of form or name, a state in which these three materials are held in perfect balance. Then the balance is disturbed, the three materials begin to mingle in various fashions, and the result is the universe. In every man, also, these three materials exist. When the Sattva material prevails, knowledge comes; when Rajas, activity; and when Tamas, darkness, lassitude, idleness, and ignorance. According to the Sankhya theory, the highest manifestation of nature, consisting of the three materials, is what they call Mahat or intelligence, universal intelligence, of which each human intellect is a part. In the Sankhya psychology there is a sharp distinction between Manas, the mind function, and the function of the Buddhi, intellect. The mind function is simply to collect and carry impressions and present them to the Buddhi, the individual Mahat, which determines upon it. Out of Mahat comes egoism, out of which again come the fine materials. The fine materials combine and become the gross materials outside — the external universe. The claim of the Sankhya philosophy is that beginning with the intellect down to a block of stone, all is the product of one substance, different only as finer to grosser states of existence. The finer is the cause, and the grosser is the effect. According. to the Sankhya philosophy, beyond the whole of nature is the Purusha, which is not material at all. Purusha is not at all similar to anything else, either Buddhi, or mind, or the Tanmatras, or the gross materials. It is not akin to any one of these, it is entirely separate, entirely different in its nature, and from this they argue that the Purusha must be immortal, because it is not the result of combination. That which is not the result of combination cannot die. The Purushas or souls are infinite in number.

Now we shall understand the aphorism that the states of the qualities are defined, undefined, indicated only, and signess. By the "defined" are meant the gross elements, which we can sense. By the "undefined" are meant the very fine materials, the Tanmatras, which cannot be sensed by ordinary men. If you practise Yoga, however, says Patanjali, after a while your perceptions will become so fine that you will actually see the Tanmatras. For instance, you have heard how every man has a certain light about him; every living being emits a certain light, and this, he says, can be seen by the Yogi. We do not all see it, but we all throw out these Tanmatras, just as a flower continuously sends out fine particles which enable us to smell it. Every day of our lives we throw out a mass of good or evil, and everywhere we go the atmosphere is full of these materials. That is how there came to the human mind, unconsciously, the idea of building temples and churches. Why should man build churches in which to worship God? Why not worship Him anywhere? Even if he did not know the reason, man found that the place where people worshipped God became full of good Tanmatras. Every day people go there, and the more they go the holier they get, and the holier that place becomes. If any man who has not much Sattva in him goes there, the place will influence him and arouse his Sattva quality. Here, therefore, is the significance of all temples and holy places, but you must remember that their holiness depends on holy people congregating there. The difficulty with man is that he forgets the original meaning, and puts the cart before the horse. It was men who made these places holy, and then the effect became the cause and made men holy. If the wicked only were to go there, it would become as bad as any other place. It is not the building, but the people that make a church, and that is what we always forget. That is why sages and holy persons, who have much of this Sattva quality, can send it out and exert a tremendous influence day and night on their surroundings. A man may become so pure that his purity will become tangible. Whosoever comes in contact with him becomes pure.

Next "the indicated only" means the Buddhi, the intellect. "The indicated only" is the first manifestation of nature; from it all other manifestations proceed. The last is "the signless". There seems to be a great difference between modern science and all religions at this point. Every religion has the idea that the universe comes out of intelligence. The theory of God, taking it in its psychological significance, apart from all ideas of personality, is that intelligence is first in the order of creation, and that out of intelligence comes what we call gross matter. Modern philosophers say that intelligence is the last to come. They say that unintelligent things slowly evolve into animals, and from animals into men. They claim that instead of everything coming out of intelligence, intelligence itself is the last to come. Both the religious and the scientific statements, though seeming directly opposed to each other are true. Take an infinite series, A—B—A—B —A—B. etc. The question is — which is first, A or B? If you take the series as A—B. you will say that A is first, but if you take it as B—A, you will say that B is first. It depends upon the way we look at it. Intelligence undergoes modification and becomes the gross matter, this again merges into intelligence, and thus the process goes on. The Sankhyas, and other religionists, put intelligence first, and the series becomes intelligence, then matter. The scientific man puts his finger on matter, and says matter, then intelligence. They both indicate the same chain. Indian philosophy, however, goes beyond both intelligence and matter, and finds a Purusha, or Self, which is beyond intelligence, of which intelligence is but the borrowed light.

द्रष्टा दृशिमात्रः शुद्धोऽपि प्रत्ययानुपश्यः ॥२०॥

20. The seer is intelligence only, and though pure, sees through the colouring of the intellect.

This is, again, Sankhya philosophy. We have seen from the same philosophy that from the lowest form up to intelligence all is nature; beyond nature are Purushas (souls), which have no qualities. Then how does the soul appear to be happy or unhappy? By reflection. If a red flower is put near a piece of pure crystal, the crystal appears to be red, similarly the appearances of happiness or unhappiness of the soul are but reflections. The soul itself has no colouring. The soul is separate from nature. Nature is one thing, soul another, eternally separate. The Sankhyas say that intelligence is a compound, that it grows and wanes, that it changes, just as the body changes, and that its nature is nearly the same as that of the body. As a finger-nail is to the body, so is body to intelligence. The nail is a part of the body, but it can be pared off hundreds of times, and the body will still last. Similarly, the intelligence lasts aeons, while this body can be "pared off," thrown off. Yet intelligence cannot be immortal because it changes — growing and waning. Anything that changes cannot be immortal. Certainly intelligence is manufactured, and that very fact shows us that there must be something beyond that. It cannot be free, everything connected with matter is in nature, and, therefore, bound for ever. Who is free? The free must certainly be beyond cause and effect. If you say that the idea of freedom is a delusion, I shall say that the idea of bondage is also a delusion. Two facts come into our consciousness, and stand or fall with each other. These are our notions of bondage and freedom. If we want to go through a wall, and our head bumps against that wall, we see we are limited by that wall. At the same time we find a willpower, and think we can direct our will everywhere. At every step these contradictory ideas come to us. We have to believe that we are free, yet at every moment we find we are not free. If one idea is a delusion, the other is also a delusion, and if one is true, the other also is true, because both stand upon the same basis — consciousness.

The Yogi says, both are true; that we are bound so far as intelligence goes, that we are free so far as the soul is concerned. It is the real nature of man, the soul, the Purusha, which is beyond all law of causation. Its freedom is percolating through layers of matter in various forms, intelligence, mind, etc. It is its light which is shining through all. Intelligence has no light of its own. Each organ has a particular centre in the brain; it is not that all the organs have one centre; each organ is separate. Why do all perceptions harmonise? Where do they get their unity? If it were in the brain, it would be necessary for all the organs, the eyes, the nose, the ears, etc., to have one centre only, while we know for certain that there are different centres for each. Both a man can see and hear at the same time, so a unity must be there at the back of intelligence. Intelligence is connected with the brain, but behind intelligence even stands the Purusha, the unit, where all different sensations and perceptions join and become one. The soul itself is the centre where all the different perceptions converge and become unified. That soul is free, and it is its freedom that tells you every moment that you are free. But you mistake, and mingle that freedom every moment with intelligence and mind. You try to attribute that freedom to the intelligence, and immediately find that intelligence is not free; you attribute that freedom to the body, and immediately nature tells you that you are again mistaken. That is why there is this mingled sense of freedom and bondage at the same time. The Yogi analyses both what is free and what is bound, and his ignorance vanishes. He finds that the Purusha is free, is the essence of that knowledge which, coming through the Buddhi, becomes intelligence, and, as such, is bound.

तदर्थ एव दृश्यस्यात्मा ॥२१॥

21. The nature of the experienced is for him.

Nature has no light of its own. As long as the Purusha is present in it, it appears as light. But the light is borrowed; just as the moon's light is reflected. According to the Yogis, all the manifestations of nature are caused by nature itself, but nature has no purpose in view, except to free the Purusha.

कृतार्थं प्रति नष्टमप्यनष्टं तदन्यसाधारणत्वात् ॥२२॥

22. Though destroyed for him whose goal has been gained, yet it is not destroyed, being common to others.

The whole activity of nature is to make the soul know that it is entirely separate from nature. When the soul knows this, nature has no more attractions for it. But the whole of nature vanishes only for that man who has become free. There will always remain an infinite number of others, for whom nature will go on working.

स्वस्वामिशक्त्योः स्वरूपोपलब्धिहेतुः संयोगः ॥२३॥

23. Junction is the cause of the realization of the nature of both the powers, the experienced and its Lord.

According to this aphorism, both the powers of soul and nature become manifest when they are in conjunction. Then all manifestations are thrown out. Ignorance is the cause of this conjunction. We see every day that the cause of our pain or pleasure is always our joining ourselves with the body. If I were perfectly certain that I am not this body, I should take no notice of heat and cold, or anything of the kind. This body is a combination. It is only a fiction to say that I have one body, you another, and the sun another. The whole universe is one ocean of matter, and you are the name of a little particle, and I of another, and the sun of another. We know that this matter is continuously changing. What is forming the sun one day, the next day may form the matter of our bodies.

तस्य हेतुरविद्या ॥२४॥

24. Ignorance is its cause.

Through ignorance we have joined ourselves with a particular body, and thus opened ourselves to misery. This idea of body is a simple superstition. It is superstition that makes us happy or unhappy. It is superstition caused by ignorance that makes us feel heat and cold, pain and pleasure. It is our business to rise above this superstition, and the Yogi shows us how we can do this. It has been demonstrated that, under certain mental conditions, a man may be burned, yet he will feel no pain. The difficulty is that this sudden upheaval of the mind comes like a whirlwind one minute, and goes away the next. If, however, we gain it through Yoga, we shall permanently attain to the separation of Self from the body.

तदभावात् संयोगाभावो हानं तद्दृशेः कैवल्यम् ॥२५॥

25. There being absence of that (ignorance) there is absence of junction, which is the thing-to-be avoided; that is the independence of the seer.

According to Yoga philosophy, it is through ignorance that the soul has been joined with nature. The aim is to get rid of nature's control over us. That is the goal of all religions. Each soul is potentially divine. The goal is to manifest this Divinity within, by controlling nature, external and internal. Do this either by work, or worship, or psychic control, or philosophy — by one or more or all of these — and be free. This is the whole of religion. Doctrines, or dogmas, or rituals, or books, or temples, or forms, are but secondary details. The Yogi tries to reach this goal through psychic control. Until we can free ourselves from nature, we are slaves; as she dictates so we must go. The Yogi claims that he who controls mind controls matter also. The internal nature is much higher than the external and much more difficult to grapple with, much more difficult to control. Therefore he who has conquered the internal nature controls the whole universe; it becomes his servant. Raja-Yoga propounds the methods of gaining this control. Forces higher than we know in physical nature will have to be subdued. This body is just the external crust of the mind. They are not two different things; they are just as the oyster and its shell. They are but two aspects of one thing; the internal substance of the oyster takes up matter from outside, and manufactures the shell. In the same way the internal fine forces which are called mind take up gross matter from outside, and from that manufacture this external shell, the body. If, then, we have control of the internal, it is very easy to have control of the external. Then again, these forces are not different. It is not that some forces are physical, and some mental; the physical forces are but the gross manifestations of the fine forces, just as the physical world is but the gross manifestation of the fine world.

विवेकख्यातिरविप्लवा हानोपायः ॥२६॥

26. The means of destruction of ignorance is unbroken practice of discrimination.

This is the real goal of practice — discrimination between the real and the unreal, knowing that the Purusha is not nature, that it is neither matter nor mind, and that because it is not nature, it cannot possibly change. It is only nature which changes, combining and re-combining, dissolving continually. When through constant practice we begin to discriminate, ignorance will vanish, and the Purusha will begin to shine in its real nature — omniscient, omnipotent, omnipresent.

तस्य सप्तधा प्रान्तभूमिः प्रज्ञा ॥२७॥

27. His knowledge is of the sevenfold highest ground.

When this knowledge comes; it will come, as it were, in seven grades, one after the other; and when one of these begins, we know that we are getting knowledge. The first to appear will be that we have known what is to be known. The mind will cease to be dissatisfied. While we are aware of thirsting after knowledge, we begin to seek here and there, wherever we think we can get some truth, and failing to find it we become dissatisfied and seek in a fresh direction. All search is vain, until we begin to perceive that knowledge is within ourselves, that no one can help us, that we must help ourselves. When we begin to practise the power of discrimination, the first sign that we are getting near truth will be that that dissatisfied state will vanish. We shall feel quite sure that we have found the truth, and that it cannot be anything else but the truth. Then we may know that the sun is rising, that the morning is breaking for us, and taking courage, we must persevere until the goal is reached. The second grade will be the absence of all pains. It will be impossible for anything in the universe, external or internal, to give us pain. The third will be the attainment of full knowledge. Omniscience will be ours. The fourth will be the attainment of the end of all duty through discrimination. Next will come what is called freedom of the Chitta. We shall realise that all difficulties and struggles, all vacillations of the mind, have fallen down, just as a stone rolls from the mountain top into the valley and never comes up again. The next will be that the Chitta itself will realise that it melts away into its causes whenever we so desire. Lastly we shall find that we are established in our Self, that we have been alone throughout the universe, neither body nor mind was ever related, much less joined, to us. They were working their own way, and we, through ignorance, joined ourselves to them. But we have been alone, omnipotent, omnipresent, ever blessed; our own Self was so pure and perfect that we required none else. We required none else to make us happy, for we are happiness itself. We shall find that this knowledge does not depend on anything else; throughout the universe there can be nothing that will not become effulgent before our knowledge. This will be the last state, and the Yogi will become peaceful and calm, never to feel any more pain, never to be again deluded, never to be touched by misery. He will know he is ever blessed, ever perfect, almighty.

योगाङ्गानुष्ठानादशुद्धिक्षये ज्ञानदीप्तिराविवेकख्यातेः ॥२८॥

28. By the practice of the different parts of Yoga the impurities being destroyed, knowledge be comes effulgent up to discrimination.

Now comes the practical knowledge. What we have just been speaking about is much higher. It is away above our heads, but it is the ideal. It is first necessary to obtain physical and mental control. Then the realization will become steady in that ideal. The ideal being known, what remains is to practice the method of reaching it.

यम – नियमासन – प्राणायाम – प्रत्याहार – धारणा – ध्यान – समाधयोऽष्टावङ्गानि ॥२९॥

29. Yama, Niyama, Âsana, Prânâyâama, Pratyâhâra, Dhâranâ, Dhyâna, and Samâdhi are the eight limbs of Yoga.

अहिंसा – सत्यास्तेय – ब्रह्मचर्यापरिग्रहा यमाः ॥३०॥

30. Non-killing, truthfulness, non-stealing, continence, and nor-receiving are called Yamas.

A man who wants to be a perfect Yogi must give up the sex idea. The soul has no sex; why should it degrade itself with sex ideas? Later on we shall understand better why these ideas must be given up. The mind of the man who receives gifts is acted on by the mind of the giver, so the receiver is likely to become degenerated. Receiving gifts is prone to destroy the independence of the mind, and make us slavish. Therefore, receive no gifts.

एते जाति - देश - काल - समयानवच्छिन्नाः सार्वभौमामहाव्रतम् ॥३१॥

31. These, unbroken by time, place, purpose, and caste-rules, are (universal) great vows.

These practices — non-killing, truthfulness, non-stealing, chastity, and non-receiving — are to be practised by every man, woman, and child; by every soul, irrespective of nation, country, or position.

शौच - सन्तोष - तपः - स्वाध्यायेश्वरप्रणिधानानि नियमाः ॥३२॥

32. Internal and external purification, contentment, mortification, study, and worship of God are the Niyamas.

External purification is keeping the body pure; a dirty man will never be a Yogi. There must be internal purification also. That is obtained by the virtues named in I.33. Of course, internal purity is of greater value than external, but both are necessary, and external purity, without internal, is of no good.

वितर्कबाधने प्रतिपक्षभावनम् ॥३३॥

33. To obstruct thoughts which are inimical to Yoga, contrary thoughts should be brought.

That is the way to practise the virtues that have been stated. For instance, when a big wave of anger has come into the mind, how are we to control that? Just by raising an opposing wave. Think of love. Sometimes a mother is very angry with her husband, and while in that state, the baby comes in, and she kisses the baby; the old wave dies out and a new wave arises, love for the child. That suppresses the other one. Love is opposite to anger. Similarly, when the idea of stealing comes, non-stealing should be thought of; when the idea of receiving gifts comes, replace it by a contrary thought.

वितर्का हिंसादयः कृतकारितानुमोदिता लोभक्रोधमोहपूर्वका मृदुमध्याधि -
मात्रा दुःखाज्ञानानन्तफला इति प्रतिपक्षभावनम् ॥३४॥

34. The obstructions to Yoga are killing, falsehood, etc., whether committed, caused, or approved; either through avarice, or anger, or

ignorance; whether slight, middling, or great; and they result in infinite ignorance and misery. This is (the method of) thinking the contrary.

If I tell a lie, or cause another to tell one, or approve of another doing so, it is equally sinful. If it is a very mild lie, still it is a lie. Every vicious thought will rebound, every thought of hatred which you may have thought, in a cave even, is stored up, and will one day come back to you with tremendous power in the form of some misery here. If you project hatred and jealousy, they will rebound on you with compound interest. No power can avert them; when once you have put them in motion, you will have to bear them. Remembering this will prevent you from doing wicked things.

अहिंसाप्रतिष्ठायां तत्सन्निधौ वैरत्यागः ॥३५॥

35. Non-killing being established, in his presence all enmities cease (in others).

If a man gets the ideal of non-injuring others, before him even animals which are by their nature ferocious will become peaceful. The tiger and the lamb will play together before that Yogi. When you have come to that state, then alone you will understand that you have become firmly established in non-injuring.

सत्यप्रतिष्ठायां क्रियाफलाश्रयत्वम् ॥३६॥

36. By the establishment of truthfulness the Yogi gets the power of attaining for himself and others the fruits of work without the works.

When this power of truth will be established with you, then even in dream you will never tell an untruth. You will be true in thought, word, and deed. Whatever you say will be truth. You may say to a man, "Be blessed," and that man will be blessed. If a man is diseased, and you say to him, "Be thou cured," he will be cured immediately.

अस्तेयप्रतिष्ठायां सर्वरत्नोपस्थानम् ॥३७॥

37. By the establishment of non-stealing all wealth comes to the Yogi.

The more you fly from nature, the more she follows you; and if you do not care for her at all, she becomes your slave.

ब्रह्मचर्यप्रतिष्ठायां वीर्यलाभः ॥३८॥

38. By the establishment of continence energy is gained.

The chaste brain has tremendous energy and gigantic will-power. Without chastity there can be no spiritual strength. Continence gives wonderful control over mankind. The spiritual leaders of men have been very continent, and this is what gave them power. Therefore the Yogi must be continent.

अपरिग्रहस्थैर्ये जन्मकथन्तासंबोधः ॥३९॥

39. When he is fixed in non-receiving, he gets the memory of past life.

When a man does not receive presents, he does not become beholden to others, but remains independent and free. His mind becomes pure. With every gift, he is likely to receive the evils of the giver. If he does not receive, the mind is purified, and the first power it gets is memory of past life. Then alone the Yogi becomes perfectly fixed in his ideal. He sees that he has been coming and going many times, so he becomes determined that this time he will be free, that he will no more come and go, and be the slave of Nature.

शौचात्स्वाङ्गजुगुप्सा परैरसंसर्गः ॥४०॥

40. Internal and external cleanliness being established, there arises disgust for one's own body, and non-intercourse with others.

When there is real purification of the body, external and internal, there arises neglect of the body, and the idea of keeping it nice vanishes. A face which others call most beautiful will appear to the Yogi as merely animal, if there is not intelligence behind it. What the world calls a very common face he regards as heavenly, if the spirit shines behind it. This thirst after body is the great bane of human life. So the first sign of the establishment of purity is that you do not care to think you are a body. It is only when purity comes that we get rid of the body idea.

सत्त्वशुद्धि-सौमनस्यैकाग्रचेन्द्रियजयात्मदर्शन-योग्यत्वानि च ॥४१॥

41. There also arises purification of the Sattva, cheerfulness of the mind, concentration, conquest of the organs, and fitness for the realisation of the Self.

By the practice of cleanliness, the Sattva material prevails, and the mind becomes concentrated and cheerful. The first sign that you are becoming religious is that you are becoming cheerful. When a man is gloomy, that may be dyspepsia, but it is not religion. A pleasurable feeling is the nature of the Sattva. Everything is pleasurable to the Sâttvika man, and when this comes, know that you are progressing in Yoga. All pain is caused by Tamas, so you must get rid of that; moroseness is one of the Exults of Tamas. The strong, the well knit, the young, the healthy, the daring alone are fit to be Yogis. To the Yogi everything is bliss, every human face that he sees brings cheerfulness to him. That is the sign of a virtuous man. Misery is caused by sin, and by no other cause. What business have you with clouded faces? It is terrible. If you have a clouded face, do not go out that day, shut yourself up in your room. What right have you to carry this disease out into the world ? When your mind has become controlled, you have control over the whole body; instead of being a slave to this machine, the machine is your slave. Instead of this machine being able to drag the soul down, it becomes its greatest helpmate.

सन्तोषादनुत्तमः सुखलाभः ॥४२॥

42. From contentment comes superlative happiness.

कायेन्द्रियसिद्धिरशुद्धिक्षयात्तपसः ॥४३॥

43. The result of mortification is bringing powers to the organs and the body, by destroying the impurity.

The results of mortification are seen immediately, sometimes by heightened powers of vision, hearing things at a distance, and so on.

स्वाध्यायादिष्टदेवतासम्प्रयोगः ॥४४॥

44. By the repetition of the Mantra comes the realisation of the intended deity.

The higher the beings that you want to get the harder is the practice.

समाधिसिद्धिरीश्वरप्रणिधानात् ॥४५॥

45. By sacrificing all to Ishvara comes Samadhi.

By resignation to the Lord, Samadhi becomes perfect.

स्थिरसुखमासनम् ॥४६॥

46. Posture is that which is firm and pleasant.

Now comes Asana, posture. Until you can get a firm seat you cannot practice the breathing and other exercises. Firmness of seat means that you do not feel the body at all. In the ordinary way, you will find that as soon as you sit for a few minutes all sorts of disturbances come into the body; but when you have got beyond the idea of a concrete body, you will lose all sense of the body. You will feel neither pleasure nor pain. And when you take your body up again, it will feel so rested. It is only perfect rest that you can give to the body. When you have succeeded in conquering the body and keeping it firm, your practice will remain firm, but while you are disturbed by the body, your nerves become disturbed, and you cannot concentrate the mind.

प्रयत्नशैथिल्यानन्तसमापत्तिभ्याम् ॥४७॥

47. By lessening the natural tendency (for restlessness) and meditating on the unlimited, posture becomes firm and pleasant.

We can make the seat firm by thinking of the infinite. We cannot think of the Absolute Infinite, but we can think of the infinite sky.

ततो द्वन्द्वानभिघातः ॥४८॥

48. Seat being conquered, the dualities do not obstruct.

The dualities, good and bad, heat and cold, and all the pairs of opposites, will not then disturb you.

तस्मिन् सति श्वासप्रश्वासयोर्गतिविच्छेदः प्राणायामः ॥४९॥

49. Controlling the motion of the exhalation and the inhalation follows after this.

When posture has been conquered, then the motion of the Prana is to be broken and controlled. Thus we come to Pranayama, the controlling of the vital forces of the body. Prana is not breath, though it is usually so translated. It is the sum total of the cosmic energy. It is the energy that is in each body, and its most apparent manifestation is the motion of the lungs. This motion is caused by Prana drawing in the breath, and it is what we seek to control in Pranayama. We begin by controlling the breath, as the easiest way of getting control of the Prana.

बाह्याभ्यन्तरस्तम्भवृत्तिः देशकालसंख्याभिः परिदृष्टो दीर्घसूक्ष्मः ॥५०॥

50. Its modifications are either external or internal, or motionless, regulated by place, terns, and number, either long or short.

The three sorts of motion of Pranayama are, one by which we draw the breath in, another by which we throw it out, and the third action is when the breath is held in the lungs, or stopped from entering the lungs. These, again, are varied by place and time. By place is meant that the Prana is held to some particular part of the body. By time is meant how long the Prana should be confined to a certain place, and so we are told how many seconds to keep one motion, and how many seconds to keep another. The result of this Pranayama is Udghâta, awakening the Kundalini.

बाह्याभ्यन्तरविषयाक्षेपी चतुर्थः ॥५१॥

51. The fourth is restraining the Prana by reflecting on external or internal object.

This is the fourth sort of Pranayama, in which the Kumbhaka is brought about by long practice attended with reflection, which is absent in the other three.

ततः क्षीयते प्रकाशावरणम् ॥५२॥

52. From that, the covering to the light of the Chitta is attenuated.

The Chitta has, by its own nature, all knowledge. It is made of Sattva particles, but is covered by Rajas and Tamas particles, and by Pranayama this covering is removed.

धारणासु च योग्यता मनसः ॥५३॥

53. The mind becomes fit for Dharana.

After this covering has been removed, we are able to concentrate the mind.

स्वस्वविषयासम्प्रयोगे चित्तस्वरूपानुकार इवेन्द्रियाणां प्रत्याहारः ॥५४॥

54. The drawing in of the organs is by their giving up their own objects and taking the form of the mind-stuff, as it were.

The organs are separate states of the mind-stuff. I see a book; the form is not in the book, it is in the mind. Something is outside which calls that form up. The real form is in the Chitta. The organs identify themselves with, and take the forms of, whatever comes to them. If you can restrain the mind-stuff from taking these forms, the mind will remain calm. This is called Pratyahara.

ततः परमा वश्यतेन्द्रियाणाम् ॥५५॥

55. Thence arises supreme control of the organs.

When the Yogi has succeeded in preventing the organs from taking the forms of external objects, and in making them remain one with the mind-stuff, then comes perfect control of the organs. When the organs are perfectly under control, every muscle and nerve will be under control, because the organs are the centres of all the sensations, and of all actions. These organs are divided into organs of work and organs of sensation. When the organs are controlled, the Yogi can control all feeling and doing; the whole of the body comes under his control. Then alone one begins to feel joy in being born; then one can truthfully say, "Blessed am I that I was born." When that control of the organs is obtained, we feel how wonderful this body really is.

Chapter III.
Powers

We have now come to the chapter in which the Yoga powers are described.'

देशबन्धश्चित्तस्य धारणा ॥१॥

1. Dhâranâ is holding the mind on to some particular object.

Dharana (concentration) is when the mind holds on to some object, either in the body, or outside the body, and keeps itself in that state.

तत्र प्रत्ययैकतानता ध्यानम् ॥२॥

2. An unbroken flow of knowledge in that object is Dhyâna.

The mind tries to think of one object, to hold itself to one particular spot, as the top of the head, the heart, etc., and if the mind succeeds in receiving the sensations only through that part of the body, and through no other part, that would be Dharana, and when the mind succeeds in keeping itself in that state for some time, it is called Dhyana (mediation).

तदेवार्थमात्रनिर्भासं स्वरूपशून्यमिव समाधिः ॥३॥

3. When that, giving up all forms, reflects only the meaning, it is Samâdhi.

That comes when in meditation the form or the external part is given up. Suppose I were meditating on a book, and that I have gradually succeeded in concentrating the mind on it, and perceiving only the internal sensations, the meaning, unexpressed in any form — that state of Dhyana is called Samadhi.

त्रैयमेकत्र संयमः ॥४॥

4. (These) three (when practiced) in regard to one object is Samyama.

When a man can direct his mind to any particular object and fix it there, and then keep it there for a long time, separating the object from the internal part, this is Samyama; or Dharana, Dhyana, and Samadhi, one following the other, and making one. The form of the thing has vanished, and only its meaning remains in the mind.

तज्जयात् प्रज्ञाऽऽलोकः ॥५॥

5. By the conquest of that comes light of knowledge.

When one has succeeded in making this Samyama, all powers come under his control. This is the great instrument of the Yogi. The objects of knowledge are infinite, and they are divided into the gross, grosser, grossest and the fine, finer, finest and so on. This Samyama should be first applied to gross things, and when you begin to get knowledge of this gross, slowly, by stages, it should be brought to finer things.

तस्य भूमिषु विनियोगः ॥६॥

6. That should be employed in stages.

This is a note of warning not to attempt to go too fast.

त्रयमन्तरङ्गं पूर्वेभ्यः ॥७॥

7. These three are more internal than those that precede.

Before these we had the Pratyâhâra, the Prânâyâma, the Âsana, the Yama and Niyama; they are external parts of the three — Dharana, Dhyana and Samadhi. When a man has attained to them, he may attain to omniscience and omnipotence, but that would not be salvation. These three would; not make the mind Nirvikalpa, changeless, but would leave the seeds for getting bodies again. Only when the seeds are, as the Yogi says, "fried", do they lose the possibility of producing further plants. These powers cannot fry the seed.

तदपि बहिरङ्गं निर्बीजस्य ॥८॥

8. But even they are external to the seedless (Samadhi).

Compared with that seedless Samadhi, therefore, even these are external. We have not yet reached the real Samadhi, the highest, but a lower stage, in which this universe still exists as we see it, and in which are all these powers.

व्युत्थान निरोधसंस्कारयोरभिभव-प्रादुर्भावौ निरोधक्षणचित्तान्वयो निरोध-परिणामः ॥९॥

9. By the suppression of the disturbed impressions of the mind, and by the rise of impressions of control, the mind, which persists in that moment of control, is said to attain the controlling modifications.

That is to say, in this first state of Samadhi the modifications of the mind have been controlled, but not perfectly, because if they were, there would be no modifications. If there is a modification which impels the mind to rush out through the senses, and the Yogi tries to control it, that very control itself will be a modification. One wave will be checked by another wave, so it will not be real Samadhi in which all the waves subside, as control itself will be a wave. Yet this lower Samadhi is very much nearer to the higher Samadhi than when the mind comes bubbling out.

तस्य प्रशान्तवाहिता संस्कारात् ॥१०॥

10. Its flow becomes steady by habit.

The flow of this continuous control of the mind becomes steady when practiced day after day, and the mind obtains the faculty of constant concentration.

सर्वार्थतैकाग्रतयोः क्षयोदयौ चित्तस्य समाधि-परिणामः ॥११॥

11. Taking in all sorts of objects, and concentrating upon one object, these two powers being destroyed and manifested respectively, the Chitta gets the modification called Samadhi.

The mind takes up various objects, runs into all sorts of things. That is the lower state. There is a higher state of the mind, when it takes up one object and excludes all others, of which Samadhi is the result.

शान्तोदितौ तुल्यप्रत्ययौ चित्तस्यैकाग्रता – परिणामः ॥१२॥

12. The one-pointedness of the Chitta is when the impression that is past and that which is present are similar.

How are we to know that the mind has become concentrated? Because the idea of time will vanish. The more time passes unnoticed the more concentrated we are. In common life we see that when we are interested in a book we do not note the time at all, and when we leave the book, we are often surprised to find how many hours have passed. All time will have the tendency to come and stand in the one present. So the definition is given: When the past and present come and stand in one, the mind is said to be concentrated.

एतेन भूतेन्द्रियेषु धर्मलक्षणावस्थापरिणामा व्याख्याताः ॥१३॥

13. By this is explained the threefold transformation of form, time and state, in fine or gross matter and in the organs.

By the threefold changes in the mind-stuff as to form, time and state are explained the corresponding changes in gross and subtle matter and in the organs. Suppose there is a lump of gold. It is transformed into a bracelet and again into an ear-ring. These are changes as to form. The same phenomena looked at from the standpoint of time give us change as to time. Again, the bracelet or the ear-ring may be bright or dull, thick or thin, and so on. This is change as to state. Now referring to the aphorisms 9, 11 and 12, the mind-stuff is changing into Vrittis — this is change as to form. That it passes through past, present and future moments of time is change as to time. That the impressions vary as to intensity within one particular period, say, present, is change as to state. The concentrations taught in the preceding aphorisms were to give the Yogi a voluntary control over the transformations of his mind-stuff, which alone will enable him to make the Samyama named in III. 4.

शान्तोदिताव्यपदेश्यधर्मानुपाती धर्मी ॥१४॥

14. That which is acted upon by transformations, either past, present, or yet to be manifested is the qualified.

That is to say, the qualified is the substance which is being acted upon by time and by the Samskâras, and getting changed and being manifested always.

क्रमान्यत्वं परिणामान्यत्वे हेतुः ॥१५॥

15. The succession of changes is the cause of manifold evolution.

परिणामत्रयसंयमादतीतानागतज्ञानम् ॥१६॥

16. By making Samyama on the three sorts of changes comes the knowledge of past and future.

We must not lose sight of the first definition of Samyama. When the mind has attained to that state when it identifies itself with the internal impression of the object, leaving the external, and when, by long practice, that is retained by the mind and the mind can get into that state in a moment, that is Samyama. If a man in that state wants to know the past and future, he has to make a Samyama on the changes in the Samskaras (III. 13). Some are working now at present, some have worked out, and some are waiting to work. So by making a Samyama on these he knows the past and future.

शब्दार्थप्रत्ययानामितरेतराध्यासात्सङ्करस्तत्प्रविभागसंयमात् सर्वभूतरुतज्ञानम् ॥१७॥

17. By making Samyama on word, meaning and knowledge, which are ordinarily confused, comes the knowledge of all animal sounds.

The word represents the external cause, the meaning represents the internal vibration that travels to the brain through the channels of the Indriyas, conveying the external impression to the mind, and knowledge represents the reaction of the mind, with which comes perception. These three, confused, make our sense-objects. Suppose I hear a word; there is first the external vibration, next the internal sensation carried to the mind by the organ of hearing, then the mind reacts, and I know the word. The word I know is a mixture of the three — vibration, sensation, and reaction. Ordinarily these three are inseparable; but by practice the Yogi can separate them. When a man has attained to this, if he makes a Samyama on any sound, he understands the meaning which that sound was intended to express, whether it was made by man or be any other animal.

संस्कारसाक्षात्करणात् पूर्वजातिज्ञानम् ॥१८॥

18. By perceiving the impressions, (comes) the knowledge of past life.

Each experience that we have, comes in the form of a wave in the Chitta, and this subsides and becomes finer and finer, but is never lost. It remains there in minute form, and if we can bring this wave up again, it becomes memory. So, if the Yogi can make a Samyama on these past impressions in the mind, he will begin to remember all his past lives.

प्रत्ययस्य परचित्तज्ञानम् ॥१९॥

19. By making Samyama on the signs in another's body, knowledge of his mind comes.

Each man has particular signs on his body, which differentiate him from others; when the Yogi makes a Samyama on these signs he knows the nature of the mind of that person.

न च तत् सालम्बनं तस्याविषयीभूतत्वात् ॥२०॥

20. But not its contents, that not being the object of the Samyama.

He would not know the contents of the mind by making a Samyama on the body. There would be required a twofold Samyama, first on the signs in the body, and then on the mind itself. The Yogi would then know everything that is in that mind.

कायरूपसंयमात्तद्ग्राह्यशक्ति स्तम्भे चक्षुः प्रकाशासंयोगेऽन्तर्धानम् ॥२१॥

21. By making Samyama on the form of the body, the perceptibility of the form being obstructed and the power of manifestation in the eye being separated, the Yogi's body becomes unseen.

A Yogi standing in the midst of this room can apparently vanish. He does not really vanish, but he will not be seen by anyone. The form and the body are, as it were, separated. You must remember that this can only be done when the Yogi has attained to that power of concentration when form and the thing formed have been separated. Then he makes a Samyama on that, and the power to perceive forms is obstructed, because the power of perceiving forms comes from the junction of form and the thing formed.

एतेन शब्दाद्यन्तर्धानमुक्तम् ॥२२॥

22. By this the disappearance or concealment of words which are being spoken and such other things are also explained.

सोपक्रमं निरुपक्रमं च कर्म तत्संयमादपरान्तज्ञानमरिष्टेभ्यो वा ॥२३॥

23. Karma is of two kinds — soon to be fructified and late to be fructified. By making Samyana on these, or by the signs called Arishta, portents, the Yogis know the exact time of separation from their bodies.

When a Yogi makes a Samyama on his own Karma, upon those impressions in his mind which are now working, and those which are just waiting to work, he knows exactly by those that are waiting when his body will fall. He knows when he will die, at what hour, even at what minute. The Hindus think very much of that knowledge or consciousness of the nearness of death, because it is taught in the Gita that the thoughts at the moment of departure are great powers in determining the next life.

मैत्र्यादिषु बलानि ॥२४॥

24. By making Samyama on friendship, mercy, etc. (I. 33), the Yogi excels in the respective qualities.

बलेषु हस्तिबलादीनि ॥२५॥

25. By making Samyama on the strength of the elephant and others, their respective strength comes to the Yogi.

When a Yogi has attained to this Samyama and wants strength, he makes a Samyama on the strength of the elephant and gets it. Infinite energy is at the disposal of everyone if he only knows how to get it. The Yogi has discovered the science of getting it.

प्रवृत्त्यालोकन्यासात् सूक्ष्म-व्यवहित-विप्रकृष्टज्ञानम् ॥२६॥

26. By making Samyama on the Effulgent Light (I. 36), comes the knowledge of the fine, the obstructed, and the remote.

When the Yogi makes Samyama on that Effulgent Light in the heart, he sees things which are very remote, things, for instance, that are happening in a distant place, and which are obstructed by mountain barriers, and also things which are very fine.

भुवनज्ञानं सूर्ये संयमात् ॥२७॥

27. By making Samyama on the sun, (comes) the knowledge of the world.

चन्द्रे ताराव्यूहज्ञानम् ॥२८॥

28. On the moon, (comes) the knowledge of the cluster of stars.

ध्रुवे तद्गतिज्ञानम् ॥२९॥

29. On the pole-star, (comes) the knowledge of the motions of the stars.

नाभिचक्रे कायव्यूहज्ञानम् ॥३०॥

30. On the navel circle, (comes) the knowledge of the constitution of the body.

कण्ठकूपे क्षुत्पिपासानिवृत्तिः ॥३१॥

31. On the hollow of the throat, (comes) cessation of hunger.

When a man is very hungry, if he can make Samyama on the hollow of the throat, hunger ceases.

कूर्मनाड्यां स्थैर्यम् ॥३२॥

32. On the nerve called Kurma, (comes) fixity of the body.

When he is practising, the body is not disturbed.

मूर्धज्योतिषि सिद्धदर्शनम् ॥३३॥

33. On the light emanating from the top of the head, sight of the Siddhas.

The Siddhas are beings who are a little above ghosts. When the Yogi concentrates his mind on the top of his head, he will see these Siddhas. The word Siddha does not refer to those men who have become free — a sense in which it is often used.

प्रातिभाद्वा सर्वम् ॥३४॥

34. Or by the power of Prâtibha, all knowledge.

All these can come without any Samyama to the man who has the power of Pratibha (spontaneous enlightenment from purity). When a man has risen to a high state of Pratibha, he has that great light. All things are apparent to him. Everything comes to him naturally without making Samyama.

हृदये चित्त-संवित् ॥३५॥

35. In the heart, knowledge of minds.

सत्त्वपुरुषयोरत्यन्तासंकीर्णयोः प्रत्ययाविशेषाद् भोगः परार्थत्वात् स्वार्थसंयमात् पुरुषज्ञानम् ॥३६॥

36. Enjoyment comes from the non-discrimination of the soul and Sattva which are totally different because the latter's actions are for another. Samyama on the self-centred one gives knowledge of the Purusha.

All action of Sattva, a modification of Prakriti characterised by light and happiness, is for the soul. When Sattva is free from egoism and illuminated with the pure intelligence of Purusha, it is called the self-centred one, because in that state it becomes independent of all relations.

ततः प्रातिभश्रावणवेदनादर्शास्वादवार्ता जायन्ते ॥३७॥

37. From that arises the knowledge belonging to Pratibha and (supernatural) hearing, touching, seeing, tasting and smelling.

ते समाधावुपसर्गा व्युत्थाने सिद्धयः ॥३८॥

38. These are obstacles to Samadhi; but they are powers in the worldly state.

To the Yogi knowledge of the enjoyments of the world comes by the junction of the Purusha and the mind. If he wants to make Samyama on the knowledge that they are two different things, nature and soul, he gets knowledge of the Purusha. From that arises discrimination. When he has got that discrimination, he gets the Pratibha, the light of supreme genius. These powers, however, are obstructions to the attainment of the highest goal, the knowledge of the pure Self, and freedom. These are, as it were, to be met in the way; and if the Yogi rejects them, he attains the highest. If he is tempted to acquire these, his further progress is barred.

बन्धकारणशैथिल्यत् प्रचारसंवेदनाच्च चित्तस्य परशरीरावेशः ॥३९॥

39. When the cause of bondage of the Chitta has become loosened, the Yogi, by his knowledge of its channels of activity (the nerves), enters another's body.

The Yogi can enter a dead body and make it get up and move, even while he himself is working in another body. Or he can enter a living body and hold that man's mind and organs in check, and for the time being act through the body of that man. That is done by the Yogi coming to this discrimination of Purusha and nature. If he wants to enter another's body, he makes a Samyama on that body and enters it, because, not only is his soul omnipresent, but his mind also, as the Yogi teaches. It is one bit of the universal mind. Now, however, it can only work; through the nerve currents in this body, but when the Yogi has loosened himself from these nerve currents, he can work through other things.

उदानजयाज्जलपङ्ककण्टकादिष्वसङ्ग उत्क्रान्तिश्च ॥४०॥

40. By conquering the current called Udâna the Yogi does not sink in water or in swamps, he can walk on thorns etc., and can, die at will.

Udana is the name of the nerve current that governs the lungs and all the upper parts of the body, and when he is master of it, he becomes light in weight. He does not sink in water; he can walk on thorns and sword blades, and stand in fire, and can depart this life whenever he likes.

समानजयात् प्रज्वलनम् ॥४१॥

41. By the conquest of the current Samâna he is surrounded by a blaze of light.

Whenever he likes, light flashes from his body.

श्रोत्राकाशयोः सम्बन्धसंयमाद्दिव्यं श्रोत्रम् ॥४२॥

42. By making Samyama on the relation between the ear and the Akâsha comes divine hearing.

There is the Akasha, the ether, and the instrument, the ear. By making Samyama on them the Yogi gets supernormal hearing; he hears everything. Anything spoken or sounded miles away he can hear.

कायाकाशयोः सम्बन्धसंयमाल्लघुतूलसमापत्तेश्चाकाशगमनम् ॥४३॥

43. By making Samyama on the relation between the Akasha and the body and becoming light as cotton-wool etc., through meditation on them, the yogi goes through the skies.

This Akasha is the material of this body; it is only Akasha in a certain form that has become the body. If the Yogi makes a Sanyama on this Akasha material of his body, it acquires the lightness of Akasha, and he can go anywhere through the air. So in the other case also.

बहिरकल्पिता वृत्तिर्महाविदेहा ततः प्रकाशावरणक्षयः ॥४४॥

44. By making Samyama on the "real modifications" of the mind, outside of the body, called great disembodiedness, comes disappearance of the covering to light.

The mind in its foolishness thinks that it is working in this body. Why should I be bound by one system of nerves, and put the Ego only in one body, if the mind is omnipresent? There is no reason why I should. The Yogi wants to feel the Ego wherever he likes. The mental waves which arise in the absence of egoism in the body are called "real modifications" or "great disembodiedness". When he has succeeded in making Samyama on these modifications, all covering to light goes away, and all darkness and ignorance vanish. Everything appears to him to be full of knowledge.

स्थूल-स्वरूप-सूक्ष्मान्वयार्थवत्त्वसंयमाद्भूतजयः ॥४५॥

45. By making Samyama on the gross and fine forms of the elements, their essential traits, the inherence of the Gunas in them and on their contributing to the experience of the soul, comes mastery of the elements.

The Yogi makes Samyama on the elements, first on the gross, and then on the finer states. This Samyama is taken up more by a sect of the Buddhists. They take a lump of clay and make Samyama on that, and gradually they begin to see the fine materials of which it is composed, and when they have known all the fine materials in it, they get power over that element. So with all the elements. The Yogi can conquer them all.

ततोऽणिमादिप्रादुर्भावः कायसम्पत्तद्धर्मानभिघातश्च ॥४६॥

46. From that comes minuteness and the rest of the powers, "glorification of the body," and indestructibleness of the bodily qualities.

This means that the Yogi has attained the eight powers. He can make himself as minute as a particle, or as huge as a mountain, as heavy as the earth, or as light as the air; he can reach anything he likes, he can rule everything he wants, he can conquer everything he wants, and so on. A lion will sit at his feet like a lamb, and all his desires will be fulfilled at will.

रूप-लावण्य-बल-वज्रसंहननत्वानि कायसम्पत् ॥४७॥

47. The "glorification of the body" is beauty, complexion, strength, adamantine hardness.

The body becomes indestructible. Nothing can injure it. Nothing can destroy it until the Yogi wishes. "Breaking the rod of time he lives in this universe with his body." In the Vedas it is written that for that man there is no more disease, death or pain.

ग्रहण-स्वरूपास्मितान्वयार्थवत्त्वसंयमादिन्द्रियजयः ॥४८॥

48. By making Samyama on the objectivity and power of illumination of the organs, on egoism, the inherence of the Gunas in them and on their contributing to the experience of the soul, comes the conquest of the organs.

In the perception of external objects the organs leave their place in the mind and go towards the object; this is followed by knowledge. Egoism also is present in the act. When the Yogi makes Samyama on these and the other two by gradation, he conquers the organs. Take up anything that you see or feel, a book for instance; first concentrate the mind on it, then on the knowledge that is in the form of a book, and then on the Ego that sees the book, and so on. By that practice all the organs will be conquered.

ततो मनोजवित्वं विकरणभावः प्रधानजयश्च ॥४९॥

49. From that comes to the body the power of rapid movement like the mind, power of the organs independently of the body, and conquest of nature.

Just as by the conquest of the elements comes glorified body, so from the conquest of the organs will come the above-mentioned powers.

सत्त्वपुरुषान्यताख्यातिमात्रस्य सर्वभावाधिष्ठातृत्वं सर्वज्ञातृत्वश्च

50. By making Samyama on the discrimination between the Sattva and the Purusha come omnipotence and omniscience.

When nature has been conquered, and the difference between the Purusha and nature realised — that the Purusha is indestructible, pure and perfect — then come omnipotence and omniscience.

तद्वैराग्यादपि दोषबीजक्षये कैवल्यम् ॥५१॥

51. By giving up even these powers comes the destruction of the very seed of evil, which leads to Kaivalya.

He attains aloneness, independence, and becomes free. When one gives up even the ideas of omnipotence and omniscience, there comes entire rejection of enjoyment, of the temptations from celestial beings. When the Yogi has seen all these wonderful powers, and rejected them, he reaches the goal. What are all these powers? Simply manifestations. They are no better than dreams. Even omnipotence is a dream. It depends on the mind. So long as there is a mind it can be understood, but the goal is beyond even the mind.

स्थान्युपनिमन्त्रणे सङ्गस्मयाकरणं पुनरनिष्टप्रसङ्गात् ॥५२॥

52. The Yogi should not feel allured or flattered by the overtures of celestial beings for fear of evil again.

There are other dangers too; gods and other beings come to tempt the Yogi. They do not want anyone to be perfectly free. They are jealous, just as we are, and worse than us sometimes. They are very much afraid of losing their places. Those Yogis who do not reach perfection die and become gods; leaving the direct road they go into one of the side streets, and get these powers. Then, again, they have to be born. But he who is strong enough to withstand these temptations and go straight to the goal, becomes free.

क्षण – तत्क्रमयोः संयमाद्विवेकजं ज्ञानम् ॥५३॥

53. By making Samyama on a particle of time and its precession and succession comes discrimination.

How are we to avoid all these things, these Devas, and heavens, and powers? By discrimination, by knowing good from evil. Therefore a Samyama is given by which the power of discrimination can be strengthened. This by making a Samyama on a particle of time, and the time preceding and following it.

जाति – लक्षण – देशैरन्यताऽनवच्छेदात्तुल्ययोस्ततः प्रतिपत्तिः ॥५४॥

54. Those things which cannot be differentiated by species, sign, and place, even they will be discriminated by the above Samyama.

The misery that we suffer comes from ignorance, from non-discrimination between the real and the unreal. We all take the bad for the good, the dream for the reality. Soul is the only reality, and we have forgotten it. Body is an unreal dream, and we think we are all bodies. This non-discrimination is the cause of misery. It is caused by ignorance. When discrimination comes, it brings strength, and then alone can we avoid all these various ideas of body, heavens, and gods. This ignorance arises through differentiating by species, sign, and place. For instance, take a cow. The cow is differentiated from the dog by species. Even with the cows alone how do we make the distinction between one cow and another? By signs. If two objects are exactly similar, they can be distinguished if they are in different places. When objects are so mixed up that even these differential will not help us, the power of discrimination acquired by the above-mentioned practice will give us the ability to distinguish them. The highest philosophy of the Yogi is based upon this fact, that the Purusha is pure and perfect, and is the only "simple" that exists in this universe. The body and mind are compounds, and yet we are ever identifying ourselves with them This is the great mistake that the distinction has been lost. When this power of discrimination has been attained, man sees that everything in this world, mental and physical, is a compound, and, as such, cannot be the Purusha.

तारकं सर्वविषयं सर्वथाविषयमक्रमश्चेति विवेकजं ज्ञानम् ॥५५॥

55. The saving knowledge is that knowledge of discrimination which simultaneously covers all objects, in all their variations.

Saving, because the knowledge takes the Yogi across the ocean of birth and death. The whole of Prakriti in all its states, subtle and gross, is within the grasp of this knowledge. There is no succession in perception by this knowledge; it takes in all things simultaneously, at a glance.

सत्त्वपुरूषयोः शुद्धिसाम्ये कैवल्यमिति ॥५६॥

56. By the similarity of purity between the Sattva and the Purusha comes Kaivalya.

When the soul realises that it depends on nothing in the universe, from gods to the lowest atom, that is called Kaivalya (isolation) and perfection. It is attained when this mixture of purity and impurity called Sattva (intellect) has been made as pure as the Purusha itself; then the Sattva reflects only the unqualified essence of purity, which is the Purusha.

Chapter IV.
Independence

जन्मौषधि – मन्त्र – तपः समाधिजाः सिद्धयः ॥१॥

1. The Siddhis (powers) are attained by birth, chemical means, power of words, mortification, or concentration.

Sometimes a man is born with the Siddhis, powers, of course, those he had earned in his previous incarnation. This time he is born, as it were, to enjoy the fruits of them. It is said of Kapila, the great father of the Sânkhya philosophy, that he was a born Siddha, which means literally a man who has attained to success.

The Yogis claim that these powers can be gained by chemical means. All of you know that chemistry originally began as alchemy; men went in search of the philosopher's stone and elixirs of life, and so forth. In India there was a sect called the Râsâyanas. Their idea was that ideality, knowledge, spirituality, and religion were all very right, but that the body was the only instrument by which to attain to all these. If the body came to an end every now and again, it would take so much more time to attain to the goal. For instance, a man wants to practice Yoga, or wants to become spiritual. Before he has advanced very far he dies. Then he takes another body and begins again, then dies, and so on. In this way much time will be lost in dying and being born again. If the body could be made strong and perfect, so that it would get rid of birth and death, we should have so much more time to become spiritual. So these Rasayanas say, first make the body very strong. They claim that this body can be made immortal. Their idea is that if the mind manufactures the body, and if it be true that each mind is only one outlet to the infinite energy, there should be no limit to each outlet getting any amount of power from outside. Why is it impossible to keep our bodies all the time? We have to manufacture all the bodies that we ever have. As soon as this body dies, we shall have to manufacture another. If we can do that, why cannot we do it just here and now, without getting out of the present body? The theory is perfectly correct. If it its possible that we live after death, and make other bodies, why is it impossible that we should have the power of making bodies here, without entirely dissolving this body, simply changing it continually? They also thought that in mercury and in sulphur was hidden the most wonderful power, and that by certain preparations of these a man could keep the body as long as he liked. Others believed that certain drugs could bring powers, such as flying through the air. Many of the most wonderful medicines of the present day we owe to the Rasayanas, notably the use of metals in medicine. Certain sects of Yogis claim that many of their principal teachers are still living in their old bodies. Patanjali, the great authority on Yoga, does not deny this.

The power of words. There are certain sacred words called Mantras, which have power, when repeated under proper conditions, produce these extraordinary powers. We are living in the midst of such a mass of miracles, day and night, that we do not think anything of them. There is no limit to man's power, the power of words and the power of mind.

Mortification. You find that in every religion mortification and asceticisms have been practised. In these religious conceptions the Hindus always go to the extremes. You will find men with their hands up all their lives, until their hands wither and die. Men keep standing, day and night, until their feet swell, and if they live, the legs become so stiff in this position that they can no more bend them, but have to stand all their lives. I once saw a man who had kept his hands raised in this way, and I asked him how it felt when he did it first. He said it was awful torture. It was such torture that he had to go to a river and put himself in water, and that allayed the pain for a little while. After a month he did not suffer much. Through such practices powers (Siddhis) can be attained.

Concentration. Concentration is Samâdhi, and that is Yoga proper; that is the principal theme of this science, and it is the highest means. The preceding ones are only secondary, and we cannot attain to the highest through them. Samadhi is the means through which we can gain anything and everything, mental, moral, or spiritual.

जात्यन्तरपरिणामः प्रकृत्यापूरात् ॥२॥

2. The change into another species is by the filling in of nature.

Patanjali has advanced the proposition that these powers come by birth, sometimes by chemical means, or through mortification. He also admits that this body can be kept for any length of time. Now he goes on to state what is the cause of the change of the body into another species. He says this is done by the filling in of nature, which he explains in the next aphorism.

निमित्तमप्रयोजकं प्रकृतीनां वरणभेदस्तु ततः क्षेत्रिकवत् ॥३॥

3. Good and bad deeds are not the direct causes in the transformations of nature, but they act as breakers of obstacles to the evolutions of nature: as a farmer breaks the obstacles to the course of water, which then runs down by its own nature.

The water for irrigation of fields is already in the canal, only shut in by gates. The farmer opens these gates, and the water flows in by itself, by the law of gravitation. So all progress and power are already in every man; perfection is man's nature, only it is barred in and prevented from taking its proper course. If anyone can take the bar off, in rushes nature. Then the man attains the powers which are his already. Those we call wicked become saints, as soon as the bar is broken and nature rushes in. It is nature that is driving us towards perfection, and eventually she will bring everyone there. All these practices and struggles to become religious are only negative work, to take off the bars, and open the doors to that perfection which is our birthright, our nature.

Today the evolution theory of the ancient Yogis will be better understood in the light of modern research. And yet the theory of the Yogis is a better explanation. The two causes of evolution advanced by the moderns, viz sexual selection and survival of the fittest, are inadequate. Suppose human knowledge to have advanced so much as to eliminate competition, both from the function of acquiring physical sustenance and of acquiring a mate. Then, according to the moderns, human progress will stop and the race will die. The result of this theory is to furnish every oppressor with an argument to calm the qualms of conscience. Men are not lacking, who, posing as philosophers, want to kill out all wicked and incompetent persons (they are, of course, the only judges of competency) and thus preserve the human race! But the great ancient evolutionist, Patanjali, declares that the true secret of evolution is the manifestation of the perfection which is already in every being; that this perfection has been barred and the infinite tide behind is struggling to express itself. These struggles and competitions are but the results of our ignorance, because we do not know the proper way to unlock the gate and let the water in. This infinite tide behind must express itself; it is the cause of all manifestation. Competitions for life or sex-gratification are only momentary, unnecessary, extraneous effects, caused by ignorance. Even when all competition has ceased, this perfect nature behind will make us go forward until everyone has become perfect. Therefore there is no reason to believe that competition is necessary to progress. In the animal the man was suppressed, but as soon as the door was opened, out rushed man. So in man there is the potential god, kept in by the locks and bars of ignorance. When knowledge breaks these bars, the god becomes manifest.

निर्माणचित्तान्यस्मितामात्रात् ॥४॥

4. From egoism alone proceed the created minds.

The theory of Karma is that we suffer for our good or bad deeds, and the whole scope of philosophy is to reach the glory of man. All the scriptures sing the glory of man, of the soul, and then, in the same breath, they preach Karma. A good deed brings such a result, and a bad deed such another, but if the soul can be acted upon by a good or a bad deed, the soul amounts to nothing. Bad deeds put a bar to the manifestation of the nature of the Purusha; good deeds take the obstacles off, and the glory of the Purusha becomes manifest. The Purusha itself is never changed. Whatever you do never destroys your own glory, your own nature, because the soul cannot be acted upon by anything, only a veil is spread before it, hiding its perfection.

With a view to exhausting their Karma quickly, Yogis create Kâya-vyuha, or groups of bodies, in which to work it out. For all these bodies they create minds from egoism. These are called "created minds", in contradistinction to their original minds.

प्रवृत्तिभेदे प्रयोजकं चित्तमेकमनेकेषाम् ॥५॥

5. Though the activities of the different created minds are various, the one original mind is the controller of them all.

These different minds, which act in these different bodies are called made-minds, and the bodies, made-bodies; that is, manufactured bodies and minds. Matter and mind are like two inexhaustible storehouses. When you become a Yogi, you learn the secret of their control. It was yours all the time, but you had forgotten it. When you become a Yogi, you recollect it. Then you can do anything with it, manipulate it in every way you like. The material out of which a manufactured mind is created is the very same material which is used for the macrocosm. It is not that mind is one thing and matter another, they are different aspects of the same thing. Asmitâ, egoism, is the material, the fine state of existence out of which these made-minds and made-bodies of the Yogi are manufactured. Therefore, when the Yogi has found the secret of these energies of nature, he can manufacture any number of bodies or minds out of the substance known as egoism.

तत्र ध्यानजमनाशयम् ॥६॥

6. Among the various Chittas, that which is attained by Samadhi is desireless.

Among all the various minds that we see in various men, only that mind which has attained to Samadhi, perfect concentration, is the highest. A man who has attained certain powers through medicines, or through words, or through mortifications, still has desires, but that man who has attained to Samadhi through concentration is alone free from all desires.

कर्माशुक्लाकृष्णं योगिनस्त्रिविधमितरेषाम् ॥७॥

7. Works are neither black nor white for the Yogis; for others they are threefold — black, white, and mixed.

When the Yogi has attained perfection, his actions, and the Karma produced by those actions, do not bind him, because he did not desire them. He just works on; he works to do good, and he does good, but does not care for the result, and it will not come to him. But, for ordinary men, who have not attained to the highest state, works are of three kinds, black (evil actions), white (good actions), and mixed.

ततस्तद्विपाकानुगुणानामेवाभिव्यक्तिर्वासनानाम् ॥८॥

8. From these threefold works are manifested in each state only those desires (which are) fitting to that state alone. (The others are held in abeyance for the time being.)

Suppose I have made the three kinds of Karma, good, bad, and mixed, and suppose I die and become a god in heaven. The desires in a god body are not the same as the desires in a human body; the god body neither eats nor drinks. What becomes of my past unworked Karmas which produce as their effect the desire to eat and drink? Where would these Karmas go when I become a god? The answer is that desires can only manifest themselves in proper environments. Only those desires will come out for which the environment is fitted; the rest will remain stored up. In this life we have many godly desires, many human desires, many animal desires. If I take a god body, only the good desires will come up, because for them the environments are suitable. And if I take an animal body, only the animal desires will come up, and the good desires will wait. What does this show? That by means of environment we can check these desires. Only that Karma which is suited to and fitted for the environments will come out. This shows that the power of environment is the great check to control even Karma itself.

जाति – देश – काल – व्यवहितानामप्यानन्तर्यं स्मृतिसंस्कारयोरेकरूपत्वात् ॥९॥

9. There is consecutiveness in desires, even though separated by species, space, and time, there being identification of memory and impressions.

Experiences becoming fine become impressions; impressions revivified become memory. The word memory here includes unconscious co-ordination of past experiences, reduced to impressions, with present conscious action. In each body, the group of impressions acquired in a similar body only becomes the cause of action in that body. The experiences of a dissimilar body are held in abeyance. Each body acts as if it were a descendant of a series of bodies of that species only; thus, consecutiveness of desires is not to be broken.

तासामनादित्वं चाशिषो नित्यत्वात् ॥१०॥

10. Thirst for happiness being eternal, desires are without beginning.

All experience is preceded by desire for happiness. There was no beginning of experience, as each fresh experience is built upon the tendency generated by past experience; therefore desire is without beginning.

हेतुफलाश्रयालम्बनैः संगृहीतत्वादेषामभावे तदभावः ॥११॥

11. Being held together by cause, effect, support, and objects, in the absence of these is its absence.

Desires are held together by cause and effect; (The causes are the "pain-bearing obstructions" (II. 3) and actions (IV. 7), and the effects are "species, life, and experience of pleasure and pain" (II. 13). — Ed.) if a desire has been raised, it does not die without producing its effect. Then, again, the mind-stuff is the great storehouse, the support of all past desires reduced to Samskara form; until they have worked themselves out, they will not die. Moreover, so long as the senses receive the external objects, fresh desires will arise. If it be possible to get rid of the cause, effect, support, and objects of desire, then alone it will vanish.

अतीतानागतं स्वरूपतोऽस्त्यध्वभेदाद्धर्माणाम् ॥१२॥

12. The past and future exist in their own nature, qualities having different ways.

The idea is that existence never comes out of nonexistence. The past and future, though not existing in a manifested form, yet exist in a fine form.

ते व्यक्त-सूक्ष्मा गुणात्मानः ॥१३॥

13. They are manifested or fine, being of the nature of the Gunas.

The Gunas are the three substances, Sattva, Rajas, and Tamas, whose gross state is the sensible universe. Past and future arise from the different modes of manifestation of these Gunas.

परिणामैकत्वाद्वस्तुतत्त्वम् ॥१४॥

14. The unity in things is from the unity in changes.

Though there are three substances, their changes being co-ordinated, all objects have their unity.

वस्तुसाम्ये चित्तभेदात्तयोर्विभक्तः पन्थाः ॥१५॥

15. Since perception and desire vary with regard to the same object, mind and object are of different nature.

That is, there is an objective world independent of our minds. This is a refutation of Buddhistic Idealism. Since different people look at the same thing differently, it cannot be a mere imagination of any particular individual.

न चैकचित्ततन्त्रं वस्तु तदप्रमाणकं तदा किं स्यात् ॥

(There is an additional aphorism here in some editions:

"The object cannot be said to be dependent on a single mind. There being no proof of its existence, it would then become nonexistent."

If the perception of an object were the only criterion of its existence, then when the mind is absorbed in anything or is in Samadhi, it would not be perceived by anybody and might as well be said to be non-existent. This is an undesirable conclusion. — Ed.)

तदुपरागापेक्षित्वाच्चित्तस्य वस्तु ज्ञाताज्ञातम् ॥१६॥

16. Things are known on unknown to the mind, being dependent on the colouring which they give to the mind.

सदा ज्ञाताश्चित्तवृत्तयस्तत्प्रभोः पुरुषस्यापरिणामित्वात् ॥१७॥

17. The states of the mind are always known, because the lord of the mind, the Purusha, is unchangeable.

The whole gist of this theory is that the universe is both mental and material. Both of these are in a continuous state of flux. What is this book? It is a combination of molecules in constant change. One lot is going out, and another coming in; it is a whirlpool, but what makes the unity? What makes it the same book? The changes are rhythmical; in harmonious order they are sending impressions to my mind, and these pieced together make a continuous picture, although the parts are continuously changing. Mind itself is continuously changing. The mind and body are like two layers in the same substance, moving at different rates of speed. Relatively, one being slower and the other quicker, we can distinguish between the two motions. For instance, a train is in motion, and a carriage is moving alongside it. It is possible to find the motion of both these to a certain extent. But still something else is necessary. Motion can only be perceived when there is something else which is not moving. But when two or three things are relatively moving, we first perceive the motion of the faster one, and then that of the slower ones. How is the mind to perceive? It is also in a flux. Therefore another thing is necessary which moves more slowly, then you must get to something in which the motion is still slower, and so on, and you will find no end. Therefore logic compels you to stop somewhere. You must complete the series by knowing something which never changes. Behind this never-ending chain of motion is the Purusha, the changeless, the colourless, the pure. All these impressions are merely reflected upon it, as a magic lantern throws images upon a screen, without in any way tarnishing it.

न तत् स्वाभासं दृश्यत्वात् ॥१८॥

18. The mind is not self-luminous, being an object.

Tremendous power is manifested everywhere in nature, but it is not self-luminous, not essentially intelligent. The Purusha alone is self-luminous, and gives its light to everything. It is the power of the Purusha that is percolating through all matter and force.

एकसमये चोभयानवधारणम् ॥१९॥

19. From its being unable to cognise both at the same time.

If the mind were self-luminous it would be able to cognise itself and its objects at the same time, which it cannot. When it cognises the object, it cannot reflect on itself. Therefore the Purusha is self-luminous, and the mind is not.

चित्तान्तरदृश्ये बुद्धिबुद्धेरतिप्रसङ्गः स्मृतिसङ्करश्च ॥२०॥

20. Another cognising mind being assumed, there will be no end to such assumptions, and confusion of memory will be the result.

Let us suppose there is another mind which cognises the ordinary mind, then there will have to be still another to cognise the former, and so there will be no end to it. It will result in confusion of memory, there will be no storehouse of memory.

चितेरप्रतिसंक्रमायास्तदाकारापत्तौ स्वबुद्धि- संवेदनम् ॥२१॥

21. The essence of knowledge (the Purusha) being unchangeable, when the mind takes its form, it becomes conscious.

Patanjali says this to make it more clear that knowledge is not a quality of the Purusha. When the mind comes near the Purusha it is reflected, as it were, upon the mind, and the mind, for the time being, becomes knowing and seems as if it were itself the Purusha.

द्रष्टृ दृश्योपरक्तं चित्तं सर्वार्थम् ॥२२॥

22. Coloured by the seer and the seen the mind is able to understand everything.

On one side of the mind the external world, the seen, is being reflected, and on the other, the seer is being reflected. Thus comes the power of all knowledge to the mind.

तदसंख्येयवासनाभिश्चित्रमपि परार्थं संहत्यकारित्वात् ॥२३॥

23. The mind, though variegated by innumerable desires, acts for another (the Purusha), because it acts in combination.

The mind is a compound of various things and therefore it cannot work for itself. Everything that is a combination in this world has some object for that combination, some third thing for which this combination is going on. So this combination of the mind is for the Purusha.

विशेषदर्शिन आत्मभाव-भावनानिवृत्तिः ॥२४॥

24. For the discriminating, the perception of the mind as Atman ceases.

Through discrimination the Yogi knows that the Purusha is not mind.

तदा विवेकनिम्नं कैवल्यप्राग्भावं चित्तम् ॥२५॥

25. Then, bent on discriminating, the mind attains the previous state of Kaivalya (isolation). (There is another reading कैवल्यप्राग्भारं ।— The meaning then would be: "Then the mind becomes deep in discrimination and gravitates towards Kaivalya." — Ed.)

Thus the practice of Yoga leads to discriminating power, to clearness of vision. The veil drops from the eyes, and we see things as they are. We find that nature is a compound, and is showing the panorama for the Purusha, who is the witness; that nature is not the Lord, that all the combinations of nature are simply for the sake of showing these phenomena to the Purusha, the enthroned king within. When discrimination comes by long practice, fear ceases, and the mind attains isolation.

तच्छिद्रेषु प्रत्ययान्तराणि संस्कारेभ्यः ॥२६॥

26. The thoughts that arise as obstructions to that are from impressions.

All the various ideas that arise, making us believe that we require something external to make us happy, are obstructions to that perfection. The Purusha is happiness and blessedness by its own nature. But that knowledge is covered over by past impressions. These impressions have to work themselves out.

हानमेषां क्लेशवदुक्तम् ॥२७॥

27. Their destruction is in the same manner as of ignorance, egoism, etc., as said before (II. 10).

प्रसंख्यानेऽप्यकुसीदस्य सर्वथा विवेकख्यातेर्धर्ममेघः समाधिः ॥२८॥

28. Even when arriving at the right discriminating knowledge of the essences, he who gives up the fruits, unto him comes, as the result of perfect domination, the Samadhi called the cloud of virtue.

When the Yogi has attained to this discrimination, all the powers mentioned in the last chapter come to him, but the true Yogi rejects them all. Unto him comes a peculiar knowledge, a particular light, called the Dharma-megha, the cloud of virtue. All the great prophets of the world whom history has recorded had this. They had found the whole foundation of knowledge within themselves. Truth to them had become real. Peace and calmness, and perfect purity became their own nature, after they had given up the vanities of powers.

ततः क्लेशकर्मनिवृत्तिः ॥२९॥

29. From that comes cessation of pain and works.

When that cloud of virtue has come, then no more is there fear of falling, nothing can drag the Yogi down. No more will there be evils for him. No more pains.

तदा सर्वावरणमलापेतस्य ज्ञानस्याऽनन्त्याज्ज्ञेयमल्पम् ॥३०॥

30. The knowledge, bereft of covering and impurities, becoming infinite, the knowable becomes small.

Knowledge itself is there; its covering is gone. One of the Buddhistic scriptures defines what is meant by the Buddha (which is the name of a state) as infinite knowledge, infinite as the sky. Jesus attained to that and became the Christ. All of you will attain to that state. Knowledge becoming infinite, the knowable becomes small. The whole universe, with all its objects of knowledge, becomes as nothing before the Purusha. The ordinary man thinks himself very small, because to him the knowable seems to be infinite.

ततः कृतार्थानां परिणामक्रमसमाप्तिर्गुणानाम् ॥३१॥

31. Then are finished the successive transformations of the qualities, they having attained the end.

Then all these various transformations of the qualities, which change from species to species, cease for ever.

क्षणप्रतियोगी परिणामापरान्तनिर्ग्राह्यः क्रमः ॥३२॥

32. The changes that exist in relation to moments and which are perceived at the other end (at the end of a series) are succession.

Patanjali here defines the word succession, the changes that exist in relation to moments. While I think, many moments pass, and with each moment there is a change of idea, but I only perceive these changes at the end of a series. This is called succession, but for the mind that has realised omnipresence there is no succession. Everything has become present for it; to it the present alone exists, the past and future are lost. Time stands controlled, all knowledge is there in one second. Everything is known like a flash.

पुरुषार्थशून्यानां गुणानां प्रतिप्रसवः कैवल्यं
स्वरूपप्रतिष्ठा वा चितिशक्तेरिति ॥३३॥

33. The resolution in the inverse order of the qualities, bereft of any motive of action for the Purusha, is Kaivalya, or it is the establishment of the power of knowledge in its own nature.

Nature's task is done, this unselfish task which our sweet nurse, nature, had imposed upon herself. She gently took the self-forgetting soul by the hand, as it were, and showed him all the experiences in the universe, all manifestations, bringing him higher and higher through various bodies, till his lost glory came back, and he remembered his own nature. Then the kind mother went back the same way she came, for others who also have lost their way in the trackless desert of life. And thus is she working, without beginning and without end. And thus through pleasure and pain, through good and evil, the infinite river of souls is flowing into the ocean of perfection, of self-realisation.

Glory unto those who have realised their own nature. May their blessings be on us all!

Appendix

References To Yoga

Shvetâshvatara Upanishad

Chapter II

अग्निर्यत्राभिमथ्यते वायुर्यत्राधिरुध्यते ।
सोमो यत्रातिरिच्यते तत्र सञ्जायते मनः ॥६॥

6. Where the fire is rubbed, where the air is controlled, where the Soma flows over, there a (perfect) mind is created.

त्रिरुन्नतं स्थाप्य समं शरीरं
हृदीन्द्रियाणि मनसा सन्निवेश्य ।
ब्रह्मोडुपेन प्रतरेत विद्वान्
स्रोतांसि सर्वाणि भयावहानि ॥८॥

8. Placing the body in a straight posture, with the chest, the throat and the head held erect, making the organs enter the mind, the sage crosses all the fearful currents by means of the raft of Brahman.

प्राणान् प्रपीड्येह संयुक्तचेष्टः
क्षीणे प्राणे नासिकयोच्छ्वसीत ।
दुष्टाश्वयुक्तमिव वाहमेनं
विद्वान् मनो धारयेताप्रमत्त ॥९॥

9. The man of well-regulated endeavours controls the Prâna; and when it has become quieted, breathes out through the nostrils. The persevering sage holds his mind as a charioteer holds the restive horses.

समे शुचौ शर्करावह्निवालुका
विवर्जिते शब्दजलाश्रयादिभिः ।
मनोनुकूले न च चक्षुपीडने
गुहानिवाताश्रयणे प्रयोजयेत् ॥१०॥

10. In (lonely) places as mountain caves where the floor is even, free of pebbles, fire, or sand, where there are no disturbing noises from men or waterfalls, in auspicious places helpful to the mind and pleasing to the eyes. Yoga is to be practised (mind is to be joined).

नीहारधूमर्कानिलानलानां
स्वद्योतविद्युत् स्फटिक – शशीनाम् ।
एतानि रूपाणि पुरःसराणि
ब्रह्मण्यभिव्यक्तिकराणि योगे ॥११॥

11. Like snowfall, smoke, sun, wind, fire, firefly, lightning, crystal, moon, these forms, coming before, gradually manifest the Brahman in Yoga.

पृथ्व्यप्तेजोऽनिलखे समुत्थिते
पञ्चात्मके योगगुणे प्रवृत्ते ।
न तस्य रोगो न जरा न मृत्युः
प्राप्तस्य योगाग्निमयं शरीरम् ॥१२॥

12. When the perceptions of Yoga, arising from earth, water, light, fire, ether, have taken place, then Yoga has begun. Unto him does not come disease, nor old age, nor death, who has got a body made up of the fire of Yoga.

लघुत्वमारोग्यमलोलुपत्वं
वर्णप्रसादः स्वरसौष्ठवञ्च ।
गन्धः शुभो मूत्रपुरीषमल्पं
योगप्रवृत्तिं प्रथमां वदन्ति ॥१३॥

13. The first signs of entering Yoga are lightness, health, non-covetousness, clearness of complexion, a beautiful voice, an agreeable odour in the body, and scantiness of excretions.

यथैव बिम्बं मृदयोपलिप्तं
तेजोमयं भ्राजते तत् सुधान्तम् ।
तद्वाऽऽत्मतत्त्वं प्रसमीक्ष्य देही
एकः कृतार्थो भवते वीतशोकः ॥१४॥

14. As gold or silver, first covered with earth, and then cleaned, shines full of light, so the embodied man seeing the truth of the Atman as one, attains the goal and becomes sorrowless.

Yâjnavalkya quoted by Shankara

(In Svetâshvatara Upanishad Bhâshya.)

आसनानि समभ्यस्य वाञ्छितानि यथाविधि ।
प्राणायामं ततो गार्गि जितासनगतोऽभ्यसेत् ॥
मृद्वासने कुशान् सम्यगास्तीर्याजिनमेव च ।
लम्बोदरं च सम्पूज्य फलमोदकभक्षणैः ॥
तदासने सुखासीनः सव्ये न्यस्येतरं करम् ।
समग्रीवशिराः सम्यक संवृतास्यः सुनिश्चलः ॥
प्राङ्मुखोदङ्मुखो वाऽपि नासाग्रन्यस्तलोचनः ।
अतिभुक्तमभुक्तं वा वर्जयित्वा प्रयत्नतः ॥
नाडीसंशोधनं कुर्यादुक्तमार्गेण यत्नतः ।
वृथा क्लेशो भवेत्तस्य तच्छोधनमकुर्वतः ॥
नासाग्रे शशभृद्बीजं चन्द्रातपवितानितम् ।
सप्तमस्य तु वर्गस्य चतुर्थं बिन्दुसंयुतम् ॥
विश्वमध्यस्थमालोक्य नासाग्रे चक्षुषी उभे ।
इडया पूरयेद्वायुं बाह्यं द्वादशमात्रकैः ॥
ततोऽग्निं पूर्ववद्ध्यायेत् स्फुरज्ज्वालावलीयुतम् ।
रकारं बिन्दुसंयुक्तं शिखिमण्डलसंस्थितम् ॥
ध्यायेद्विरेचयेद्वायुं मन्दं पिङ्गलया पुनः ।
पुनः पिङ्गलयापूर्य घ्राणं दक्षिणतः सुधीः ॥
तद्वद्विरेचयेद्वायुमिडया तु शनैः शनैः ।
त्रिचतुर्वत्सरं चापि त्रिचतुर्मासमेव वा ॥
गुरुणोक्तप्रकारेण रहस्येवं समभ्यसेत् ।
प्रातर्मध्यन्दिने सायं स्नात्वा षट्कृत्व आचरेत् ॥
सन्ध्यादिकर्म कृत्वैवं मध्यरात्रेऽपि नित्यशः ।
नाडीशुद्धिमवाप्नोति तच्चिह्नं दृश्यते पृथक् ॥
शरीरलघुता दीप्तिर्जठराग्निविवर्धनम् ।
नादाभिव्यक्तिरित्येतच्चिह्नं तच्छुद्धिसूचनम् ॥
प्राणायामं ततः कुर्याद्रेचपूरककुम्भकैः ।
प्राणापानसमायोगः प्राणायामः प्रकीर्तितः ॥

* * *

पूरयेत् षोडशैर्मात्रैरापादतलमस्तकम् ।
मात्रैर्द्वात्रिंशकैः पश्चाद्रेचयेत् सुसमाहितः ॥
सम्पूर्णकुम्भवद्वायोर्निश्चलं मूर्ध्नि देशतः ।
कुम्भकं धारणं गार्गि चतुःषष्ट्या तु मात्रया ॥
ऋषयस्तु वदन्त्यन्ये प्राणायामपरायणाः ।
पवित्रीभूता पूतान्ताः प्रभञ्जनजये रताः ॥
तत्रादौ कुम्भकं कृत्वा चतुःषष्ट्या तु मात्रया ।
रेचयेत् षोडशैर्मात्रैर्नासेनैकेन सुन्दरि ।
ततश्च पूरयेद्वायुं शनैः षोडशमात्रया ॥
प्राणायामैर्दहेद्दोषान् धारणाभिश्च किल्बिषान् ।
प्रत्याहाराच्च संसर्गान्ध्यानेनानीश्वरान् गुणान् ॥

"After practicing the postures as desired, according to rules, then, O Gârgi, the man who has conquered the posture will practice Prânâyâma.

"Seated in an easy posture, on a (deer or tiger) skin, placed on Kusha grass, worshipping Ganapati with fruits and sweetmeats, placing the right palm on the left, holding the throat and head in the same line, the lips closed and firm, facing the east or the north, the eyes fixed on the tip of the nose, avoiding too much food or fasting, the Nâdis should be purified, without which the practice will be fruitless. Thinking of the (seed-word) "Hum," at the junction of Pingalâ and Idâ (the right and the left nostrils), the Ida should be filled with external air in twelve Mâtrâs (seconds); then the Yogi meditates on fire in the same place with the word "Rung," and while meditating thus, slowly ejects the air through the Pingala (right nostril). Again filling in through the Pingala the air should be slowly ejected through the Ida, in the same way. This should be practiced for three or four years, or three or four months, according to the directions of a Guru, in secret (alone in a room), in the early morning, at midday, in the evening, and at midnight (until) the nerves become purified. Lightness of body, clear complexion, good appetite, hearing of the Nâda, are the signs of the purification of nerves. Then should be practiced Pranayama composed of Rechaka (exhalation), Kumbhaka (retention), and Puraka (inhalation). Joining the Prâna with the Apâna is Pranayama.

"In sixteen Matras filling the body from the head to the feet, in thirty-two Matras the Prana is to be thrown out, and with sixty-four the Kurnbhaka should be made.

"There is another Pranayama in which the Kumbhaka should first be made with sixty-four Matras, then the Prana should be thrown out with sixteen, and the body next filled with sixteen Matras.

"By Pranayama impurities of the body are thrown out; by Dhâranâ the impurities of the mind; by Pratyâhâra impurities of attachment; and by Samadhi is taken off everything that hides the lordship of the Soul."

Sânkhya

Book III

भावनोपचयात् शुद्धस्य सर्वं ॥२९॥

29. By the achievement of meditation, there come to the pure one (the Purusha) all powers of nature.

रागोपहतिर्ध्यानम् ॥३०॥

30. Meditation is the removal of attachment.

वृत्तिनिरोधात्तत्सिद्धिः ॥३१॥

31. It is perfected by the suppression of the modifications.

धारणाऽऽसनस्वकर्मणा तत्सिद्धिः ॥३२॥

32. By Dhâranâ, posture, and performance of one's duties, it is perfected.

निरोधश्छर्दिविधारणाभ्याम् ॥३३॥

33. Restraint of the Prâna is by means of expulsion and retention.

स्थिरसुखमासनम् ॥३४॥

34. Posture is that which is steady and easy.

वैराग्यादभ्यासाच्च ॥३६॥

36. Also by non-attachment and practice, meditation is perfected.

तत्वाभ्यासान्नेति नेतीति त्यागाद्विवेकसिद्धिः ॥७४॥

74. By reflection on the principles of nature, and by giving them up as "not It, not It" discrimination is perfected.

Book IV

आवृत्तिरसकृदुपदेशात् ॥३॥

3. Instruction is to be repeated.

श्येनवत् सुखःदुखी त्यागवियोगाभ्याम् ॥५॥

5. As the hawk becomes unhappy if the food is taken away from him and happy if he gives it up himself (so he who gives up everything voluntarily is happy).

अहिनिर्ल्वयनीवत् ॥६॥

6. As the snake is happy in giving up his old skin.

असाधनानुचिन्तनं बन्धाय भरतवत् ॥८॥

8. That which is not a means of liberation is not to be thought of; it becomes a cause of bondage, as in the case of Bharata.

बहुभिर्योगे विरोधो रागादिभिः कुमारीशङ्खवत् ॥९॥

9. From the association of many things there is obstruction to meditation, through passion, aversion, etc., like the shell bracelets on the virgin's hand.

द्वाभ्यामपि तथैव ॥१०॥

10. It is the same even in the case of two.

निराशः सुखी पिङ्गलावत् ॥११॥

11. The renouncers of hope are happy, like the girl Pingalâ.

बहुशास्त्रगुरूपासनेऽपि सारादानं षट्पदवत् ॥१३॥

13. Although devotion is to be given to many institutes and teachers, the essence is to be taken from them all as the bee takes the essence from many flowers.

इषुकारवन्नैकचित्तस्य समाधिहानिः ॥१४॥

14. One whose mind has become concentrated like the arrowmaker's does not get his meditation disturbed.

कृतनियमलङ्घनादानर्थक्यं लोकवत् ॥१५॥

15. Through transgression of the original rules there is non-attainment of the goal, as in other worldly things.

प्रणतिब्रह्मचर्योपसर्पणानि कृत्वा सिद्धिर्बहुकालात्तद्वत् ॥१९॥

19. By continence, reverence, and devotion to Guru, success comes after a long time (as in the case of Indra).

न कालनियमो वामदेववत् ॥२०॥

20. There is no law as to time, as in the case of Vâmadeva.

लब्धातिशययोगाद्वा तद्वत् ॥२४॥

24. Or through association with one who has attained perfection.

न भोगात् रागशान्तिर्मुनिवत् ॥२७॥

27. Not by enjoyments is desire appeased even with sages (who have practiced Yoga for long).

Book V

योगसिद्धयोऽप्यौषधादिसिद्धिवन्नापलपनीयाः ॥१२८॥

128. The Siddhis attained by Yoga are not to be denied like recovery through medicines etc.

Book VI

स्थिरसुखमासनमिति न नियमः ॥२४॥

24. Any posture which is easy and steady is an Âsana; there is no other rule.

Vyâsa-Sutras

Chapter IV, Section I

आसीनः सम्भवात् ॥७॥

7. Worship is possible in a sitting posture.

ध्यानाच्च ॥८॥

8. Because of meditation.

अचलत्वञ्चापेक्ष्य ॥९॥

9. Because the meditating (person) is compared to the immovable earth.

स्मरन्ति च ॥१०॥

10. Also because the Smritis say so.

यत्रैकाग्रता तत्राविशेषात् ॥११॥

11. There is no law of place; wherever the mind is concentrated, there worship should be performed.

These several extracts give an idea of what other systems of Indian Philosophy have to say upon Yoga.

Lectures and Discourses

Soul, God And Religion

Through the vistas of the past the voice of the centuries is coming down to us; the voice of the sages of the Himalayas and the recluses of the forest; the voice that came to the Semitic races; the voice that spoke through Buddha and other spiritual giants; the voice that comes from those who live in the light that accompanied man in the beginning of the earth — the light that shines wherever man goes and lives with him for ever — is coming to us even now. This voice is like the little rivulets; that come from the mountains. Now they disappear, and now they appear again in stronger flow till finally they unite in one mighty majestic flood. The messages that are coming down to us from the prophets and holy men and women of all sects and nations are joining their forces and speaking to us with the trumpet voice of the past. And the first message it brings us is: Peace be unto you and to all religions. It is not a message of antagonism, but of one united religion.

Let us study this message first. At the beginning of this century it was almost feared that religion was at an end. Under the tremendous sledge-hammer blows of scientific research, old superstitions were crumbling away like masses of porcelain. Those to whom religion meant only a bundle of creeds and meaningless ceremonials were in despair; they were at their wit's end. Everything was slipping between their fingers. For a time it seemed inevitable that the surging tide of agnosticism and materialism would sweep all before it. There were those who did not dare utter what they thought. Many thought the case hopeless and the cause of religion lost once and for ever. But the tide has turned and to the rescue has come — what? The study of comparative religions. By the study of different religions we find that in essence they are one. When I was a boy, this scepticism reached me, and it seemed for a time as if I must give up all hope of religion. But fortunately for me I studied the Christian religion, the Mohammedan, the Buddhistic, and others, and what was my surprise to find that the same foundation principles taught by my religion were also taught by all religions. It appealed to me this way. What is the truth? I asked. Is this world true? Yes. Why? Because I see it. Are the beautiful sounds we just heard (the vocal and instrumental music) true? Yes. Because we heard them. We know that man has a body, eyes, and ears, and he has a spiritual nature which we cannot see. And with his spiritual faculties he can study these different religions and find that whether a religion is taught in the forests and jungles of India or in a Christian land, in essentials all religions are one. This only shows us that religion is a constitutional necessity of the human mind. The proof of one religion depends on the proof of all the rest. For instance, if I have six fingers, and no one else has, you may well say that is abnormal. The same reasoning may be applied to the argument that only one religion is true and all others false. One religion only, like one set of six fingers in the world, would be unnatural. We see, therefore, that if one religion is true, all others must be true. There are differences in non-essentials, but in essentials they are all one. If my five fingers are true, they prove that your five fingers are true too. Wherever man is, he must develop a belief, he must develop his religious nature.

And another fact I find in the study of the various religions of the world is that there are three different stages of ideas with regard to the soul and God. In the first place, all religions admit that, apart from the body which perishes, there is a certain part or something which does not change like the body, a part that is immutable, eternal, that never dies; but some of the later religions teach that although there is a part of us that never dies, it had a beginning. But anything that has a beginning must necessarily have an end. We — the essential part of us — never had a beginning, and will never have an end. And above us all, above this eternal nature, there is another eternal Being, without end — God. People talk about the beginning of the world, the beginning of man. The word *beginning* simply means the beginning of the cycle. It nowhere means the beginning of the whole Cosmos. It is impossible that creation could have a beginning. No one of you can imagine a time of beginning. That which has a beginning must have an end. "Never did I not exist, nor you, nor will any of us ever hereafter cease to be," says the Bhagavad-Gita. Wherever the beginning of creation is mentioned, it means the beginning of a cycle. Your body will meet with death, but your soul, never.

Along with this idea of the soul we find another group of ideas in regard to its perfection. The soul in itself is perfect. The Old Testament of the Hebrews admits man perfect at the beginning. Man made himself impure by his own actions. But he is to regain his old nature, his pure nature. Some speak of these things in allegories, fables, and symbols. But when we begin to analyse these statements, we find that they all teach that the human soul is in its very nature perfect, and that man is to regain that original purity. How? By knowing God. Just as the Bible says, "No man can see God but through the Son." What is meant by it? That seeing God is the aim and goal of all human life. The sonship must come before we become one with the Father. Remember that man lost his purity through his own actions. When we suffer, it is because of our own acts; God is not to be blamed for it.

Closely connected with these ideas is the doctrine — which was universal before the Europeans mutilated it — the doctrine of reincarnation. Some of you may have heard of and ignored it. This idea of reincarnation runs parallel with the other doctrine of the eternity of the human soul. Nothing which ends at one point can be without a beginning and nothing that begins at one point can be without an end. We cannot believe in such a monstrous impossibility as the beginning of the human soul. The doctrine of reincarnation asserts the freedom of the soul. Suppose there was an absolute beginning. Then the whole burden of this impurity in man falls upon God. The all-merciful Father responsible for the sins of the world! If sin comes in this way, why should one suffer more than another? Why such partiality, if it comes from an all-merciful God? Why are millions trampled underfoot? Why do people starve who never did anything to cause it? Who is responsible? If they had no hand in it, surely, God would be responsible. Therefore the better explanation is that one is responsible for the miseries one suffers. If I set the wheel in motion, I am responsible for the result. And if I can bring misery, I can also stop it. It necessarily follows that we are free. There is no such thing as fate. There is nothing to compel us. What we have done, that we can undo.

To one argument in connection with this doctrine I will ask your patient attention, as it is a little intricate. We gain all our knowledge through experience; that is the only way. What we call experiences are on the plane of consciousness. For illustration: A man plays a tune on a piano, he places each finger on each key consciously. He repeats this process till the movement of the fingers becomes a habit. He then plays a tune without having to pay special attention to each particular key. Similarly, we find in regard to ourselves that our tendencies are the result of past conscious actions. A child is born with certain tendencies. Whence do they come? No child is born with a *tabula rasa* — with a clean, blank page — of a mind. The page has been written on previously. The old Greek and Egyptian philosophers taught that no child came with a vacant mind. Each child comes with a hundred tendencies generated by past conscious actions. It did not acquire these in this life, and we are bound to admit that it must have had them in past lives. The rankest materialist has to admit that these tendencies are the result of past actions, only they add that these tendencies come through heredity. Our parents, grandparents, and great-grandparents come down to us through this law of heredity. Now if heredity alone explains this, there is no necessity of believing in the soul at all, because body explains everything. We need not go into the different arguments and discussions on materialism and spiritualism. So far the way is clear for those who believe in an individual soul. We see that to come to a reasonable conclusion we must admit that we have had past lives. This is the belief of the great philosophers and sages of the past and of modern times. Such a doctrine was believed in among the Jews. Jesus Christ believed in it. He says in the Bible, "Before Abraham was, I am." And in another place it is said, "This is Elias who is said to have come."

All the different religions which grew among different nations under varying circumstances and conditions had their origin in Asia, and the Asiatics understand them well. When they came out from the motherland, they got mixed up with errors. The most profound and noble ideas of Christianity were never understood in Europe, because the ideas and images used by the writers of the Bible were foreign to it. Take for illustration the pictures of the Madonna. Every artist paints his Madonna according to his own pre-conceived ideas. I have been seeing hundreds of pictures of the Last Supper of Jesus Christ, and he is made to sit at a table. Now, Christ never sat at a table; he squatted with others, and they had a bowl in which they dipped bread — not the kind of bread you eat today. It is hard for any nation to understand the unfamiliar customs of other people. How much more difficult was it for Europeans to understand the Jewish customs after centuries of changes and accretions from Greek, Roman, and other sources! Through all the myths and mythologies by which it is surrounded it is no wonder that the people get very little of the beautiful religion of Jesus, and no wonder that they have made of it a modern shop-keeping religion.

To come to our point. We find that all religions teach the eternity of the soul, as well as that its lustre has been dimmed, and that its primitive purity is to be regained by the knowledge of God. What is the idea of God in these different religions? The primary idea of God was very vague. The most ancient nations had different Deities — sun, earth, fire, water. Among the ancient Jews we find numbers of these gods ferociously fighting with each other. Then we find Elohim whom the Jews and the Babylonians worshipped. We next find one God standing supreme. But the idea differed according to different tribes. They each asserted that their God was the greatest. And they tried to prove it by fighting. The one that could do the best fighting proved thereby that its God was the greatest. Those races were more or less savage. But gradually better and better ideas took the place of the old ones. All those old ideas are gone or going into the lumber-room.

All those religions were the outgrowth of centuries; not one fell from the skies. Each had to be worked out bit by bit. Next come the monotheistic ideas: belief in one God, who is omnipotent and omniscient, the one God of the universe. This one God is extra-cosmic; he lies in the heavens. He is invested with the gross conceptions of His originators. He has a right side and a left side, and a bird in His hand, and so on and so forth. But one thing we find, that the tribal gods have disappeared for ever, and the one God of the universe has taken their place: the God of gods. Still He is only an extra-cosmic God. He is unapproachable; nothing can come near Him. But slowly this idea has changed also, and at the next stage we find a God immanent in nature.

In the New Testament it is taught, "Our Father who art in heaven" — God living in the heavens separated from men. We are living on earth and He is living in heaven. Further on we find the teaching that He is a God immanent in nature; He is not only God in heaven, but on earth too. He is the God in us. In the Hindu philosophy we find a stage of the same proximity of God to us. But we do not stop there. There is the non-dualistic stage, in which man realises that the God he has been worshipping is not only the Father in heaven, and on earth, but that "I and my Father are one." He realises in his soul that he is God Himself, only a lower expression of Him. All that is real in me is He; all that is real in Him is I. The gulf between God and man is thus bridged. Thus we find how, by knowing God, we find the kingdom of heaven within us.

In the first or dualistic stage, man knows he is a little personal soul, John, James, or Tom; and he says, "I will be John, James, or Tom to all eternity, and never anything else." As well might the murderer come along and say, "I will remain a murderer for ever." But as time goes on, Tom vanishes and goes back to the original pure Adam.

"Blessed are the pure in heart, for they shall see God." Can we see God? Of course not. Can we know God? Of course not. If God can be known, He will be God no longer. Knowledge is limitation. But I and my Father are one: I find the reality in my soul. These ideas are expressed in some religions, and in others only hinted. In some they were expatriated. Christ's teachings are now very little understood in this country. If you will excuse me, I will say that they have never been very well understood.

The different stages of growth are absolutely necessary to the attainment of purity and perfection. The varying systems of religion are at bottom founded on the same ideas. Jesus says the kingdom of heaven is within you. Again he says, "Our father who art in Heaven." How do you reconcile the two sayings? In this way: He was talking to the uneducated masses when he said the latter, the masses who were uneducated in religion. It was necessary to speak to them in their own language. The masses want concrete ideas, something the senses can grasp. A man may be the greatest philosopher in the world, but a child in religion. When a man has developed a high state of spirituality he can understand that the kingdom of heaven is within him. That is the real kingdom of the mind. Thus we see that the apparent contradictions and perplexities in every religion mark but different stages of growth. And as such we have no right to blame anyone for his religion. There are stages of growth in which forms and symbols are necessary; they are the language that the souls in that stage can understand.

The next idea that I want to bring to you is that religion does not consist in doctrines or dogmas. It is not what you read, nor what dogmas you believe that is of importance, but what you realise. "Blessed are the pure in heart, for they shall see God," yea, in this life. And that is salvation. There are those who teach that this can be gained by the mumbling of words. But no great Master ever taught that external forms were necessary for salvation. The power of attaining it is within ourselves. We live and move in God. Creeds and sects have their parts to play, but they are for children, they last but temporarily. Books never make religions, but religions make books. We must not forget that. No book ever created God, but God inspired all the great books. And no book ever created a soul. We must never forget that. The end of all religions is the realising of God in the soul. That is the one universal religion. If there is one universal truth in all religions, I place it here — in realising God. Ideals and methods may differ, but that is the central point. There may be a thousand different radii, but they all converge to the one centre, and that is the realisation of God: something behind this world of sense, this world of eternal eating and drinking and talking nonsense, this world of false shadows and selfishness. There is that beyond all books, beyond all creeds, beyond the vanities of this world and it is the realisation of God within yourself. A man may believe in all the churches in the world, he may carry in his head all the sacred books ever written, he may baptise himself in all the rivers of the earth, still, if he has no perception of God, I would class him with the rankest atheist. And a man may have never entered a church or a mosque, nor performed any ceremony, but if he feels God within himself and is thereby lifted above the vanities of the world, that man is a holy man, a saint, call him what you will. As soon as a man stands up and says he is right or his church is right, and all others are wrong, he is himself all wrong. He does not know that upon the proof of all the others depends the proof of his own. Love and charity for the whole human race, that is the test of true religiousness. I do not mean the sentimental statement that all men are brothers, but that one must feel the oneness of human life. So far as they are not exclusive, I see that the sects and creeds are all mine; they are all grand. They are all helping men towards the real religion. I will add, it is good to be born in a church, but it is bad to die there. It is good to be born a child, but bad to remain a child. Churches, ceremonies, and symbols are good for children, but when the child is grown, he must burst the church or himself. We must not remain children for ever. It is like trying to fit one coat to all sizes and growths. I do not deprecate the existence of sects in the world. Would to God there were twenty millions more, for the more there are, there will be a greater field for selection. What I do object to is trying to fit one religion to every case. Though all religions are essentially the same, they must have the varieties of form produced by dissimilar circumstances among different nations. We must each have our own individual religion, individual so far as the externals of it go.

Many years ago, I visited a great sage of our own country, a very holy man. We talked of our revealed book, the Vedas, of your Bible, of the Koran, and of revealed books in general. At the close of our talk, this good man asked me to go to the table and take up a book; it was a book which, among other things, contained a forecast of the rainfall during the year. The sage said, "Read that." And I read out the quantity of rain that was to fall. He said, "Now take the book and squeeze it." I did so and he said, "Why, my boy, not a drop of water comes out. Until the water comes out, it is all book, book. So until your religion makes you realise God, it is useless. He who only studies books for religion reminds one of the fable of the ass which carried a heavy load of sugar on its back, but did not know the sweetness of it."

Shall we advise men to kneel down and cry, "O miserable sinners that we are!" No, rather let us remind them of their divine nature. I will tell you a story. A lioness in search of prey came upon a flock of sheep, and as she jumped at one of them, she gave birth to a cub and died on the spot. The young lion was brought up in the flock, ate grass, and bleated like a sheep, and it never knew that it was a lion. One day a lion came across the flock and was astonished to see in it a huge lion eating grass and bleating like a sheep. At his sight the flock fled and the lion-sheep with them. But the lion watched his opportunity and one day found the lion-sheep asleep. He woke him up and said, "You are a lion." The other said, "No," and began to bleat like a sheep. But the stranger lion took him to a lake and asked him to look in the water at his own image and see if it did not resemble him, the stranger lion. He looked and acknowledged that it did. Then the stranger lion began to roar and asked him to do the same. The lion-sheep tried his voice and was soon roaring as grandly as the other. And he was a sheep no longer.

My friends, I would like to tell you all that you are mighty as lions.

If the room is dark, do you go about beating your chest and crying, "It is dark, dark, dark!" No, the only way to get the light is to strike a light, and then the darkness goes. The only way to realise the light above you is to strike the spiritual light within you, and the darkness of sin and impurity will flee away. Think of your higher self, not of your lower.

* * *

Some questions and answers here followed.

Q. A man in the audience said, "If ministers stop preaching hell-fire, they will have no control over their people."

A. They had better lose it then. The man who is frightened into religion has no religion at all. Better teach him of his divine nature than of his animal.

Q. What did the Lord mean when he said, "The kingdom of heaven is not of this world?"

A. That the kingdom of heaven is within us. The Jewish idea was a kingdom of heaven upon this earth. That was not the idea of Jesus.

Q. Do you believe we come up from the animals?

A. I believe that, by the law of evolution, the higher beings have come up from the lower kingdoms.

Q. Do you know of anyone who remembers his previous life ?

A. I have met some who told me they did remember their previous life. They had reached a point where they could remember their former incarnations.

Q. Do you believe in Christ's crucifixion?

A. Christ was God incarnate; they could not kill him. That which was crucified was only a semblance, a mirage.

Q. If he could have produced such a semblance as that, would not that have been the greatest miracle of all?

A. I look upon miracles as the greatest stumbling-blocks in the way of truth. When the disciples of Buddha told him of a man who had performed a so-called miracle — had taken a bowl from a great height without touching it — and showed him the bowl, he took it and crushed it under his feet and told them never to build their faith on miracles, but to look for truth in everlasting principles. He taught them the true inner light — the light of the spirit, which is the only safe light to go by. Miracles are only stumbling-blocks. Let us brush them aside.

Q. Do you believe Jesus preached the Sermon on the Mount?

A. I do believe he did. But in this matter I have to go by the books as others do, and I am aware that mere book testimony is rather shaky ground. But we are all safe in taking the teachings of the Sermon on the Mount as a guide. We have to take what appeals to our inner spirit. Buddha taught five hundred years before Christ, and his words were full of blessings: never a curse came from his lips, nor from his life; never one from Zoroaster, nor from Confucius.

The Hindu Religion

My religion is to learn. I read my Bible better in the light of your Bible and the dark prophecies of my religion become brighter when compared with those of your prophets. Truth has always been universal. If I alone were to have six fingers on my hand while all of you had only five, you would not think that my hand was the true intent of nature, but rather that it was abnormal and diseased. Just so with religion. If one creed alone were to be true and all the others untrue, you would have a right to say that that religion was diseased; if one religion is true, all the others must be true. Thus the Hindu religion is your property as well as mine. Of the two hundred and ninety millions of people inhabiting India, only two millions are Christians, sixty millions Mohammedans and all the rest are Hindus.

The Hindus found their creed upon the ancient Vedas, a word derived from Vid, "to know". These are a series of books which, to our minds, contain the essence of all religion; but we do not think they alone contain the truths. They teach us the immortality of the soul. In every country and every human breast there is a natural desire to find a stable equilibrium — something that does not change. We cannot find it in nature, for all the universe is nothing but an infinite mass of changes. But to infer from that that nothing unchanging exists is to fall into the error of the Southern school of Buddhists and the Chârvâkas, which latter believe that all is matter and nothing mind, that all religion is a cheat, and morality and goodness, useless superstitions. The Vedanta philosophy teaches that man is not bound by his five senses. They only know the present, and neither the future nor the past; but as the present signifies both past and future, and all three are only demarcations of time, the present also would be unknown if it were not for something above the senses, something independent of time, which unifies the past and the future in the present.

But what is independent? Not our body, for it depends upon outward conditions; nor our mind, because the thoughts of which it is composed are caused. It is our soul. The Vedas say the whole world is a mixture of independence and dependence, of freedom and slavery, but through it all shines the soul independent, immortal, pure, perfect, holy. For if it is independent, it cannot perish, as death is but a change, and depends upon conditions; if independent, it must be perfect, for imperfection is again but a condition, and therefore dependent. And this immortal and perfect soul must be the same in the highest God as well as in the humblest man the difference between them being only in the degree in which this soul manifests itself.

But why should the soul take to itself a body? For the same reason that I take a looking-glass — to see myself. Thus, in the body, the soul is reflected The soul is God, and every human being has a perfect divinity within himself, and each one must show his divinity sooner or later. If I am in a dark room, no amount of protestation will make it any brighter — I must light a match. Just so, no amount of grumbling and wailing will make our imperfect body more perfect. But the Vedanta teaches — call forth your soul show your divinity. Teach your children that they are divine, that religion is a positive something and not a negative nonsense; that it is not subjection to groans when under oppression, but expansion and manifestation.

Every religion has it that man's present and future are modified by the past, and that the present is but the effect of the past. How is it, then, that every child is born with an experience that cannot be accounted for by hereditary transmission? How is it that one is born of good parents receives a good education and becomes a good man, while another comes from besotted parents and ends on the gallows? How do you explain this inequality without implicating God? Why should a merciful Father set His child in such conditions which must bring forth misery? It is no explanation to say God will make amends; later on — God has no blood-money. Then too, what becomes of my liberty, if this be my first birth? Coming into this world without the experience of a former life, my independence would be gone, for my path would be marked out by the experience of others. If I cannot be the maker of my own fortune, then I am not free. I take upon myself the blame for the misery of this existence, and say I will unmake the evil I have done in another existence. This, then, is our philosophy of the migration of the soul. We come into this life with the experience of another, and the fortune or misfortune of this existence is the result of our acts in a former existence, always becoming better, till at last perfection is reached.

We believe in a God, the Father of the universe, infinite and omnipotent But if our soul at last becomes perfect, it also must become infinite. But there is no room for two infinite unconditional beings, and hence we believe in a Personal God, and we ourselves are He. These are the three stages which every religion has taken. First we see God in the far beyond, then we come nearer to Him and give Him omnipresence so that we live in Him; and at last we recognise that we are He. The idea of an Objective God is not untrue — in fact, every idea of God, and hence every religion, is true, as each is but a different stage in the journey, the aim of which is the perfect conception of the Vedas. Hence, too, we not only tolerate, but we Hindus accept every religion, praying in the mosque of the Mohammedans, worshipping before the fire of the Zoroastrians, and kneeling before the cross of the Christians, knowing that all the religions, from the lowest fetishism to the highest absolutism, mean so many attempts of the human soul to grasp and realise the infinite, each determined by the conditions of its birth and association, and each of them marking a stage of progress. We gather all these flowers and bind them with the twine of love, making a wonderful bouquet of worship.

If I am God, then my soul is a temple of the Highest, and my every motion should be a worship — love for love's sake, duty for duty's sake, without hope of reward or fear of punishment. Thus my religion means expansion, and expansion means realisation and perception in the highest sense — no mumbling words or genuflections. Man is to become divine, realising the divine more and more from day to day in an endless progress.

(Summary of a lecture delivered before the Ethical Society, Brooklyn, at the Pouch Gallery in Clinton Avenue, on the 30th December, 1894. Reproduced from the *Brooklyn Standard Union.*)

What Is Religion?

A huge locomotive has rushed on over the line and a small worm that was creeping upon one of the rails saved its life by crawling out of the path of the locomotive. Yet this little worm, so insignificant that it can be crushed in a moment, is a living something, while this locomotive, so huge, so immense, is only an engine, a machine. You say the one has life and the other is only dead matter and all its powers and strength and speed are only those of a dead machine, a mechanical contrivance. Yet the poor little worm which moved upon the rail and which the least touch of the engine would have deprived of its life is a majestic being compared to that huge locomotive. It is a small part of the Infinite and, therefore, it is greater than this powerful engine. Why should that be so? How do we know the living from the dead? The machine mechanically performs all the movements its maker made it to perform, its movements are not those of life. How can we make the distinction between the living and the dead, then? In the living there is freedom, there is intelligence; in the dead all is bound and no freedom is possible, because there is no intelligence. This freedom that distinguishes us from mere machines is what we are all striving for. To be more free is the goal of all our efforts, for only in perfect freedom can there be perfection. This effort to attain freedom underlies all forms of worship, whether we know it or not.

If we were to examine the various sorts of worship all over the world, we would see that the rudest of mankind are worshipping ghosts, demons, and the spirits of their forefathers — serpent worship, worship of tribal gods, and worship of the departed ones. Why do they do this? Because they feel that in some unknown way these beings are greater, more powerful than themselves, and limit their freedom. They, therefore, seek to propitiate these beings in order to prevent them from molesting them, in other words, to get more freedom. They also seek to win favour from these superior beings, to get by gift of the gods what ought to be earned by personal effort.

On the whole, this shows that the world is expecting a miracle. This expectation never leaves us, and however we may try, we are all running after the miraculous and extraordinary. What is mind but that ceaseless inquiry into the meaning and mystery of life? We may say that only uncultivated people are going after all these things, but the question still is there: Why should it be so? The Jews were asking for a miracle. The whole world has been asking for the same these thousands of years. There is, again, the universal dissatisfaction. We make an ideal but we have rushed only half the way after it when we make a newer one. We struggle hard to attain to some goal and then discover we do not want it. This dissatisfaction we are having time after time, and what is there in the mind if there is to be only dissatisfaction? What is the meaning of this universal dissatisfaction? It is because freedom is every man's goal. He seeks it ever, his whole life is a struggle after it. The child rebels against law as soon as it is born. Its first utterance is a cry, a protest against the bondage in which it finds itself. This longing for freedom produces the idea of a Being who is absolutely free. The concept of God is a fundamental element in the human constitution. In the Vedanta, Sat-chit-ânanda (Existence-Knowledge-Bliss) is the highest concept of God possible to the mind. It is the essence of knowledge and is by its nature the essence of bliss. We have been stifling that inner voice long enough, seeking to follow law and quiet the human nature, but there is that human instinct to rebel against nature's laws. We may not understand what the meaning is, but there is that unconscious struggle of the human with the spiritual, of the lower with the higher mind, and the struggle attempts to preserve one's separate life, what we call our "individuality".

Even hells stand out with this miraculous fact that we are born rebels; and the first fact of life — the inrushing of life itself — against this we rebel and cry out, "No law for us." As long as we obey the laws we are like machines, and on goes the universe, and we cannot break it. Laws as laws become man's nature. The first inkling of life on its higher level is in seeing this struggle within us to break the bond of nature and to be free. "Freedom, O Freedom! Freedom, O Freedom!" is the song of the soul. Bondage, alas, to be bound in nature, seems its fate.

Why should there be serpent, or ghost, or demon worship and all these various creeds and forms for having miracles? Why do we say that there is life, there is being in anything? There must be a meaning in all this search, this endeavour to understand life, to explain being. It is not meaningless and vain. It is man's ceaseless endeavour to become free. The knowledge which we now call science has been struggling for thousands of years in its attempt to gain freedom, and people ask for freedom. Yet there is no freedom in nature. It is all law. Still the struggle goes on. Nay, the whole of nature from the very sun to the atoms is under law, and even for man there is no freedom. But we cannot believe it. We have been studying laws from the beginning and yet cannot — nay, will not — believe that man is under law. The soul cries ever, "Freedom, O Freedom!" With the conception of

God as a perfectly free Being, man cannot rest eternally in this bondage. Higher he must go, and unless the struggle were for himself, he would think it too severe. Man says to himself, "I am a born slave, I am bound; nevertheless, there is a Being who is not bound by nature. He is free and Master of nature."

The conception of God, therefore, is as essential and as fundamental a part of mind as is the idea of bondage. Both are the outcome of the idea of freedom. There cannot be life, even in the plant, without the idea of freedom. In the plant or in the worm, life has to rise to the individual concept. It is there, unconsciously working, the plant living its life to preserve the variety, principle, or form, not nature. The idea of nature controlling every step onward overrules the idea of freedom. Onward goes the idea of the material world, onward moves the idea of freedom. Still the fight goes on. We are hearing about all the quarrels of creeds and sects, yet creeds and sects are just and proper, they must be there. The chain is lengthening and naturally the struggle increases, but there need be no quarrels if we only knew that we are all striving to reach the same goal.

The embodiment of freedom, the Master of nature, is what we call God. You cannot deny Him. No, because you cannot move or live without the idea of freedom. Would you come here if you did not believe you were free? It is quite possible that the biologist can and will give some explanation of this perpetual effort to be free. Take all that for granted, still the idea of freedom is there. It is a fact, as much so as the other fact that you cannot apparently get over, the fact of being under nature.

Bondage and liberty, light and shadow, good and evil must be there, but the very fact of the bondage shows also this freedom hidden there. If one is a fact, the other is equally a fact. There must be this idea of freedom. While now we cannot see that this idea of bondage, in uncultivated man, is his struggle for freedom, yet the idea of freedom is there. The bondage of sin and impurity in the uncultivated savage is to his consciousness very small, for his nature is only a little higher than the animal's. What he struggles against is the bondage of physical nature, the lack of physical gratification, but out of this lower consciousness grows and broadens the higher conception of a mental or moral bondage and a longing for spiritual freedom. Here we see the divine dimly shining through the veil of ignorance. The veil is very dense at first and the light may be almost obscured, but it is there, ever pure and undimmed — the radiant fire of freedom and perfection. Man personifies this as the Ruler of the Universe, the One Free Being. He does not yet know that the universe is all one, that the difference is only in degree, in the concept.

The whole of nature is worship of God. Wherever there is life, there is this search for freedom and that freedom is the same as God. Necessarily this freedom gives us mastery over all nature and is impossible without knowledge. The more we are knowing, the more we are becoming masters of nature. Mastery alone is making us strong and if there be some being entirely free and master of nature, that being must have a perfect knowledge of nature, must be omnipresent and omniscient. Freedom must go hand in hand with these, and that being alone who has acquired these will be beyond nature.

Blessedness, eternal peace, arising from perfect freedom, is the highest concept of religion underlying all the ideas of God in Vedanta — absolutely free Existence, not bound by anything, no change, no nature, nothing that can produce a change in Him. This same freedom is in you and in me and is the only real freedom.

God is still, established upon His own majestic changeless Self. You and I try to be one with Him, but plant ourselves upon nature, upon the trifles of daily life, on money, on fame, on human love, and all these changing forms in nature which make for bondage. When nature shines, upon what depends the shining? Upon God and not upon the sun, nor the moon, nor the stars. Wherever anything shines, whether it is the light in the sun or in our own consciousness, it is He. He shining, all shines after Him.

Now we have seen that this God is self-evident, impersonal, omniscient, the Knower and Master of nature, the Lord of all. He is behind all worship and it is being done according to Him, whether we know it or not. I go one step further. That at which all marvel, that which we call evil, is His worship too. This too is a part of freedom. Nay, I will be terrible even and tell you that, when you are doing evil, the impulse behind is also that freedom. It may have been misguided and misled, but it was there; and there cannot be any life or any impulse unless that freedom be behind it. Freedom breathes in the throb of the universe. Unless there is unity at the universal heart, we cannot understand variety. Such is the conception of the Lord in the Upanishads. Sometimes it rises even higher, presenting to us an ideal before which at first we stand aghast — that we are in essence one with God. He who is the colouring in the wings of the butterfly, and the blossoming of the rose-bud, is the power that is in the plant and in the butterfly. He who gives us life is the power within us. Out of His fire comes life, and the direst death is also His power. He whose shadow is death, His shadow is immortality also. Take a still higher conception. See how we are flying like hunted hares from all that is terrible, and like them, hiding our heads and thinking we are safe. See how the whole world is flying from everything terrible. Once when I was in Varanasi, I was passing through a place where there was a large tank of water on one side and a high wall on the other. It was in the grounds where there were many monkeys. The monkeys of Varanasi are huge brutes and are sometimes surly. They now took it into their heads not to allow me to pass through their street, so they howled and shrieked and clutched at my feet as I passed. As they pressed closer, I began to run, but the faster I ran, the faster came the monkeys and they began to bite at me. It seemed impossible to escape, but just then I met a stranger who called out to me, "Face the brutes." I turned and faced the monkeys, and they fell back and finally fled. That is a lesson for all life — face the terrible, face it boldly. Like the monkeys, the hardships of life fall back when we cease to flee before them. If we are ever to gain freedom, it must be by conquering nature, never by running away. Cowards never win victories. We have to fight fear and troubles and ignorance if we expect them to flee before us.

What is death? What are terrors? Do you not see the Lord's face in them? Fly from evil and terror and misery, and they will follow you. Face them, and they will flee. The whole world worships ease and pleasure, and very few dare to worship that which is painful. To rise above both is the idea of freedom. Unless man passes through this gate he cannot be free. We all have to face these. We strive to worship the Lord, but the body rises between, nature rises between Him and us and blinds our vision. We must learn how to worship and love Him in the thunderbolt, in shame, in sorrow, in sin. All the world has ever been preaching the God of virtue. I preach a God of virtue and a God of sin in one. Take Him if you dare — that is the one way to salvation; then alone will come to us the Truth Ultimate which comes from the idea of oneness. Then will be lost the idea that one is greater than another. The nearer we approach the law of freedom, the more we shall come under the Lord, and troubles will vanish. Then we shall not differentiate the door of hell from the gate of heaven, nor differentiate between men and say, "I am greater than any being in the universe." Until we see nothing in the world but the Lord Himself, all these evils will beset us and we shall make all these distinctions; because it is only in the Lord, in the Spirit, that we are all one; and until we see God everywhere, this unity will not exist for us.

Two birds of beautiful plumage, inseparable companions, sat upon the same tree, one on the top and one below. The beautiful bird below was eating the fruits of the tree, sweet and bitter, one moment a sweet one and another a bitter. The moment he ate a bitter fruit, he was sorry, but after a while he ate another and when it too was bitter, he looked up and saw the other bird who ate neither the sweet nor the bitter, but was calm and majestic, immersed in his own glory. And then the poor lower bird forgot and went on eating the sweet and bitter fruits again, until at last he ate one that was extremely bitter; and then he stopped again and once more looked up at the glorious bird above. Then he came nearer and nearer to the other bird; and when he had come near enough, rays of light shone upon him and enveloped him, and he saw he was transformed into the higher bird. He became calm, majestic, free, and found that there had been but one bird all the time on the tree. The lower bird was but the reflection of the one above. So we are in reality one with the Lord, but the reflection makes us seem many, as when the one sun reflects in a million dew-drops and seems a million tiny suns. The reflection must vanish if we are to identify ourselves with our real nature which is divine. The universe itself can never be the limit of our satisfaction. That is why the miser gathers more and more money, that is why the robber robs, the sinner sins, that is why you are learning philosophy. All have one purpose. There is no other purpose in life, save to reach this freedom. Consciously or unconsciously, we are all striving for perfection. Every being must attain to it.

The man who is groping through sin, through misery, the man who is choosing the path through hells, will reach it, but it will take time. We cannot save him. Some hard knocks on his head will help him to turn to the Lord. The path of virtue, purity, unselfishness, spirituality, becomes known at last and what all are doing unconsciously, we are trying to do consciously. The idea is expressed by St. Paul, "The God that ye ignorantly worship, Him declare I unto you." This is the lesson for the whole world to learn. What have these philosophies and theories of nature to do, if not to help us to attain to this one goal in life? Let us come to that consciousness of the identity of everything and let man see himself in everything. Let us be no more the worshippers of creeds or sects with small limited notions of God, but see Him in everything in the universe. If you are knowers of God, you will everywhere find the same worship as in your own heart.

Get rid, in the first place, of all these limited ideas and see God in every person — working through all hands, walking through all feet, and eating through every mouth. In every being He lives, through all minds He thinks. He is self-evident, nearer unto us than ourselves. To know this is religion, is faith, and may it please the Lord to give us this faith! When we shall feel that oneness, we shall be immortal. We are physically immortal even, one with the universe. So long as there is one that breathes throughout the universe, I live in that one. I am not this limited little being, I am the universal. I am the life of all the sons of the past. I am the soul of Buddha, of Jesus, of Mohammed. I am the soul of the teachers, and I am all the robbers that robbed, and all the murderers that were hanged, I am the universal. Stand up then; this is the highest worship. You are one with the universe. That only is humility — not crawling upon all fours and calling yourself a sinner.

That is the highest evolution when this veil of differentiation is torn off. The highest creed is Oneness. I am so-and-so is a limited idea, not true of the real "I". I am the universal; stand upon that and ever worship the Highest through the highest form, for God is Spirit and should be worshipped in spirit and in truth. Through lower forms of worship, man's material thoughts rise to spiritual worship and the Universal Infinite One is at last worshipped in and through the spirit. That which is limited is material. The Spirit alone is infinite. God is Spirit, is infinite; man is Spirit and, therefore, infinite, and the Infinite alone can worship the Infinite. We will worship the Infinite; that is the highest spiritual worship. The grandeur of realising these ideas, how difficult it is! I theorise, talk, philosophize; and the next moment something comes against me, and I unconsciously become angry, I forget there is anything in the universe but this little limited self, I forget to say, "I am the Spirit, what is this trifle to me? I am the Spirit." I forget it is all myself playing, I forget God, I forget freedom.

Sharp as the blade of a razor, long and difficult and hard to cross, is the way to freedom. The sages have declared this again and again. Yet do not let these weaknesses and failures bind you. The Upanishads have declared, "Arise ! Awake ! and stop not until the goal is reached." We will then certainly cross the path, sharp as it is like the razor, and long and distant and difficult though it be. Man becomes the master of gods and demons. No one is to blame for our miseries but ourselves. Do you think there is only a dark cup of poison if man goes to look for nectar? The nectar is there and is for every man who strives to reach it. The Lord Himself tells us, "Give up all these paths and struggles. Do thou take refuge in Me. I will take thee to the other shore, be not afraid." We hear that from all the scriptures of the world that come to us. The same voice teaches us to say, "Thy will be done upon earth, as it is in heaven," for "Thine is the kingdom and the power and the glory." It is difficult, all very difficult. I say to myself, "This moment I will take refuge in Thee, O Lord. Unto Thy love I will sacrifice all, and on Thine altar I will place all that is good and virtuous. My sins, my sorrows, my actions, good and evil, I will offer unto Thee; do Thou take them and I will never forget." One moment I say, "Thy will be done," and the next moment something comes to try me and I spring up in a rage. The goal of all religions is the same, but the language of the teachers differs. The attempt is to kill the false "I", so that the real "I", the Lord, will reign. "I the Lord thy God am a jealous God. Thou shalt have no other gods before me," say the Hebrew scriptures. God must be there all alone. We must say, "Not I, but Thou," and then we should give up everything but the Lord. He, and He alone, should reign. Perhaps we struggle hard, and yet the next moment our feet slip, and then we try to stretch out our hands to Mother. We find we cannot stand alone. Life is infinite, one chapter of which is, "Thy will be done," and unless we realise all the chapters we cannot realise the whole. "Thy will be done" — every moment the traitor mind rebels against it, yet it must be said, again and again, if we are to conquer the lower self. We cannot serve a traitor and yet be saved. There is salvation for all except the traitor and we stand condemned as traitors, traitors against our own selves, against the majesty of Mother, when we refuse to obey the voice of our higher Self. Come what will, we must give our bodies and minds up to the Supreme Will. Well has it been said by the Hindu philosopher, "If man says twice, 'Thy will be done,' he commits sin." "Thy will be done," what more is needed, why say it twice? What is good is good. No more shall we take it back. "Thy will be done on earth as it is in heaven, for Thine is the kingdom and the power and the glory for evermore."

Vedic Religious Ideals

What concerns us most is the religious thought — on soul and God and all that appertains to religion. We will take the Samhitâs. These are collections of hymns forming, as it were, the oldest Aryan literature, properly speaking, the oldest literature in the world. There may have been some scraps of literature of older date here and there, older than that even, but not books, or literature properly so called. As a collected book, this is the oldest the world has, and herein is portrayed the earliest feeling of the Aryans, their aspirations, the questions that arose about their manners and methods, and so on. At the very outset we find a very curious idea. These hymns are sung in praise of different gods, Devas as they are called, the bright ones. There is quite a number of them. One is called Indra, another Varuna, another Mitra, Parjanya, and so on. Various mythological and allegorical figures come before us one after the other — for instance, Indra the thunderer, striking the serpent who has withheld the rains from mankind. Then he lets fly his thunderbolt, the serpent is killed, and rain comes down in showers. The people are pleased, and they worship Indra with oblations. They make a sacrificial pyre, kill some animals, roast their flesh upon spits, and offer that meat to Indra. And they had a popular plant called Soma. What plant it was nobody knows now; it has entirely disappeared, but from the books we gather that, when crushed, it produced a sort of milky juice, and that was fermented; and it can also be gathered that this fermented Soma juice was intoxicating. This also they offered to Indra and the other gods, and they also drank it themselves. Sometimes they drank a little too much, and so did the gods. Indra on occasions got drunk. There are passages to show that Indra at one time drank so much of this Soma juice that he talked irrelevant words. So with Varuna. He is another god, very powerful, and is in the same way protecting his votaries, and they are praising him with their libations of Soma. So is the god of war, and so on. But the popular idea that strikes one as making the mythologies of the Samhitas entirely different from the other mythologies is, that along with every one of these gods is the idea of an infinity. This infinite is abstracted, and sometimes described as Âditya. At other times it is affixed, as it were, to all the other gods. Take, for example, Indra. In some of the books you will find that Indra has a body, is very strong, sometimes is wearing golden armour, and comes down, lives and eats with his votaries, fights the demons, fights the snakes, and so on. Again, in one hymn we find that Indra has been given a very high position; he is omnipresent and omnipotent, and Indra sees the heart of every being. So with Varuna. This Varuna is god of the air and is in charge of the water, just as Indra was previously; and then, all of a sudden, we find him raised up and said to be omnipresent, omnipotent, and so on. I will read one passage about this Varuna in his highest form, and you will understand what I mean. It has been translated into English poetry, so it is better that I read it in that form.

> The mighty Lord on high our deeds, as if at hand, espies;
> The gods know all men do, though men would fain their acts disguise;
> Whoever stands, whoever moves, or steals from place to place,
> Or hides him in his secret cell — the gods his movements trace.
> Wherever two together plot, and deem they are alone,
> King Varuna is there, a third, and all their schemes are known.
> This earth is his, to him belong those vast and boundless skies;
> Both seas within him rest, and yet in that small pool he lies,
> Whoever far beyond the sky should think his way to wing.
> He could not there elude the grasp of Varuna the King.
> His spies, descending from the skies, glide all this world around;
> Their thousand eyes all-scanning sweep to earth's remotest bound.

So we can multiply examples about the other gods; they all come, one after the other, to share the same fate — they first begin as gods, and then they are raised to this conception as the Being in whom the whole universe exists, who sees every heart, who is the ruler of the universe. And in the case of Varuna, there is another idea, just the germ of one idea which came, but was immediately suppressed by the Aryan mind, and that was the idea of fear. In another place we read they are afraid they have sinned and ask Varuna for pardon. These ideas were never allowed, for reasons you will come to understand later on, to grow on Indian soil, but the germs were there sprouting, the idea of fear, and the idea of sin. This is the idea, as you all know, of what is called monotheism. This monotheism, we see, came to India at a very early period. Throughout the Samhitas, in the first and oldest part, this monotheistic idea prevails, but we shall find that it did not prove sufficient for the Aryans; they threw it aside, as it were, as a very primitive sort of idea and went further on, as we Hindus think. Of course in reading books and criticisms on the Vedas written by Europeans, the Hindu cannot help smiling when he reads, that the writings of our authors are saturated with this previous education alone. Persons who have sucked in as their mother's milk the idea that the highest ideal of God is the idea of a Personal God, naturally dare not think on the lines of these ancient thinkers of India, when they find that just after the Samhitas, the monotheistic idea with which the Samhita portion is replete was thought by the Aryans to be useless and not worthy of philosophers and thinkers, and that they struggled hard for a more philosophical and transcendental idea. The monotheistic idea was much too human for them, although they gave it such descriptions as "The whole universe rests in Him," and "Thou art the keeper of all hearts." The Hindus were bold, to their great credit be it said, bold thinkers in all their ideas, so bold that one spark of their thought frightens the so-called bold thinkers of the West. Well has it been said by Prof. Max Müller about these thinkers that they climbed up to heights where their lungs only could breathe, and where those of other beings would have burst. These brave people followed reason wherever it led them, no matter at what cost, never caring if all their best superstitions were smashed to pieces, never caring what society would think about them, or talk about them; but what they thought was right and true, they preached and they talked.

Before going into all these speculations of the ancient Vedic sages, we will first refer to one or two very curious instances in the Vedas. The peculiar fact — that these gods are taken up, as it were, one after the other, raised and sublimated, till each has assumed the proportions of the infinite Personal God of the Universe — calls for an explanation. Prof. Max Müller creates for it a new name, as he thinks it peculiar to the Hindus: he calls it "Henotheism". We need not go far for the explanation. It is within the book. A few steps from the very place where we find those gods being raised and sublimated, we find the explanation also. The question arises how the Hindu mythologies should be so unique, so different from all others. In Babylonian or Greek mythologies we find one god struggling upwards, and he assumes a position and remains there, while the other gods die out. Of all the Molochs, Jehovah becomes supreme, and the other Molochs are forgotten, lost for ever; he is the God of gods. So, too, of all the Greek gods, Zeus comes to the front and assumes big proportions, becomes the God of the Universe, and all the other gods become degraded into minor angels. This fact was repeated in later times. The Buddhists and the Jains raised one of their prophets to the Godhead, and all the other gods they made subservient to Buddha, or to Jina. This is the world-wide process, but there we find an exception, as it were. One god is praised, and for the time being it is said that all the other gods obey his commands, and the very one who is said to be raised up by Varuna, is himself raised up, in the next book, to the highest position. They occupy the position of the Personal God in turns. But the explanation is there in the book, and it is a grand explanation, one that has given the theme to all subsequent thought in India, and one that will be the theme of the whole world of religions: "Ekam Sat Viprâ Bahudhâ Vadanti — That which exists is One; sages call It by various names." In all these cases where hymns were written about all these gods, the Being perceived was one and the same; it was the perceiver who made the difference. It was the hymnist, the sage, the poet, who sang in different languages and different words, the praise of one and the same Being. "That which exists is One; sages call It by various names." Tremendous results have followed from that one verse. Some of you, perhaps, are surprised to think that India is the only country where there never has been a religious persecution, where never was any man disturbed for his religious faith. Theists or atheists, monists, dualists, monotheists are there and always live unmolested. Materialists were allowed to preach from the steps of Brahminical temples, against the gods, and against God Himself; they went preaching all over the land that the idea of God was a mere superstition, and that gods, and Vedas, and religion were simply superstitions invented by the priests for their own benefit, and they were allowed to do this unmolested. And so, wherever he went, Buddha tried to pull down every old thing sacred to the Hindus to the dust, and Buddha died of ripe old age. So did the Jains, who laughed at the idea of God. "How can it be that there is a God?" they asked; "it must be a mere superstition." So on, endless examples there are. Before the Mohammedan wave came into India, it was never known what religious persecution was; the Hindus had only experienced it as made by foreigners on themselves. And even now it is a patent fact how much Hindus have helped to build Christian churches, and how much readiness there is to help them. There never has been bloodshed. Even heterodox religions that have come out of India have been likewise affected; for instance, Buddhism. Buddhism is a great religion in some respects, but to confuse Buddhism with Vedanta is without meaning; anyone may mark just the difference that exists between Christianity and the Salvation Army. There are great and good points in Buddhism, but these great points fell into hands which were not able to keep them safe. The jewels which came from philosophers fell into the hands of mobs, and the mobs took up their ideas. They had a great deal of enthusiasm, some marvellous ideas, great and humanitarian ideas, but, after all, there is something else that is necessary — thought and intellect — to keep everything safe. Wherever you see the most humanitarian ideas fall into the hands of the multitude, the first result, you may notice, is degradation. It is learning and intellect that keep things sure. Now this

Buddhism went as the first missionary religion to the world, penetrated the whole of the civilised world as it existed at that time, and never was a drop of blood shed for that religion. We read how in China the Buddhist missionaries were persecuted, and thousands were massacred by two or three successive emperors, but after that, fortune favoured the Buddhists, and one of the emperors offered to take vengeance on the persecutors, but the missionaries refused. All that we owe to this one verse. That is why I want you to remember it: "Whom they call Indra, Mitra, Varuna — That which exists is One; sages call It by various names."

It was written, nobody knows at what date, it may be 8,000 years ago, in spite of all modern scholars may say, it may be 9,000 years ago. Not one of these religious speculations is of modern date, but they are as fresh today as they were when they were written, or rather, fresher, for at that distant date man was not so civilised as we know him now. He had not learnt to cut his brother's throat because he differed a little in thought from himself; he had not deluged the world in blood, he did not become demon to his own brother. In the name of humanity he did not massacre whole lots of mankind then. Therefore these words come to us today very fresh, as great stimulating, life-giving words, much fresher than they were when they were written: "That which exists is One; sages call It by various names." We have to learn yet that all religions, under whatever name they may be called, either Hindu, Buddhist, Mohammedan, or Christian, have the same God, and he who derides any one of these derides his own God.

That was the solution they arrived at. But, as I have said, this ancient monotheistic idea did not satisfy the Hindu mind. It did not go far enough, it did not explain the visible world: a ruler of the world does not explain the world — certainly not. A ruler of the universe does not explain the universe, and much less an external ruler, one outside of it. He may be a moral guide, the greatest power in the universe, but that is no explanation of the universe; and the first question that we find now arising, assuming proportions, is the question about the universe: "Whence did it come?" "How did it come?" "How does it exist?" Various hymns are to be found on this question struggling forward to assume form, and nowhere do we find it so poetically, so wonderfully expressed as in the following hymn:

"Then there was neither aught nor naught, nor air, nor sky, nor anything. What covered all? Where rested all? Then death was not, nor deathlessness, nor change to night and day." The translation loses a good deal of the poetical beauty. "Then death was not, nor deathlessness, nor change to night and day;" the very sound of the Sanskrit is musical. "*That* existed, that breath, covering as it were, that God's existence; but it did not begin to move." It is good to remember this one idea that it existed motionless, because we shall find how this idea sprouts up afterwards in the cosmology, how according to the Hindu metaphysics and philosophy, this whole universe is a mass of vibrations, as it were, motions; and there are periods when this whole mass of motions subsides and becomes finer and finer, remaining in that state for some time. That is the state described in this hymn. It existed unmoved, without vibration, and when this creation began, this began to vibrate and all this creation came out of it, that one breath, calm, self-sustained, naught else beyond it.

"Gloom existed first." Those of you who have ever been in India or any tropical country, and have seen the bursting of the monsoon, will understand the majesty of these words. I remember three poets' attempts to picture this. Milton says, "No light, but rather darkness visible." Kalidasa says, "Darkness which can be penetrated with a needle," but none comes near this Vedic description, "Gloom hidden in gloom." Everything is parching and sizzling, the whole creation seems to be burning away, and for days it has been so, when one afternoon there is in one corner of the horizon a speck of cloud, and in less than half an hour it has extended unto the whole earth, until, as it were, it is covered with cloud, cloud over cloud, and then it bursts into a tremendous deluge of rain. The cause of creation was described as will. That which existed at first became changed into will, and this will began to manifest itself as desire. This also we ought to remember, because we find that this idea of desire is said to be the cause of all we have. This idea of will has been the corner-stone of both the Buddhist and the Vedantic system, and later on, has penetrated into German philosophy and forms the basis of Schopenhauer's system of philosophy. It is here we first hear of it.

> Now first arose desire, the primal seed of mind.
> Sages, searching in their hearts by wisdom, found the bond,
> Between existence and non-existence.

It is a very peculiar expression; the poet ends by saying that "perhaps He even does not know." We find in this hymn, apart from its poetical merits, that this questioning about the universe has assumed quite definite proportions, and that the minds of these sages must have advanced to such a state, when all sorts of common answers would not satisfy them. We find that they were not even satisfied with this Governor above. There are various other hymns where the same idea, comes in, about how this all came, and just as we have seen, when they were trying to find a Governor of the universe, a Personal God, they were taking up one Deva after another, raising him up to that position, so now we shall find that in various hymns one or other idea is taken up, and expanded infinitely and made responsible for everything in the universe. One particular idea is taken as the support, in which everything rests and exists, and that support has become all this. So on with various ideas. They tried this method with Prâna, the life principle. They expanded the idea of the life principle until it became universal and infinite. It is the life principle that is supporting everything; not only the human body, but it is the light of the sun and the moon, it is the power moving everything, the universal motive energy. Some of these attempts are very beautiful, very poetical. Some of them as, "He ushers the beautiful morning," are marvellously lyrical in the way they picture things. Then this very desire, which, as we have just read, arose as the first primal germ of creation, began to be stretched out, until it became the universal God. But none of these ideas satisfied.

Here the idea is sublimated and finally abstracted into a personality. "He alone existed in the beginning; He is the one Lord of all that exists; He supports this universe; He who is the author of souls, He who is the author of strength, whom all the gods worship, whose shadow is life, whose shadow is death; whom else shall we worship? Whose glory the snow-tops of the Himalayas declare, whose glory the oceans with all their waters proclaim." So on it goes, but, as I told you just now, this idea did not satisfy them.

At last we find a very peculiar position. The Aryan mind had so long been seeking an answer to the question from outside. They questioned everything they could find, the sun, the moon, and stars, and they found all they could in this way. The whole of nature at best could teach them only of a personal Being who is the Ruler of the universe; it could teach nothing further. In short, out of the external world we can only get the idea of an architect, that which is called the Design Theory. It is not a very logical argument, as we all know; there is something childish about it, yet it is the only little bit of anything we can know about God from the external world, that this world required a builder. But this is no explanation of the universe. The materials of this world were before Him, and this God wanted all these materials, and the worst objection is that He must be limited by the materials. The builder could not have made a house without the materials of which it is composed. Therefore he was limited by the materials; he could only do what the materials enabled him to. Therefore the God that the Design Theory gives is at best only an architect, and a limited architect of the universe; He is bound and restricted by the materials; He is not independent at all. That much they had found out already, and many other minds would have rested at that. In other countries the same thing happened; the human mind could not rest there; the thinking, grasping minds wanted to go further, but those that were backward got hold of them and did not allow them to grow. But fortunately these Hindu sages were not the people to be knocked on the head; they wanted to get a solution, and now we find that they were leaving the external for the internal. The first thing that struck them was, that it is not with the eyes and the senses that we perceive that external world, and know anything about religion; the first idea, therefore, was to find the deficiency, and that deficiency was both physical and moral, as we shall see. You do not know, says one of these sages, the cause of this universe; there has arisen a tremendous difference between you and me — why? Because you have been talking sense things and are satisfied with sense-objects and with the mere ceremonials of religion, while I have known the Purusha beyond.

Along with this progress of spiritual ideas that I am trying to trace for you, I can only hint to you a little about the other factor in the growth, for that has nothing to do with our subject, therefore I need not enlarge upon it — the growth of rituals. As those spiritual ideas progressed in arithmetical progression, so the ritualistic ideas progressed in geometrical progression. The old superstitions had by this time developed into a tremendous mass of rituals, which grew and grew till it almost killed the Hindu life And it is still there, it has got hold of and permeated every portion of our life and made us born slaves. Yet, at the same time, we find a fight against this advance of ritual from the very earliest days. The one objection raised there is this, that love for ceremonials, dressing at certain times, eating in a certain way, and shows and mummeries of religion like these are only external religion, because you are satisfied with the senses and do not want to go beyond them. This is a tremendous difficulty with us, with every human being. At best when we want to hear of spiritual things our standard is the senses; or a man hears things about philosophy, and God, and transcendental things, and after hearing about them for days, he asks: After all, how much money will they bring, how much sense-enjoyment will they bring? For his enjoyment is only in the senses, quite naturally. But that satisfaction in the senses, says our sage, is one of the causes which have spread the veil between truth and ourselves. Devotion to ceremonials, satisfaction in the senses, and forming various theories, have drawn a veil between ourselves and truth. This is another great landmark, and we shall have to trace this ideal to the end, and see how it developed later on into that wonderful theory of Mâyâ of the Vedanta, how this veil will be the real explanation of the Vedanta, how the truth was there all the time, it was only this veil that had covered it.

Thus we find that the minds of these ancient Aryan thinkers had begun a new theme. They found out that in the external world no search would give an answer to their question. They might seek in the external world for ages, but there would be no answer to their questions. So they fell back upon this other method; and according to this, they were taught that these desires of the senses, desires for ceremonials and externalities have caused a veil to come between themselves and the truth, and that this cannot be removed by any ceremonial. They had to fall back on their own minds, and analyse the mind to find the truth in themselves. The outside world failed and they turned back upon the inside world, and then it became the real philosophy of the Vedanta; from here the Vedanta philosophy begins. It is the foundation-stone of Vedanta philosophy. As we go on, we find that all its inquiries are inside. From the very outset they seemed to declare — look not for the truth in any religion; it is here in the human soul, the miracle of all miracles in the human soul, the emporium of all knowledge, the mine of all existence — seek here. What is not here cannot be there. And they found out step by step that that which is external is but a dull reflection at best of that which is inside. We shall see how they took, as it were, this old idea of God, the Governor of the universe, who is external to the universe, and first put Him inside the universe. He is not a God outside, but He is inside; and they took Him from there into their own hearts. Here He is in the heart of man, the Soul of our souls, the Reality in us.

Several great ideas have to be understood, in order to grasp properly the workings of the Vedanta philosophy. In the first place it is not philosophy in the sense we speak of the philosophy of Kant and Hegel. It is not one book, or the work of one man. Vedanta is the name of a series of books written at different times. Sometimes in one of these productions there will be fifty different things. Neither are they properly arranged; the thoughts, as it were, have been jotted down. Sometimes in the midst of other extraneous things, we find some wonderful idea. But one fact is remarkable, that these ideas in the Upanishads would be always progressing. In that crude old language, the working of the mind of every one of the sages has been, as it were, painted just as it went; how the ideas are at first very crude, and they become finer and finer till they reach the goal of the Vedanta, and this goal assumes a philosophical name. Just at first it was a search after the Devas, the bright ones, and then it was the origin of the universe, and the very same search is getting another name, more philosophical, clearer — the unity of all things — "Knowing which everything else becomes known."

The Vedanta Philosophy

The Vedanta philosophy, as it is generally called at the present day, really comprises all the various sects that now exist in India. Thus there have been various interpretations, and to my mind they have been progressive, beginning with the dualistic or Dvaita and ending with the non-dualistic or Advaita. The word Vedanta literally means the end of the Vedas — the Vedas being the scriptures of the Hindus. Sometimes in the West by the Vedas are meant only the hymns and rituals of the Vedas. But at the present time these parts have almost gone out of use, and usually by the word Vedas in India, the Vedanta is meant. All our commentators, when they want to quote a passage from the scriptures, as a rule, quote from the Vedanta, which has another technical name with the commentators — the Shrutis. (The term Shruti — meaning "that which is heard" — though including the whole of the Vedic literature, is chiefly applied by the commentators to the Upanishads.) Now, all the books known by the name of the Vedanta were not entirely written after the ritualistic portions of the Vedas. For instance, one of them — the Ishâ Upanishad — forms the fortieth chapter of the Yajur-Veda, that being one of the oldest parts of the Vedas. There are other Upanishads which form portions of the Brahmanas or ritualistic writings; and the rest of the Upanishads are independent, not comprised in any of the Brahmanas or other parts of the Vedas; but there is no reason to suppose that they were entirely independent of other parts, for, as we well know, many of these have been lost entirely and many of the Brahmanas have become extinct. So it is quite possible that the independent Upanishads belonged to some Brahmanas, which in course of time fell into disuse, while the Upanishads remained. These Upanishads are also called Forest Books or Aranyakas.

The Vedanta, then, practically forms the scriptures of the Hindus, and all systems of philosophy that are orthodox have to take it as their foundation. Even the Buddhists and Jains, when it suits their purpose, will quote a passage from the Vedanta as authority. All schools of philosophy in India, although they claim to have been based upon the Vedas, took different names for their systems. The last one, the system of Vyâsa, took its stand upon the doctrines of the Vedas more than the previous systems did, and made an attempt to harmonise the preceding philosophies, such as the

Sânkhya and the Nyâya, with the doctrines of the Vedanta. So it is especially called the Vedanta philosophy; and the Sutras or aphorisms of Vyasa are, in modern India, the basis of the Vedanta philosophy. Again, these Sutras of Vyasa have been variously explained by different commentators. In general there are three sorts of commentators in India now; from their interpretations have arisen three systems of philosophy and sects. One is the dualistic, or Dvaita; a second is the qualified non-dualistic, or Vishishtâdvaita; and a third is the non-dualistic, or Advaita. Of these the dualistic and the qualified non-dualistic include the largest number of the Indian people. The non-dualists are comparatively few in number. Now I will try to lay before you the ideas that are contained in all these three sects; but before going on, I will make one remark — that these different Vedanta systems have one common psychology, and that is, the psychology of the Sankhya system. The Sankhya psychology is very much like the psychologies of the Nyaya and Vaisheshika systems, differing only in minor particulars.

All the Vedantists agree on three points. They believe in God, in the Vedas as revealed, and in cycles. We have already considered the Vedas. The belief about cycles is as follows: All matter throughout the universe is the outcome of one primal matter called Âkâsha; and all force, whether gravitation, attraction or repulsion, or life, is the outcome of one primal force called Prâna. Prana acting on Akasha is creating or projecting the universe. At the beginning of a cycle, Akasha is motionless, unmanifested. Then Prana begins to act, more and more, creating grosser and grosser forms out of Akasha — plants, animals, men, stars, and so on. After an incalculable time this evolution ceases and involution begins, everything being resolved back through finer and finer forms into the original Akasha and Prana, when a new cycle follows. Now there is something beyond Akasha and Prana. Both can be resolved into a third thing called Mahat — the Cosmic Mind. This Cosmic Mind does not create Akasha and Prana, but changes itself into them.

We will now take up the beliefs about mind, soul, and God. According to the universally accepted Sankhya psychology, in perception — in the case of vision, for instance — there are, first of all, the instruments of vision, the eyes. Behind the instruments — the eyes — is the organ of vision or Indriya — the optic nerve and its centres — which is not the external instrument, but without which the eyes will not see. More still is needed for perception. The mind or Manas must come and attach itself to the organ. And besides this, the sensation must be carried to the intellect or Buddhi — the determinative, reactive state of the mind. When the reaction comes from Buddhi, along with it flashes the external world and egoism. Here then is the will; but everything is not complete. Just as every picture, being composed of successive impulses of light, must be united on something stationary to form a whole, so all the ideas in the mind must be gathered and projected on something that is stationary — relatively to the body and mind — that is, on what is called the Soul or Purusha or Âtman.

According to the Sankhya philosophy, the reactive state of the mind called Buddhi or intellect is the outcome, the change, or a certain manifestation of the Mahat or Cosmic Mind. The Mahat becomes changed into vibrating thought; and that becomes in one part changed into the organs, and in the other part into the fine particles of matter. Out of the combination of all these, the whole of this universe is produced. Behind even Mahat, the Sankhya conceives of a certain state which is called Avyakta or unmanifested, where even the manifestation of mind is not present, but only the causes exist. It is also called Prakriti. Beyond this Prakriti, and eternally separate from it, is the Purusha, the soul of the Sankhya which is without attributes and omnipresent. The Purusha is not the doer but the witness. The illustration of the crystal is used to explain the Purusha. The latter is said to be like a crystal without any colour, before which different colours are placed, and then it seems to be coloured by the colours before it, but in reality it is not. The Vedantists reject the Sankhya ideas of the soul and nature. They claim that between them there is a huge gulf to be bridged over. On the one hand the Sankhya system comes to nature, and then at once it has to jump over to the other side and come to the soul, which is entirely separate from nature. How can these different colours, as the Sankhya calls them, be able to act on that soul which by its nature is colourless? So the Vedantists, from the very first affirm that this soul and this nature are one. Even the dualistic Vedantists admit that the Atman or God is not only the efficient cause of this universe, but also the material cause. But they only say so in so many words. They do not really mean it, for they try to escape from their conclusions, in this way: They say there are three existences in this universe — God, soul, and nature. Nature and soul are, as it were, the body of God, and in this sense it may be said that God and the whole universe are one. But this nature and all these various souls remain different from each other through all eternity. Only at the beginning of a cycle do they become manifest; and when the cycle ends, they become fine, and remain in a fine state. The Advaita Vedantists — the non-dualists — reject this theory of the soul, and, having nearly the whole range of the Upanishads in their favour, build their philosophy entirely upon them. All the books contained in me Upanishads have one subject, one task before them — to prove the following theme: "Just as by the knowledge of one lump of clay we have the knowledge of all the clay in the universe, so what is that, knowing which we know everything in the universe?" The idea of the Advaitists is to generalise the whole universe into one — that something which is really the whole of this universe. And they claim that this whole universe is one, that it is one Being manifesting itself in all these various forms. They admit that what the Sankhya calls nature exists, but say that nature is God. It is this Being, the Sat, which has become converted into all this — the universe, man, soul, and everything that exists. Mind and Mahat are but the manifestations of that one Sat. But then the difficulty arises that this would be pantheism. How came that Sat which is unchangeable, as they admit (for that which is absolute is unchangeable), to be changed into that which is changeable, and perishable? The Advaitists here have a theory which they call Vivarta Vâda or apparent manifestation. According to the dualists and the Sankhyas, the whole of this universe is the evolution of primal nature. According to some of the Advaitists and some of the dualists, the whole of this universe is evolved from God. And according to the Advaitists proper, the followers of Shankaracharya, the whole universe is the *apparent* evolution of God. God is the material cause of this universe, but not really, only apparently. The celebrated illustration used is that of the rope and the snake, where the rope appeared to be the snake, but was not really so. The rope did not really change into the snake. Even so this whole universe as it exists is that Being. It is unchanged, and all the changes we see in it are only apparent. These changes are caused by Desha, Kâla and Nimitta (space, time, and causation), or, according to a higher psychological generalization, by Nâma and Rupa (name and form). It is by name and form that one thing is differentiated from another. The name and form alone cause the difference. In reality they are one and the same. Again, it is not, the Vedantists say, that there is something as phenomenon and something as noumenon. The rope is changed into the snake apparently only; and when the delusion ceases, the snake vanishes. When one is in ignorance, he sees the phenomenon and does not see God. When he sees God, this universe vanishes entirely for him. Ignorance or Mâyâ, as it is called, is the cause of all this phenomenon — the Absolute, the Unchangeable, being taken as this manifested universe. This Maya is not absolute zero, nor non-existence. It is defined as neither existence nor non-existence. It is not existence, because that can be said only of the Absolute, the Unchangeable, and in this sense, Maya is non-existence. Again, it cannot be said it is non-existence; for if it were, it could never produce phenomenon. So it is something which is neither; and in the Vedanta philosophy it is called Anirvachaniya or inexpressible. Maya, then, is the real cause of this universe. Maya gives the name and form to what Brahman or God gives the material; and the latter seems to have been transformed into all this. The Advaitists, then, have no place for the individual soul. They say individual souls are created by Maya. In reality they cannot exist. If there were only one existence throughout, how could it be that I am one, and you are one, and so forth? We are all one, and the cause of evil is the perception of duality. As soon as I begin to feel that I am separate from this universe, then first comes fear, and then comes misery. "Where one hears another, one sees another, that is small. Where one does not see another, where one does not hear another, that is the greatest, that is God. In that greatest is perfect happiness. In small things there is no happiness."

According to the Advaita philosophy, then, this differentiation of matter, these phenomena, are, as it were, for a time, hiding the real nature of man; but the latter really has not been changed at all. In the lowest worm, as well as in the highest human being, the same divine nature is present. The worm form is the lower form in which the divinity has been more overshadowed by Maya; that is the highest form in which it has been least overshadowed. Behind everything the same divinity is existing, and out of this comes the basis of morality. Do not injure another. Love everyone as your own self, because the whole universe is one. In injuring another, I am injuring myself; in loving another, I am loving myself. From this also springs that principle of Advaita morality which has been summed up in one word — self-abnegation. The Advaitist says, this little personalised self is the cause of all my misery. This individualised self, which makes me different from all other beings, brings hatred and jealousy and misery, struggle and all other evils. And when this idea has been got rid of, all struggle will cease, all misery vanish. So this is to be given up. We must always hold ourselves ready, even to give up our lives for the lowest beings. When a man has become ready even to give up his life for a little insect, he has reached the perfection which the Advaitist wants to attain; and at that moment when he has become thus ready, the veil of ignorance falls away from him, and he will feel his own nature. Even in this life, he will feel that he is one with the universe. For a time, as it were, the whole of this phenomenal world will disappear for him, and he will realise what he is. But so long as the Karma of this body remains, he will have to live. This state, when the veil has vanished and yet the body remains for some time, is what the Vedantists call the Jivanmukti, the living freedom. If a man is deluded by a mirage for some time, and one day the mirage disappears — if it comes back again the next day, or at some future time, he will not be deluded. Before the mirage first broke, the man could not distinguish between the reality and the deception. But when it has once broken, as long as he has organs and eyes to work with, he will see the image, but will no more be deluded. That fine distinction between the actual world and the mirage he has caught, and the latter cannot delude him any more. So when the Vedantist has realised his own nature, the whole world has vanished for him. It will come back again, but no more the same world of misery. The prison of misery has become changed into Sat, Chit, Ânanda — Existence Absolute, Knowledge Absolute, Bliss Absolute — and the attainment of this is the goal of the Advaita Philosophy.

(The above address was delivered before the Graduate Philosophical Society of Harvard University, on March 25, 1896.)

(A discussion following this is available at Vol. V.)

Reason And Religion

(Delivered in England)

A sage called Nârada went to another sage named Sanatkumâra to learn about truth, and Sanatkumara inquired what he had studied already. Narada answered that he had studied the Vedas, Astronomy, and various other things, yet he had got no satisfaction. Then there was a conversation between the two, in the course of which Sanatkumara remarked that all this knowledge of the Vedas, of Astronomy, and of Philosophy, was but secondary; sciences were but secondary. That which made us realise the Brahman was the supreme, the highest knowledge. This idea we find in every religion, and that is why religion always claimed to be supreme knowledge. Knowledge of the sciences covers, as it were, only part of our lives, but the knowledge which religion brings to us is eternal, as infinite as the truth it preaches. Claiming this superiority, religions have many times looked down, unfortunately, on all secular knowledge, and not only so, but many times have refused to be justified by the aid of secular knowledge. In consequence, all the world over there have been fights between secular knowledge and religious knowledge, the one claiming infallible authority as its guide, refusing to listen to anything that secular knowledge has to say on the point, the other, with its shining instrument of reason, wanting to cut to pieces everything religion could bring forward. This fight has been and is still waged in every country. Religions have been again and again defeated, and almost exterminated. The worship of the goddess of Reason during the French Revolution was not the first manifestation of that phenomenon in the history of humanity, it was a re-enactment of what had happened in ancient times, but in modern times it has assumed greater proportions. The physical sciences are better equipped now than formerly, and religions have become less and less equipped. The foundations have been all undermined, and the modern man, whatever he may say in public, knows in the privacy of his heart that he can no more "believe". Believing certain things because an organised body of priests tells him to believe, believing because it is written in certain books, believing because his people like him to believe, the modern man knows to be impossible for him. There are, of course, a number of people who seem to acquiesce in the so-called popular faith, but we also know for certain that they do not think. Their idea of belief may be better translated as "not-thinking-carelessness". This fight cannot last much longer without breaking to pieces all the buildings of religion.

The question is: Is there a way out? To put it in a more concrete form: Is religion to justify itself by the discoveries of reason, through which every other science justifies itself? Are the same methods of investigation, which we apply to sciences and knowledge outside, to be applied to the science of Religion? In my opinion this must be so, and I am also of opinion that the sooner it is done the better. If a religion is destroyed by such investigations, it was then all the time useless, unworthy superstition; and the sooner it goes the better. I am thoroughly convinced that its destruction would be the best thing that could happen. All that is dross will be taken off, no doubt, but the essential parts of religion will emerge triumphant out of this investigation. Not only will it be made scientific — as scientific, at least, as any of the conclusions of physics or chemistry — but will have greater strength, because physics or chemistry has no internal mandate to vouch for its truth, which religion has.

People who deny the efficacy of any rationalistic investigation into religion seem to me somewhat to be contradicting themselves. For instance, the Christian claims that his religion is the only true one, because it was revealed to so-and-so. The Mohammedan makes the same claim for his religion; his is the only true one, because it was revealed to so-and-so. But the Christian says to the Mohammedan, "Certain parts of your ethics do not seem to be right. For instance, your books say, my Mohammedan friend, that an infidel may be converted to the religion of Mohammed by force, and if he will not accept the Mohammedan religion he may be killed; and any Mohammedan who kills such an infidel will get a sure entry into heaven, whatever may have been his sins or misdeeds." The Mohammedan will retort by saying, "It is right for me to do so, because my book enjoins it. It will be wrong on my part not to do so." The Christian says, "But my book does not say so." The Mohammedan replies, "I do not know; I am not bound by the authority of your book; my book says, 'Kill all the infidels'. How do you know which is right and which is wrong? Surely what is written in my book is right and what your book says, 'Do not kill,' is wrong. You also say the same thing, my Christian friend; you say that what Jehovah declared to the Jews is right to do, and what he forbade them to do is wrong. So say I, Allah declared in my book that certain things should be done, and that certain things should not be done, and that is all the test of right and wrong." In spite of that the Christian is not satisfied; he insists on a comparison of the morality of the Sermon on the Mount with the morality of the Koran. How is this to be decided? Certainly not by the books, because the books, fighting between themselves, cannot be the judges. Decidedly then we have to admit that there is something more universal than these books, something higher than all the ethical codes that are in the world, something which can judge between the strength of inspirations of different nations. Whether we declare it boldly, clearly, or not — it is evident that here we appeal to reason.

Now, the question arises if this light of reason is able to judge between inspiration and inspiration, and if this light can uphold its standard when the quarrel is between prophet and prophet, if it has the power of understanding anything whatsoever of religion. If it has not, nothing can determine the hopeless fight of books and prophets which has been going on through ages; for it means that all religions are mere lies, hopelessly contradictory, without any constant idea of ethics. The proof of religion depends on the truth of the constitution of man, and not on any books. These books are the outgoings, the effects of man's constitution; man made these books. We are yet to see the books that made man. Reason is equally an effect of that common cause, the constitution of man, where our appeal must be. And yet, as reason alone is directly connected with this constitution, it should be resorted to, as long as it follows faithfully the same. What do I mean by reason? I mean what every educated man or woman is wanting to do at the present time, to apply the discoveries of secular knowledge to religion. The first principle of reasoning is that the particular is explained by the general, the general by the more general, until we come to the universal. For instance, we have the idea of law. If something happens and we believe that it is the effect of such and such a law, we are satisfied; that is an explanation for us. What we mean by that explanation is that it is proved that this one effect, which had dissatisfied us, is only one particular of a general mass of occurrences which we designate by the word "law". When one apple fell, Newton was disturbed; but when he found that all apples fell, it was gravitation, and he was satisfied. This is one principle of human knowledge. I see a particular being, a human being, in the street. I refer him to the bigger conception of man, and I am satisfied; I know he is a man by referring him to the more general. So the particulars are to be referred to the general, the general to the more general, and everything at last to the universal, the last concept that we have, the most universal — that of existence. Existence is the most universal concept.

We are all human beings; that is to say, each one of us, as it were, a particular part of the general concept, humanity. A man, and a cat, and a dog, are all animals. These particular examples, as man, or dog, or cat, are parts of a bigger and more general concept, animal. The man, and the cat, and the dog, and the plant, and the tree, all come under the still more general concept, life. Again, all these, all beings and all materials, come under the one concept of existence, for we all are in it. This explanation merely means referring the particular to a higher concept, finding more of its kind. The mind, as it were, has stored up numerous classes of such generalisations. It is, as it were, full of pigeon-holes where all these ideas are grouped together, and whenever we find a new thing the mind immediately tries to find out its type in one of these pigeon-holes. If we find it, we put the new thing in there and are satisfied, and we are said to have known the thing. This is what is meant by knowledge, and no more. And if we do not find that there is something like it, we are dissatisfied, and have to wait until we find a further classification for it, already existing in the mind. Therefore, as I have already pointed out, knowledge is more or less classification. There is something more. A second explanation of knowledge is that the explanation of a thing must come from inside and not from outside. There had been the belief that, when a man threw up a stone and it fell, some demon dragged it down. Many occurrences which are really natural phenomena are attributed by people to unnatural beings. That a ghost dragged down the stone was an explanation that was not in the thing itself, it was an explanation from outside; but the second explanation of gravitation is something in the nature of the stone; the explanation is coming from inside. This tendency you will find throughout modern thought; in one word, what is meant by science is that the explanations of things are in their own nature, and that no external beings or existences are required to explain what is going on in the universe. The chemist never requires demons, or ghosts, or anything of that sort, to explain his phenomena. The physicist never requires any one of these to explain the things he knows, nor does any other scientist. And this is one of the features of science which I mean to apply to religion. In this religions are found wanting and that is why they are crumbling into pieces. Every science wants its explanations from inside, from the very nature of things; and the religions are not able to supply this. There is an ancient theory of a personal deity entirely separate from the universe, which has been held from the very earliest time. The arguments in favour of this have been repeated again and again, how it is necessary to have a God entirely separate from the universe, an extra-cosmic deity, who has created the universe out of his will, and is conceived by religion to be its ruler. We find, apart from all these arguments, the Almighty God painted as the All-merciful, and at the same time, inequalities remain in the world. These things do not concern the philosopher at all, but he says the heart of the thing was wrong; it was an explanation from outside, and not inside. What is the cause of the universe? Something outside of it, some being who is moving this universe! And just as it was found insufficient to explain the phenomenon of the falling stone, so this was found insufficient to explain religion. And religions are falling to pieces, because they cannot give a better explanation than that.

Another idea connected with this, the manifestation of the same principle, that the explanation of everything comes from inside it, is the modern law of evolution. The whole meaning of evolution is simply that the nature of a thing is reproduced, that the effect is nothing but the cause in another form, that all the potentialities of the effect were present in the cause, that the whole of creation is but an evolution and not a creation. That is to say, every effect is a reproduction of a preceding cause, changed only by the circumstances, and thus it is going on throughout the universe, and we need not go outside the universe to seek the causes of these changes; they are within. It is unnecessary to seek for any cause outside. This also is breaking down religion. What I mean by breaking down religion is that religions that have held on to the idea of an extra-cosmic deity, that he is a very big man and nothing else, can no more stand on their feet; they have been pulled down, as it were.

Can there be a religion satisfying these two principles? I think there can be. In the first place we have seen that we have to satisfy the principle of generalisation. The generalisation principle ought to be satisfied along with the principle of evolution. We have to come to an ultimate generalisation, which not only will be the most universal of all generalisations, but out of which everything else must come. It will be of the same nature as the lowest effect; the cause, the highest, the ultimate, the primal cause, must be the same as the lowest and most distant of its effects, a series of evolutions. The Brahman of the Vedanta fulfils that condition, because Brahman is the last generalisation to which we can come. It has no attributes but is Existence, Knowledge, and Bliss — Absolute. Existence, we have seen, is the very ultimate generalisation which the human mind can come to. Knowledge does not mean the knowledge we have, but the essence of that, that which is expressing itself in the course of evolution in human beings or in other animals as knowledge. The essence of that knowledge is meant, the ultimate fact beyond, if I may be allowed to say so, even consciousness. That is what is meant by knowledge and what we see in the universe as the essential unity of things. To my mind, if modern science is proving anything again and again, it is this, that we are one — mentally, spiritually, and physically. It is wrong to say we are even physically different. Supposing we are materialists, for argument's sake, we shall have to come to this, that the whole universe is simply an ocean of matter, of which you and I are like little whirlpools. Masses of matter are coming into each whirlpool, taking the whirlpool form, and coming out as matter again. The matter that is in my body may have been in yours a few years ago, or in the sun, or may have been the matter in a plant, and so on, in a continuous state of flux. What is meant by your body and my body? It is the oneness of the body.

So with thought. It is an ocean of thought, one infinite mass, in which your mind and my mind are like whirlpools. Are you not seeing the effect now, how my thoughts are entering into yours, and yours into mine? The whole of our lives is one; we are one, even in thought. Coming to a still further generalisation, the essence of matter and thought is their potentiality of spirit; this is the unity from which all have come, and that must essentially be one. We are absolutely one; we are physically one, we are mentally one, and as spirit, it goes without saying, that we are one, if we believe in spirit at all. This oneness is the one fact that is being proved every day by modern science. To proud man it is told: You are the same as that little worm there; think not that you are something enormously different from it; you are the same. You have been that in a previous incarnation, and the worm has crawled up to this man state, of which you are so proud. This grand preaching, the oneness of things, making us one with everything that exists, is the great lesson to learn, for most of us are very glad to be made one with higher beings, but nobody wants to be made one with lower beings. Such is human ignorance, that if anyone's ancestors were men whom society honoured, even if they were brutish, if they were robbers, even robber barons, everyone of us would try to trace our ancestry to them; but if among our ancestors we had poor, honest gentlemen, none of us wants to trace our ancestry to them. But the scales are falling from our eyes, truth is beginning to manifest itself more and more, and that is a great gain to religion. That is exactly the teaching of the Advaita, about which I am lecturing to you. The Self is the essence of this universe, the essence of all souls; He is the essence of your own life, nay, "Thou art That". You are one with this universe. He who says he is different from others, even by a hair's breadth, immediately becomes miserable. Happiness belongs to him who knows this oneness, who knows he is one with this universe.

Thus we see that the religion of the Vedanta can satisfy the demands of the scientific world, by referring it to the highest generalisation and to the law of evolution. That the explanation of a thing comes from within itself is still more completely satisfied by Vedanta. The Brahman, the God of the Vedanta, has nothing outside of Himself; nothing at all. All this indeed is He: He is in the universe: He is the universe Himself. "Thou art the man, Thou art the woman, Thou art the young man walking in the pride of youth, Thou art the old man tottering in his step." He is here. Him we see and feel: in Him we live, and move, and have our being. You have that conception in the New Testament. It is that idea, God immanent in the universe, the very essence, the heart, the soul of things. He manifests Himself, as it were, in this universe. You and I are little bits, little points, little channels, little expressions, all living inside of that infinite ocean of Existence, Knowledge, and Bliss. The difference between man and man, between angels and man, between man and animals, between animals and plants, between plants and stones is not in kind, because everyone from the highest angel to the lowest particle of matter is but an expression of that one infinite ocean, and the difference is only in degree. I am a low manifestation, you may be a higher, but in both the materials are the same. You and I are both outlets of the same channel, and that is God; as such, your nature is God, and so is mine. You are of the nature of God by your birthright; so am I. You may be an angel of purity, and I may be the blackest of demons. Nevertheless, my birthright is that infinite ocean of Existence, Knowledge, and Bliss. So is yours. You have manifested yourself more today. Wait; I will manifest myself more yet, for I have it all within me. No extraneous explanation is sought; none is asked for. The sum total of this whole universe is God Himself. Is God then matter? No, certainly not, for matter is that God perceived by the five senses; that God as perceived through the intellect is mind; and when the spirit sees, He is seen as spirit. He is not matter, but whatever is real in matter is He. Whatever is real in this chair is He, for the chair requires two things to make it. Something was outside which my senses brought to me, and to which my mind contributed something else, and the combination of these two is the chair. That which existed eternally, independent of the senses and of the intellect, was the Lord Himself. Upon Him the senses are painting chairs, and tables, and rooms, houses, and worlds, and moons, and suns, and stars, and everything else. How is it, then, that we all see this same chair, that we are all alike painting these various things on the Lord, on this Existence, Knowledge, and Bliss? It need not be that all paint the same way, but those who paint the same way are on the same plane of existence and therefore they see one another's paintings as well as one another. There may be millions of beings between you and me who do not paint the Lord in the same way, and them and their paintings we do not see.

On the other hand, as you all know, the modern physical researches are tending more and more to demonstrate that what is real is but the finer; the gross is simply appearance. However that may be, we have seen that if any theory of religion can stand the test of modern reasoning, it is the Advaita, because it fulfils its two requirements. It is the highest generalisation, beyond even personality, generalisation which is common to every being. A generalisation ending in the Personal God can never be universal, for, first of all, to conceive of a Personal God we must say, He is all-merciful, all-good. But this world is a mixed thing, some good and some bad. We cut off what we like, and generalise that into a Personal God! Just as you say a Personal God is this and that, so you have also to say that He is not this and not that. And you will always find that the idea of a Personal God has to carry with it a personal devil. That is how we clearly see that the idea of a Personal God is not a true generalisation, we have to go beyond, to the Impersonal. In that the universe exists, with all its joys and miseries, for whatever exists in it has all come from the Impersonal. What sort of a God can He be to whom we attribute evil and other things? The idea is that both good and evil are different aspects, or manifestations of the same thing. The idea that they were two was a very wrong idea from the first, and it has been the cause of a good deal of the misery in this world of ours — the idea that right and wrong are two separate things, cut and dried, independent of each other, that good and evil are two eternally separable and separate things. I should be very glad to see a man who could show me something which is good all the time, and something which is bad all the time. As if one could stand and gravely define some occurrences in this life of ours as good and good alone, and some which are bad and bad alone. That which is good today may be evil tomorrow. That which is bad today may be good tomorrow. What is good for me may be bad for you. The conclusion is, that like every other thing, there is an evolution in good and evil too. There is something which in its evolution, we call, in one degree, good, and in another, evil. The storm that kills my friend I call evil, but that may have saved the lives of hundreds of thousands of people by killing the bacilli in the air. They call it good, but I call it evil. So both good and evil belong to the relative world, to phenomena. The Impersonal God we propose is not a relative God; therefore it cannot be said that It is either good or bad, but that It is something beyond, because It is neither good nor evil. Good, however, is a nearer manifestation of It than evil.

What is the effect of accepting such an Impersonal Being, an Impersonal Deity? What shall we gain? Will religion stand as a factor in human life, our consoler, our helper? What becomes of the desire of the human heart to pray for help to some being? That will all remain. The Personal God will remain, but on a better basis. He has been strengthened by the Impersonal. We have seen that without the Impersonal, the Personal cannot remain. If you mean to say there is a Being entirely separate from this universe, who has created this universe just by His will, out of nothing, that cannot be proved. Such a state of things cannot be. But if we understand the idea of the Impersonal, then the idea of the Personal can remain there also. This universe, in its various forms, is but the various readings of the same Impersonal. When we read it with the five senses, we call it the material world. If there be a being with more senses than five, he will read it as something else. If one of us gets the electrical sense, he will see the universe as something else again. There are various forms of that same Oneness, of which all these various ideas of worlds are but various readings, and the Personal God is the highest reading that can be attained to, of that Impersonal, by the human intellect. So that the Personal God is true as much as this chair is true, as much as this world is true, but no more. It is not absolute truth. That is to say, the Personal God is that very Impersonal God and, therefore, it is true, just as I, as a human being, am true and not true at the same time. It is not true that I am what you see I am; you can satisfy yourself on that point. I am not the being that you take me to be. You can satisfy your reason as to that, because light, and various vibrations, or conditions of the atmosphere, and all sorts of motions inside me have contributed to my being looked upon as what I am, by you. If any one of these conditions change, I am different again. You may satisfy yourself by taking a photograph of the same man under different conditions of light. So I am what I appear in relation to your senses, and yet, in spite of all these facts, there is an unchangeable something of which all these are different states of existence, the impersonal me, of which thousands of me's are different persons. I was a child, I was young, I am getting older. Every day of my life, my body and thoughts are changing, but in spite of all these changes, the sum-total of them constitutes a mass which is a constant quantity. That is the impersonal me, of which all these manifestations form, as it were, parts.

Similarly, the sum-total of this universe is immovable, we know, but everything pertaining to this universe consists of motion, everything is in a constant state of flux, everything changing and moving. At the same time, we see that the universe as a whole is immovable, because motion is a relative term. I move with regard to the chair, which does not move. There must be at least two to make motion. If this whole universe is taken as a unit there is no motion; with regard to what should it move? Thus the Absolute is unchangeable and immovable, and all the movements and changes are only in the phenomenal world, the limited. That whole is Impersonal, and within this Impersonal are all these various persons beginning with the lowest atom, up to God, the Personal God, the Creator, the Ruler of the Universe, to whom we pray, before whom we kneel, and so on. Such a Personal God can be established with a great deal of reason. Such a Personal God is explicable as the highest manifestation of the Impersonal. You and I are very low manifestations, and the Personal God is the highest of which we can conceive. Nor can you or I become that Personal God. When the Vedanta says you and I are God, it does not mean the Personal God. To take an example. Out of a mass of clay a huge elephant of clay is manufactured, and out of the same clay, a little clay mouse is made. Would the clay mouse ever be able to become the clay elephant? But put them both in water and they are both clay; as clay they are both one, but as mouse and elephant there will be an eternal difference between them. The Infinite, the Impersonal, is like the clay in the example. We and the Ruler of the Universe are one, but as manifested beings, men, we are His eternal slaves, His worshippers. Thus we see that the Personal God remains. Everything else in this relative world remains, and religion is made to stand on a better foundation. Therefore it is necessary, that we first know the Impersonal in order to know the Personal.

As we have seen, the law of reason says, the particular is only known through the general. So all these particulars, from man to God, are only known through the Impersonal, the highest generalisation. Prayers will remain, only they will get a better meaning. All those senseless ideas of prayer, the low stages of prayer, which are simply giving words to all sorts of silly desire in our minds, perhaps, will have to go. In all sensible religions, they never allow prayers to God; they allow prayers to gods. That is quite natural. The Roman Catholics pray to the saints; that is quite good. But to pray to God is senseless. To ask God to give you a breath of air, to send down a shower of rain, to make fruits grow in your garden, and so on, is quite unnatural. The saints, however, who were little beings like ourselves, may help us. But to pray to the Ruler of the Universe, prating every little need of ours, and from our childhood saying, "O Lord, I have a headache; let it go," is ridiculous. There have been millions of souls that have died in this world, and they are all here; they have become gods and angels; let them come to your help. But God! It cannot be. Unto Him we must go for higher things. A fool indeed is he who, resting on the banks of the Gangâ, digs a little well for water; a fool indeed is he who, living near a mine of diamonds, digs for bits of crystal.

And indeed we shall be fools if we go to the Father of all mercy, Father of all love, for trivial earthly things. Unto Him, therefore, we shall go for light, for strength, for love. But so long as there is weakness and a craving for servile dependence in us, there will be these little prayers and ideas of the worship of the Personal God. But those who are highly advanced do not care for such little helps, they have wellnigh forgotten all about this seeking things for themselves, wanting things for themselves. The predominant idea in them is — not I, but thou, my brother. Those are the fit persons to worship the Impersonal God. And what is the worship of the Impersonal God? No slavery there — "O Lord, I am nothing, have mercy on me." You know the old Persian poem, translated into English: "I came to see my beloved. The doors were closed. I knocked and a voice came from inside. 'Who art thou?' 'I am so-and-so' The door was not opened. A second time I came and knocked; I was asked the same question, and gave the same answer. The door opened not. I came a third time, and the same question came. I answered, 'I am thee, my love,' and the door opened." Worship of the Impersonal God is through truth. And what is truth? That I am He. When I say that I am not Thou, it is untrue. When I say I am separate from you it is a lie, a terrible lie. I am one with this universe, born one. It is self evident to my senses that I am one with the universe. I am one with the air that surrounds me, one with heat, one with light, eternally one with the whole Universal Being, who is called this universe, who is mistaken for the universe, for it is He and nothing else, the eternal subject in the heart who says, "I am," in every heart — the deathless one, the sleepless one, ever awake, the immortal, whose glory never dies, whose powers never fail. I am one with That.

This is all the worship of the Impersonal, and what is the result? The whole life of man will be changed. Strength, strength it is that we want so much in this life, for what we call sin and sorrow have all one cause, and that is our weakness. With weakness comes ignorance, and with ignorance comes misery. It will make us strong. Then miseries will be laughed at, then the violence of the vile will be smiled at, and the ferocious tiger will reveal, behind its tiger's nature, my own Self. That will be the result. That soul is strong that has become one with the Lord; none else is strong. In your own Bible, what do you think was the cause of that strength of Jesus of Nazareth, that immense, infinite strength which laughed at traitors, and blessed those that were willing to murder him? It was that, "I and my Father are one"; it was that prayer, "Father, just as I am one with you, so make them all one with me." That is the worship of the Impersonal God. Be one with the universe, be one with Him. And this Impersonal God requires no demonstrations, no proofs. He is nearer to us than even our senses, nearer to us than our own thoughts; it is in and through Him that we see and think. To see anything, I must first see Him. To see this wall I first see Him, and then the wall, for He is the eternal subject. Who is seeing whom? He is here in the heart of our hearts. Bodies and minds change; misery, happiness, good and evil come and go; days and years roll on; life comes and goes; but He dies not. The same voice, "I am, I am," is eternal, unchangeable. In Him and through Him we know everything. In Him and through Him we see everything. In Him and through Him we sense, we think, we live, and we are. And that "I," which we mistake to be a little "I," limited, is not only my "I," but yours, the "I" of everyone, of the animals, of the angels, of the lowest of the low. That "I am" is the same in the murderer as in the saint, the same in the rich as in the poor, the same in man as in woman, the same in man as in animals. From the lowest amoeba to the highest angel, He resides in every soul, and eternally declares, "I am He, I am He." When we have understood that voice eternally present there, when we have learnt this lesson, the whole universe will have expressed its secret. Nature will have given up her secret to us. Nothing more remains to be known. Thus we find the truth for which all religions search, that all this knowledge of material sciences is but secondary. That is the only true knowledge which makes us one with this Universal God of the Universe.

Vedanta As A Factor In Civilisation

(Extract from an address delivered at Airlie Lodge, Ridgeway Gardens, England)

People who are capable of seeing only the gross external aspect of things can perceive in the Indian nation only a conquered and suffering people, a race of dreamers and philosophers. They seem to be incapable of perceiving that in the spiritual realm India conquers the world. No doubt it is true that just as the too active Western mind would profit by an admixture of Eastern introspect ion and the meditative habit, so the Eastern would benefit by a somewhat greater activity and energy. Still we must ask: What may be that force which causes this afflicted and suffering people, the Hindu, and the Jewish too (the two races from which have originated all the great religions of the world) to survive, when other nations perish? The cause can only be their spiritual force. The Hindus are still living though silent, the Jews are more numerous today than when they lived in Palestine. The philosophy of India percolates throughout the whole civilised world, modifying and permeating as it goes. So also in ancient times, her trade reached the shores of Africa before Europe was known, and opened communication with the rest of the world, thus disproving the belief that Indians never went outside of their own country.

It is remarkable also that the possession of India by a foreign power has always been a turning-point in the history of that power, bringing to it wealth, prosperity, dominion, and spiritual ideas. While the Western man tries to measure how much it is possible for him to possess and to enjoy, the Eastern seems to take the opposite course, and to measure how little of material possessions he can do with. In the Vedas we trace the endeavour of that ancient people to find God. In their search for Him they came upon different strata; beginning with ancestor worship, they passed on to the worship of Agni, the fire-god, of Indra, the god of thunder, and of Varuna, the God of gods. We find the growth of this idea of God, from many gods to one God, in all religions; its real meaning is that He is the chief of the tribal gods, who creates the world, rules it, and sees into every heart; the stages of growth lead up from a multiplicity of gods to monotheism. This anthropomorphic conception, however, did not satisfy the Hindus, it was too human for them who were seeking the Divine. Therefore they finally gave up searching for God in the outer world of sense and matter, and turned their attention to the inner world. Is there an inner world? And what is it? It is Âtman. It is the Self, it is the only thing an individual can be sure of. If he knows himself, he can know the universe, and not otherwise. The same question was asked in the beginning of time, even in the Rig-Veda, in another form: "Who or what existed from the beginning?" That question was gradually solved by the Vedanta philosophy. The Atman existed. That is to say, what we call the Absolute, the Universal Soul, the Self, is the force by which from the beginning all things have been and are and will be manifested.

While the Vedanta philosophers solved that question, they at the same time discovered the basis of ethics. Though all religions have taught ethical precepts, such as, "Do not kill, do not injure; love your neighbour as yourself," etc., yet none of these has given the reason. Why should I not injure my neighbour? To this question there was no satisfactory or conclusive answer forthcoming, until it was evolved by the metaphysical speculations of the Hindus who could not rest satisfied with mere dogmas. So the Hindus say that this Atman is absolute and all-pervading, therefore infinite. There cannot be two infinites, for they would limit each other and would become finite. Also each individual soul is a part and parcel of that Universal Soul, which is infinite. Therefore in injuring his neighbour, the individual actually injures himself. This is the basic metaphysical truth underlying all ethical codes. It is too often believed that a person in his progress towards perfection passes from error to truth; that when he passes on from one thought to another, he must necessarily reject the first. But no error can lead to truth. The soul passing through its different stages goes from truth to truth, and each stage is true; it goes from lower truth to higher truth. This point may be illustrated in the following way. A man is journeying towards the sun and takes a photograph at each step. How different would be the first photograph from the second and still more from the third or the last, when he reaches the real sun! But all these, though differing so widely from each other, are true, only they are made to appear different by the changing conditions of time and space. It is the recognition of this truth, which has enabled the Hindus to perceive the universal truth of all religions, from the lowest to the highest; it has made of them the only people who never had religious persecutions. The shrine of a Mohammedan saint which is at the present day neglected and forgotten by Mohammedans, is worshipped by Hindus! Many instances may be quoted, illustrating the same spirit of tolerance.

The Eastern mind could not rest satisfied till it had found that goal, which is the end sought by all humanity, namely, Unity. The Western scientist seeks for unity in the atom or the molecule. When he finds it, there is nothing further for him to discover, and so when we find that Unity of Soul or Self, which is called Atman, we can go no further. It becomes clear that everything in the sense world is a manifestation of that One Substance. Further, the scientist is brought to the necessity of recognising metaphysics, when he supposes that atoms having neither breadth nor length yet become, when combined, the cause of extension, length, and breadth. When one atom acts upon another, some medium is necessary. What is that medium? It will be a third atom. If so, then the question still remains unanswered, for how do these two act on the third? A manifest *reductio ad absurdum*. This contradiction in terms is also found in the hypothesis necessary to all physical science that a point is that which has neither parts nor magnitude, and a line has length without breadth. These cannot be either seen or conceived. Why? Because they do not come within the range of the senses. They are metaphysical conceptions. So we see, it is finally the mind which gives the form to all perception. When I see a chair, it is not the real chair external to my eye which I perceive, but an external something plus the mental image formed. Thus even the materialist is driven to metaphysics in the last extremity.

The Spirit And Influence Of Vedanta

(Delivered at the Twentieth Century Club, Boston)

Before going into the subject of this afternoon, will you allow me to say a few words of thanks, now that I have the opportunity? I have lived three years amongst you. I have travelled over nearly the whole of America, and as I am going back from here to my own country, it is meet that I should take this opportunity of expressing my gratitude in this Athens of America. When I first came to this country, after a few days I thought I would be able to write a book on the nation. But after three years' stay here, I find I am not able to write even a page. On the other hand, I find in travelling in various countries that beneath the surface differences that we find in dress and food and little details of manners, man is man all the world over; the same wonderful human nature is everywhere represented. Yet there are certain characteristics, and in a few words I would like to sum up all my experiences here. In this land of America, no question is asked about a man's peculiarities. If a man is a man, that is enough, and they take him into their hearts, and that is one thing I have never seen in any other country in the world.

I came here to represent a philosophy of India, which is called the Vedanta philosophy. This philosophy is very, very ancient; it is the outcome of that mass of ancient Aryan literature known by the name of the Vedas. It is, as it were, the very flower of all the speculations and experiences and analyses, embodied in that mass of literature — collected and culled through centuries. This Vedanta philosophy has certain peculiarities. In the first place, it is perfectly impersonal; it does not owe its origin to any person or prophet: it does not build itself around one man as a centre. Yet it has nothing to say against philosophies which do build themselves around certain persons. In later days in India, other philosophies and systems arose, built around certain persons — such as Buddhism, or many of our present sects. They each have a certain leader to whom they owe allegiance, just as the Christians and Mohammedans have. But the Vedanta philosophy stands at the background of all these various sects, and there is no fight and no antagonism between the Vedanta and any other system in the world.

One principle it lays down — and that, the Vedanta claims, is to be found in every religion in the world — that man is divine, that all this which we see around us is the outcome of that consciousness of the divine. Everything that is strong, and good, and powerful in human nature is the outcome of that divinity, and though potential in many, there is no difference between man and man essentially, all being alike divine. There is, as it were, an infinite ocean behind, and you and I are so many waves, coming out of that infinite ocean; and each one of us is trying his best to manifest that infinite outside. So, potentially, each one of us has that infinite ocean of Existence, Knowledge, and Bliss as our birthright, our real nature; and the difference between us is caused by the greater or lesser power to manifest that divine. Therefore the Vedanta lays down that each man should be treated not as what he manifests, but as what he stands for. Each human being stands for the divine, and, therefore, every teacher should be helpful, not by condemning man, but by helping him to call forth the divinity that is within him.

It also teaches that all the vast mass of energy that we see displayed in society and in every plane of action is really from inside out; and, therefore, what is called inspiration by other sects, the Vedantist begs the liberty to call the *expiration* of man. At the same time it does not quarrel with other sects; the Vedanta has no quarrel with those who do not understand this divinity of man. Consciously or unconsciously, every man is trying to unfold that divinity.

Man is like an infinite spring, coiled up in a small box, and that spring is trying to unfold itself; and all the social phenomena that we see the result of this trying to unfold. All the competitions and struggles and evils that we see around us are neither the causes of these unfoldments, nor the effects. As one of our great philosophers says — in the case of the irrigation of a field, the tank is somewhere upon a higher level, and the water is trying to rush into the field, and is barred by a gate. But as soon as the gate is opened, the water rushes in by its own nature; and if there is dust and dirt in the way, the water rolls over them. But dust and dirt are neither the result nor the cause of this unfolding of the divine nature of man. They are coexistent circumstances, and, therefore, can be remedied.

Now, this idea, claims the Vedanta, is to be found in all religions, whether in India or outside of it; only, in some of them, the idea is expressed through mythology, and in others, through symbology. The Vedanta claims that there has not been one religious inspiration, one manifestation of the divine man, however great, but it has been the expression of that infinite oneness in human nature; and all that we call ethics and morality and doing good to others is also but the manifestation of this oneness. There are moments when every man feels that he is one with the universe, and he rushes forth to express it, whether he knows it or not. This expression of oneness is what we call love and sympathy, and it is the basis of all our ethics and morality. This is summed up in the Vedanta philosophy by the celebrated aphorism, Tat Tvam Asi, "Thou art That".

To every man, this is taught: Thou art one with this Universal Being, and, as such, every soul that exists is your soul; and every body that exists is your body; and in hurting anyone, you hurt yourself, in loving anyone, you love yourself. As soon as a current of hatred is thrown outside, whomsoever else it hurts, it also hurts yourself; and if love comes out from you, it is bound to come back to you. For I am the universe; this universe is my body. I am the Infinite, only I am not conscious of it now; but I am struggling to get this consciousness of the Infinite, and perfection will be reached when full consciousness of this Infinite comes.

Another peculiar idea of the Vedanta is that we must allow this infinite variation in religious thought, and not try to bring everybody to the same opinion, because the goal is the same. As the Vedantist says in his poetical language, "As so many rivers, having their source in different mountains, roll down, crooked or straight, and at last come into the ocean — so, all these various creeds and religions, taking their start from different standpoints and running through crooked or straight courses, at last come unto THEE."

As a manifestation of that, we find that this most ancient philosophy has, through its influence, directly inspired Buddhism, the first missionary religion of the world, and indirectly, it has also influenced Christianity, through the Alexandrians, the Gnostics, and the European philosophers of the middle ages. And later, influencing German thought, it has produced almost a revolution in the regions of philosophy and psychology. Yet all this mass of influence has been given to the world almost unperceived. As the gentle falling of the dew at night brings support to all vegetable life, so, slowly and imperceptibly, this divine philosophy has been spread through the world for the good of mankind. No march of armies has been used to preach this religion. In Buddhism, one of the most missionary religions of the world, we find inscriptions remaining of the great Emperor Asoka — recording how missionaries were sent to Alexandria, to Antioch, to Persia, to China, and to various other countries of the then civilised world. Three hundred years before Christ, instructions were given them not to revile other religions: "The basis of all religions is the same, wherever they are; try to help them all you can, teach them all you can, but do not try to injure them."

Thus in India there never was any religious persecution by the Hindus, but only that wonderful reverence, which they have for all the religions of the world. They sheltered a portion of the Hebrews, when they were driven out of their own country; and the Malabar Jews remain as a result. They received at another time the remnant of the Persians, when they were almost annihilated; and they remain to this day, as a part of us and loved by us, as the modern Parsees of Bombay. There were Christians who claimed to have come with St. Thomas, the disciple of Jesus Christ; and they were allowed to settle in India and hold their own opinions; and a colony of them is even now in existence in India. And this spirit of toleration has not died out. It will not and cannot die there.

This is one of the great lessons that the Vedanta has to teach. Knowing that, consciously or unconsciously, we are struggling to reach the same goal, why should we be impatient? If one man is slower than another, we need not be impatient, we need not curse him, or revile him. When our eyes are opened and the heart is purified, the work of the same divine influence, the unfolding of the same divinity in every human heart, will become manifest; and then alone we shall be in a position to claim the brotherhood of man.

When a man has reached the highest, when he sees neither man nor woman, neither sect nor creed, nor colour, nor birth, nor any of these differentiations, but goes beyond and finds that divinity which is the real man behind every human being — then alone he has reached the universal brotherhood, and that man alone is a Vedantist.

Such are some of the practical historical results of the Vedanta.

Steps Of Hindu Philosophic Thought

The first group of religious ideas that we see coming up — I mean recognised religious ideas, and not the very low ideas, which do not deserve the name of religion — all include the idea of inspiration and revealed books and so forth. The first group of religious ideas starts with the idea of God. Here is the universe, and this universe is created by a certain Being. Everything that is in this universe has been created by Him. Along with that, at a later stage, comes the idea of soul — that there is this body, and something inside this body which is not the body. This is the most primitive idea of religion that we know. We can find a few followers of that in India, but it was given up very early. The Indian religions take a peculiar start. It is only by strict analysis, and much calculation and conjecture, that we can ever think that that stage existed in Indian religions. The tangible state in which we find them is the next step, not the first one. At the earliest step the idea of creation is very peculiar, and it is that the whole universe is created out of zero, at the will of God; that all this universe did not exist, and out of this nothingness all this has come. In the next stage we find this conclusion is questioned. How can existence be produced out of nonexistence? At the first step in the Vedanta this question is asked. If this universe is existent it must have come out of something, because it was very easy to see that nothing comes out of nothing, anywhere. All work that is done by human hands requires materials. If a house is built, the material was existing before; if a boat is made the material existed before; if any implements are made, the materials were existing before. So the effect is produced. Naturally, therefore, the first idea that this world was created out of nothing was rejected, and some material out of which this world was created was wanted. The whole history of religion, in fact, is this search after that material.

Out of what has all this been produced? Apart from the question of the efficient cause, or God, apart from the question that God created the universe, the great question of all questions is: Out of what did He create it? All the philosophies are turning, as it were, on this question. One solution is that nature, God, and soul are eternal existences, as if three lines are running parallel eternally, of which nature and soul comprise what they call the dependent, and God the independent Reality. Every soul, like every particle of matter, is perfectly dependent on the will of God. Before going to the other steps we will take up the idea of soul, and then find that with all the Vedantic philosophers, there is one tremendous departure from all Western philosophy. All of them have a common psychology. Whatever their philosophy may have been, their psychology is the same in India, the old Sânkhya psychology. According to this, perception occurs by the transmission of the vibrations which first come to the external sense-organs, from the external to the internal organs, from the internal organs to the mind, from the mind to the Buddhi, from the Buddhi or intellect, to something which is a unit, which they call the Âtman. Coming to modern physiology, we know that it has found centres for all the different sensations. First it finds the lower centres, and then a higher grade of centres, and these two centres exactly correspond with the internal organs and the mind, but not one centre has been found which controls all the other centres. So physiology cannot tell what unifies all these centres. Where do the centres get united? The centres in the brain are all different. and there is not one centre which controls all the other centres; therefore, so far as it goes, the Indian psychology stands unchallenged upon this point. We must have this unification, some thing upon which the sensations will be reflected, to form a complete whole. Until there is that something, I cannot have any idea of you, or a picture, or anything else. If we had not that unifying something, we would only see, then after a while breathe, then hear, and so on, and while I heard a man talking I would not see him at all, because all the centres are different.

This body is made of particles which we call matter, and it is dull and insentient. So is what the Vedantists call the fine body. The fine body, according to them, is a material but transparent body, made of very fine particles, so fine that no microscope can see them. What is the use of that? It is the receptacle of the fine forces. Just as this gross body is the receptacle of the gross forces, so the fine body is the receptacle of the fine forces, which we call thought, in its various modifications. First is the body, which is gross matter, with gross force. Force cannot exist without matter. It must require some matter to exist, so the grosser forces work in the body; and those very forces become finer; the very force which is working in a gross form, works in a fine form, and becomes thought. There is no distinction between them, simply one is the gross and the other the fine manifestation of the same thing. Neither is there any distinction between this fine body and the gross body. The fine body is also material, only very fine matter; and just as this gross body is the instrument that works the gross forces, so the fine body is the instrument that works the fine forces. From where do all these forces come? According to Vedanta philosophy, there are two things in nature, one of which they call Âkâsha, which is the substance, infinitely fine, and the other they call Prâna, which is the force. Whatever you see, or feel, or hear, as air, earth, or anything, is material — the product of Akasha. It goes on and becomes finer and finer, or grosser and grosser, changing under the action of Prana. Like Akasha, Prana is omnipresent, and interpenetrating everything. Akasha is like the water, and everything else in the universe is like blocks of ice, made out of that water, and floating in the water, and Prana is the power that changes this Akasha into all these various forms. The gross body is the instrument made out of Akasha, for the manifestation of Prana in gross forms, as muscular motion, or walking, sitting, talking, and so forth. That fine body is also made of Akasha, a very fine form of Akasha, for the manifestation of the same Prana in the finer form of thought. So, first there is this gross body. Beyond that is this fine body, and beyond that is the Jiva, the real man. Just as the nails can be pared off many times and yet are still part of our bodies, not different, so is our gross body related to the fine. It is not that a man has a fine and also a gross body; it is the one body only, the part which endures longer is the fine body, and that which dissolves sooner is the gross. Just as I can cut this nail any number of times, so, millions of times I can shed this gross body, but the fine body will remain. According to the dualists, this Jiva or the real man is very fine, minute.

So far we see that man is a being, who has first a gross body which dissolves very quickly, then a fine body which remains through aeons, and then a Jiva. This Jiva, according to the Vedanta philosophy, is eternal, just as God is eternal. Nature is also eternal, but changefully eternal. The material of nature — Prana and Akasha — is eternal, but it is changing into different forms eternally. But the Jiva is not manufactured either of Akasha or Prana; it is immaterial and, therefore, will remain for ever. It is not the result of any combination of Prana and Akasha, and whatever is not the result of combination, will never be destroyed, because destruction is going back to causes. The gross body is a compound of Akasha and Prana and, therefore, will be decomposed. The fine body will also be decomposed, after a long time, but the Jiva is simple, and will never be destroyed. It was never born for the same reason. Nothing simple can be born. The same argument applies. That which is a compound only can be born. The whole of nature comprising millions and millions of souls is under the will of God. God is all-pervading, omniscient, formless, and He is working through nature day and night. The whole of it is under His control. He is the eternal Ruler. So say the dualists. Then the question comes: If God is the ruler of this universe, why did He create such a wicked universe, why must we suffer so much? They say, it is not God's fault. It is our fault that we suffer. Whatever we sow we reap. He did not do anything to punish us. Man is born poor, or blind, or some other way. What is the reason? He had done something before, he was born that way. The Jiva has been existing for all time, was never created. It has been doing all sorts of things all the time. Whatever we do reacts upon us. If we do good, we shall have happiness, and if evil, unhappiness. So the Jiva goes on enjoying and suffering, and doing all sorts of things.

What comes after death? All these Vedanta philosophers admit that this Jiva is by its own nature pure. But ignorance covers its real nature, they say. As by evil deeds it has covered itself with ignorance, so by good deeds it becomes conscious of its own nature again. Just as it is eternal, so its nature is pure. The nature of every being is pure.

When through good deeds all its sins and misdeeds have been washed away, then the Jiva becomes pure again, and when it becomes pure, it goes to what is called Devayâna. Its organ of speech enters the mind. You cannot think without words. Wherever there is thought, there must be words. As words enter the mind, so the mind is resolved into the Prana, and the Prana into the Jiva. Then the Jiva gets quickly out of the body, and goes to the solar regions. This universe has sphere after sphere. This earth is the world sphere, in which are moons, suns, and stars. Beyond that here is the solar sphere, and beyond that another which they call the lunar sphere. Beyond that there is the sphere which they call the sphere of lightning, the electric sphere, and when the Jiva goes there, there comes another Jiva, already perfect, to receive it, and takes it to another world, the highest heaven, called the Brahmaloka, where the Jiva lives eternally, no more to be born or to die. It enjoys through eternity, and gets all sorts of powers, except the power of creation. There is only one ruler of the universe, and that is God. No one can become God; the dualists maintain that if you say you are God, it is a blasphemy. All powers except the creative come to the Jiva, and if it likes to have bodies, and work in different parts of the world, it can do so. If it orders all the gods to come before it, if it wants its forefathers to come, they all appear at its command. Such are its powers that it never feels any more pain, and if it wants, it can live in the Brahmaloka through all eternity. This is the highest man, who has attained the love of God, who has become perfectly unselfish, perfectly purified, who has given up all desires, and who does not want to do anything except worship and love God.

There are others that are not so high, who do good works, but want some reward. They say they will give so much to the poor, but want to go to heaven in return. When they die, what becomes of them? The speech enters the mind, the mind enters the Prana, the Prana enters the Jiva, and the Jiva gets out, and goes to the lunar sphere, where it has a very good time for a long period. There it enjoys happiness, so long as the effect of its good deeds endures. When the same is exhausted, it descends, and once again enters life on earth according to its desires. In the lunar sphere the Jiva becomes what we call a god, or what the Christians or Mohammedans call an angel. These gods are the names of certain positions; for instance, Indra, the king of the gods, is the name of a position; thousands of men get to that position. When a virtuous man who has performed the highest of Vedic rites dies, he becomes a king of the gods; by that time the old king has gone down again, and become man. Just as kings change here, so the gods, the Devas, also have to die. In heaven they will all die. The only deathless place is Brahmaloka, where alone there is no birth and death.

So the Jivas go to heaven, and have a very good time, except now and then when the demons give them chase. In our mythology it is said there are demons, who sometimes trouble the gods. In all mythologies, you read how these demons and the gods fought, and the demons sometimes conquered the gods, although many times, it seems, the demons did not do so many wicked things as the gods. In all mythologies, for instance, you find the Devas fond of women. So after their reward is finished, they fall down again, come through the clouds, through the rains, and thus get into some grain or plant and find their way into the human body, when the grain or plant is eaten by men. The father gives them the material out of which to get a fitting body. When the material suits them no longer, they have to manufacture other bodies. Now there are the very wicked fellows, who do, all sorts of diabolical things; they are born again as animals, and if they are very bad, they are born as very low animals, or become plants, or stones.

In the Deva form they make no Karma at all; only man makes Karma. Karma means work which will produce effect. When a man dies and becomes a Deva, he has only a period of pleasure, and during that time makes no fresh Karma; it is simply a reward for his past good Karma. When the good Karma is worked out, then the remaining Karma begins to take effect, and he comes down to earth. He becomes man again, and if he does very good works, and purifies himself, he goes to Brahmaloka and comes back no more.

The animal is a state of sojourn for the Jiva evolving from lower forms. In course of time the animal becomes man. It is a significant fact that as the human population is increasing, the animal population is decreasing. The animal souls are all becoming men. So many species of animals have become men already. Where else have they gone?

In the Vedas, there is no mention of hell. But our Purânas, the later books of our scriptures, thought that no religion could be complete, unless hells were attached to it, and so they invented all sorts of hells. In some of these, men are sawed in half, and continually tortured, but do not die. They are continually feeling intense pain, but the books are merciful enough to say it is only for a period. Bad Karma is worked out in that state and then they come back on earth, and get another chance. So this human form is the great chance. It is called the Karma-body, in which we decide our fate. We are running in a huge circle, and this is the point in the circle which determines the future. So this is considered the most important form that there is. Man is greater than the gods.

So far with dualism, pure and simple. Next comes the higher Vedantic philosophy which says, that this cannot be. God is both the material and the efficient cause of this universe. If you say there is a God who is an infinite Being, and a soul which is also infinite, and a nature which is also infinite, you can go on multiplying infinites without limit which is simply absurd; you smash all logic. So God is both the material and the efficient cause of the universe; He projects this universe out of Himself. Then how is it that God has become these walls and this table, that God has become the pig, and the murderer, and all the evil things in the world? We say that God is pure. How can He become all these degenerate things? Our answer is: just as I am a soul and have a body, and in a sense, this body is not different from me, yet I, the real I, in fact, am not the body. For instance, I say, I am a child, a young man, or an old man, but my soul has not changed. It remains the same soul. Similarly, the whole universe, comprising all nature and an infinite number of souls, is, as it were, the infinite body of God. He is interpenetrating the whole of it. He alone is unchangeable, but nature changes, and soul changes. He is unaffected by changes in nature and soul. In what way does nature change? In its forms; it takes fresh forms. But the soul cannot change that way. The soul contracts and expands in knowledge. It contracts by evil deeds. Those deeds which contract the real natural knowledge and purity of the soul are called evil deeds. Those deeds, again, which bring out the natural glory of the soul, are called good deeds. All these souls were pure, but they have become contracted; through the mercy of God, and by doing good deeds, they will expand and recover their natural purity. Everyone has the same chance, and in the long run, must get out. But this universe will not cease, because it is eternal. This is the second theory. The first is called dualism. The second holds that there are God, soul, and nature, and soul and nature form the body of God, and, therefore, these three form one unit. It represents a higher stage of religious development and goes by the name of qualified monism. In dualism, the universe is conceived as a large machine set going by God while in qualified monism, it is conceived as an organism, interpenetrated by the Divine Self.

The last are the non-dualists. They raise the question also, that God must be both the material and the efficient cause of this universe. As such, God has become the whole of this universe and there is no going against it. And when these other people say that God is the soul, and the universe is the body, and the body is changing, but God is changeless, the non-dualists say, all this is nonsense. In that case what is the use of calling God the material cause of this universe? The material cause is the cause become effect; the effect is nothing but the cause in another form. Wherever you see an effect, it is the cause reproduced. If the universe is the effect, and God the cause, it must be the reproduction of God. If you say that the universe is the body of God, and that the body becomes contracted and fine and becomes the cause, and out of that the universe is evolved, the non-dualists say that it is God Himself who has become this universe. Now comes a very fine question. If this God has become this universe, you and all these things are God. Certainly. This book is God, everything is God. My body is God, and my mind is God, and my soul is God. Then why are there so many Jivas? Has God become divided into millions of Jivas? Does that one God turn into millions of Jivas? Then how did it become so? How can that infinite power and substance, the one Being of the universe, become divided? It is impossible to divide infinity. How can that pure Being become this universe? If He has become the universe, He is changeful, and if He is changeful, He is part of nature, and whatever is nature and changeful is born and dies. If our God is changeful, He must die some day. Take note of that. Again, how much of God has become this universe? If you say X (the unknown algebraical quantity), then God is God minus X now, and, therefore, not the same God as before this creation, because so much has become this universe.

So the non-dualists say, "This universe does not exist at all; it is all illusion. The whole of this universe, these Devas, gods, angels, and all the other beings born and dying, all this infinite number of souls coming up and going down, are all dreams." There is no Jiva at all. How can there be many? It is the one Infinity. As the one sun, reflected on various pieces of water, appears to be many, and millions of globules of water reflect so many millions of suns, and in each globule will be a perfect image of the sun, yet there is only one sun, so are all these Jivas but reflections in different minds.

These different minds are like so many different globules, reflecting this one Being. God is being reflected in all these different Jivas. But a dream cannot be without a reality, and that reality is that one Infinite Existence. You, as body, mind, or soul, are a dream, but what you really are, is Existence, Knowledge, Bliss. You are the God of this universe. You are creating the whole universe and drawing it in. Thus says the Advaitist. So all these births and rebirths, coming and going are the figments of Mâyâ. You are infinite. Where can you go? The sun, the moon, and the whole universe are but drops in your transcendent nature. How can you be born or die? I never was born, never will be born. I never had father or mother, friends or foes, for I am Existence, Knowledge, Bliss Absolute. I am He, I am He. So, what is the goal, according to this philosophy? That those who receive this knowledge are one with the universe. For them, all heavens and even Brahmaloka are destroyed, the whole dream vanishes, and they find themselves the eternal God of the universe. They attain their real individuality, with its infinite knowledge and bliss, and become free. Pleasures in little things cease. We are finding pleasure in this little body, in this little individuality. How much greater the pleasure when this whole universe is my body! If there is pleasure in one body, how much more when all bodies are mine! Then is freedom attained. And this is called Advaita, the non-dualistic Vedanta philosophy.

These are the three steps which Vedanta philosophy has taken, and we cannot go any further, because we cannot go beyond unity. When a science reaches a unity, it cannot by any manner of means go any further. You cannot go beyond this idea of the Absolute.

All people cannot take up this Advaita philosophy; it is hard. First of all, it is very hard to understand it intellectually. It requires the sharpest of intellects, a bold understanding. Secondly, it does not suit the vast majority of people. So there are these three steps. Begin with the first one. Then by thinking of that and understanding it, the second will open itself. Just as a race advances, so individuals have to advance. The steps which the human race has taken to reach to the highest pinnacles of religious thought, every individual will have to take. Only, while the human race took millions of years to reach from one step to another, individuals may live the whole life of the human race in a much shorter duration. But each one of us will have to go through these steps. Those of you who are non-dualists look back to the period of your lives when you were strong dualists. As soon as you think you are a body and a mind, you will have to take the whole of this dream. If you take one portion, you must take the whole. The man who says, here is this world, and there is no (Personal) God, is a fool; because if there is a world, there will have to be a cause, and that is what is called God. You cannot have an effect without knowing that there is a cause. God will only vanish when this world vanishes; then you will become God (Absolute), and this world will be no longer for you. So long as the dream that you are a body exists, you are bound to see yourself as being born and dying; but as soon as that dream vanishes, so will the dream vanish that you are being born and dying, and so will the other dream that there is a universe vanish. That very thing which we now see as the universe will appear to us as God (Absolute), and that very God who has so long been external will appear to be internal, as our own Self.

Steps To Realisation

(A class-lecture delivered in America)

First among the qualifications required of the aspirant for Jnâna, or wisdom, come Shama and Dama, which may be taken together. They mean the keeping of the organs in their own centres without allowing them to stray out. I shall explain to you first what the word "organ" means. Here are the eyes; the eyes are not the organs of vision but only the instruments. Unless the organs also are present, I cannot see, even if I have eyes. But, given both the organs and the instruments, unless the mind attaches itself to these two, no vision takes place. So, in each act of perception, three things are necessary — first, the external instruments, then, the internal organs, and lastly, the mind. If any one of them be absent, then there will be no perception. Thus the mind acts through two agencies — one external, and the other internal. When I see things, my mind goes out, becomes externalised; but suppose I close my eyes and begin to think, the mind does not go out, it is internally active. But, in either case, there is activity of the organs. When I look at you and speak to you, both the organs and the instruments are active. When I close my eyes and begin to think, the organs are active, but not the instruments. Without the activity of these organs, there will be no thought. You will find that none of you can think without some symbol. In the case of the blind man, he has also to think through some figure. The organs of sight and hearing are generally very active. You must bear in mind that by the word "organ" is meant the nerve centre in the brain. The eyes and ears are only the instruments of seeing and hearing, and the organs are inside. If the organs are destroyed by any means, even if the eyes or the ears be there, we shall not see or hear. So in order to control the mind, we must first be able to control these organs. To restrain the mind from wandering outward or inward, and keep the organs in their respective centres, is what is meant by the words Shama and Dama. Shama consists in not allowing the mind to externalise, and Dama, in checking the external instruments.

Now comes Uparati which consists in not thinking of things of the senses. Most of our time is spent in thinking about sense-objects, things which we have seen, or we have heard, which we shall see or shall hear, things which we have eaten, or are eating, or shall eat, places where we have lived, and so on. We think of them or talk of them most of our time. One who wishes to be a Vedantin must give up this habit.

Then comes the next preparation (it is a hard task to be a philosopher!), Titikshâ, the most difficult of all. It is nothing less than the ideal forbearance — "Resist not evil." This requires a little explanation. We may not resist an evil, but at the same time we may feel very miserable. A man may say very harsh things to me, and I may not outwardly hate him for it, may not answer him back, and may restrain myself from apparently getting angry, but anger and hatred may be in my mind, and I may feel very badly towards that man. That is not non-resistance; I should be without any feeling of hatred or anger, without any thought of resistance; my mind must then be as calm as if nothing had happened. And only when I have got to that state, have I attained to non-resistance, and not before. Forbearance of all misery, without even a thought of resisting or driving it out, without even any painful feeling in the mind, or any remorse — this is Titiksha. Suppose I do not resist, and some great evil comes thereby; if I have Titiksha, I should no feel any remorse for not having resisted. When the mind has attained to that state, it has become established in Titiksha. People in India do extraordinary things in order to practice this Titiksha. They bear tremendous heat and cold without caring, they do not even care for snow, because they take no thought for the body; it is left to itself, as if it were a foreign thing.

The next qualification required is Shraddhâ, faith. One must have tremendous faith in religion and God. Until one has it, one cannot aspire to be a Jnâni. A great sage once told me that not one in twenty millions in this world believed in God. I asked him why, and he told me, "Suppose there is a thief in this room, and he gets to know that there is a mass of gold in the next room, and only a very thin partition between the two rooms; what will be the condition of that thief?" I answered, "He will not be able to sleep at all; his brain will be actively thinking of some means of getting at the gold, and he will think of nothing else." Then he replied, "Do you believe that a man could believe in God and not go mad to get him? If a man sincerely believes that there is that immense, infinite mine of Bliss, and that It can be reached, would not that man go mad in his struggle to reach it ?" Strong faith in God and the consequent eagerness to reach Him constitute Shraddha.

Then comes Samâdhâna, or constant practice, to hold the mind in God. Nothing is done in a day. Religion cannot be swallowed in the form of a pill. It requires hard and constant practice. The mind can be conquered only by slow and steady practice.

Next is Mumukshutva, the intense desire to be free. Those of you who have read Edwin Arnold's *Light of Asia* remember his translation of the first sermon of Buddha, where Buddha says,

> Ye suffer from yourselves. None else compels.
> None other holds you that ye live and die,
> And whirl upon the wheel, and hug and kiss
> Its spokes of agony,
> Its tire of tears, its nave of nothingness.

All the misery we have is of our own choosing; such is our nature. The old Chinaman, who having been kept in prison for sixty years was released on the coronation of a new emperor, exclaimed, when he came out, that he could not live; he must go back to his horrible dungeon among the rats and mice; he could not bear the light. So he asked them to kill him or send him back to the prison, and he was sent back. Exactly similar is the condition of all men. We run headlong after all sorts of misery, and are unwilling to be freed from them. Every day we run after pleasure, and before we reach it, we find it is gone, it has slipped through our fingers. Still we do not cease from our mad pursuit, but on and on we go, blinded fools that we are.

In some oil mills in India, bullocks are used that go round and round to grind the oil-seed. There is a yoke on the bullock's neck. They have a piece of wood protruding from the yoke, and on that is fastened a wisp of straw. The bullock is blindfolded in such a way that it can only look forward, and so it stretches its neck to get at the straw; and in doing so, it pushes the piece of wood out a little further; and it makes another attempt with the same result, and yet another, and so on. It never catches the straw, but goes round and round in the hope of getting it, and in so doing, grinds out the oil. In the same way you and I who are born slaves to nature, money and wealth, wives and children, are always chasing a wisp of straw, a mere chimera, and are going through an innumerable round of lives without obtaining what we seek. The great dream is love; we are all going to love and be loved, we are all going to be happy and never meet with misery, but the more we go towards happiness, the more it goes away from us. Thus the world is going on, society goes on, and we, blinded slaves, have to pay for it without knowing. Study your own lives, and find how little of happiness there is in them, and how little in truth you have gained in the course of this wild-goose chase of the world.

Do you remember the story of Solon and Croesus? The king said to the great sage that Asia Minor was a very happy place. And the sage asked him, "Who is the happiest man? I have not seen anyone very happy." "Nonsense," said Croesus, "I am the happiest man in the world." "Wait, sir, till the end of your life; don't be in a hurry," replied the sage and went away. In course of time that king was conquered by the Persians, and they ordered him to be burnt alive. The funeral pyre was prepared and when poor Croesus saw it, he cried aloud "Solon! Solon!" On being asked to whom he referred, he told his story, and the Persian emperor was touched, and saved his life.

Such is the life-story of each one of us; such is the tremendous power of nature over us. It repeatedly kicks us away, but still we pursue it with feverish excitement. We are always hoping against hope; this hope, this chimera maddens us; we are always hoping for happiness.

There was a great king in ancient India who was once asked four questions, of which one was: "What is the most wonderful thing in the world?" "Hope," was the answer. This is the most wonderful thing. Day and nights we see people dying around us, and yet we think we shall not die; we never think that we shall die, or that we shall suffer. Each man thinks that success will be his, hoping against hope, against all odds, against all mathematical reasoning. Nobody is ever really happy here. If a man be wealthy and have plenty to eat, his digestion is: out of order, and he cannot eat. If a man's digestion be good, and he have the digestive power of a cormorant, he has nothing to put into his mouth. If he be rich, he has no children. If he be hungry and poor, he has a whole regiment of children, and does not know what to do with them. Why is it so? Because happiness and misery are the obverse and reverse of the same coin; he who takes happiness, must take misery also. We all have this foolish idea that we can have happiness without misery, and it has taken such possession of us that we have no control over the senses.

When I was in Boston, a young man came up to me, and gave me a scrap of paper on which he had written a name and address, followed by these words: "All the wealth and all the happiness of the world are yours, if you only know how to get them. If you come to me, I will teach you how to get them. Charge, $ 5." He gave me this and said, "What do you think of this?" I said, "Young man, why don't you get the money to print this? You have not even enough money to get this printed !" He did not understand this. He was infatuated with the idea that he could get immense wealth and happiness without any trouble. There are two extremes into which men are running; one is extreme optimism, when everything is rosy and nice and good; the other, extreme pessimism, when everything seems to be against them. The majority of men have more or less undeveloped brains. One in a million we see with a well-developed brain; the rest either have peculiar idiosyncrasies, or are monomaniacs.

Naturally we run into extremes. When we are healthy and young, we think that all the wealth of the world will be ours, and when later we get kicked about by society like footballs and get older, we sit in a corner and croak and throw cold water on the enthusiasm of others. Few men know that with pleasure there is pain, and with pain, pleasure; and as pain is disgusting, so is pleasure, as it is the twin brother of pain. It is derogatory to the glory of man that he should be going after pain, and equally derogatory, that he should be going after pleasure. Both should be turned aside by men whose reason is balanced. Why will not men seek freedom from being played upon? This moment we are whipped, and when we begin to weep, nature gives us a dollar; again we are whipped, and when we weep, nature gives us a piece of ginger-bread, and we begin to laugh again.

The sage wants liberty; he finds that sense-objects are all vain and that there is no end to pleasures and pains. How many rich people in the world want to find fresh pleasures! All pleasures are old, and they want new ones. Do you not see how many foolish things they are inventing every day, just to titillate the nerves for a moment, and that done, how there comes a reaction? The majority of people are just like a flock of sheep. If the leading sheep falls into a ditch, all the rest follow and break their necks. In the same way, what one leading member of a society does, all the others do, without thinking what they are doing. When a man begins to see the vanity of worldly things, he will feel he ought not to be thus played upon or borne along by nature. That is slavery. If a man has a few kind words said to him, he begins to smile, and when he hears a few harsh words, he begins to weep. He is a slave to a bit of bread, to a breath of air; a slave to dress, a slave to patriotism, to country, to name, and to fame. He is thus in the midst of slavery and the real man has become buried within, through his bondage. What you call man is a slave. When one realises all this slavery, then comes the desire to be free; an intense desire comes. If a piece of burning charcoal be placed on a man's head, see how he struggles to throw it off. Similar will be the struggles for freedom of a man who really understands that he is a slave of nature.

We have now seen what Mumukshutva, or the desire to be free, is. The next training is also a very difficult one. Nityânitya-Viveka — discriminating between that which is true and that which is untrue, between the eternal and the transitory. God alone is eternal, everything else is transitory. Everything dies; the angels die, men die, animals die, earths die, sun, moon, and stars, all die; everything undergoes constant change. The mountains of today were the oceans of yesterday and will be oceans tomorrow. Everything is in a state of flux. The whole universe is a mass of change. But there is One who never changes, and that is God; and the nearer we get to Him, the less will be the change for us, the less will nature be able to work on us; and when we reach Him, and stand with Him, we shall conquer nature, we shall be masters of phenomena of nature, and they will have no effect on us.

You see, if we really have undergone the above discipline, we really do not require anything else in this world. All knowledge is within us. All perfection is there already in the soul. But this perfection has been covered up by nature; layer after layer of nature is covering this purity of the soul. What have we to do? Really we do not develop our souls at all. What can develop the perfect? We simply take the evil off; and the soul manifests itself in its pristine purity, its natural, innate freedom.

Now begins the inquiry: Why is this discipline so necessary? Because religion is not attained through the ears, nor through the eyes, nor yet through the brain. No scriptures can make us religious. We may study all the books that are in the world, yet we may not understand a word of religion or of God. We may talk all our lives and yet may not be the better for it; we may be the most intellectual people the world ever saw, and yet we may not come to God at all. On the other hand, have you not seen what irreligious men have been produced from the most intellectual training? It is one of the evils of your Western civilisation that you are after intellectual education alone, and take no care of the heart. It only makes men ten times more selfish, and that will be your destruction. When there is conflict between the heart and the brain, let the heart be followed, because intellect has only one state, reason, and within that, intellect works, and cannot get beyond. It is the heart which takes one to the highest plane, which intellect can never reach; it goes beyond intellect, and reaches to what is called inspiration. Intellect can never become inspired; only the heart when it is enlightened, becomes inspired. An intellectual, heartless man never becomes an inspired man. It is always the heart that speaks in the man of love; it discovers a greater instrument than intellect can give you, the instrument of inspiration. Just as the intellect is the instrument of knowledge, so is the heart the instrument of inspiration. In a lower state it is a much weaker instrument than intellect. An ignorant man knows nothing, but he is a little emotional by nature. Compare him with a great professor — what wonderful power the latter possesses! But the professor is bound by his intellect, and he can be a devil and an intellectual man at the same time; but the man of heart can never be a devil; no man with emotion was ever a devil. Properly cultivated, the heart can be changed, and will go beyond intellect; it will be changed into inspiration. Man will have to go beyond intellect in the end. The knowledge of man, his powers of perception, of reasoning and intellect and heart, all are busy churning this milk of the world. Out of long churning comes butter, and this butter is God. Men of heart get the "butter", and the "buttermilk" is left for the intellectual.

These are all preparations for the heart, for that love, for that intense sympathy appertaining to the heart. It is not at all necessary to be educated or learned to get to God. A sage once told me, "To kill others one must be equipped with swords and shields, but to commit suicide a needle is sufficient; so to teach others, much intellect and learning are necessary, but not so for your own self-illumination." Are on pure? If you are pure, you will reach God. "Blessed are the pure in heart, for they shall see God." If you are not pure, and you know all the sciences in the world, that will not help you at all; you may be buried in all the books you read, but that will not be of much use. It is the heart that reaches the goal. Follow the heart. A pure heart sees beyond the intellect; it gets inspired; it knows things that reason can never know, and whenever there is conflict between the pure heart and the intellect, always side with the pure heart, even if you think what your heart is doing is unreasonable. When it is desirous of doing good to others, your brain may tell you that it is not politic to do so, but follow your heart, and you will find that you make less mistakes than by following your intellect. The pure heart is the best mirror for the reflection of truth, so all these disciplines are for the purification of the heart. And as soon as it is pure, all truths flash upon it in a minute; all truth in the universe will manifest in your heart, if you are sufficiently pure.

The great truths about atoms, and the finer elements, and the fine perceptions of men, were discovered ages ago by men who never saw a telescope, or a microscope, or a laboratory. How did they know all these things? It was through the heart; they purified the heart. It is open to us to do the same today; it is the culture of the heart, really, and not that of the intellect that will lessen the misery of the world.

Intellect has been cultured with the result that hundreds of sciences have been discovered, and their effect has been that the few have made slaves of the many — that is all the good that has been done. Artificial wants have been created; and every poor man, whether he has money or not, desires to have those wants satisfied, and when he cannot, he struggles, and dies in the struggle. This is the result. Through the intellect is not the way to solve the problem of misery, but through the heart. If all this vast amount of effort had been spent in making men purer, gentler, more forbearing, this world would have a thousandfold more happiness than it has today. Always cultivate the heart; through the heart the Lord speaks, and through the intellect you yourself speak.

You remember in the Old Testament where Moses was told, "Take off thy shoes from off thy feet, for the place whereon thou standest is holy ground." We must always approach the study of religion with that reverent attitude. He who comes with a pure heart and a reverent attitude, his heart will be opened; the doors will open for him, and he will see the truth.

If you come with intellect only, you can have a little intellectual gymnastics, intellectual theories, but not truth. Truth has such a face that any one who sees that face becomes convinced. The sun does not require any torch to show it; the sun is self-effulgent. If truth requires evidence, what will evidence that evidence? If something is necessary as witness for truth, where is the witness for that witness? We must approach religion with reverence and with love, and our heart will stand up and say, this is truth, and this is untruth.

The field of religion is beyond our senses, beyond even our consciousness. We cannot *sense* God. Nobody has seen God with his eyes or ever will see; nobody has God in his consciousness. I am not conscious of God, nor you, nor anybody. Where is God? Where is the field of religion? It is beyond the senses, beyond consciousness. Consciousness is only one of the many planes in which we work; you will have to transcend the field of consciousness, to go beyond the senses, approach nearer and nearer to your own centre, and as you do that, you will approach nearer and nearer to God. What is the proof of God? Direct perception, Pratyaksha. The proof of this wall is that I perceive it. God has been perceived that way by thousands before, and will be perceived by all who want to perceive Him. But this perception is no sense-perception at all; it is supersensuous, superconscious, and all this training is needed to take us beyond the senses. By means of all sorts of past work and bondages we are being dragged downwards; these preparations will make us pure and light. Bondages will fall off by themselves, and we shall be buoyed up beyond this plane of sense-perception to which we are tied down, and then we shall see, and hear, and feel things which men in the three ordinary states (viz waking, dream, and sleep) neither feel, nor see, nor hear. Then we shall speak a strange language, as it were, and the world will not understand us, because it does not know anything but the senses. True religion is entirely transcendental. Every being that is in the universe has the potentiality of transcending the senses; even the little worm will one day transcend the senses and reach God. No life will be a failure; there is no such thing as failure in the universe. A hundred times man will hurt himself, a thousand times he will tumble, but in the end he will realise that he is God. We know there is no progress in a straight line. Every soul moves, as it were, in a circle, and will have to complete it, and no soul can go so low but there will come a time when it will have to go upwards. No one will be lost. We are all projected from one common centre, which is God. The highest as well as the lowest life God ever projected, will come back to the Father of all lives. "From whom all beings are projected, in whom all live, and unto whom they all return; that is God."

Vedanta And Privilege

(Delivered in London)

We have nearly finished the metaphysical portion of the Advaita. One point, and perhaps the most difficult to understand, remains. We have seen so far that, according to the Advaita theory, all we see around us, and the whole universe in fact, is the evolution of that one Absolute. This is called, in Sanskrit, Brahman. The Absolute has become changed into the whole of nature. But here comes a difficulty. How is it possible for the Absolute to change? What made the Absolute to change? By its very definition, the Absolute is unchangeable. Change of the unchangeable would be a contradiction. The same difficulty applies to those who believe in a Personal God. For instance, how did this creation arise? It could not have arisen out of nothing; that would be a contradiction – something coming out of nothing can never be. The effect is the cause in another form. Out of the seed, the big tree grows; the tree is the seed, plus air and water taken in. And if there were any method of testing the amount of the air, and water taken to make the body of the tree, we should find that it is exactly the same as the effect, the tree. Modern science has proved beyond doubt that it is so, that the cause is the effect in another form. The adjustment of the parts of the cause changes and becomes the effect. So, we have to avoid this difficulty of having a universe without a cause, and we are bound to admit that God has become the universe.

But we have avoided one difficulty, and landed in another. In every theory, the idea of God comes through the idea of unchangeability. We have traced historically how the one idea which we have always in mind in the search for God, even in its crudest form, is the idea of freedom; and the idea of freedom and of unchangeability is one and the same. It is the free alone which never changes, and the unchangeable alone which is free; for change is produced by something exterior to a thing, or within itself, which is more powerful than the surroundings. Everything which can be changed is necessarily bound by certain cause or causes, which cannot be unchangeable. Supposing God has become this universe, then God is here and has changed. And suppose the Infinite has become this finite universe, so much of the Infinite has gone, and, therefore, God is Infinite minus the universe. A changeable God would be no God. To avoid this doctrine of pantheism, there is a very bold theory of the Vedanta. It is that this universe, as we know and think it, does not exist, that the unchangeable has not changed, that the whole of this universe is mere appearance and not reality, that this idea of parts, and little beings, and differentiations is only apparent, not the nature of the thing itself. God has not changed at all, and has not become the universe at all. We see God as the universe, because we have to look through time, space, and causation. It is time, space, and causation that make this differentiation apparently, but not really. This is a very bold theory indeed. Now this theory ought to be explained a little more clearly. It does not mean idealism in the sense in which it is generally understood. It does not say that this universe does not exist; it exists, but at the same time it is not what we take it for. To illustrate this, the example given by the Advaita philosophy is well known. In the darkness of night, a stump of a tree is looked upon as a ghost by some superstitious person, as a policeman by a robber, as a friend by some one waiting for his companion. In all these cases, the stump of the tree did not change, but there are apparent changes, and these changes were in the minds of those who saw it. From the subjective side we can understand it better through psychology. There is something outside of ourselves, the true nature of which is unknown and unknowable to us; let us call it x. And there is something inside, which is also unknown and unknowable to us; let us call it y. The knowable is a combination of x plus y, and everything that we know, therefore, must have two parts, the x outside, and the y inside; and the x plus y is the thing we know. So, every form in the universe is partly our creation and partly something outside. Now what the Vedanta holds is that this x and this y are one and the same.

A very similar conclusion has been arrived at by some western philosophers, especially by Herbert Spencer, and some other modern philosophers. When it is said that the same power which is manifesting itself in the flower is welling up in my own consciousness, it is the very same idea which the Vedantist wants to preach, that the reality of the external world and the reality of the internal world are one and the same. Even the ideas of the internal and external exist by differentiation and do not exist in the things themselves. For instance, if we develop another sense, the whole world will change for us, showing that it is the subject which will change the object. If I change, the external world changes. The theory of the Vedanta, therefore, comes to this, that you and I and everything in the universe are that Absolute, not parts, but the whole. You are the whole of that Absolute, and so are all others, because the idea of part cannot come into it. These divisions, these limitations, are only apparent, not in the thing itself. I am complete and perfect, and I was never bound, boldly preaches the

Vedanta. If you think you are bound, bound you will remain; if you know that you are free, free you are. Thus the end and aim of this philosophy is to let us know that we have been free always, and shall remain free for ever. We never change, we never die, and we are never born. What are all these changes then? What becomes of this phenomenal world? This world is admitted as an apparent world, bound by time, space, and causation, and it comes to what is called the Vivarta-vâda in Sanskrit, evolution of nature, and manifestation of the Absolute. The Absolute does not change, or re-evolve. In the little amoeba is that infinite perfection latent. It is called amoeba from its amoeba covering, and from the amoeba to the perfect man the change is not in what is inside — that remains the same, unchangeable — but the change occurs in the covering.

There is a screen here, and some beautiful scenery outside. There is a small hole in the screen through which we can only catch a glimpse of it. Suppose this hole begins to increase; as it grows larger and larger, more and more of the scenery comes into view, and when the screen has vanished, we come face to face with the whole of the scenery. This scene outside is the soul, and the screen between us and the scenery is Mâyâ — time, space, and causation. There is a little hole somewhere, through which I can catch only a glimpse of the soul. When the hole is bigger, I see more and more, and when the screen has vanished, I know that I am the soul. So changes in the universe are not in the Absolute; they are in nature. Nature evolves more and more, until the Absolute manifests Itself. In everyone It exists; in some It is manifested more than in others. The whole universe is really one. In speaking of the soul, to say that one is superior to another has no meaning. In speaking of the soul, to say that man is superior to the animal or the plant, has no meaning; the whole universe is one. In plants the obstacle to soul-manifestation is very great; in animals a little less; and in man still less; in cultured, spiritual men still less; and in perfect men, it has vanished altogether. All our struggles, exercises, pains, pleasures, tears, and smiles, all that we do and think tend towards that goal, the tearing up of the screen, making the hole bigger, thinning the layers that remain between the manifestation and the reality behind. Our work, therefore, is not to make the soul free, but to get rid of the bondages. The sun is covered by layers of clouds, but remains unaffected by them. The work of the wind is to drive the clouds away, and the more the clouds disappear, the more the light of the sun appears. There is no change whatsoever in the soul — Infinite, Absolute, Eternal, Knowledge, Bliss, and Existence. Neither can there be birth or death for the soul. Dying, and being born, reincarnation, and going to heaven, cannot be for the soul. These are different appearances, different mirages, different dreams. If a man who is dreaming of this world now dreams of wicked thoughts and wicked deeds, after a certain time the thought of that very dream will produce the next dream. He will dream that he is in a horrible place, being tortured. The man who is dreaming good thoughts and good deeds, after that period of dream is over, will dream he is in a better place; and so on from dream to dream. But the time will come when the whole of this dream will vanish. To everyone of us there must come a time when the whole universe will be found to have been a mere dream, when we shall find that the soul is infinitely better than its surroundings. In this struggle through what we call our environments, there will come a time when we shall find that these environments were almost zero in comparison with the power of the soul. It is only a question of time, and time is nothing in the Infinite. It is a drop in the ocean. We can afford to wait and be calm.

Consciously or unconsciously, therefore, the whole universe is going towards that goal. The moon is struggling to get out of the sphere of attraction of other bodies, and will come out of it, in the long run. But those who consciously strive to get free hasten the time. One benefit from this theory we practically see is that the idea of a real universal love is only possible from this point of view. All are our fellow passengers, our fellow travellers — all life, plants, animals; not only my brother man, but my brother brute, my brother plant; not only my brother the good, but my brother the evil, my brother the spiritual and my brother the wicked. They are all going to the same goal. All are in the same stream, each is hurrying towards that infinite freedom. We cannot stay the course, none can stay it, none can go back, however he may try; he will be driven forward, and in the end he will attain to freedom. Creation means the struggle to get back to freedom, the centre of our being, whence we have been thrown off, as it were. The very fact that we are here, shows that we are going towards the centre, and the manifestation of this attraction towards the centre is what we call love.

The question is asked: From what does this universe come, in what does it remain, to what does it go back? And the answer is: From love it comes, in love it remains, back it goes unto love. Thus we are in a position to understand that, whether one likes it or not, there is no going back for anyone. Everyone has to get to the centre, however he may struggle to go back. Yet if we struggle consciously, knowingly, it will smooth the passage, it will lessen the jar, and quicken the time. Another conclusion we naturally arrive at from this is that all knowledge and all power are within and not without. What we call nature is a reflecting glass — that is all the use of nature — and all knowledge is this reflection of the within on this glass of nature. What we call powers, secrets of nature, and force, are all within. In the external world are only a series of changes. There is no knowledge in nature; all knowledge comes from the human soul. Man manifests knowledge, discovers it within himself, which is pre-existing through eternity. Everyone is the embodiment of Knowledge, everyone is the embodiment of eternal Bliss, and eternal Existence. The ethical effect is just the same, as we have seen elsewhere, with regard to equality.

But the idea of privilege is the bane of human life. Two forces, as it were, are constantly at work, one making caste, and the other breaking caste; in other words, the one making for privilege, the other breaking down privilege. And whenever privilege is broken down, more and more light and progress come to a race. This struggle we see all around us. Of course there is first the brutal idea of privilege, that of the strong over the weak. There is the privilege of wealth. If a man has more money than another, he wants a little privilege over those who have less. There is the still subtler and more powerful privilege of intellect; because one man knows more than others, he claims more privilege. And the last of all, and the worst, because the most tyrannical, is the privilege of spirituality. If some persons think they know more of spirituality, of God, they claim a superior privilege over everyone else. They say, "Come down and worships us, ye common herds; we are the messengers of God, and you have to worship us." None can be Vedantists, and at the same time admit of privilege to anyone, either mental, physical, or spiritual; absolutely no privilege for anyone. The same power is in every man, the one manifesting more, the other less; the same potentiality is in everyone. Where is the claim to privilege? All knowledge is in every soul, even in the most ignorant; he has not manifested it, but, perhaps, he has not had the opportunity, the environments were not, perhaps, suitable to him. When he gets the opportunity, he will manifest it. The idea that one man is born superior to another has no meaning in the Vedanta; that between two nations one is superior and the other inferior has no meaning whatsoever. Put them in the same circumstances, and see whether the same intelligence comes out or not. Before that you have no right to say that one nation is superior to another. And as to spirituality, no privilege should be claimed there. It is a privilege to serve mankind, for this is the worship of God. God is here, in all these human souls. He is the soul of man. What privilege can men ask? There are no special messengers of God, never were, and never can be. All beings, great or small, are equally manifestations of God; the difference is only in the manifestation. The same eternal message, which has been eternally given, comes to them little by little. The eternal message has been written in the heart of every being; it is there already, and all are struggling to express it. Some, in suitable circumstances, express it a little better than others, but as bearers of the message they are all one. What claim to superiority is there? The most ignorant man, the most ignorant child, is as great a messenger of God as any that ever existed, and as great as any that are yet to come. For the infinite message is there imprinted once for all in the heart of every being. Wherever there is a being, that being contains the infinite message of the Most High. It is there. The work of the Advaita, therefore, is to break down all these privileges. It is the hardest work of all, and curious to say, it has been less active than anywhere else in the land of its birth. If there is any land of privilege, it is the land which gave birth to this philosophy — privilege for the spiritual man as well as for the man of birth. There they have not so much privilege for money (that is one of the benefits, I think), but privilege for birth and spirituality is everywhere.

Once a gigantic attempt was made to preach Vedantic ethics, which succeeded to a certain extent for several hundred years, and we know historically that those years were the best times of that nation. I mean the Buddhistic attempt to break down privilege. Some of the most beautiful epithets addressed to Buddha that I remember are, "Thou the breaker of castes, destroyer of privileges, preacher of equality to all beings." So, he preached this one idea of equality. Its power has been misunderstood to a certain extent in the brotherhood of Shramanas, where we find that hundreds of attempts have been made to make them into a church, with superiors and inferiors. Your cannot make much of a church when you tell people they are all gods. One of the good effects of Vedanta has been freedom of religious thought, which India enjoyed throughout all times of its history. It is something to glory in, that it is the land where there was never a religious persecution, where people are allowed perfect freedom in religion.

This practical side of Vedanta morality is necessary as much today as it ever was, more necessary, perhaps, than it ever was, for all this privilege-claiming has become tremendously intensified with the extension of knowledge. The idea of God and the devil, or Ahura Mazda and Ahriman, has a good deal of poetry in it. The difference between God and the devil is in nothing except in unselfishness and selfishness. The devil knows as much as God, is as powerful as God; only he has no holiness — that makes him a devil. Apply the same idea to the modern world: excess of knowledge and power, without holiness, makes human beings devils. Tremendous power is being acquired by the manufacture of machines and other appliances, and privilege is claimed today as it never has been claimed in the history of the world. That is why the Vedanta wants to preach against it, to break down this tyrannising over the souls of men.

Those of you who have studied the Gita will remember the memorable passages: "He who looks upon the learned Brahmin, upon the cow, the elephant, the dog, or the outcast with the same eye, he indeed is the sage, and the wise man"; "Even in this life he has conquered relative existence whose mind is firmly fixed on this sameness, for the Lord is one and the same to all, and the Lord is pure; therefore those who have this sameness for all, and are pure, are said to be living in God." This is the gist of Vedantic morality — this sameness for all. We have seen that it is the subjective world that rules the objective. Change the subject, and the object is bound to change; purify yourself, and the world is bound to be purified. This one thing requires to be taught now more than ever before. We are becoming more and more busy about our neighbours, and less and less about ourselves. The world will change if we change; if we are pure, the world will become pure. The question is why I should see evil in others. I cannot see evil unless I be evil. I cannot be miserable unless I am weak. Things that used to make me miserable when I was a child, do not do so now. The subject changed, so the object was bound to change; so says the Vedanta. All these things which we call causes of misery and evil, we shall laugh at when we arrive at that wonderful state of equality, that sameness. This is what is called in Vedanta attaining to freedom. The sign of approaching that freedom is more and more of this sameness and equality. In misery and happiness the same, in success and defeat the same — such a mind is nearing that state of freedom.

The mind cannot be easily conquered. Minds that rise into waves at the approach of every little thing at the slightest provocation or danger, in what a state they must be! What to talk of greatness or spirituality, when these changes come over the mind? This unstable condition of the mind must be changed. We must ask ourselves how far we can be acted upon by the external world, and how far we can stand on our own feet, in spite of all the forces outside us. When we have succeeded in preventing all the forces in the world from throwing us off our balance, then alone we have attained to freedom, and not before. That is salvation. It is here and nowhere else; it is this moment. Out of this idea, out of this fountain-head, all beautiful streams of thought have flowed upon the world, generally misunderstood in their expression, apparently contradicting each other. We find hosts of brave and wonderfully spiritual souls, in every nation, taking to caves or forests for meditation, severing their connection with the external world. This is the one idea. And, on the other hand, we find bright, illustrious beings coming into society, trying to raise their fellow men, the poor, the miserable. Apparently these two methods are contradictory. The man who lives in a cave, apart from his fellow-beings, smiles contemptuously upon those who are working for the regeneration of their fellow men. "How foolish!" he says; "what work is there? The world of Maya will always remain the world of Maya; it cannot be changed." If I ask one of our priests in India, "Do you believe in Vedanta?" — he says, "That is my religion; I certainly do; that is my life." "Very well, do you admit the equality of all life, the sameness of everything?" "Certainly, I do." The next moment, when a low-caste man approaches this priest, he jumps to one side of the street to avoid that man. "Why do you jump?" "Because his very touch would have polluted me." "But you were just saying we are all the same, and you admit there is no difference in souls." He says, "Oh, that is in theory only for householders; when I go into a forest, then I will look upon everyone as the same." You ask one of your great men in England, of great birth and wealth, if he believes as a Christian in the brotherhood of mankind, since all came from God. He answers in the affirmative, but in five minutes he shouts something uncomplimentary about the common herd. Thus, it has been a theory only for several thousand years and never came into practice. All understand it, declare it as the truth, but when you ask them to practice it, they say, it will take millions of years.

There was a certain king who had a huge number of courtiers, and each one of these courtiers declared he was ready to sacrifice his life for his master, and that he was the most sincere being ever born. In course of time, a Sannyâsin came to the king. The king said to him that there never was a king who had so many sincere courtiers as he had. The Sannyasin smiled and said he did not believe that. The king said the Sannyasin could test it if he liked. So the Sannyasin declared that he would make a great sacrifice by which the king's reign would be extended very long, with the condition that there should be made a small tank into which each one of his courtiers should pour a pitcher of milk, in the dark of night. The king smiled and said, "Is this the test?" And he asked his courtiers to come to him, and told them what was to be done. They all expressed their joyful assent to the proposal and returned. In the dead of night, they came and emptied their pitchers into the tank. But in the morning, it was found full of water only. The courtiers were assembled and questioned about the matter. Each one of them had thought there would be so many pitchers of milk that his water would not be detected. Unfortunately most of us have the same idea and we do our share of work as did the courtiers in the story.

There is so much idea of equality, says the priest, that my little privilege will not be detected. So say our rich men, so say the tyrants of every country. There is more hope for the tyrannised over, than for the tyrants. It will take a very long time for tyrants to arrive at freedom, but less time for the others. The cruelty of the fox is much more terrible than the cruelty of the lion. The lion strikes a blow and is quiet for some time afterwards, but the fox trying persistently to follow his prey never misses an opportunity. Priestcraft is in its nature cruel and heartless. That is why religion goes down where priestcraft arises. Says the Vedanta, we must give up the idea of privilege, then will religion come. Before that there is no religion at all.

Do you believe what Christ says, "Sell all that thou hast, and give to the poor?" Practical equality there; no trying to torture the texts, but taking the truth as it is. Do not try to torture texts. I have heard it said that that was preached only to the handful of Jews who listened to Jesus. The same argument will apply to other things also. Do not torture texts; dare to face truth as it is. Even if we cannot reach to it, let us confess our weakness, but let us not destroy the ideal. Let us hope that we shall attain to it sometime, and strive for it. There it is — "Sell all that thou hast, and give to the poor, and follow me." Thus, trampling on every privilege and everything in us that works for privilege, let us work for that knowledge which will bring the feeling of sameness towards all mankind. You think that because you talk a little more polished language you are superior to the man in the street. Remember that when you are thinking this, you are not going towards freedom, but are forging a fresh chain for your feet. And, above all, if the pride of spirituality enters into you, woe unto you. It is the most awful bondage that ever existed. Neither can wealth nor any other bondage of the human heart bind the soul so much as this. "I am purer than others", is the most awful idea that can enter into the human heart. In what sense are you pure? The God in you is the God in all. If you have not known this, you have known nothing. How can there be difference? It is all one. Every being is the temple of the Most High; if you can see that, good, if not, spirituality has yet to come to you.

Privilege

(Delivered at the Sesame Club, London)

Two forces seem to be working throughout nature. One of these is constantly differentiating, and the other is as constantly unifying; the one making more and more for separate individuals, the other, as it were, bringing the individuals into a mass, bringing out sameness in the midst of all this differentiation. It seems that the action of these two forces enters into every department of nature and of human life. On the physical plane, we always find the two forces most distinctly at work, separating the individuals, making them more and more distinct from other individuals, and again making them into species and classes, and bringing out similarities of expressions, and form. The same holds good as regards the social life of man. Since the time when society began, these two forces have been at work, differentiating and unifying. Their action appears in various forms, and is called by various names, in different places, and at different times. But the essence is present in all, one making for differentiation, and the other for sameness; the one making for caste, and the other breaking it down; one making for classes and privileges, and the other destroying them. The whole universe seems to be the battle-ground of these two forces. On the one hand, it is urged, that though this unifying process exists, we ought to resist it with all our might, because it leads towards death, that perfect unity is perfect annihilation, and that when the differentiating process that is at work in this universe ceases, the universe comes to an end. It is differentiation that causes the phenomena that are before us; unification would reduce them all to a homogeneous and lifeless matter. Such a thing, of course, mankind wants to avoid. The same argument is applied to all the things and facts that we see around us. It is urged that even in physical body and social classification, absolute sameness would produce natural death and social death. Absolute sameness of thought and feeling would produce mental decay and degeneration. Sameness, therefore, is to be avoided. This has been the argument on the one side, and it has been urged in every country and in various times, with only a change of language. Practically it is the same argument which is urged by the Brahmins of India, when they want to uphold the divisions and castes, when they want to uphold the privileges of a certain portion of the community, against everybody else. The destruction of caste, they declare, would lead to destruction of society, and boldly they produce the historical fact that theirs has been the longest-lived society. So they, with some show of force, appeal to this argument. With some show of authority they declare that that alone which makes the individual live the longest life must certainly be better than that which produces shorter lives.

On the other hand, the idea of oneness has had its advocates throughout all times. From the days of the Upanishads, the Buddhas, and Christs, and all other great preachers of religion, down to our present day, in the new political aspirations, and in the claims of the oppressed and the downtrodden, and of all those who find themselves bereft of privileges — comes out the one assertion of this unity and sameness. But human nature asserts itself. Those who have an advantage want to keep it, and if they find an argument, however one-sided and crude, they must cling to it. This applies to both sides.

Applied to metaphysics, this question also assumes another form. The Buddhist declares that we need not look for anything which brings unity in the midst of these phenomena, we ought to be satisfied with this phenomenal world. This variety is the essence of life, however miserable and weak it may seem to be; we can have nothing more. The Vedantist declares that unity is the only thing that exists; variety is but phenomenal, ephemeral and apparent. "Look not to variety," says the Vedantist, "go back to unity." "Avoid unity; it is a delusion," says the Buddhist, "go to variety." The same differences of opinion in religion and metaphysics have come down to our own day, for, in fact, the sum-total of the principles of knowledge is very small. Metaphysics and metaphysical knowledge, religion and religious knowledge, reached their culmination five thousand years ago, and we are merely reiterating the same truths in different languages, only enriching them sometimes by the accession of fresh illustrations. So this is the fight, even today. One side wants us to keep to the phenomenal, to all this variation, and points out, with great show of argument, that variation has to remain, for when that stops, everything is gone. What we mean by life has been caused by variation. The other side, at the same time, valiantly points to unity.

Coming to ethics, we find a tremendous departure. It is, perhaps, the only science which makes a bold departure from this fight. For ethics is unity; its basis is love. It will not look at this variation. The one aim of ethics is this unity, this sameness. The highest ethical codes that mankind has discovered up to the present time know no variation; they have no time to stop to look into it; their one end is to make for that sameness. The Indian mind, being more analytical — I mean the Vedantic mind — found this unity as the result of all its analyses, and wanted to base everything upon this one idea of unity. But as we have seen, in the same country, there were other minds (the Buddhistic) who could not find that unity anywhere. To them all truth was a mass of variation, there was no connection between one thing and another.

I remember a story told by Prof. Max Müller in one of his books, an old Greek story, of how a Brahmin visited Socrates in Athens. The Brahmin asked, "What is the highest knowledge?" And Socrates answered, "To know man is the end and aim of all knowledge." "But how can you know man without knowing God?" replied the Brahmin. The one side, the Greek side, which is represented by modern Europe, insisted upon the knowledge of man; the Indian side, mostly represented by the old religions of the world, insisted upon the knowledge of God. The one sees God in nature, and the other sees nature in God. To us, at the present time, perhaps, has been given the privilege of standing aside from both these aspects, and taking an impartial view of the whole. This is a fact that variation exists, and so it must, if life is to be. This is also a fact that in and through these variations unity must be perceived. This is a fact that God is perceived in nature. But it is also a fact that nature is perceived in God. The knowledge of man is the highest knowledge, and only by knowing man, can we know God. This is also a fact that the knowledge of God is the highest knowledge, and knowing God alone we can know man. Apparently contradictory though these statements may appear, they are the necessity of human nature. The whole universe is a play of unity in variety, and of variety in unity. The whole universe is a play of differentiation and oneness; the whole universe is a play of the finite in the Infinite. We cannot take one without granting the other. But we cannot take them both as facts of the same perception, as facts of the same experience; yet in this way it will always go on.

Therefore, coming to our more particular purpose, which is religion rather than ethics, a state of things, where all variation has died down, giving place to a uniform, dead homogeneity, is impossible so long as life lasts. Nor is it desirable. At the same time, there is the other side of the fact, viz that this unity already exists. That is the peculiar claim — not that this unity has to be made, but that it already exists, and that you could not perceive the variety at all, without it. God is not to be made, but He already exists. This has been the claim of all religions. Whenever one has perceived the finite, he has also perceived the Infinite. Some laid stress on the finite side, and declared that they perceived the finite without; others laid stress on the Infinite side, and declared they perceived the Infinite only. But we know that it is a logical necessity that we cannot perceive the one without the other. So the claim is that this sameness, this unity, this perfection — as we may call it — is not to be made, it already exists, and is here. We have only to recognise it, to understand it. Whether we know it or not, whether we can express it in clear language or not, whether this perception assumes the force and clearness of a sense-perception or not, it is there. For we are bound by the logical necessity of our minds to confess that it is there, else, the perception of the finite would not be. I am not speaking of the old theory of substance and qualities, but of oneness; that in the midst of all this mass of phenomena, the very fact of the consciousness that you and I are different brings to us, at the same moment, the consciousness that you and I are not different. Knowledge would be impossible without that unity. Without the idea of sameness there would be neither perception nor knowledge. So both run side by side.

Therefore the absolute sameness of conditions, if that be the aim of ethics, appears to be impossible. That all men should be the same, could never be, however we might try. Men will be born differentiated; some will have more power than others; some will have natural capacities, others not; some will have perfect bodies, others not. We can never stop that. At the same time ring in our ears the wonderful words of morality proclaimed by various teachers: "Thus, seeing the same God equally present in all, the sage does not injure Self by the Self, and thus reaches the highest goal. Even in this life they have conquered relative existence whose minds are firmly fixed on this sameness; for God is pure, and God is the same to all. Therefore such are said to be living in God." We cannot deny that this is the real idea; yet at the same time comes the difficulty that the sameness as regards external forms and position can never be attained.

But what can be attained is elimination of privilege. That is really the work before the whole world. In all social lives, there has been that one fight in every race and in every country. The difficulty is not that one body of men are naturally more intelligent than another, but whether this body of men, because they have the advantage of intelligence, should take away even physical enjoyment from those who do not possess that advantage. The fight is to destroy that privilege. That some will be stronger physically than others, and will thus naturally be able to subdue or defeat the weak, is a self-evident fact, but that because of this strength they should gather unto themselves all the attainable happiness of this life, is not according to law, and the fight has been against it. That some people, through natural aptitude, should be able to accumulate more wealth than others, is natural: but that on account of this power to acquire wealth they should tyrannize and ride roughshod over those who cannot acquire so much wealth, is not a part of the law, and the fight has been against that. The enjoyment of advantage over another is privilege, and throughout ages, the aim of morality has been its destruction. This is the work which tends towards sameness, towards unity, without destroying variety.

Let all these variations remain eternally; it is the very essence of life. We shall all play in this way, eternally. You will be wealthy, and I shall be poor; you will be strong, and I shall be weak; you will be learned and I ignorant; you will be spiritual, and I, less so. But what of that? Let us remain so, but because you are physically or intellectually stronger, you must not have more privilege than I, and that you have more wealth is no reason why you should be considered greater than I, for that sameness is here, in spite of the different conditions.

The work of ethics has been, and will be in the future, not the destruction of variation and the establishment of sameness in the external world — which is impossible for it would bring death and annihilation — but to recognise the unity in spite of all these variations, to recognise the God within, in spite of everything that frightens us, to recognise that infinite strength as the property of everyone in spite of all apparent weakness, and to recognise the eternal, infinite, essential purity of the soul in spite of everything to the contrary that appears on the surface. This we have to recognise. Taking one side alone, one half only of the position, is dangerous and liable to lead to quarrels. We must take the whole thing as it is, stand on it as our basis and work it out in every part of our lives, as individuals and as unit members of society.

Krishna

This article was recorded by Ida Ansell in shorthand. As, however, Swamiji's speed was too great for her in her early days, dots are put in the articles to indicate the omissions, while the words within square brackets are added by way of linking up the disconnected parts.

(Delivered in California, on April 1, 1900)

Almost the same circumstances which gave birth to Buddhism in India surrounded the rise of Krishna. Not only this, the events of that day we find happening in our own times.

There is a certain ideal. At the same time there must always be a large majority of the human race who cannot come up to the ideal, not even intellectually. ... The strong ones carry it out and many times have no sympathy for the weak. The weak to the strong are only beggars. The strong ones march ahead. ... Of course, we see at once that the highest position to take is to be sympathetic and helpful to those who are weak. But then, in many cases the philosopher bars the way to our being sympathetic. If we go by the theory that the whole of this infinite life has to be determined by the few years' existence here and now, ... then it is very hopeless for us, ... and we have no time to look back upon those who are weak. But if these are not the conditions — if the world is only one of the many schools through which we have to pass, if the eternal life is to be moulded and fashioned and guided by the eternal law, and eternal law, eternal chances await everyone — then we need not be in a hurry. We have time to sympathise, to look around, stretch out a helping hand to the weak and bring them up.

With Buddhism we have two words in Sanskrit: one is translated religion, the other, a sect. It is the most curious fact that the disciples and descendants of Krishna have no name for their religion [although] foreigners call it Hinduism or Brâhmanism. There is one religion, and there are many sects. The moment you give it a name, individualise it and separate it from the rest, it is a sect, no more a religion. A sect [proclaims] its own truth and declares that there is no truth anywhere else. Religion believes that there has been, and still is, one religion in the world. There never were two religions. It is the same religion [presenting] different aspects in different places.

The task is to conceive the proper understanding of the goal and scope of humanity.

This was the great work of Krishna: to clear our eyes and make us look with broader vision upon humanity in its march upward and onward. His was the first heart that was large enough to see truth in all, his the first lips that uttered beautiful words for each and all.

This Krishna preceded Buddha by some thousand years. ... A great many people do not believe that he ever existed. Some believe that [the worship of Krishna grew out of] the old sun worship. There seem to be several Krishnas: one was mentioned in the Upanishads, another was king, another a general. All have been lumped into one Krishna. It does not matter much. The fact is, some individual comes who is unique in spirituality. Then all sorts of legends are invented around him. But, all the Bibles and stories which come to be cast upon this one person have to be recast in [the mould of] his character. All the stories of the New Testament have to be modelled upon the accepted life [and] character of Christ. In all of the Indian stories about Buddha the one central note of that whole life is kept up — sacrifice for others. ...

In Krishna we find ... two ideas [stand] supreme in his message: The first is the harmony of different ideas; the second is non-attachment. A man can attain to perfection, the highest goal, sitting on a throne, commanding armies, working out big plans for nations. In fact, Krishna's great sermon was preached on the battlefield.

Krishna saw plainly through the vanity of all the mummeries, mockeries, and ceremonials of the old priests; and yet he saw some good in them.

If you are a strong man, very good! But do not curse others who are not strong enough for you. ... Everyone says, "Woe unto you people! !" Who says, "Woe unto me that I cannot help you?" The people are doing all right to the best of their ability and means and knowledge. Woe unto me that I cannot lift them to where I am!

So the ceremonials, worship of gods, and myths, are all right, Krishna says. ... Why? Because they all lead to the same goal. Ceremonies, books, and forms— all these are links in the chain. Get hold! That is the one thing. If you are sincere and have really got hold of one link, do not let go; the rest is bound to come. [But people] do not get hold. They spend the time quarrelling and determining what they should get hold of, and do not get hold of anything. ... We are always after truth, but never want to get it. We simply want the pleasure to go about and ask. We have a lot of energy and spend it that way. That is why Krishna says: Get hold of any one of these chains that are stretched out from the common centre. No one step is greater than another. ... Blame no view of religion so far as it is sincere. Hold on to one of these links, and it will pull you to the centre. Your heart itself will teach all the rest. The teacher within will teach all the creeds, all the philosophies. ...

Krishna talks of himself as God, as Christ does. He sees the Deity in himself. And he says, "None can go a day out of my path. All have to come to me. Whosoever wants to worship in whatsoever form, I give him faith in that form, and through that I meet him. ..."(Gita, IV. 12.) His heart is all for the masses.

Independent, Krishna stands out. The very boldness of it frightens us. We depend upon everything — ... upon a few good words, upon circumstances. When the soul wants to depend upon nothing, not even upon life, that is the height of philosophy, the height of manhood. Worship leads to the same goal. Krishna lays great stress upon worship. Worship God!

Various sorts of worship we see in this world. The sick man is very worshipful to God. ... There is the man who loses his fortune; he also prays very much, to get money. The highest worship is that of the man who loves God for God's sake. [The question may be asked :] "Why should there be so much sorrow if there is a God?" The worshipper replies! " ... There is misery in the world; [but] because of that I do not cease to love God. I do not worship Him to take away my [misery]. I love Him because He is love itself." The other [types of worship] are lower-grade; but Krishna has no condemnation for anything. It is better to do something than to stand still. The man who begins to worship God will grow by degrees and begin to love God for love's sake. ...

How to attain purity living this life? Shall we all go to the forest caves? What good would it do? If the mind is not under control, it is no use living in a cave because the same mind will bring all disturbances there. We will find twenty devils in the cave because all the devils are in the mind. If the mind is under control, we can have the cave anywhere, wherever we are.

It is our own mental attitude which makes the world what it is for us. Our thoughts make things beautiful, our thoughts make things ugly. The whole world is in our own minds. Learn to see things in the proper light. First, believe in this world — that there is meaning behind everything. Everything in the world is good, is holy and beautiful. If you see something evil, think that you are not understanding it in the right light. Throw the burden on yourselves! ... Whenever we are tempted to say that the world is going to the dogs, we ought to analyse ourselves, and we shall find that we have lost the faculty of seeing things as they are.

Work day and night! "Behold, I am the Lord of the Universe. I have no duty. Every duty is bondage. But I work for work's sake. If I ceased to work for a minute, [there would be chaos]."(Ibid. III. 22-23.) So do thou work, without any idea of duty. ...

This world is a play. You are His playmates. Go on and work, without any sorrow, without any misery. See His play in the slums, in the saloons! Work to lift people! Not that they are vile or degraded; Krishna does not say that.

Do you know why so little good work is done? My lady goes to the slum. ... She gives a few ducats and says, "My poor men, take that and be happy!" ... Or my fine woman, walking through the street, sees a poor fellow and throws him five cents. Think of the blasphemy of it! Blessed are we that the Lord has given us his teaching in your own Testament. Jesus says, "Inasmuch as ye have done it unto the least of these my brethren, ye have done it unto me." It is blasphemy to think that you can help anyone. First root out this idea of helping, and then go to worship. God's children are your Master's children. [And children are but different forms of the father.] You are His servant. ... Serve the living God! God comes to you in the blind, in the halt, in the poor, in the weak, in the diabolical. What a glorious chance for you to worship! The moment you think you are "helping", you undo the whole thing and degrade yourself. Knowing this, work. "What follows?" you say. You do not get that heartbreak, that awful misery. ... Then work is no more slavery. It becomes a play, and joy itself. ... Work! Be unattached! That is the whole secret. If you get attached, you become miserable. ...

With everything we do in life we identify ourselves. Here is a man who says harsh words to me. I feel anger coming on me. In a few seconds anger and I are one, and then comes misery. Attach yourselves to the Lord and to nothing else, because everything else is unreal. Attachment to the unreal will bring misery. There is only one Existence that is real, only one Life in which there is neither object nor [subject]. ...

But unattached love will not hurt you. Do anything — marry, have children. ... Do anything you like — nothing will hurt you. Do nothing with the idea of "mine". Duty for duty's sake; work for work's sake. What is that to you? You stand aside.

When we come to that non-attachment, then we can understand the marvellous mystery of the universe; how it is intense activity and vibration, and at the same time intensest peace and calm; how it is work every moment and rest every moment. That is the mystery of the universe — the impersonal and personal in one, the infinite and finite in one. Then we shall find the secret. "He who finds in the midst of intense activity the greatest rest, and in the midst of the greatest rest intense activity, he has become a Yogi." (Ibid. IV. 18.) He alone is a real worker, none else. We do a little work and break ourselves. Why? We become attached to that work. If we do not become attached, side by side with it we have infinite rest. ...

How hard it is to arrive at this sort of non-attachment! Therefore Krishna shows us the lower ways and methods. The easiest way for everyone is to do [his or her] work and not take the results. It is our desire that binds us. If we take the results of actions, whether good or evil, we will have to bear them. But if we work not for ourselves, but all for the glory of the Lord, the results will take care of themselves. "To work you have the right, but not to the fruits thereof." (Ibid. II. 47.) The soldier works for no results. He does his duty. If defeat comes, it belongs to the general, not to the soldier. We do our duty for love's sake — love for the general, love for the Lord. ...

If you are strong, take up the Vedanta philosophy and be independent. If you cannot do that, worship God; if not, worship some image. If you lack strength even to do that, do some good works without the idea of gain. Offer everything you have unto the service of the Lord. Fight on! "Leaves and water and one flower — whosoever lays anything on my altar, I receive it with equal delights."(Ibid IX. 26.) If you cannot do anything, not a single good work, then take refuge [in the Lord]. "The Lord resides within the heart of the being, making them turn upon His wheel. Do thou with all thy soul and heart take refuge in Him. ...(Ibid XVIII. 61-62.)

These are some of the general ideas that Krishna preached on this idea of love [in the Gita]. There are [in] other great books, sermons on love — as with Buddha, as with Jesus. ...

A few words about the life of Krishna. There is a great deal of similarity between the lives of Jesus and Krishna. A discussion is going on as to which borrowed of the other. There was the tyrannical king in both places. Both were born in a manger. The parents were bound in both cases. Both were saved by angels. In both cases all the boys born in that year were killed. The childhood is the same. ... Again, in the end, both were killed. Krishna was killed by accident; he took the man who killed him to heaven. Christ was killed, and blessed the robber and took him to heaven.

There are a great many similarities in of the New Testament and the Gita. The human thought goes the same way. ... I will find you the answer in the words of Krishna himself: "Whenever virtue subsides and irreligion prevails, I come down. Again and again I come. Therefore, whenever thou seest a great soul struggling to uplift mankind, know that I am come, and worship. ..."(Ibid. IV. 8; X. 41.)

At the same time, if he comes as Jesus or as Buddha, why is there so much schism? The preachings must be followed! A Hindu devotee would say: It is God himself who became Christ and Krishna and Buddha and all these [great teachers]. A Hindu philosopher would say: These are the great souls; they are already free. And though free, they refuse to accept their liberation while the whole world is suffering. They come again and again, take a human embodiment and help mankind. They know from their childhood what they are and what they come for. ... They do not come through bondage like we do. ... They come out of their own free will, and cannot help having tremendous spiritual power. We cannot resist it. The vast mass of mankind is dragged into the whirlpool of spirituality, and the vibration goes on and on because one of these [great souls] gives a push. So it continues until all mankind is liberated and the play of this planet is finished.

Glory unto the great souls whose lives we have been studying! They are the living gods of the world. They are the persons whom we ought to worship. If He comes to me, I can only recognise Him if He takes a human form. He is everywhere, but do we see Him? We can only see Him if He takes the limitation of man. .... If men and ... animals are manifestations of God, these teachers of mankind are leaders, are Gurus. Therefore, salutations unto you, whose footstool is worshipped by angels! Salutations unto you leaders of the human race! Salutations unto you great teachers! You leaders have our salutations for ever and ever!

The Gita I

This article was recorded by Ida Ansell in shorthand. As, however, Swamiji's speed was too great for her in her early days, dots are put in the articles to indicate the omissions, while the words within square brackets are added by way of linking up the disconnected parts.

(Delivered in San Francisco, on May 26, 1900)

To understand the Gita requires its historical background. The Gita is a commentary on the Upanishads. The Upanishads are the Bible of India. They occupy the same place as the New Testament does. There are [more than] a hundred books comprising the Upanishads, some very small and some big, each a separate treatise. The Upanishads do not reveal the life of any teacher, but simply teach principles. They are [as it were] shorthand notes taken down of discussion in [learned assemblies], generally in the courts of kings. The word Upanishad may mean "sittings" [or "sitting near a teacher"]. Those of you who may have studied some of the Upanishads can understand how they are condensed shorthand sketches. After long discussions had been held, they were taken down, possibly from memory. The difficulty is that you get very little of the background. Only the luminous points are mentioned there. The origin of ancient Sanskrit is 5000 B.C.; the Upanishads [are at least] two thousand years before that. Nobody knows [exactly] how old they are. The Gita takes the ideas of the Upanishads and in [some] cases the very words. They are strung together with the idea of bringing out, in a compact, condensed, and systematic form, the whole subject the Upanishads deal with.

The [original] scriptures of the Hindus are called the Vedas. They were so vast — the mass of writings — that if the texts alone were brought here, this room would not contain them. Many of them are lost. They were divided into branches, each branch put into the head of certain priests and kept alive by memory. Such men still exist. They will repeat book after book of the Vedas without missing a single intonation. The larger portion of the Vedas has disappeared. The small portion left makes a whole library by itself. The oldest of these contains the hymns of the Rig-Veda. It is the aim of the modern scholar to restore [the sequence of the Vedic compositions]. The old, orthodox idea is quite different, as your orthodox idea of the Bible is quite different from the modern scholar's. The Vedas are divided into two portions: one the Upanishads, the philosophical portion, the other the work portion.

We will try to give a little idea of the work portion. It consists of rituals and hymns, various hymns addressed to various gods. The ritual portion is composed of ceremonies, some of them very elaborate. A great many priests are required. The priestly function became a science by itself, owing to the elaboration of the ceremonials. Gradually the popular idea of veneration grew round these hymns and rituals. The gods disappeared and in their place were left the rituals. That was the curious development in India. The orthodox Hindu [the Mimâmsaka] does not believe in gods, the unorthodox believe in them. If you ask the orthodox Hindu what the meaning is of these gods in the Vedas, [he will not be able to give any satisfactory answer]. The priests sing these hymns and pour libations and offering into the fire. When you ask the orthodox Hindu the meaning of this, he says that words have the power to produce certain effects. That is all. There is all the natural and supernatural power that ever existed. The Vedas are simply words that have the mystical power to produce effects if the sound intonation is right. If one sound is wrong it will not do. Each one must be perfect. [Thus] what in other religions is called prayer disappeared and the Vedas became the gods. So you see the tremendous importance that was attached to the words of the Vedas. These are the eternal words out of which the whole universe has been produced. There cannot be any thought without the word. Thus whatever there is in this world is the manifestation of thought, and thought can only manifest itself through words. This mass of words by which the unmanifested thought becomes manifest, that is what is meant by the Vedas. It follows that the external existence of everything [depends on the Vedas, for thought] does not exist without the word. If the word "horse" did not exist, none could think of a horse. [So] there must be [an intimate relation between] thought, word, and the external object. What are these words [in reality]? The Vedas. They do not call it Sanskrit language at all. It is Vedic language, a divine language. Sanskrit is a degenerate form. So are all other languages. There is no language older than Vedic. You may ask, "Who wrote the Vedas?" They were not written. The words are the Vedas. A word is Veda, if I can pronounce it rightly. Then it will immediately produce the [desired] effect.

This mass of Vedas eternally exists and all the world is the manifestation of this mass of words. Then when the cycle ends, all this manifestation of energy becomes finer and finer, becomes only words, then thought. In the next cycle, first the thought changes into words and then out of those words [the whole universe] is produced. If there is something here that is not in the Vedas, that is your delusion. It does not exist.

[Numerous] books upon that subject alone defend the Vedas. If you tell [their authors] that the Vedas must have been pronounced by men first, [they will simply laugh]. You never heard of any [man uttering them for the first time]. Take Buddha's words. There is a tradition that he lived and spoke these words [many times before]. If the Christian stands up and says, "My religion is a historical religion and therefore yours is wrong and ours is true," [the Mimamsaka replies], "Yours being historical, you confess that a man invented it nineteen hundred years ago. That which is true must be infinite and eternal. That is the one test of truth. It never decays, it is always the same. You confess your religion was created by such-and-such a man. The Vedas were not. By no prophets or anything. ... Only infinite words, infinite by their very nature, from which the whole universe comes and goes." In the abstract it is perfectly correct. ... The sound must be the beginning of creation. There must be germ sounds like germ plasm. There cannot be any ideas without the words. ... Wherever there are sensations, ideas, emotions, there must be words. The difficulty is when they say that these four books are the Vedas and nothing else. [Then] the Buddhist will stand up and say, "Ours are Vedas. They were revealed to us later on." That cannot be. Nature does not go on in that way. Nature does not manifest her laws bit by bit, an inch of gravitation today and [another inch] tomorrow. No, every law is complete. There is no evolution in law at all. It is [given] once and for ever. It is all nonsense, this "new religion and better inspiration," and all that. It means nothing. There may be a hundred thousand laws and man may know only a few today. We discover them — that is all. Those old priests with their tremendous [claims about eternal words], having dethroned the gods, took the place of the gods. [They said], "You do not understand the power of words. We know how to use them. We are the living gods of the world. Pay us; we will manipulate the words, and you will get what you want. Can you pronounce the words yourself? You cannot, for, mind you, one mistake will produce the opposite effect. You want to be rich, handsome, have a long life, a fine husband?" Only pay the priest and keep quiet!

Yet there is another side. The ideal of the first part of the Vedas is entirely different from the ideal of the other part, the Upanishads. The ideal of the first part coincides with [that of] all other religions of the world except the Vedanta. The ideal is enjoyment here and hereafter — man and wife, husband and children. Pay your dollar, and the priest will give you a certificate, and you will have a happy time afterwards in heaven. You will find all your people there and have this merry-go-round without end. No tears, no weeping — only laughing. No stomach-ache, but yet eating. No headache, but yet [parties]. That, considered the priests, was the highest goal of man.

There is another idea in this philosophy which is according to your modern ideas. Man is a slave of nature, and slave eternally he has got to remain. We call it Karma. Karma means law, and it applies everywhere. Everything is bound by Karma. "Is there no way out?" "No! Remain slaves all through the years — fine slaves. We will manipulate the words so that you will only have the good and not the bad side of all — if you will pay [us] enough." That was the ideal of [the Mimamsakas]. These are the ideals which are popular throughout the ages. The vast mass of mankind are never thinkers. Even if they try to think, the [effect of the] vast mass of superstitions on them is terrible. The moment they weaken, one blow comes, and the backbone breaks into twenty pieces. They can only be moved by lures and threats. They can never move of their own accord. They must be frightened, horrified, or terrorised, and they are your slaves for ever. They have nothing else to do but to pay and obey. Everything else is done by the priest. ... How much easier religion becomes! You see, you have nothing to do. Go home and sit quietly. Somebody is doing the whole thing for you. Poor, poor animals!

Side by side, there was the other system. The Upanishads are diametrically opposite in all their conclusions. First of all, the Upanishads believe in God, the creator of the universe, its ruler. You find later on [the idea of a benign Providence]. It is an entirely opposite [conception]. Now, although we hear the priest, the ideal is much more subtle. Instead of many gods they made one God.

The second idea, that you are all bound by the law of Karma, the Upanishads admit, but they declare the way out. The goal of man is to go beyond law. And enjoyment can never be the goal, because enjoyment can only be in nature.

In the third place, the Upanishads condemn all the sacrifices and say that is mummery. That may give you all you want, but it is not desirable, for the more you get, the more you [want], and you run round and round in a circle eternally, never getting to the end — enjoying and weeping. Such a thing as eternal happiness is impossible anywhere. It is only a child's dream. The same energy becomes joy and sorrow.

I have changed my psychology a bit today. I have found the most curious fact. You have a certain idea and you do not want to have it, and you think of something else, and the idea you want to suppress is entirely suppressed. What is that idea? I saw it come out in fifteen minutes. It came out and staggered me. It was strong, and it came in such a violent and terrible fashion [that] I thought here was a madman. And when it was over, all that had happened [was a suppression of the previous emotion]. What came out? It was my own bad impression which had to be worked out. "Nature will have her way. What can suppression do?" (Gita, III. 33.) That is a terrible [statement] in the Gita. It seems it may be a vain struggle after all. You may have a hundred thousand [urges competing] at the same time. You may repress [them], but the moment the spring rebounds, the whole thing is there again.

[But there is hope]. If you are powerful enough, you can divide your consciousness into twenty parts all at the same time. I am changing my psychology. Mind grows. That is what the Yogis say. There is one passion and it rouses another, and the first one dies. If you are angry, and then happy, the next moment the anger passes away. Out of that anger you manufactured the next state. These states are always interchangeable. Eternal happiness and misery are a child's dream. The Upanishads point out that the goal of man is neither misery nor happiness, but we have to be master of that out of which these are manufactured. We must be masters of the situation at its very root, as it were.

The other point of divergence is: the Upanishads condemn all rituals, especially those that involve the killing of animals. They declare those all nonsense. One school of old philosophers says that you must kill such an animal at a certain time if the effect is to be produced. [You may reply], "But [there is] also the sin of taking the life of the animal; you will have to suffer for that." They say that is all nonsense. How do you know what is right and what is wrong? Your mind says so? Who cares what your mind says? What nonsense are you talking? You are setting your mind against the scriptures. If your mind says something and the Vedas say something else, stop your mind and believe in the Vedas. If they say, killing a man is right, that is right. If you say, "No, my conscience says [otherwise," it won't do]. The moment you believe in any book as the eternal word, as sacred, no more can you question. I do not see how you people here believe in the Bible whenever you say about [it], "How wonderful those words are, how right and how good!" Because, if you believe in the Bible as the word of God, you have no right to judge at all. The moment you judge, you think you are higher than the Bible. [Then] what is the use of the Bible to you? The priests say, "We refuse to make the comparison with your Bible or anybody's. It is no use comparing, because — what is the authority? There it ends. If you think something is not right, go and get it right according to the Vedas."

The Upanishads believe in that, [but they have a higher standard too]. On the one hand, they do not want to overthrow the Vedas, and on the other they see these animal sacrifices and the priests stealing everybody's money.

But in the psychology they are all alike. All the differences have been in the philosophy, [regarding] the nature of the soul. Has it a body and a mind? And is the mind only a bundle of nerves, the motor nerves and the sensory nerves? Psychology, they all take for granted, is a perfect science. There cannot be any difference there. All the fight has been regarding philosophy — the nature of the soul, and God, and all that.

Then another great difference between the priests and the Upanishads. The Upanishads say, renounce. That is the test of everything. Renounce everything. It is the creative faculty that brings us into all this entanglement. The mind is in its own nature when it is calm. The moment you can calm it, that [very] moment you will know the truth. What is it that is whirling the mind? Imagination, creative activity. Stop creation and you know the truth. All power of creation must stop, and then you know the truth at once.

On the other hand, the priests are all for [creation]. Imagine a species of life [in which there is no creative activity. It is unthinkable]. The people had to have a plan [of evolving a stable society. A system of rigid selection was adopted. For instance,] no people who are blind and halt can be married. [As a result] you will find so much less deformity [in India] than in any other country in the world. Epileptics and insane [people] are very rare [there]. That is owing to direct selection. The priests say, "Let them become Sannyâsins." On the other hand, the Upanishads say, "Oh no, [the] earth's best and finest [and] freshest flowers should be laid upon the altar. The strong, the young, with sound intellect and sound body — they must struggle for the truth."

So with all these divergences of opinion, I have told you that the priests already differentiated themselves into a separate caste. The second is the caste of the kings. ... All the Upanishadic philosophy is from the brains of kings, not priests. There [runs] an economic struggle through every religious struggle. This animal called man has some religious influence, but he is guided by economy. Individuals are guided by something else, but the mass of mankind never made a move unless economy was [involved]. You may [preach a religion that may not be perfect in every detail], but if there is an economic background [to it], and you have the most [ardent champions] to preach it, you can convince a whole country. ...

Whenever any religion succeeds, it must have economic value. Thousands of similar sects will be struggling for power, but only those who meet the real economic problem will have it. Man is guided by the stomach. He walks and the stomach goes first and the head afterwards. Have you not seen that? It will take ages for the head to go first. By the time a man is sixty years of age, he is called out of [the world]. The whole of life is one delusion, and just when you begin to see things the way they are, you are snatched off. So long as the stomach went first you were all right. When children's dreams begin to vanish and you begin to look at things the way they are, the head goes. Just when the head goes first, [you go out].

[For] the religion of the Upanishads to be popularised was a hard task. Very little economy is there, but tremendous altruism. ...

The Upanishads had very little kingdom, although they were discovered by kings that held all the royal power in their hands. So the struggle ... began to be fiercer. Its culminating point came two thousand years after, in Buddhism. The seed of Buddhism is here, [in] the ordinary struggle between the king and the priest; and [in the struggle] all religion declined. One wanted to sacrifice religion, the other wanted to cling to the sacrifices, to Vedic gods, etc. Buddhism ... broke the chains of the masses. All castes and creeds alike became equal in a minute. So the great religious ideas in India exist, but have yet to be preached: otherwise they do no good. ...

In every country it is the priest who is conservative, for two reasons — because it is his bread and because he can only move with the people. All priests are not strong. If the people say, "Preach two thousand gods," the priests will do it. They are the servants of the congregation who pay them. God does not pay them. So blame yourselves before blaming the priests. You can only get the government and the religion and the priesthood you deserve, and no better.

So the great struggle began in India and it comes to one of its culminating points in the Gita. When it was causing fear that all India was going to be broken up between [the] two ... [groups], there rose this man Krishna, and in the Gita he tries to reconcile the ceremony and the philosophy of the priests and the people. Krishna is loved and worshipped in the same way as you do Christ. The difference is only in the age. The Hindus keep the birthday of Krishna as you do Christ's. Krishna lived five thousand years ago and his life is full of miracles, some of them very similar to those in the life of Christ. The child was born in prison. The father took him away and put him with the shepherds. All children born in that year were ordered to be killed. ... He was killed; that was his fate.

Krishna was a married man. There are thousands of books about him. They do not interest me much. The Hindus are great in telling stories, you see. [If] the Christian missionaries tell one story from their Bible, the Hindus will produce twenty stories. You say the whale swallowed Jonah; the Hindus say someone swallowed an elephant. ... Since I was a child I have heard about Krishna's life. I take it for granted there must have been a man called Krishna, and his Gita shows he has [left] a wonderful book. I told you, you can understand the character of a man by analysing the fables about him. The fables have the nature [of decorations]. You must find they are all polished and manipulated to fit into the character. For instance, take Buddha. The central idea [is] sacrifice. There are thousands of folklore, but in every case the sacrifice must have been kept up. There are thousands of stories about Lincoln, about some characteristic of that great man. You take all the fables and find the general idea and [know] that that was the central character of the man. You find in Krishna that non-attachment is the central idea. He does not need anything. He does not want anything. He works for work's sake. "Work for work's sake. Worship for worship's sake. Do good because it is good to do good. Ask no more." That must have been the character of the man. Otherwise these fables could not be brought down to the one idea of non-attachment. The Gita is not his only sermon. ...

He is the most rounded man I know of, wonderfully developed equally in brain and heart and hand. Every moment [of his] is alive with activity, either as a gentleman, warrior, minister, or something else. Great as a gentleman, as a scholar, as a poet. This all-rounded and wonderful activity and combination of brain and heart you see in the Gita and other books. Most wonderful heart, exquisite language, and nothing can approach it anywhere. This tremendous activity of the man — the impression is still there. Five thousand years have passed and he has influenced millions and millions. Just think what an influence this man has over the whole world, whether you know it or not. My regard for him is for his perfect sanity. No cobwebs in that brain, no superstition. He knows the use of everything, and when it is necessary to [assign a place to each], he is there. Those that talk, go everywhere, question about the mystery of the Vedas, etc., they do not know the truth. They are no better than frauds. There is a place in the Vedas [even] for superstition, for ignorance. The whole secret is to find out the proper place for everything.

Then that heart! He is the first man, way before Buddha, to open the door of religion to every caste. That wonderful mind! That tremendously active life! Buddha's activity was on one plane, the plane of teaching. He could not keep his wife and child and become a teacher at the same time. Krishna preached in the midst of the battlefield. "He who in the midst of intense activity finds himself in the greatest calmness, and in the greatest peace finds intense activity, that is the greatest [Yogi as well as the wisest man]." (Ibid. IV. 18.) It means nothing to this man — the flying of missiles about him. Calm and sedate he goes on discussing the problems of life and death. Each one of the prophets is the best commentary on his own teaching. If you want to know what is meant by the doctrine of the New Testament, you go to Mr. So-and-so. [But] read again and again [the four Gospels and try to understand their import in the light of the wonderful life of the Master as depicted there]. The great men think, and you and I [also] think. But there is a difference. We think and our bodies do not follow. Our actions do not harmonise with our thoughts. Our words have not the power of the words that become Vedas. ... Whatever they think must be accomplished. If they say, "I do this," the body does it. Perfect obedience. This is the end. You can think yourself God in one minute, but you cannot be [God]. That is the difficulty. They become what they think. We will become [only] by [degrees].

You see, that was about Krishna and his time. In the next lecture we will know more of his book.

The Gita II

This article was recorded by Ida Ansell in shorthand. As, however, Swamiji's speed was too great for her in her early days, dots are put in the articles to indicate the omissions, while the words within square brackets are added by way of linking up the disconnected parts.

(Delivered in San Francisco, on May 28, 1900)

The Gitâ requires a little preliminary introduction. The scene is laid on the battlefield of Kurukshetra. There were two branches of the same race fighting for the empire of India about five thousand years ago. The Pândavas had the right, but the Kauravas had the might. The Pandavas were five brothers, and they were living in a forest. Krishna was the friend of the Pandavas. The Kauravas would not grant them as much land as would cover the point of a needle.

The opening scene is the battlefield, and both sides see their relatives and friends — one brother on one side and another on the other side; a grandfather on one side, grandson on the other side. ... When Arjuna sees his own friends and relatives on the other side and knows that he may have to kill them, his heart gives way and he says that he will not fight. Thus begins the Gita.

For all of us in this world life is a continuous fight. ... Many a time comes when we want to interpret our weakness and cowardice as forgiveness and renunciation. There is no merit in the renunciation of a beggar. If a person who can [give a blow] forbears, there is merit in that. If a person who has, gives up, there is merit in that. We know how often in our lives through laziness and cowardice we give up the battle and try to hypnotise our minds into the belief that we are brave.

The Gita opens with this very significant verse: "Arise, O Prince! Give up this faint-heartedness, this weakness! Stand up and fight!" (Gita, II. 3.) Then Arjuna, trying to argue the matter [with Krishna], brings higher moral ideas, how non-resistance is better than resistance, and so on. He is trying to justify himself, but he cannot fool Krishna. Krishna is the higher Self, or God. He sees through the argument at once. In this case [the motive] is weakness. Arjuna sees his own relatives and he cannot strike them. ...

There is a conflict in Arjuna's heart between his emotionalism and his duty. The nearer we are to [beasts and] birds, the more we are in the hells of emotion. We call it love. It is self-hypnotisation. We are under the control of our [emotions] like animals. A cow can sacrifice its life for its young. Every animal can. What of that? It is not the blind, birdlike emotion that leads to perfection. ... [To reach] the eternal consciousness, that is the goal of man! There emotion has no place, nor sentimentalism, nor anything that belongs to the senses — only the light of pure reason. [There] man stands as spirit.

Now, Arjuna is under the control of this emotionalism. He is not what he should be — a great self-controlled, enlightened sage working through the eternal light of reason. He has become like an animal, like a baby, just letting his heart carry away his brain, making a fool of himself and trying to cover his weakness with the flowery names of "love" and so on. Krishna sees through that. Arjuna talks like a man of little learning and brings out many reasons, but at the same time he talks the language of a fool.

"The sage is not sorry for those that are living nor for those that die." (Ibid. 11.) [Krishna says :] "You cannot die nor can I. There was never a time when we did not exist. There will never be a time when we shall not exist. As in this life a man begins with childhood, and [passes through youth and old age, so at death he merely passes into another kind of body]. Why should a wise man be sorry?" (Ibid. 12-13.) And where is the beginning of this emotionalism that has got hold of you? It is in the senses. "It is the touch of the senses that brings all this quality of existence: heat and cold, pleasure and pain. They come and go." (Ibid. 14.) Man is miserable this moment, happy the next. As such he cannot experience the nature of the soul. ...

"Existence can never be non-existence, neither can non-existence ever become existence. ... Know, therefore, that that which pervades all this universe is without beginning or end. It is unchangeable. There is nothing in the universe that can change [the Changeless]. Though this body has its beginning and end, the dweller in the body is infinite and without end." (Ibid. 16-18.)

Knowing this, stand up and fight! Not one step back, that is the idea. ... Fight it out, whatever comes. Let the stars move from the sphere! Let the whole world stand against us! Death means only a change of garment. What of it? Thus fight! You gain nothing by becoming cowards. ... Taking a step backward, you do not avoid any misfortune. You have cried to all the gods in the world. Has misery ceased? The masses in India cry to sixty million gods, and still die like dogs. Where are these gods? ... The gods come to help you when you have succeeded. So what is the use? Die game. ... This bending the knee to superstitions, this selling yourself to your own mind does not befit you, my soul. You are infinite, deathless, birthless. Because you are infinite spirit, it does not befit you to be a slave. ... Arise! Awake! Stand up and fight! Die if you must. There is none to help you. You are all the world. Who can help you?

"Beings are unknown to our human senses before birth and after death. It is only in the interim that they are manifest. What is there to grieve about? (Ibid. 28.)

"Some look at It [the Self] with wonder. Some talk of It as wonderful. Others hear of It as wonderful. Others, hearing of It, do not understand." (Ibid. 29.)

But if you say that killing all these people is sinful, then consider this from the standpoint of your own caste-duty. ... "Making pleasure and misery the same, making success and defeat the same, do thou stand up and fight. (Ibid. 38.)

This is the beginning of another peculiar doctrine of the Gita — the doctrine of non-attachment. That is to say, we have to bear the result of our own actions because we attach ourselves to them. ... "Only what is done as duty for duty's sake ... can scatter the bondage of Karma." (Ibid. 39.) There is no danger that you can overdo it. ... "If you do even a little of it, [this Yoga will save you from the terrible round of birth and death]. (Ibid. 40.)

"Know, Arjuna, the mind that succeeds is the mind that is concentrated. The minds that are taken up with two thousand subjects (have) their energies dispersed. Some can talk flowery language and think there is nothing beyond the Vedas. They want to go to heaven. They want good things through the power of the Vedas, and so they make sacrifices." (Ibid. 41-43.) Such will never attain any success [in spiritual life] unless they give up all these materialistic ideas. (Ibid. 44.)

That is another great lesson. Spirituality can never be attained unless all material ideas are given up. ... What is in the senses? The senses are all delusion. People wish to retain them [in heaven] even after they are dead — a pair of eyes, a nose. Some imagine they will have more organs than they have now. They want to see God sitting on a throne through all eternity — the material body of God. ... Such men's desires are for the body, for food and drink and enjoyment. It is the materialistic life prolonged. Man cannot think of anything beyond this life. This life is all for the body. "Such a man never comes to that concentration which leads to freedom." (Ibid. 44.)

"The Vedas only teach things belonging to the three Gunas, to Sattva, Rajas, and Tamas." (Ibid. 45.) The Vedas only teach about things in nature. People cannot think anything they do not see on earth. If they talk about heaven, they think of a king sitting on a throne, of people burning incense. It is all nature, nothing beyond nature. The Vedas, therefore, teach nothing but nature. "Go beyond nature, beyond the dualities of existence, beyond your own consciousness, caring for nothing, neither for good nor for evil." (Ibid. 45.)

We have identified ourselves with our bodies. We are only body, or rather, possessed of a body. If I am pinched, I cry. All this is nonsense, since I am the soul. All this chain of misery, imagination, animals, gods, and demons, everything, the whole world all this comes from the identification of ourselves with the body. I am spirit. Why do I jump if you pinch me? ... Look at the slavery of it. Are you not ashamed? We are religious! We are philosophers! We are sages! Lord bless us! What are we? Living hells, that is what we are. Lunatics, that is what we are!

We cannot give up the idea [of body]. We are earth-bound. ... Our ideas are burial grounds. When we leave the body we are bound by thousands of elements to those [ideas].

Who can work without any attachment? That is the real question. Such a man is the same whether his work succeeds or fails. His heart does not give one false beat even if his whole life-work is burnt to ashes in a moment. "This is the sage who always works for work's sake without caring for the results. Thus he goes beyond the pain of birth and death. Thus he becomes free." (Ibid. 51.) Then he sees that this attachment is all delusion. The Self can never be attached. ... Then he goes beyond all the scriptures and philosophies. (Ibid. 52.) If the mind is deluded and pulled into a whirlpool by books and scriptures, what is the good of all these scriptures? One says this, another says that. What book shall you take? Stand alone! See the glory of your own soul, and see that you will have to work. Then you will become a man of firm will. (Ibid. 53.)

Arjuna asks: "Who is a person of established will?" (Ibid. 54.)

[Krishna answers:] "The man who has given up all desires, who desires nothing, not even this life, nor freedom, nor gods, nor work, nor anything. When he has become perfectly satisfied, he has no more cravings." (Ibid. 55.) He has seen the glory of the Self and has found that the world, and the gods, and heaven are ... within his own Self. Then the gods become no gods; death becomes no death; life becomes no life. Everything has changed. "A man is said to be [illumined] if his will has become firm, if his mind is not disturbed by misery, if he does not desire any happiness, if he is free of all [attachment], of all fear, of all anger. (Ibid. 56.) ...

"As the tortoise can draw in his legs, and if you strike him, not one foot comes out, even so the sage can draw all his sense-organs inside," (Ibid. 58.)

and nothing can force them out. Nothing can shake him, no temptation or anything. Let the universe tumble about him, it does not make one single ripple in his mind.

Then comes a very important question. Sometimes people fast for days. ... When the worst man has fasted for twenty days, he becomes quite gentle. Fasting and torturing themselves have been practiced by people all over the world. Krishna's idea is that this is all nonsense. He says that the senses will for the moment recede from the man who tortures himself, but will emerge again with twenty times more [power]. ... What should you do? The idea is to be natural — no asceticism. Go on, work, only mind that you are not attached. The will can never be fixed strongly in the man who has not learnt and practiced the secret of non-attachment.

I go out and open my eyes. If something is there, I must see it. I cannot help it. The mind runs after the senses. Now the senses must give up any reaction to nature.

"Where it is dark night for the [sense-bound] world, the self controlled [man] is awake. It is daylight for him. ... And where the world is awake, the sage sleeps." (Ibid. 69.) Where is the world awake? In the senses. People want to eat and drink and have children, and then they die a dog's death. ... They are always awake for the senses. Even their religion is just for that. They invent a God to help them, to give them more women, more money, more children — never a God to help them become more godlike! "Where the whole world is awake, the sage sleeps. But where the ignorant are asleep, there the sage keeps awake" (Ibid. 69.) — in the world of light where man looks upon himself not as a bird, not as an animal, not as a body, but as infinite spirit, deathless, immortal. There, where the ignorant are asleep, and do not have time, nor intellect, nor power to understand, there the sage is awake. That is daylight for him.

"As all the rivers of the world constantly pour their waters into the ocean, but the ocean's grand, majestic nature remains undisturbed and unchanged, so even though all the senses bring in sensations from nature, the ocean-like heart of the sage knows no disturbance, knows no fear." (Ibid. 70.) Let miseries come in millions of rivers and happiness in hundreds! I am no slave to misery! I am no slave to happiness!

The Gita III

This article was recorded by Ida Ansell in shorthand. As, however, Swamiji's speed was too great for her in her early days, dots are put in the articles to indicate the omissions, while the words within square brackets are added by way of linking up the disconnected parts.

(Delivered in San Francisco, on May 29, 1900)

Arjuna asks: "You just advised action, and yet you uphold knowledge of Brahman as the highest form of life. Krishna, if you think that knowledge is better than action, why do you tell me to act?" (Gita III. 1.)

[Shri Krishna]: "From ancient times these two systems have come down to us. The Sânkhya philosophers advance the theory of knowledge. The Yogis advance the theory of work. But none can attain to peace by renouncing actions. None in this life can stop activity even for a moment. Nature's qualities [Gunas] will make him act. He who stops his activities and at the same time is still thinking about them attains to nothing; he only becomes a hypocrite. But he who by the power of his mind gradually brings his sense-organs under control, employing them in work, that man is better. Therefore do thou work." (Ibid. 2-8.) ...

"Even if you have known the secret that you have no duty, that you are free, still you have to work for the good of others. Because whatever a great man does, ordinary people will do also. (Ibid. 20-21.) If a great man who has attained peace of mind and freedom ceases to work, then all the rest without that knowledge and peace will try to imitate him, and thus confusion would arise. (Ibid. 22-24.)

"Behold, Arjuna, there is nothing that I do not possess and nothing that I want to acquire. And yet I continue to work. If I stopped work for a moment, the whole universe would [be destroyed]. (Ibid. 22-24.) That which the ignorant do with desire for results and gain, let the wise do without any attachment and without any desire for results and gain." (Ibid. 25.)

Even if you have knowledge, do not disturb the childlike faith of the ignorant. On the other hand, go down to their level and gradually bring them up. (Ibid. 26, 29.) That is a very powerful idea, and it has become the ideal in India. That is why you can see a great philosopher going into a temple and worshipping images. It is not hypocrisy.

Later on we read what Krishna says, "Even those who worship other deities are really worshipping me." (Ibid. IX. 23.) It is God incarnate whom man is worshipping. Would God be angry if you called Him by the wrong name? He would be no God at all! Can't you understand that whatever a man has in his own heart is God — even if he worships a stone? What of that!

We will understand more clearly if we once get rid of the idea that religion consists in doctrines. One idea of religion has been that the whole world was born because Adam ate the apple, and there is no way of escape. Believe in Jesus Christ — in a certain man's death! But in India there is quite a different idea. [There] religion means realisation, nothing else. It does not matter whether one approaches the destination in a carriage with four horses, in an electric car, or rolling on the ground. The goal is the same. For the [Christians] the problem is how to escape the wrath of the terrible God. For the Indians it is how to become what they really are, to regain their lost Selfhood. ...

Have you realised that you are spirit? When you say, "I do," what is meant by that — this lump of flesh called the body or the spirit, the infinite, ever blessed, effulgent, immortal? You may be the greatest philosopher, but as long as you have the idea that you are the body, you are no better than the little worm crawling under your foot! No excuse for you! So much the worse for you that you know all the philosophies and at the same time think you are the body! Body-gods, that is what you are! Is that religion?

Religion is the realisation of spirit as spirit. What are we doing now? Just the opposite, realising spirit as matter. Out of the immortal God we manufacture death and matter, and out of dead dull matter we manufacture spirit. ...

If you [can realise Brahman] by standing on your head, or on one foot, or by worshipping five thousand gods with three heads each — welcome to it! ... Do it any way you can! Nobody has any right to say anything. Therefore, Krishna says, if your method is better and higher, you have no business to say that another man's method is bad, however wicked you may think it.

Again, we must consider, religion is a [matter of] growth, not a mass of foolish words. Two thousand years ago a man saw God. Moses saw God in a burning bush. Does what Moses did when he saw God save you? No man's seeing God can help you the least bit except that it may excite you and urge you to do the same thing. That is the whole value of the ancients' examples. Nothing more. [Just] signposts on the way. No man's eating can satisfy another man. No man's seeing God can save another man. You have to see God yourself. All these people fighting about what God's nature is — whether He has three heads in one body or five heads in six bodies. Have you seen God? No. ... And they do not believe they can ever see Him. What fools we mortals be! Sure, lunatics!

[In India] it has come down as a tradition that if there is a God, He must be your God and my God. To whom does the sun belong! You say Uncle Sam is everybody's uncle. If there is a God, you ought to be able to see Him. If not, let Him go.

Each one thinks his method is best. Very good! But remember, it may be good for you. One food which is very indigestible to one is very digestible to another. Because it is good for you, do not jump to the conclusion that your method is everybody's method, that Jack's coat fits John and Mary. All the uneducated, uncultured, unthinking men and women have been put into that sort of strait jacket! Think for yourselves. Become atheists! Become materialists! That would be better. Exercises the mind! ... What right have you to say that this man's method is wrong? It may be wrong for you. That is to say, if you undertake the method, you will be degraded; but that does not mean that he will be degraded. Therefore, says Krishna, if you have knowledge and see a man weak, do not condemn him. Go to his level and help him if you can. He must grow. I can put five bucketfuls of knowledge into his head in five hours. But what good will it do? He will be a little worse than before.

Whence comes all this bondage of action? Because we chain the soul with action. According to our Indian system, there are two existences: nature on the one side and the Self, the Atman, on the other. By the word nature is meant not only all this external world, but also our bodies, the mind, the will, even down to what says "I". Beyond all that is the infinite life and light of the soul — the Self, the Atman. ... According to this philosophy the Self is entirely separate from nature, always was and always will be. ... There never was a time, when the spirit could be identified even with the mind. ...

It is self-evident that the food you eat is manufacturing the mind all the time. It is matter. The Self is above any connection with food. Whether you eat or not does not matter. Whether you think or not ... does not matter. It is infinite light. Its light is the same always. If you put a blue or a green glass [before a light], what has that to do with the light? Its colour is unchangeable. It is the mind which changes and gives the different colours. The moment the spirit leaves the body, the whole thing goes to pieces.

The reality in nature is spirit. Reality itself — the light of the spirit — moves and speaks and does everything [through our bodies, minds, etc.].

It is the energy and soul and life of the spirit that is being worked upon in different ways by matter.... The spirit is the cause of all our thoughts and body-action and everything, but it is untouched by good or evil, pleasure or pain, heat or cold, and all the dualism of nature, although it lends its light to everything.

"Therefore, Arjuna, all these actions are in nature. Nature ... is working out her own laws in our bodies and minds. We identify ourselves with nature and say, 'I am doing this.' This way delusion seizes us." (Ibid. III. 27.)

We always act under some compulsion. When hunger compels me, I eat. And suffering is still worse — slavery. That real "I" is eternally free. What can compel it to do anything? The sufferer is in nature. It is only when we identify ourselves with the body that we say, "I am suffering; I am Mr. So and-so" — all such nonsense. But he who has known the truth, holds himself aloof. Whatever his body does, whatever his mind does, he does not care. But mind you, the vast majority of mankind are under this delusion; and whenever they do any good, they feel that they are [the doers]. They are not yet able to understand higher philosophy. Do not disturb their faith! They are shunning evil and doing good. Great idea! Let them have it! ... They are workers for good. By degrees they will think that there is greater glory than that of doing good. They will only witness, and things are done.... Gradually they will understand. When they have shunned all evil and done all good, then they will begin to realise that they are beyond all nature. They are not the doers. They stand [apart]. They are the ... witness. They simply stand and look. Nature is begetting all the universe.... They turn their backs. "In the beginning, O beloved, there only existed that Existence. Nothing else existed. And That [brooding], everything else was created." (Chhândogya, VI. ii. 2-3.)

"Even those who know the path act impelled by their own nature. Everyone acts according to his nature. He cannot transcend it."(Gita, III. 33.) The atom cannot disobey the law. Whether it is the mental or the physical atom, it must obey the law. "What is the use of [external restraint]?" (Gita, III. 33.)

What makes the value of anything in life? Not enjoyment, not possessions. Analyse everything. You will find there is no value except in experience, to teach us something. And in many cases it is our hardships that give us better experience than enjoyment. Many times blows give us better experience than the caresses of nature.... Even famine has its place and value....

According to Krishna, we are not new beings just come into existence. Our minds are not new minds.... In modern times we all know that every child brings [with him] all the past, not only of humanity, but of the plant life. There are all the past chapters, and this present chapter, and there are a whole lot of future chapters before him. Everyone has his path mapped and sketched and planned out for him. And in spite of all this darkness, there cannot be anything uncaused — no event, no circumstance.... It is simply our ignorance. The whole infinite chain of causation ... is bound one link to another back to nature. The whole universe is bound by that sort of chain. It is the universal [chain of] cause and effect, you receiving one link, one part, I another.... And that [part] is our own nature.

Now Shri Krishna says: "Better die in your own path than attempt the path of another."(Ibid. 35.) This is my path, and I am down here. And you are way up there, and I am always tempted to give up my path thinking I will go there and be with you. And if I go up, I am neither there nor here. We must not lose sight of this doctrine. It is all [a matter of] growth. Wait and grow, and you attain everything; otherwise there will be [great spiritual danger]. Here is the fundamental secret of teaching religion.

What do you mean by "saving people" and all believing in the same doctrine? It cannot be. There are the general ideas that can be taught to mankind. The true teacher will be able to find out for you what your own nature is. Maybe you do not know it. It is possible that what you think is your own nature is all wrong. It has not developed to consciousness. The teacher is the person who ought to know.... He ought to know by a glance at your face and put you on [your path]. We grope about and struggle here and there and do all sorts of things and make no progress until the time comes when we fall into that life-current and are carried on. The sign is that the moment we are in that stream we will float. Then there is no more struggle. This is to be found out. Then die in that [path] rather than giving it up and taking hold of another.

Instead, we start a religion and make a set of dogmas and betray the goal of mankind and treat everyone [as having] the same nature. No two persons have the same mind or the same body. ... No two persons have the same religion....

If you want to be religious, enter not the gate of any organised religions. They do a hundred times more evil than good, because they stop the growth of each one's individual development. Study everything, but keep your own seat firm. If you take my advice, do not put your neck into the trap. The moment they try to put their noose on you, get your neck out and go somewhere else. [As] the bee culling honey from many flowers remains free, not bound by any flower, be not bound.... Enter not the door of any organised religion. [Religion] is only between you and your God, and no third person must come between you. Think what these organised religions have done! What Napoleon was more terrible than those religious persecutions? . . . If you and I organise, we begin to hate every person. It is better not to love, if loving only means hating others. That is no love. That is hell! If loving your own people means hating everybody else, it is the quintessence of selfishness and brutality, and the effect is that it will make you brutes. Therefore, better die working out your own natural religion than following another's natural religion, however great it may appear to you. (Ibid. 35.)

"Beware, Arjuna, lust and anger are the great enemies. These are to be controlled. These cover the knowledge even of those [who are wise]. This fire of lust is unquenchable. Its location is in the sense-organs and in the mind. The Self desires nothing. (Ibid. 37, 40.)

"This Yoga I taught in ancient times [to Vivaswân; Vivaswan taught it to Manu]. ... Thus it was that the knowledge descended from one thing to another. But in time this great Yoga was destroyed. That is why I am telling it to you again today." (Ibid. IV. 1-3.)

Then Arjuna asks, "Why do you speak thus? You are a man born only the other day, and [Vivaswan was born long before you]. What do you mean that you taught him?" (Ibid. 4.)

Then Krishna says, "O Arjuna, you and I have run the cycle of births and deaths many times, but you are not conscious of them all. I am without beginning, birthless, the absolute Lord of all creation. I through my own nature take form. Whenever virtue subsides and wickedness prevails, I come to help mankind. For the salvation of the good, for the destruction of wickedness, for the establishment of spirituality I come from time to time. Whosoever wants to reach me through whatsoever ways, I reach him through that. But know, Arjuna, none can ever swerve from my path." (Ibid. 5-8, 11.) None ever did. How can we? None swerves from His path.

... All societies are based upon bad generalisation. The law can only be formed upon perfect generalisation. What is the old saying: Every law has its exception? ... If it is a law, it cannot be broken. None can break it. Does the apple break the law of gravitation? The moment a law is broken, no more universe exists. There will come a time when you will break the law, and that moment your consciousness, mind, and body will melt away.

There is a man stealing there. Why does he steal? You punish him. Why can you not make room for him and put his energy to work? ... You say, "You are a sinner," and many will say he has broken the law. All this herd of mankind is forced [into uniformity] and hence all trouble, sin, and weakness.... The world is not as bad as you think. It is we fools who have made it evil. We manufacture our own ghosts and demons, and then ... we cannot get rid of them. We put our hands before our eyes and cry: "Somebody give us light." Fools! Take your hands from your eyes! That is all there is to it.... We call upon the gods to save us and nobody blames himself. That is the pity of it. Why is there so much evil in society? What is it they say? Flesh and the devil and the woman. Why make these things [up]? Nobody asks you to make them [up]. "None, O Arjuna, can swerve from my path." (Ibid. 11.) We are fools, and our paths are foolish. We have to go through all this Mâyâ. God made the heaven, and man made the hell for himself.

"No action can touch me. I have no desire for the results of action. Whosoever knows me thus knows the secret and is not bound by action. The ancient sages, knowing this secret [could safely engage in action]. Do thou work in the same fashion. (Ibid. 14-15.)

"He who sees in the midst of intense activity, intense calm, and in the midst of intensest peace is intensely active [is wise indeed]. (Ibid 18.) ... This is the question: With every sense and every organ active, have you that tremendous peace [so that] nothing can disturb you? Standing on Market Street, waiting for the car with all the rush ... going on around you, are you in meditation — calm and peaceful? In the cave, are you intensely active there with all quiet about you? If you are, you are a Yogi, otherwise not.

"[The seers call him wise] whose every attempt is free, without any desire for gain, without any selfishness." (Ibid. 19). Truth can never come to us as long as we are selfish. We colour everything with our own selves. Things come to us as they are. Not that they are hidden, not at all! *We* hide them. We have the brush. A thing comes, and we do not like it, and we brush a little and then look at it. ... We do not want to know. We paint everything with ourselves. In all action the motive power is selfishness. Everything is hidden by ourselves. We are like the caterpillar which takes the thread out of his own body and of that makes the cocoon, and behold, he is caught. By his own work he imprisons himself. That is what we are doing. The moment I say "me" the thread makes a turn. "I and mine," another turn. So it goes. ...

We cannot remain without action for a moment. Act! But just as when your neighbour asks you, "Come and help me!" have you exactly the same idea when you are helping yourself. No more. Your body is of no more value than that of John. Don't do anything more for your body than you do for John. That is religion.

"He whose efforts are bereft of all desire and selfishness has burnt all this bondage of action with the fire of knowledge. He is wise." (Ibid. 19.) Reading books cannot do that. The ass can be burdened with the whole library; that does not make him learned at all. What is the use of reading many books? "Giving up all attachment to work, always satisfied, not hoping for gain, the wise man acts and is beyond action." (Ibid. 20.) ...

Naked I came out of my mother's womb and naked I return. Helpless I came and helpless I go. Helpless I am now. And we do not know [the goal]. It is terrible for us to think about it. We get such odd ideas! We go to a medium and see if the ghost can help us. Think of the weakness! Ghosts, devils, gods, anybody — come on! And all the priests, all the charlatans! That is just the time they get hold of us, the moment we are weak. Then they bring in all the gods.

I see in my country a man becomes strong, educated, becomes a philosopher, and says, "All this praying and bathing is nonsense." ... The man's father dies, and his mother dies. That is the most terrible shock a Hindu can have. You will find him bathing in every dirty pool, going into the temple, licking the dust. ... Help anyone! But we are helpless. There is no help from anyone. That is the truth. There have been more gods than human beings; and yet no help. We die like dogs — no help. Everywhere beastliness, famine, disease, misery, evil! And all are crying for help. But no help. And yet, hoping against hope, we are still screaming for help. Oh, the miserable condition! Oh, the terror of it! Look into your own heart! One half of [the trouble] is not our fault, but the fault of our parents. Born with this weakness, more and more of it was put into our heads. Step by step we go beyond it.

It is a tremendous error to feel helpless. Do not seek help from anyone. We are our own help. If we cannot help ourselves, there is none to help us. ... "Thou thyself art thy only friend, thou thyself thy only enemy. There is no other enemy but this self of mine, no other friend but myself." (Ibid. VI. 5.) This is the last and greatest lesson, and Oh, what a time it takes to learn it! We seem to get hold of it, and the next moment the old wave comes. The backbone breaks. We weaken and again grasp for that superstition and help. Just think of that huge mass of misery, and all caused by this false idea of going to seek for help!

Possibly the priest says his routine words and expects something. Sixty thousand people look to the skies and pray and pay the priest. Month after month they still look, still pay and pray. ... Think of that! Is it not lunacy? What else is it? Who is responsible? You may preach religion, but to excite the minds of undeveloped children... ! You will have to suffer for that. In your heart of hearts, what are you? For every weakening thought you have put into anybody's head you will have to pay with compound interest. The law of Karma must have its pound of flesh. ...

There is only one sin. That is weakness. When I was a boy I read Milton's*Paradise Lost*. The only good man I had any respect for was Satan. The only saint is that soul that never weakens, faces everything, and determines to die game.

Stand up and die game! ... Do not add one lunacy to another. Do not add your weakness to the evil that is going to come. That is all I have to say to the world. Be strong! ... You talk of ghosts and devils. We are the living devils. The sign of life is strength and growth. The sign of death is weakness. Whatever is weak, avoid! It is death. If it is strength, go down into hell and get hold of it! There is salvation only for the brave. "None but the brave deserves the fair." None but the bravest deserves salvation. Whose hell? Whose torture? Whose sin? Whose weakness? Whose death? Whose disease?

You believe in God. If you do, believe in the real God. "Thou art the man, thou the woman, thou the young man walking in the strength of youth, ... thou the old man tottering with his stick." (Shvetâshvatara, IV. 3.) Thou art weakness. Thou art fear. Thou art heaven, and Thou art hell. Thou art the serpent that would sting. Come thou as fear! Come thou as death! Come thou as misery! ...

All weakness, all bondage is imagination. Speak one word to it, it must vanish. Do not weaken! There is no other way out.... Stand up and be strong! No fear. No superstition. Face the truth as it is! If death comes — that is the worst of our miseries — let it come! We are determined to die game. That is all the religion I know. I have not attained to it, but I am struggling to do it. I may not, but you may. Go on!

Where one sees another, one hears another so long as there are two, there must be fear, and fear is the mother of all [misery]. Where none sees another, where it is all One, there is none to be miserable, none to be unhappy. (Chhândogya, VII. xxiii-xxiv, (adapted)) [There is only] the One without a second. Therefore be not afraid. Awake, arise, and stop not till the goal is reached!

Mohammed

This article was recorded by Ida Ansell in shorthand. As, however, Swamiji's speed was too great for her in her early days, dots are put in the articles to indicate the omissions, while the words within square brackets are added by way of linking up the disconnected parts.

(Delivered on March 25, 1900, in the San Francisco Bay Area)

The ancient message of Krishna is one harmonising three — Buddha's, Christ's and Mohammed's. Each of the three started an idea and carried it to its extreme. Krishna antedates all the other prophets. [Yet, we might say,] Krishna takes the old ideas and synthesises them, [although] his is the most ancient message. His message was for the time being submerged by the advance wave of Buddhism. Today it is the message peculiar to India. If you will have it so, this afternoon I will take Mohammed and bring out the particular work of the great Arabian prophet....

Mohammed [as] a young man ... did not [seem to] care much for religion. He was inclined to make money. He was considered a nice young man and very handsome. There was a rich widow. She fell in love with this young man, and they married. When Mohammed had become emperor over the larger part of the world, the Roman and Persian empires were all under his feet, and he had a number of wives. When one day he was asked which wife he liked best, he pointed to his first wife: "Because she believed [in] me first." Women have faith.... Gain independence, gain everything, but do not lose that characteristic of women! ...

Mohammed's heart was sick at the sin, idolatry and mock worship, superstitions and human sacrifices, and so on. The Jews were degraded by the Christians. On the other hand, the Christians were worse degraded than his own countrymen.

We are always in a hurry. [But] if any great work is to be done, there must be great preparation. ... After much praying, day and night, Mohammed began to have dreams and visions. Gabriel appeared to him in a dream and told him that he was the messenger of truth. He told him that the message of Jesus, of Moses, and all the prophets would be lost and asked him to go and preach. Seeing the Christians preaching politics in the name of Jesus, seeing the Persians preaching dualism, Mohammed said: "Our God is one God. He is the Lord of all that exists. There is no comparison between Him and any other."

God is God. There is no philosophy, no complicated code of ethics. "Our God is one without a second, and Mohammed is the Prophet." ... Mohammed began to preach it in the streets of Mecca. ... They began to persecute him, and he fled into the city of [Medina]. He began to fight, and the whole race became united. [Mohammedanism] deluged the world in the name of the Lord. The tremendous conquering power! ...

You ... people have very hard ideas and are so superstitious and prejudiced! These messengers must have come from God, else how could they have been so great? You look at every defect. Each one of us has his defects. Who hasn't? I can point out many defects in the Jews. The wicked are always looking for defects. ... Flies come and seek for the [ulcer], and bees come only for the honey in the flower. Do not follow the way of the fly but that of the bee....

Mohammed married quite a number of wives afterwards. Great men may marry two hundred wives each. "Giants" like you, I would not allow to marry one wife. The characters of the great souls are mysterious, their methods past our finding out. We must not judge them. Christ may judge Mohammed. Who are you and I? Little babies. What do we understand of these great souls? ...

[Mohammedanism] came as a message for the masses. ... The first message was equality. ... There is one religion — love. No more question of race, colour, [or] anything else. Join it! That practical quality carried the day. ... The great message was perfectly simple. Believe in one God, the creator of heaven and earth. All was created out of nothing by Him. Ask no questions. ...

Their temples are like Protestant churches. ... no music, no paintings, no pictures. A pulpit in the corner; on that lies the Koran. The people all stand in line. No priest, no person, no bishop. ... The man who prays must stand at the side of the audience. Some parts are beautiful. ...

These old people were all messengers of God. I fall down and worship them; I take the dust of their feet. But they are dead! ... And we are alive. We must go ahead! ... Religion is not an imitation of Jesus or Mohammed. Even if an imitation is good, it is never genuine. Be not an imitation of Jesus, but be Jesus, You are quite as great as Jesus, Buddha, or anybody else. If we are not ... we must struggle and be. I would not be exactly like Jesus. It is unnecessary that I should be born a Jew. ...

The greatest religion is to be true to your own nature. Have faith in yourselves! If you do not exist, how can God exist, or anybody else? Wherever you are, it is this mind that perceives even the Infinite. I see God, therefore He exists. If I cannot think of God, He does not exist [for me]. This is the grand march of our human progress.

These [great souls] are signposts on the way. That is all they are. They say, "Onward, brothers!" We cling to them; we never want to move. We do not want to think; we want others to think for us. The messengers fulfil their mission. They ask to be up and doing. A hundred years later we cling to the message and go to sleep.

Talking about faith and belief and doctrine is easy, but it is so difficult to build character and to stem the tide of the senses. We succumb. We become hypocrites. ...

[Religion] is not a doctrine, [not] a rule. It is a process. That is all. [Doctrines and rules] are all for exercise. By that exercise we get strong and at last break the bonds and become free. Doctrine is of no use except for gymnastics. ... Through exercise the soul becomes perfect. That exercise is stopped when you say, "I believe." ...

"Whenever virtue subsides and immorality abounds, I take human form. In every age I come for the salvation of the good, for the destruction of the wicked, for the establishment of spirituality." (Gita, IV. 7-8.)

[Such] are the great messengers of light. They are our great teachers, our elder brothers. But we must go our own way!

Vilvamangala

(Found in the papers of Miss S. E. Waldo by Swami Raghavananda when he was in the U.S.A.)

This is a story from one of the books of India, called "Lives of Saints". There was a young man, a Brahmin by birth, in a certain village. The man fell in love with a bad woman in another village. There was a big river between the two villages, and this man, every day, used to go to that girl, crossing this river in a ferry boat. Now, one day he had to perform the obsequies of his father, and so, although he was longing, almost dying to go to the girl, he could not. The ceremonies had to be performed, and all those things had to be undergone; it is absolutely necessary in Hindu society. He was fretting and fuming and all that, but could not help it. At last the ceremony ended, and night came, and with the night, a tremendous howling storm arose. The rain was pouring down, and the river was lashed into gigantic waves. It was very dangerous to cross. Yet he went to the bank of the river. There was no ferry boat. The ferrymen were afraid to cross, but he would go; his heart was becoming mad with love for the girl, so he would go. There was a log floating down, and he got that, and with the help of it, crossed the river, and getting to the other side dragged the log up, threw it on the bank, and went to the house. The doors were closed. He knocked at the door, but the wind was howling, and nobody heard him. So he went round the walls and at last found what he thought to be a rope, hanging from the wall. He clutched at it, saying to himself, "Oh, my love has left a rope for me to climb." By the help of that rope he climbed over the wall, got to the other side, missed his footing, and fell, and noise aroused the inmates of the house, and the came out and found the man there in a faint. She revived him, and noticing that he was smelling very unpleasantly, she said, "What is the matter with you? Why this stench on your body? How did you come into the house?" He said, "Why, did not my love put that rope there?" She smiled, and said, "What love? We are for money, and do you think that I let down a rope for you, fool that you are? How did you cross the river?" "Why, I got hold of a log of wood." "Let us go and see," said the girl. The rope was a cobra, a tremendously poisonous serpent, whose least touch is death. It had its head in a hole, and was getting in when the man caught hold of its tail, and he thought it was a rope. The madness of love made him do it. When the serpent has its head in its hole, and its body out, and you catch hold of it, it will not let its head come out; so the man climbed up by it, but the force of the pull killed the serpent. "Where did you get the log?" "It was floating down the river." It was a festering dead body; the stream had washed it down and that he took for a log, which explained why he had such an unpleasant odour. The woman looked at him and said, "I never believed in love; we never do; but, if this is not love, the Lord have mercy on me. We do not know what love is. But, my friend, why do you give that heart to a woman like me? Why do you not give it to God? You will be perfect." It was a thunderbolt to the man's brain. He got a glimpse of the beyond for a moment. "Is there a God?" "Yes, yes, my friend, there is," said the woman. And the man walked on, went into a forest, began to weep and pray. "I want Thee, Oh Lord! This tide of my love cannot find a receptacle in little human beings. I want to love where this mighty river of my love can go, the ocean of love; this rushing tremendous river of my love cannot enter into little pools, it wants the infinite ocean. Thou art there; come Thou to me." So he remained there for years. After years he thought he had succeeded, he became a Sannyasin and he came into the cities. One day he was sitting on the bank of a river, at one of the bathing places, and a beautiful young girl, the wife of a merchant of the city, with her servant, came and passed the place. The old man was again up in him, the beautiful face again attracted him. The Yogi looked and looked, stood up and followed the girl to her home. Presently the husband came by, and seeing the Sannyasin in the yellow garb he said to him, "Come in, sir, what can I do for you?" The Yogi said, "I will ask you a terrible thing." "Ask anything, sir, I am a Grihastha (householder), and anything that one asks I am ready to give." "I want to see your wife." The man said, "Lord, what is this! Well, I am pure, and my wife is pure, and the Lord is a protection to all. Welcome; come in sir." He came in, and the husband introduced him to his wife. "What can I do for you?" asked the lady. He looked and looked, and then said, "Mother, will you give me two pins from your hair?" "Here they are." He thrust them into his two eyes saying "Get away, you rascals! Henceforth no fleshy things for you. If you are to see, see the Shepherd of the groves of Vrindaban with the eyes of the soul. Those are all the eyes you have." So he went back into the forest. There again he wept and wept and wept. It was all that great flow of love in the man that was struggling to get at the truth, and at last he succeeded; he gave his soul, the river of his love, the right direction, and it came to the Shepherd. The story goes that he saw God in the form of Krishna. Then, for once, he was sorry that he had lost his eyes, and that he could only have the internal vision. He wrote some beautiful poems of love. In all Sanskrit books, the writers first of all salute their Gurus. So he saluted that girl as his first Guru.

The Soul And God

This article was recorded by Ida Ansell in shorthand. As, however, Swamiji's speed was too great for her in her early days, dots are put in the articles to indicate the omissions, while the words within square brackets are added by way of linking up the disconnected parts.

(Delivered in San Francisco, March 23, 1900)

Whether it was fear or mere inquisitiveness which first led man to think of powers superior to himself, we need not discuss. ... These raised in the mind peculiar worship tendencies, and so on. There never have been [times in the history of mankind] without [some ideal] of worship. Why? What makes us all struggle for something beyond what we see — whether it be a beautiful morning or a fear of dead spirits? ... We need not go back into prehistoric times, for it is a fact present today as it was two thousand years ago. We do not find satisfaction here. Whatever our station in life — [even if we are] powerful and wealthy — we cannot find satisfaction.

Desire is infinite. Its fulfilment is very limited.. There is no end to our desires; but when we go to fulfil them, the difficulty comes. It has been so with the most primitive minds, when their desires were [few]. Even [these] could not be accomplished. Now, with our arts and sciences improved and multiplied, our desires cannot be fulfilled [either]. On the other hand, we are struggling to perfect means for the fulfilment of desires, and the desires are increasing. ...

The most primitive man naturally wanted help from outside for things which he could not accomplish. ...He desired something, and it could not be obtained. He wanted help from other powers. The most ignorant primitive man and the most cultivated man today, each appealing to God and asking for the fulfilment of some desire, are exactly the same. What difference? [Some people] find a great deal of difference. We are always finding much difference in things when there is no difference at all. Both [the primitive man and the cultivated man] plead to the same [power]. You may call it God or Allah or Jehovah. Human beings want something and cannot get it by their own powers, and are after someone who will help them. This is primitive, and it is still present with us. ... We are all born savages and gradually civilise ourselves. ... All of us here, if we search, will find the same fact. Even now this fear does not leave us. We may talk big, become philosophers and all that; but when the blow comes, we find that we must beg for help. We believe in all the superstitions that ever existed. [But] there is no superstition in the world [that does not have some basis of truth]. If I cover my face and only the tip of my [nose] is showing, still it is a bit of my face. So [with] the superstitions — the little bits are true.

You see, the lowest sort of manifestation of religion came with the burial of the departed. ... First they wrapped them up and put them in mounds, and the spirits of the departed came and lived in the [mounds, at night]. ... Then they began to bury them. ... At the gate stands a terrible goddess with a thousand teeth. ... Then [came] the burning of the body and the flames bore the spirit up. ... The Egyptians brought food and water for the departed.

The next great idea was that of the tribal gods. This tribe had one god and that tribe another. The Jews had their God Jehovah, who was their own tribal god and fought against all the other gods and tribes. That god would do anything to please his own people. If he killed a whole tribe not protected by him, that was all right, quite good. A little love was given, but that love was confined to a small section.

Gradually, higher ideals came. The chief of the conquering tribe was the Chief of chiefs, God of gods. ... So with the Persians when they conquered Egypt. The Persian emperor was the Lord of [lords], and before the emperor nobody could stand. Death was the penalty for anyone who looked at the Persian emperor.

Then came the ideal of God Almighty and All-powerful, the omnipotent, omniscient Ruler of the universe: He lives in heaven, and man pays special tribute to his Most Beloved, who creates everything for man. The whole world is for man. The sun and moon and stars are [for him]. All who have those ideas are primitive men, not civilised and not cultivated at all. All the superior religions had their growth between the Ganga and the Euphrates. ... Outside of India we will find no further development [of religion beyond this idea of God in heaven]. That was the highest knowledge ever obtained outside of India. There is the local heaven where he is and [where] the faithful shall go when they die. ... As far as I have seen, we should call it a very primitive idea. ... Mumbo jumbo in Africa [and] God in heaven — the same. He moves the world, and of course his will is being done everywhere.

The old Hebrew people did not care for any heaven. That is one of the reasons they [opposed] Jesus of Nazareth — because he taught life after death. Paradise in Sanskrit means land beyond this life. So the paradise was to make up for all this evil. The primitive man does not care [about] evil. ... He never questions why there should be any. ...

... The word devil is a Persian word. ... The Persians and Hindus [share the Aryan ancestry] upon religious grounds, and ... they spoke the same language, only the words one sect uses for good the other uses for bad. The word Deva is an old Sanskrit word for God, the same word in the Aryan languages. Here the word means the devil. ...

Later on, when man developed [his inner life], he began to question, and to say that God is good. The Persians said that there were two gods — one was bad and one was good. [Their idea was that] everything in this life was good: beautiful country, where there was spring almost the whole year round and nobody died; there was no disease, everything was fine. Then came this Wicked One, and he touched the land, and then came death and disease and mosquitoes and tigers and lions. Then the Aryans left their fatherland and migrated southward. The old Aryans must have lived way to the north. The Jews learnt it [the idea of the devil] from the Persians. The Persians also taught that there will come a day when this wicked god will be killed, and it is our duty to stay with the good god and add our force to him in this eternal struggle between him and the wicked one. ... The whole world will be burnt out and everyone will get a new body.

The Persian idea was that even the wicked will be purified and not be bad any more. The nature of the Aryan was love and poetry. They cannot think of their being burnt [for eternity]. They will all receive new bodies. Then no more death. So that is the best about [religious] ideas outside of India. ...

Along with that is the ethical strain. All that man has to do is to take care of three things: good thought, good word, good deed. That is all. It is a practical, wise religion. Already there has come a little poetry in it. But there is higher poetry and higher thought.

In India we see this Satan in the most ancient part of the Vedas. He just (appears) and immediately disappears. ... In the Vedas the bad god got a blow and disappeared. He is gone, and the Persians took him. We are trying to make him leave the world [al]together. Taking the Persian idea, we are going to make a decent gentleman of him; give him a new body. There was the end of the Satan idea in India.

But the idea of God went on; but mind you, here comes another fact. The idea of God grew side by side with the idea of [materialism] until you have traced it up to the emperor of Persia. But on the other hand comes in metaphysics, philosophy. There is another line of thought, the idea of [the non-dual Âtman, man's] own soul. That also grows. So, outside of India ideas about God had to remain in that concrete form until India came to help them out a bit. ... The other nations stopped with that old concrete idea. In this country [America], there are millions who believe that God is [has?] a body. ... Whole sects say it. [They believe that] He rules the world, but there is a place where He has a body. He sits upon a throne. They light candles and sing songs just as they do in our temples.

But in India they are sensible enough never to make [their God a physical being]. You never see in India a temple of Brahmâ. Why? Because the idea of the soul always existed. The Hebrew race never questioned about the soul. There is no soul idea in the Old Testament at all. The first is in the New Testament. The Persians, they became so practical — wonderfully practical people — a fighting, conquering race. They were the English people of the old time, always fighting and destroying their neighbours — too much engaged in that sort of thing to think about the soul. ...

The oldest idea of [the] soul [was that of] a fine body inside this gross one. The gross one disappears and the fine one appears. In Egypt that fine one also dies, and as soon as the gross body disintegrates, the fine one also disintegrates. That is why they built those pyramids [and embalmed the dead bodies of their ancestors, thus hoping to secure immortality for the departed]. ...

The Indian people have no regard for the dead body at all. [Their attitude is:] "Let us take it and burn it." The son has to set fire to his father's body. ...

There are two sorts of races, the divine and the demonic. The divine think that they are soul and spirit. The demonic think that they are bodies. The old Indian philosophers tried to insist that the body is nothing. "As a man emits his old garment and takes a new one, even so the old body is [shed] and he takes a new one" (Gita, II. 22). In my case, all my surrounding and education were trying to [make me] the other way. I was always associated with Mohammedans and Christians, who take more care of the body. ...

It is only one step from [the body] to the spirit. ... [In India] they became insistent on this ideal of the soul. It became [synonymous with] the idea of God. ... If the idea of the soul begins to expand, [man must arrive at the conclusion that it is beyond name and form]. ... The Indian idea is that the soul is formless. Whatever is form must break some time or other. There cannot be any form unless it is the result of force and matter; and all combinations must dissolve. If such is the case, [if] your soul is [made of name and form, it disintegrates], and you die, and you are no more immortal. If it is double, it has form and it belongs to nature and it obeys nature's laws of birth and death. ... They find that this [soul] is not the mind ... neither a double. ...

Thoughts can be guided and controlled. ... [The Yogis of India] practiced to see how far the thoughts can be guided and controlled. By dint of hard work, thoughts may be silenced altogether. If thoughts were [the real man], as soon as thought ceases, he ought to die. Thought ceases in meditation; even the mind's elements are quite quiet. Blood circulation stops. His breath stops, but he is not dead. If thought were he, the whole thing ought to go, but they find it does not go. That is practical [proof]. They came to the conclusion that even mind and thought were not the real man. Then speculation showed that it could not be.

I come, I think and talk. In the midst of all [this activity is] this unity [of the Self]. My thought and action are varied, many [fold] ... but in and through them runs ... that one unchangeable One. It cannot be the body. That is changing every minute. It cannot be the mind; new and fresh thoughts [come] all the time. It is neither the body nor the mind. Both body and mind belong to nature and must obey nature's laws. A free mind never will. ...

Now, therefore, this real man does not belong to nature. It is the person whose mind and body belong to nature. So much of nature we are using. Just as you come to use the pen and ink and chair, so he uses so much of nature in fine and in gross form; gross form, the body, and fine form, the mind. If it is simple, it must be formless. In nature alone are forms. That which is not of nature cannot have any forms, fine or gross. It must be formless. It must be omnipresent. Understand this. [Take] this glass on the table. The glass is form and the table is form. So much of the glass-ness goes off, so much of table-ness [when they break]. ...

The soul ... is nameless because it is formless. It will neither go to heaven nor [to hell] any more than it will enter this glass. It takes the form of the vessel it fills. If it is not in space, either of two things is possible. Either the [soul permeates] space or space is in [it]. You are in space and must have a form. Space limits us, binds us, and makes a form of us. If you are not in space, space is in you. All the heavens and the world are in the person. ...

So it must be with God. God is omnipresent. "Without hands [he grasps] everything; without feet he can move. ... " (Shvetâshvatara Upanishad, III. 19.) He [is] the formless, the deathless, the eternal. The idea of God came. ... He is the Lord of souls, just as my soul is the [lord] of my body. If my soul left the body, the body would not be for a moment. If He left my soul, the soul would not exist. He is the creator of the universe; of everything that dies He is the destroyer. His shadow is death; His shadow is life.

[The ancient Indian philosophers] thought: ... This filthy world is not fit for man's attention. There is nothing in the universe that is [permanent — neither good nor evil]. ...

I told you ... Satan ... did not have much chance [in India]. Why? Because they were very bold in religion. They were not babies. Have you seen that characteristic of children? They are always trying to throw the blame on someone else. Baby minds [are] trying, when they make a mistake, to throw the blame upon someone [else]. On the one hand, we say, "Give me this; give me that." On the other hand, we say, "I did not do this; the devil tempted me. The devil did it." That is the history of mankind, weak mankind. ...

Why is evil? Why is [the world] the filthy, dirty hole? We have made it. Nobody is to blame. We put our hand in the fire. The Lord bless us, [man gets] just what he deserves. Only He is merciful. If we pray to Him, He helps us. He gives Himself to us.

That is their idea. They are [of a] poetic nature. They go crazy over poetry. Their philosophy is poetry. This philosophy is a poem. ... All [high thought] in the Sanskrit is written in poetry. Metaphysics, astronomy — all in poetry.

We are responsible, and how do we come to mischief? [You may say], "I was born poor and miserable. I remember the hard struggle all my life." Philosophers say that you are to blame. You do not mean to say that all this sprang up without any cause whatever? You are a rational being. Your life is not without cause, and you are the cause. You manufacture your own life all the time. ... You make and mould your own life. You are responsible for yourself. Do not lay the blame upon anybody, any Satan. You will only get punished a little more. ...

[A man] is brought up before God, and He says, "Thirty-one stripes for you," ... when comes another man. He says, "Thirty stripes: fifteen for that fellow, and fifteen for the teacher — that awful man who taught him." That is the awful thing in teaching. I do not know what I am going to get. I go all over the world. If I have to get fifteen for each one I have taught!...

We have to come to this idea: "This My Mâyâ is divine." It is My activity [My] divinity. "[My Maya] is hard to cross, but those that take refuge in me [go beyond maya]." (Gita, VII. 14.) But you find out that it is very difficult to cross this ocean [of Maya by] yourself. You cannot. It is the old question - hen and egg. If you do any work, that work becomes the cause and produces the effect. That effect [again] becomes the cause and produces the effect. And so on. If you push this down, it never stops. Once you set a thing in motion, there is no more stopping. I do some work, good or bad, [and it sets up a chain reaction].... I cannot stop now.

It is impossible for us to get out from this bondage [by ourselves]. It is only possible if there is someone more powerful than this law of causation, and if he takes mercy on us and drags us out.

And we declare that there is such a one - God. There is such a being, all merciful.... If there is a God, then it is possible for me to be saved. How can you be saved by your own will? Do you see the philosophy of the doctrine of salvation by grace? You Western people are wonderfully clever, but when you undertake to explain philosophy, you are so wonderfully complicated. How can you save yourself by work, if by salvation you mean that you will be taken out of all this nature? Salvation means just standing upon God, but if you understand what is meant by salvation, then you are the Self.... You are not nature. You are the only thing outside of souls and gods and nature. These are the external existences, and God [is] interpenetrating both nature and soul.

Therefore, just as my soul is [to] my body, we, as it were, are the bodies of God. God-souls-nature — it is one. The One, because, as I say, I mean the body, soul, and mind. But, we have seen, the law of causation pervades every bit of nature, and once you have got caught you cannot get out. When once you get into the meshes of law, a possible way of escape is not [through work done] by you. You can build hospitals for every fly and flea that ever lived.... All this you may do, but it would never lead to salvation.... [Hospitals] go up and they come down again. [Salvation] is only possible if there is some being whom nature never caught, who is the Ruler of nature. He rules nature instead of being ruled by nature. He wills law instead of being downed by law. ... He exists and he is all merciful. The moment you seek Him [He will save you].

Why has He not taken us out? You do not want Him. You want everything but Him. The moment you want Him, that moment you get Him. We never want Him. We say, "Lord, give me a fine house." We want the house, not Him. "Give me health! Save me from this difficulty!" When a man wants nothing but Him, [he gets Him]. "The same love which wealthy men have for gold and silver and possessions, Lord, may I have the same love for Thee. I want neither earth nor heaven, nor beauty nor learning. I do not want salvation. Let me go to hell again and again. But one thing I want: to love Thee, and for love's sake — not even for heaven."

Whatever man desires, he gets. If you always dream of having a body, [you will get another body]. When this body goes away he wants another, and goes on begetting body after body. Love matter and you become matter. You first become animals. When I see a dog gnawing a bone, I say, "Lord help us!" Love body until you become dogs and cats! Still degenerate, until you become minerals — all body and nothing else....

There are other people, who would have no compromise. The road to salvation is through truth. That was another watchword. ...

[Man began to progress spiritually] when he kicked the devil out. He stood up and took the responsibility of the misery of the world upon his own shoulders. But whenever he looked [at the] past and future and [at the] law of causation, he knelt down and said, "Lord, save me, [thou] who [art] our creator, our father, and dearest friend." That is poetry, but not very good poetry, I think. Why not? It is the painting of the Infinite [no doubt]. You have it in every language how they paint the Infinite. [But] it is the infinite of the senses, of the muscles. ...

"[Him] the sun [does not illumine], nor the moon, nor the stars, [nor] the flash of lightning." (Katha Upanishad, II. ii. 15.) That is another painting of the Infinite, by negative language. ... And the last Infinite is painted in [the] spirituality of the Upanishads. Not only is Vedanta the highest philosophy in the world, but it is the greatest poem....

Mark today, this is the ... difference between the first part of the Vedas and the second. In the first, it is all in [the domain of] sense. But all religions are only [concerned with the] infinite of the external world — nature and nature's God.... [Not so Vedanta]. This is the first light that the human mind throws back [of] all that. No satisfaction [comes] of the infinite [in] space. "[The] Self-exisent [One] has [created] the [senses as turned] ... to the outer world. Those therefore who [seek] outside will never find that [which is within]. There are the few who, wanting to know the truth, turn their eyes inward and in their own souls behold the glory [of the Self]." (Katha Upanishad, II. i. 1.)

It is not the infinite of space, but the real Infinite, beyond space, beyond time.... Such is the world missed by the Occident.... Their minds have been turned to external nature and nature's God. Look within yourself and find the truth that you had [forgotten]. Is it possible for mind to come out of this dream without the help of the gods? Once you start the action, there is no help unless the merciful Father takes us out.

That would not be freedom, [even] at the hands of the merciful God. Slavery is slavery. The chain of gold is quite as bad as the chain of iron. Is there a way out?

You are not bound. No one was ever bound. [The Self] is beyond. It is the all. You are the One; there are no two. God was your own reflection cast upon the screen of Maya. The real God [is the Self]. He [whom man] ignorantly worships is that reflection. [They say that] the Father in heaven is God. Why God? [It is because He is] your own reflection that [He] is God. Do you see how you are seeing God all the time? As you unfold yourself, the reflection grows [clearer].

"Two beautiful birds are there sitting upon the same tree. The one [is] calm, silent, majestic; the one below [the individual self], is eating the fruits, sweet and bitter, and becoming happy and sad. [But when the individual self beholds the worshipful Lord as his own true Self, he grieves no more.]" (Mundaka Upanishad, III. i. 1-2.)

... Do not say "God". Do not say "Thou". Say "I". The language of [dualism] says, "God, Thou, my Father." The language of [non-dualism] says, "Dearer unto me than I am myself. I would have no name for Thee. The nearest I can use is I....

"God is true. The universe is a dream. Blessed am I that I know this moment that I [have been and] shall be free all eternity; ... that I know that I am worshipping only myself; that no nature, no delusion, had any hold on me. Vanish nature from me, vanish [these] gods; vanish worship; ... vanish superstitions, for I know myself. I am the Infinite. All these — Mrs. So-and-so, Mr. So-and-so, responsibility, happiness, misery — have vanished. I am the Infinite. How can there be death for me, or birth? Whom shall I fear? I am the One. Shall I be afraid of myself? Who is to be afraid of [whom]? I am the one Existence. Nothing else exists. I am everything."

It is only the question of memory [of your true nature], not salvation by work. Do you *get* salvation? You are [already] free.

Go on saying, "I am free". Never mind if the next moment delusion comes and says, "I am bound." Dehypnotise the whole thing.

[This truth] is first to be heard. Hear it first. Think on it day and night. Fill the mind [with it] day and night: "I am It. I am the Lord of the universe. Never was there any delusion.... " Meditate upon it with all the strength of the mind till you actually see these walls, houses, everything, melt away — [until] body, everything, vanishes. "I will stand alone. I am the One." Struggle on! "Who cares! We want to be free; [we] do not want any powers. Worlds we renounce; heavens we renounce; hells we renounce. What do I care about all these powers, and this and that! What do I care if the mind is controlled or uncontrolled! Let it run on. What of that! I am not the mind, Let it go on!"

The sun [shines on the just and on the unjust]. Is he touched by the defective [character] of anyone? "I am He. Whatever [my] mind does, I am not touched. The sun is not touched by shining on filthy places, I am Existence."

This is the religion of [non-dual] philosophy. [It is] difficult. Struggle on! Down with all superstitions! Neither teachers nor scriptures nor gods [exist]. Down with temples, with priests, with gods, with incarnations, with God himself! I am all the God that ever existed! There, stand up philosophers! No fear! Speak no more of God and [the] superstition of the world. Truth alone triumphs, and this is true. I am the Infinite.

All religious superstitions are vain imaginations. ... This society, that I see you before me, and [that] I am talking to you — this is all superstition; all must be given up. Just see what it takes to become a philosopher! This is the [path] of [Jnâna-] Yoga, the way through knowledge. The other [paths] are easy, slow, ... but this is pure strength of mind. No weakling [can follow this path of knowledge. You must be able to say:] "I am the Soul, the ever free; [I] never was bound. Time is in me, not I in time. God was born in my mind. God the Father, Father of the universe — he is created by me in my own mind...."

Do you call yourselves philosophers? Show it! Think of this, talk [of] this, and [help] each other in this path, and give up all superstition!

Breathing

This article was recorded by Ida Ansell in shorthand. As, however, Swamiji's speed was too great for her in her early days, dots are put in the articles to indicate the omissions, while the words within square brackets are added by way of linking up the disconnected parts.

(Delivered in San Francisco, March 28, 1900)

Breathing exercises have been very popular in India from the most ancient times, so much so [that] they form a part of their religion, just as going to church and repeating certain prayers.... I will try to bring those ideas before you.

I have told you how the Indian philosopher reduces the whole universe into two parts — Prâna and Âkâsha.

Prana means force — all that is manifesting itself as movement or possible movement, force, or attraction. ... Electricity, magnetism, all the movements in the body, all [the movements] in the mind — all these are various manifestations of one thing called Prana. The best form of Prana, however, is in [the brain], manifesting itself as light [of understanding]. This light is under the guidance of thought.

The mind ought to control every bit of Prana that has been worked up in the body.... [The] mind should have entire control of the body. That is not [the case] with all. With most of us it is the other way. The mind should be able to control every part of [the body] just at will. That is reason, philosophy; but [when] we come to matters of fact, it is not so. For you, on the other hand, the cart is before the horse. It is the body mastering the mind. If my finger gets pinched, I become sorry. The body works upon the mind. If anything happens which I do not like to happen, I am worried; my mind [is] thrown off its balance. The body is master of the mind. We have become bodies. We are nothing else but bodies just now.

Here [comes] the philosopher to show us the way out, to teach us what we really are. You may reason it out and understand it intellectually, but there is a long way between intellectual understanding and the practical realisation of it. Between the plan of the building and the building itself there is quite a long distance. Therefore there must be various methods [to reach the goal of religion]. In the last course, we have been studying the method of philosophy, trying to bring everything under control, once more asserting the freedom of the soul. ... "It is very difficult. This way is not for [every]body. The embodied mind tries it with great trouble" (Gita, XII. 5).

A little physical help will make the mind comfortable. What would be more rational than to have the mind itself accomplish the thing? But it cannot. The physical help is necessary for most of us. The system of Râja-Yoga is to utilise these physical helps, to make use of the powers and forces in the body to produce certain mental states, to make the mind stronger and stronger until it regains its lost empire. By sheer force of will if anyone can attain to that, so much the better. But most of us cannot, so we will use physical means, and help the will on its way.

... The whole universe is a tremendous case of unity in variety. There is only one mass of mind. Different [states] of that mind have different names. [They are] different little whirlpools in this ocean of mind. We are universal and individual at the same time. Thus is the play going on.... In reality this unity is never broken. [Matter, mind, spirit are all one.]

All these are but various names. There is but one fact in the universe, and we look at it from various standpoints. The same [fact] looked at from one standpoint becomes matter. The same one from another standpoint becomes mind. There are not two things. Mistaking the rope for the snake, fear came [to a man] and made him call somebody else to kill the snake. [His] nervous system began to shake; his heart began to beat.... All these manifestations [came] from fear, and he discovered it was a rope, and they all vanished. This is what we see in reality. What even the senses see — what we call matter — that [too] is the Real; only not as we have seen it. The mind [which] saw the rope [and] took it for a snake was not under a delusion. If it had been, it would not have seen anything. One thing is taken for another, not as something that does not exist. What we see here is body, and we take the Infinite as matter.... We are but seeking that Reality. We are never deluded. We always know truth, only our reading of truth is mistaken at times. You can perceive only one thing at a time. When I see the snake, the rope has vanished entirely. And when I see the rope, the snake has vanished. It must be one thing....

When we see the world, how can we see God? Think in your own mind. What is meant by the world is God as seen as all things [by] our senses. Here you see the snake; the rope is not. When you know the Spirit, everything else will vanish. When you see the Spirit itself, you see no matter, because that which you called matter is the very thing that is Spirit. All these variations are [superimposed] by our senses. The same sun, reflected by a thousand little wavelets, will represent to us thousands of little suns. If I am looking at the universe with my senses, I interpret it as matter and force. It is one and many at the same time. The manifold does not destroy the unity. The millions of waves do not destroy the unity of the ocean. It remains the same ocean. When you look at the universe, remember that we can reduce it to matter or to force. If we increase the velocity, the mass decreases. ... On the other hand, we can increase the mass and decrease the velocity.... We may almost come to a point where all the mass will entirely disappear. ...

Matter cannot be said to cause force nor [can] force [be] the cause of matter. Both are so [related] that one may disappear in the other. There must be a third [factor], and that third something is the mind. You cannot produce the universe from matter, neither from force. Mind is something [which is] neither force nor matter, yet begetting force and matter all the time. In the long run, mind is begetting all force, and that is what is meant by the universal mind, the sum total of all minds. Everyone is creating, and [in] the sum total of all these creations you have the universe — unity in diversity. It is one and it is many at the same time.

The Personal God is only the sum total of all, and yet it is an individual by itself, just as you are the individual body of which each cell is an individual part itself.

Everything that has motion is included in Prana or force. [It is] this Prana which is moving the stars, sun, moon; Prana is gravitation. ...

All forces of nature, therefore, must be created by the universal mind. And we, as little bits of mind, [are] taking out that Prana from nature, working it out again in our own nature, moving our bodies and manufacturing our thought. If [you think] thought cannot be manufactured, stop eating for twenty days and see how you feel. Begin today and count. ... Even thought is manufactured by food. There is no doubt about it.

Control of this Prana that is working everything, control of this Prana in the body, is called Prânâyâma. We see with our common sense that it is the breath [that] is setting everything in motion. If I stop breathing, I stop. If the breath begins, [the body] begins to move. What we want to get at is not the breath itself; it is something finer behind the breath.

[There was once a minister to a great king. The] king, displeased with the minister, ordered him to be confined in the top of [a very high tower. This was done, and the minister was left there to perish. His wife came to the tower at night and called to her husband.] The minister said to her, "No use weeping." He told her to take a little honey, [a beetle], a pack of fine thread, a ball of twine, and a rope. She tied the fine thread to one of the legs of the beetle and put honey on the top of its head and let it go [with its head up]. [The beetle slowly crept onwards, in the hope of reaching the honey, until at last it reached the top of the tower, when the minister grasped the beetle, and got possession of the silken thread, then the pack thread, then the stout twine, and lastly of the rope. The minister descended from the tower by means of the rope, and made his escape. In this body of ours the breath motion is the "silken thread"; by laying hold of it we grasp the pack thread of the nerve currents, and from these the stout twine of our thoughts, and lastly the rope of Prana, controlling which we reach freedom. (Vide ante.)

By the help of things on the material plane, we have to come to finer and finer [perceptions]. The universe is one, whatever point you touch. All the points are but variations of that one point. Throughout the universe is a unity (at bottom).... Even through such a gross thing as breath I can get hold of the Spirit itself.

By the exercise of breathing we begin to feel all the movements of the body that we [now] do not feel. As soon as we begin to feel them, we begin to master them. Thoughts in the germ will open to us, and we will be able to get hold of them. Of course, not all of us have the opportunity nor the will nor the patience nor the faith to pursue such a thing; but there is the common sense idea that is of some benefit to everyone.

The first benefit is health. Ninety-nine per cent of us do not at all breathe properly. We do not inflate the lungs enough.... Regularity [of breath] will purify the body. It quiets the mind.... When you are peaceful, your breath is going on peacefully, [it is] rhythmic. If the breath is rhythmic, you must be peaceful. When the mind is disturbed, the breath is broken. If you can bring the breath into rhythm forcibly by practice, why can you not become peaceful? When you are disturbed, go into the room and close the door. Do not try to control the mind, but go on with rhythmic breathing for ten minutes. The heart will become peaceful. These are common sense benefits that come to everyone. The others belong to the Yogi....

Deep-breathing exercises [are only the first step]. There are about eighty-four [postures for] various exercises. Some [people] have taken up this breathing as the whole [pursuit] of life. They do not do anything without consulting the breath. They are all the time [observing] in which nostril there is more breath. When it is the right, [they] will do certain things, and when [it is] the left, they do other things. When [the breath is] flowing equally through both nostrils, they will worship.

When the breath is coming rhythmically through both nostrils, that is the time to control your mind. By means of the breath you can make the currents of the body move through any part of the body, just [at] will. Whenever [any] part of the body is ill, send the Prana to that part, all by the breath.

Various other things are done. There are sects who are trying not to breathe at all. They would not do anything that would make them breathe hard. They go into a sort of trance.... Scarcely any part of the body [functions]. The heart almost ceases [to beat].... Most of these exercises are very dangerous; the higher methods [are] for acquiring higher powers. There are whole sects trying to [lighten] the whole body by withdrawal of breath and then they will rise up in the air. I have never seen anyone rise.... I have never seen anyone fly through the air, but the books say so. I do not pretend to know everything. All the time I am seeing most wonderful things.... [Once I observed a] man bringing out fruits and flowers, etc. [out of nowhere].

... The Yogi, when he becomes perfect, can make his body so small it will pass through this wall — this very body. He can become so heavy, two hundred persons cannot lift him. He will be able to fly through the air if he likes. [But] nobody can be as powerful as God Himself. If they could, and one created, another would destroy....

This is in the books. I can [hardly] believe them, nor do I disbelieve them. What I have seen I take....

If the study [improvement?] of things in this world is possible, it is not by competition, it is by regulating the mind. Western people say, "That is our nature; we cannot help it." Studying your social problems, [I conclude] you cannot solve them either. In some things you are worse off than we are, ... and all these things do not bring the world anywhere at all...

The strong take everything; the weak go to the wall. The poor are waiting.... The man who can take, will take everything. The poor hate that man. Why? Because they are waiting their turn. All the systems they invent, they all teach the same thing. The problem can only be solved in the mind of man.... No law will ever make him do what he does not want to do. ... It is only if [man] wills to be good that he will be good. All the law and juries ... cannot make him good. The almighty man says, "I do not care." ... The only solution is if we all want to be good. How can that be done?

All knowledge is within [the] mind. Who saw knowledge in the stone, or astronomy in the star? It is all in the human being.

Let us realise [that] we are the infinite power. Who put a limit to the power of mind? Let us realise we are all mind. Every drop has the whole of the ocean in it. That is the mind of man. The Indian mind reflects upon these [powers and potentialities] and wants to bring [them] all out. For himself he doesn't care what happens. It will take a great length of time [to reach perfection]. If it takes fifty thousand years, what of that! ...

The very foundation of society, the formation of it, makes the defect. [Perfection] is only possible if the mind of man is changed, if he, of his own sweet will, changes his mind; and the great difficulty is, neither can he force his own mind.

You may not believe in all the claims of this Raja-Yoga. It is absolutely necessary that every individual can become divine. That is only [possible] when every individual has absolute mastery over his own thoughts.... [The thoughts, the senses] should be all my servants, not my masters. Then only is it possible that evils will vanish....

Education is not filling the mind with a lot of facts. Perfecting the instrument and getting complete mastery of my own mind [is the ideal of education]. If I want to concentrate my mind upon a point, it goes there, and the moment I call, it is free [again]....

That is the great difficulty. By great struggle we get a certain power of concentration, the power of attachment of the mind to certain things. But then there is not the power of detachment. I would give half my life to take my mind off that object! I cannot. It is the power of concentration and attachment as well as the power of detachment [that we must develop]. [If] the man [is] equally powerful in both — that man has attained manhood. You cannot make him miserable even if the whole universe tumbles about his ears. What books can teach you that? You may read any amount of books.... Crowd into the child fifty thousand words a moment, teach him all the theories and philosophies.... There is only one science that will teach him facts, and that is psychology.... And the work begins with control of the breath.

Slowly and gradually you get into the chambers of the mind and gradually get control of the mind. It is a long, [hard struggle]. It must not be taken up as something curious. When one wants to do something, he has a plan. [Raja-Yoga] proposes no faith, no belief, no God. If you believe in two thousand gods, you can try that. Why not? ... [But in Raja-Yoga] it is impersonal principles.

The greatest difficulty is what? We talk and theorise The vast majority of mankind must deal with things that are concrete. For the dull people cannot see all the highest philosophy. Thus it ends. You may be graduates [in] all sciences in the world, ... but if you have not realised, you must become a baby and learn.

... If you give them things in the abstract and infinite, they get lost. Give them things [to do,] a little at a time [Tell them,] "You take [in] so many breaths, you do this." They go on, [they] understand it, and find pleasure in it. These are the kindergartens of religion. That is why breathing exercises will be so beneficial. I beg you all not to be merely curious. Practise a few days, and if you do not find any benefit, then come and curse me....

The whole universe is a mass of energy, and it is present at every point. One grain is enough for all of us, if we know how to get what there is....

This having to *do* is the poison that is killing us.... [Duty is] what pleases slaves.... [But] I am free! What I do is my play. [I am not a slave. I am] having a little fun — that is all....

The departed spirits — they are weak, are trying to get vitality from us....

Spiritual vitality can be given from one mind to another. The man who gives is the Guru. The man who receives is the disciple. That is the only way spiritual truth is brought into the world.

[At death] all the senses go into the [mind] and the mind goes into Prana, vitality. The soul goes out and carries part of the mind out with him. He carries a certain part of the vitality, and he carries a certain amount of very fine material also, as the germ of the spiritual body. The Prana cannot exist without some sort of [vehicle].... It gets lodgement in the thoughts, and it will come out again. So you manufacture this new body and new brain. Through that it will manifest....

[Departed spirits] cannot manufacture a body; and those that are very weak do not remember that they are dead.... They try to get more enjoyment from this [spirit] life by getting into the bodies of others, and any person who opens his body to them runs a terrible risk. They seek his vitality....

In this world nothing is permanent except God.... Salvation means knowing the truth. We do not become anything; we are what we are. Salvation [comes] by faith and not by work. It is a question of *knowledge*! You must *know* what you are, and it is done. The dream vanishes. This you [and others] are dreaming here. When they die, they go to [the] heaven [of their dream]. They live in that dream, and [when it ends], they take a nice body [here], and they are good people....

[The wise man says,] "All these [desires] have vanished from me. This time I will not go through all this paraphernalia." He tries to get knowledge and struggles hard, and he sees what a dream, what a nightmare this is - [this dreaming], and working up heavens and worlds and worse. He laughs at it.

[According to SWAMI VIVEKANANDA HIS SECOND VISIT TO THE WEST (P. 461), this address was delivered on 29 March 1900 under the title "The Science of Breathing". — Ed.]

Practical Religion: Breathing And Meditation

This article was recorded by Ida Ansell in shorthand. As, however, Swamiji's speed was too great for her in her early days, dots are put in the articles to indicate the omissions, while the words within square brackets are added by way of linking up the disconnected parts.

(Delivered in San Francisco, April 5, 1900)

Everyone's idea of practical religion is according to his theory of practicality and the standpoint he starts from. There is work. There is the system of worship. There is knowledge.

The philosopher thinks ... the difference between bondage and freedom is only caused by knowledge and ignorance. To him, knowledge is the goal, and his practicality is gaining that knowledge.... The worshipper's practical religion is the power of love and devotion. The worker's practical religion consists in doing good works. And so, as in every other thing, we are always trying to ignore the standard of another, trying to bind the whole world to our standard.

Doing good to his fellow-beings is the practical religion of the man full of love. If men do not help to build hospitals, he thinks that they have no religion at all. But there is no reason why everyone should do that. The philosopher, in the same way, may denounce every man who does not have knowledge. People may build twenty thousand hospitals, and the philosopher declares they are but ... the beasts of burden of the gods. The worshipper has his own idea and standard: Men who cannot love God are no good, whatever work they do. The [Yogi believes in] psychic [control and] the conquest of [internal] nature. "How much have you gained towards that? How much control over your senses, over your body?" — that is all the Yogi asks. And, as we said, each one judges the others by his own standard. Men may have given millions of dollars and fed rats and cats, as some do in India. They say that men can take care of themselves, but the poor animals cannot. That is their idea. But to the Yogi the goal is conquest of [internal] nature, and he judges man by that standard....

We are always talking [about] practical religion. But it must be practical in our sense. Especially [so] in the Western countries. The Protestants' ideal is good works. They do not care much for devotion and philosophy. They think there is not much in it. "What is your knowledge!" [they say]. "Man has to do something!" ... A little humanitarianism! The churches rail day and night against callous agnosticism. Yet they seem to be veering rapidly towards just that. Callous slaves! Religion of utility! That is the spirit just now. And that is why some Buddhists have become so popular in the West. People do not know whether there is a God or not, whether there is a soul or not. [They think :] This world is full of misery. Try to help this world.

The Yoga doctrine, which we are having our lecture on, is not from that standpoint. [It teaches that] there is the soul, and inside this soul is all power. It is already there, and if we can master this body, all the power will be unfolded. All knowledge is in the soul. Why are people struggling? To lessen the misery.... All unhappiness is caused by our not having mastery over the body.... We are all putting the cart before the horse.... Take the system of work, for instance. We are trying to do good by ... comforting the poor. We do not get to the cause which created the misery. It is like taking a bucket to empty out the ocean, and more [water] comes all the time. The Yogi sees that this is nonsense. [He says that] the way out of misery is to know the cause of misery first.... We try to do the good we can. What for? If there is an incurable disease, why should we struggle and take care of ourselves? If the utilitarians say: "Do not bother about soul and God!" what is that to the Yogi and what is it to the world? The world does not derive any good [from such an attitude]. More and more misery is going on all the time....

The Yogi says you are to go to the root of all this. Why is there misery in the world? He answers: "It is all our own foolishness, not having proper mastery of our own bodies. That is all." He advises the means by which this misery can be [overcome]. If you can thus get mastery of your body, all the misery of the world will vanish. Every hospital is praying that more and more sick people will come there. Every time you think of doing some charity, you think there is some beggar to take your charity. If you say, "O Lord, let the world be full of charitable people!" — you mean, let the world be full of beggars also. Let the world be full of good works - let the world be full of misery. This is out-and-out slavishness!

... The Yogi says, religion is practical if you know first why misery exists. All the misery in the world is in the senses. Is there any ailment in the sun, moon, and stars? The same fire that cooks your meal burns the child. Is it the fault of the fire? Blessed be the fire! Blessed be this electricity! It gives light.... Where can you lay the blame? Not on the elements. The world is neither good nor bad; the world is the world. The fire is the fire. If you burn your finger in it, you are a fool. If you [cook your meal and with it satisfy your hunger,] you are a wise man. That is all the difference. Circumstances can never be good or bad. Only the individual man can be good or bad. What is meant by the world being good or bad? Misery and happiness can only belong to the sensuous individual man.

The Yogis say that nature is the enjoyed; the soul is the enjoyer. All misery and happiness — where is it? In the senses. It is the touch of the senses that causes pleasure and pain, heat and cold. If we can control the senses and order what they shall feel — not let them order us about as they are doing now — if they can obey our commands, become our servants, the problem is solved at once. We are bound by the senses; they play upon us, make fools of us all the time.

Here is a bad odour. It will bring me unhappiness as soon as it touches my nose. I am the slave of my nose. If I am not its slave, I do not care. A man curses me. His curses enter my ears and are retained in my mind and body. If I am the master, I shall say: "Let these things go; they are nothing to me. I am not miserable. I do not bother." This is the outright, pure, simple, clear-cut truth.

The other problem to be solved is — is it practical? Can man attain to the power of mastery of the body? ... Yoga says it is practical .... Supposing it is not — suppose there are doubts in your mind. You have got to try it. There is no other way out....

You may do good works all the time. All the same, you will be the slave of your senses, you will be miserable and unhappy. You may study the philosophy of every religion. Men in this country carry loads and loads of books on their backs. They are mere scholars, slaves of the senses, and therefore happy and unhappy. They read two thousand books, and that is all right; but as soon as a little misery comes, they are worried, anxious.... You call yourselves men! You stand up ... and build hospitals. You are fools!

What is the difference between men and animals? ... "Food and [sleep], procreation of the species, and fear exist in common with the animals. There is one difference: Man can control all these and become God, the master." Animals cannot do it. Animals can do charitable work. Ants do it. Dogs do it. What is the difference then? Men can be masters of themselves. They can resist the reaction to anything.... The animal cannot resist anything. He is held ... by the string of nature everywhere. That is all the distinction. One is the master of nature, the other the slave of nature. What is nature? The five senses....

[The conquest of internal nature] is the only way out, according to Yoga.... The thirst for God is religion.... Good works and all that [merely] make the mind a little quiet. To practice this — to be perfect — all depends upon our past. I have been studying [Yoga] all my life and have made very little progress yet. But I have got enough [result] to believe that this is the only true way. The day will come when I will be master of myself. If not in this life, [in another life]. I will struggle and never let go. Nothing is lost. If I die this moment, all my past struggles [will come to my help]. Have you not seen what makes the difference between one man and another? It is their past. The past habits make one man a genius and another man a fool. You may have the power of the past and can succeed in five minutes. None can predict the moment of time. We all have to attain [perfection] some time or other.

The greater part of the practical lessons which the Yogi gives us is in the mind, the power of concentration and meditation.... We have become so materialistic. When we think of ourselves, we find only the body. The body has become the ideal, nothing else. Therefore a little physical help is necessary....

First, to sit in the posture In which you can sit still for a long time. All the nerve currents which are working pass along the spine. The spine is not intended to support the weight of the body. Therefore the posture must be such that the weight of the body is not on the spine. Let it be free from all pressure.

There are some other preliminary things. There is the great question of food and exercise....

The food must be simple and taken several times [a day] instead of once or twice. Never get very hungry. "He who eats too much cannot be a Yogi. He who fasts too much cannot be a Yogi. He who sleeps too much cannot be a Yogi, nor he who keeps awake too much." (Gita, VI. 16.) He who does not do any work and he who works too hard cannot succeed. Proper food, proper exercise, proper sleep, proper wakefulness — these are necessary for any success.

What the proper food is, what kind, we have to determine ourselves. Nobody can determine that [for us]. As a general practice, we have to shun exciting food.... We do not know how to vary our diet with our occupation. We always forget that it is the food out of which we manufacture everything we have. So the amount and kind of energy that we want, the food must determine....

Violent exercises are not all necessary.... If you want to be muscular, Yoga is not for you. You have to manufacture a finer organism than you have now. Violent exercises are positively hurtful.... Live amongst those who do not take too much exercise. If you do not take violent exercise, you will live longer. You do not want to burn out your lamp in muscles! People who work with their brains are the longest-lived people.... Do not burn the lamp quickly. Let it bum slowly and gently.... Every anxiety, every violent exercise — physical and mental — [means] you are burning the lamp.

The proper diet means, generally, simply do not eat highly spiced foods. There are three sorts of mind, says the Yogi, according to the elements of nature. One is the dull mind, which covers the luminosity of the soul. Then there is that which makes people active, and lastly, that which makes them calm and peaceful.

Now there are persons born with the tendency to sleep all the time. Their taste will be towards that type of food which is rotting — crawling cheese. They will eat cheese that fairly jumps off the table. It is a natural tendency with them.

Then active people. Their taste is for everything hot and pungent, strong alcohol....

Sâttvika people are very thoughtful, quiet, and patient. They take food in small quantities, and never anything bad.

I am always asked the question: "Shall I give up meat?" My Master said, "Why should you give up anything? It will give you up." Do not give up anything in nature. Make it so hot for nature that she will give you up. There will come a time when you cannot possibly eat meat. The very sight of it will disgust you. There will come a time when many things you are struggling to give up will be distasteful, positively loathsome.

Then there are various sorts of breathing exercises. One consists of three parts: the drawing in of the breath, the holding of the breath — stopping still without breathing — and throwing the breath out. [Some breathing exercises] are rather difficult, and some of the complicated ones are attended with great danger if done without proper diet. I would not advise you to go through any one of these except the very simple ones.

Take a deep breath and fill the lungs. Slowly throw the breath out. Take it through one nostril and fill the lungs, and throw it out slowly through the other nostril. Some of us do not breathe deeply enough. Others cannot fill the lungs enough. These breathings will correct that very much. Half an hour in the morning and half an hour in the evening will make you another person. This sort of breathing is never dangerous. The other exercises should be practiced very slowly. And measure your strength. If ten minutes are a drain, only take five.

The Yogi is expected to keep his own body well. These various breathing exercises are a great help in regulating the different parts of the body. All the different parts are inundated with breath. It is through breath that we gain control of them all. Disharmony in parts of the body is controlled by more flow of the nerve currents towards them. The Yogi ought to be able to tell when in any part pain is caused by less vitality or more. He has to equalise that....

Another condition [for success in Yoga] is chastity. It is the corner-stone of all practice. Married or unmarried — perfect chastity. It is a long subject, of course, but I want to tell you: Public discussions of this subject are not to the taste of this country. These Western countries are full of the most degraded beings in the shape of teachers who teach men and women that if they are chaste they will be hurt. How do they gather all this? ... People come to me — thousands come every year — with this one question. Someone has told them that if they are chaste and pure they will be hurt physically.... How do these teachers know it? Have they been chaste? Those unchaste, impure fools, lustful creatures, want to drag the whole world down to their [level]! ...

Nothing is gained except by sacrifice.... The holiest function of our human consciousness, the noblest, do not make it unclean! Do not degrade it to the level of the brutes.... Make yourselves decent men! ... Be chaste and pure! ... There is no other way. Did Christ find any other way? ... If you can conserve and use the energy properly, it leads you to God. Inverted, it is hell itself ....

It is much easier to do anything upon the external plane, but the greatest conqueror in the world finds himself a mere child when he tries to control his own mind. This is the world he has to conquer — the greater and more difficult world to conquer. Do not despair! Awake, arise, and stop not until the goal is reached!...